FAVORITE
FOLKTALES
from
AROUND
the WORLD

FAVORITE FOLKTALES from AROUND the WORLD

Edited by
JANE YOLEN

PANTHEON BOOKS

NEW YORK

Library of Congress Cataloging-in-Publication Data
Favorite folktales from around the world.
Includes bibliographical notes.
1. Tales.   I. Yolen, Jane.
GR76.F38   1986   398.2   86-42644
ISBN 0-394-54382-3

BOOK DESIGN BY MARYSARAH QUINN

For the members of the

WESTERN NEW ENGLAND
STORYTELLERS' GUILD

When the heart overflows,
it comes out through the mouth.
—ETHIOPIAN PROVERB

CONTENTS

◆   ◆   ◆

◆   ◆   ◆

CONTENTS

◆   ◆   ◆

TRUE LOVES AND FALSE   65

◆   ◆   ◆

TRICKSTERS, ROGUES, AND CHEATS   125

◆   ◆   ◆

THE FOOL: NUMBSKULLS AND NOODLEHEADS   167

◆   ◆   ◆

HEROES: LIKELY AND UNLIKELY   199

◆   ◆   ◆

WONDER TALES, TALL TALES, AND BRAG   243

◆   ◆   ◆

SHAPE SHIFTERS   297

◆   ◆   ◆

NOT QUITE HUMAN   329

◆   ◆   ◆

FOOLING THE DEVIL   355

◆   ◆   ◆

THE GETTING OF WISDOM   401

ACKNOWLEDGMENTS

I would like to thank the following people who have helped in the preparation of this book: my patient husband, David Stemple, who has read every single word of every single book I have written; my editor, Wendy Wolf, who knows more about folktales—and folklorists—than is healthy; Dan Cullen, for his second eye at Pantheon and his endless patience on the phone; and all the storytellers whose performances and friendships have contributed enormously to this work: Connie Regan, Barbara Freeman, Laura Simms, Carol Birch, Ellin Greene, Diane Wolkstein, Doug Lipman, LeeEllen Marvin, Maggi Peirce, Susan Fleischman, Susan Klein, Michale Gabriel, Robert Harris, John Porcino, Cynthia Payne, Tim Van Egmond, Mara Capy, Jay Goldspinner, Rochelle Wildfong, Pamela Van der Ploeg, Jay O'Callahan, Brother Blue, Cynthia Orr, Milbre Burch, Jill Oxendine, Kay Stone, Anne Pellowski, Michael Parent, David Holt—and all the others.

INTRODUCTION

I

Tales are meant to be told. That simple statement is correct both in the etymological sense—*tale* comes from the Anglo-Saxon *talu*, which means "speech"—and in a historical sense. Storytelling, that oldest of arts, has always been both an entertainment and a cultural necessity. Laws, news, customs, even royal successions encapsulated within the bodies of tales were passed on and on, down through the years. As the stories were kept alive by this process of mouth-to-mouth resuscitation, the storytellers breathed life into human cultures.

So stories are history—of a sort. But after a while stories become nonisomorphic, no longer corresponding point for point to the thing they originally symbolized. This does not mean that stories lie but rather that they look at humanity's history obliquely, through slotted eyes. Emily Dickinson once wrote something to that effect: "Tell all the Truth but tell it slant."

In a world of sunlight, stories are the shadows cast by humankind, for it is humans, of course, who are the storytellers. Stories distinguish us from animals more than any opposable thumb. And though Vachel Lindsay has it that language began in imitation of nature—

> *Whining like forest dogs,*
> *Rustling like budding trees,*
> *Bubbling like thawing springs,*
> *Humming like little bees,*
> *Crooning like Maytime tides,*
> *Chattering parrot words,*

Crying the panther's cry,
Chirping like mating birds,
Thus, thus, we learned to speak . . .
—"Eden in Winter"

—animals have but a marginal language: the tilt of head, the twitch of ear, the placement of forepaws or tail. Scientists watching wolves have distinguished a whole variety of signals, primitive language tricks. Ornithologists can tell a southern crow from a northern crow by its caws. Dolphins have been studied and their clicking signals searched for meaning. Whale "song" has been charted. Jane Goodall has learned to decipher chimpanzee sounds. Others, following her techniques, have worked with mountain gorillas. Washoe and Nim and other captive apes have been taught hand signing. But though there is evidence of a rudimentary language in animal species, it is a language that is concerned only with the moment. It can treat with neither the past nor the future. Only humans can create tales that change or structure the world in which they live.

It is because of that ability to structure and change, a seemingly magical ability to hold past, present, and future in the Word, that storytellers have been venerated in oral cultures all over the earth. Except in times of war, the Irish shanachies were second only to the king. In Siberia, skilled tale tellers were hired by artels of lumbermen, fishermen, and hunters to tell stories to while away their leisure hours. Ivan the Terrible, like some avatar of Sheherazade's sultan, required three blind old men to tell him folktales before he fell asleep. The African *griot*, a key member of his society, chanted genealogies, advised rulers, and told stories that recorded history. Even today Hungarian soldiers, by a centuries-old custom, can be required to tell stories after lights out or pay the penalty of shouting into the stove, "Oh, Mother, haven't you brought me up to be a big brute of an ass, who hasn't even been taught to tell a tale!"

And what kinds of tales did these tellers recite? Wonder tales, tales of transformations, noodlehead and numbskull stories, jocular tales, cautionary stories to keep children in line, stories of ghosts and revenants to make the listener shiver, long adventures of heroes and heroines, amusing exploits of animals who could talk and had interesting things to say, touching accounts of love lost or won, frightening tales of rapine and murder, horrifying stories of cannibal kings and ogres on mountaintops and trolls under bridges who cracked bone and sucked marrow. There were stories that seemed almost straightforward recordings of battles or of matters of belief, teaching tales that enabled marginal tribes to survive, and stories that detailed in fascinating ways the proper method for propitiating the local gods. These tales could be as short as the English ghost story reported by the venerable English collector Katharine Briggs:

He woke up frightened and reached for the matches, and the matches were put into his hand.

Or they could be days-long recitations that were part devotion, part history, part mystery, and part entertainment, like the tales told about Gilgamesh, Inanna, Hercules, or Mwindo.

The accumulated stories from the world's many societies are a veritable Sears catalogue of people, places, events—and wonder. Often such tales are described as "cultural history," as if they constituted a fixed body of lore. However, this is a fluid tradition that is as migratory as a winter bird, feeding as it goes from place to place and leaving something of itself behind. Those of us with gardens can attest to the hardiness of "volunteers" that spring up from seeds that have been carried in a bird's body over countless miles.

In the very center of these stories, of course, is human truth. But as in the old story of the man who searched for truth, it is served up to us in different guises, capped and belled or wrapped in a cloth of gold. As folklorist Roger Abrahams puts it, "Tales are, in the ears of their hearers, permissible lies."

THE OLD LADY IN THE CAVE

There was once a man who was successful in all things. He had a fine wife, a loving family, and a craft for which he was justly famous. But still he was not happy.

"I want to know Truth," he said to his wife.

"Then you should seek her," she replied.

So the man put his house and all his worldly goods in his wife's name (she being adamant on that point) and went out on the road a beggar after Truth.

He searched up the hills and down in the valleys for her. He went into small villages and large towns; into the forests and along the coasts of the great wide sea; into dark, grim wastes and lush meadows pied with flowers. He looked for days and for weeks and for months.

And then one day, atop a high mountain, in a small cave, he found her.

Truth was a wizened old woman with but a single tooth left in her head. Her hair hung down onto her shoulders in lank, greasy strands. The skin on her face was the brown of old parchment and as dry, stretched over prominent bones. But when she signaled to him with a hand crabbed with age, her voice was low and lyrical and pure and it was then that he knew he had found Truth.

He stayed a year and a day with her and he learned all that she had to teach. And when the year and a day was up, he stood at the mouth of the cave ready to leave for home.

"My Lady Truth," he said, "you have taught me so much and I would do something for you before I leave. Is there anything you wish?"

Truth put her head to one side and considered. Then she raised an ancient finger. "When you speak of me," she said, "tell them I am young and beautiful!"

II

"There is a kind of death to every story," Ruth Sawyer has written in *The Way of the Storyteller*, "when it leaves the speaker and becomes impaled for all time on clay tablets or the written and printed page."

Well, yes—and no. There are stories wrenched from the lips of a storyteller that die miserably on the page. But other stories, set down by a particularly able transcriber, actually take on greater life in a book. And some stories are born directly in print and suffer from being spoken aloud, though they may trace a common ancestor back to the oral tradition. Perhaps it would be wiser to say that there are some stories meant only to be read and some meant only to be heard, and some that are felicitous to either eye or ear.

Basically there are three kinds of folk stories: the oral, the transcribed, and the literary or art tale. No one kind of story is better than another; there is no contest since there are no set or even settable standards. A good story is simply one that lasts because the listeners or readers like it and demand it again. Told and retold or read and reread, the story exists neither in the mouth nor on the page, neither in the ear nor the eye. It is created *between*. No two listeners hear exactly the same tale. Each brings something of himself to the story, and the story is then re-created between the teller and the listener, between the writer and the reader.

We can actually hear oral tales being changed by different tellers, though we cannot, of course, observe the re-creation by the listener. But by looking at tale variants, one can get a sense of the kind of metamorphosis a story undergoes in the listening ear. Folktales from the oral tradition carry with them the thumbprints of history. Each place, each culture, each teller leaves a mark. As Italo Calvino has written, the folktale "tends to absorb something of the place where it is narrated—a landscape, a custom, a moral outlook, or else merely a very faint accent or flavor of that locality." Reading as many tales as I had to in order to make the selections for this book, I was reminded again and again how bits and pieces of stories—archetypal characters, situations, magical hats or sticks or rings—have been lifted from one teller's quilt and sewn into another. The patchworking of Story is endless. How many variations of the crop-division story (tale type 1030) have I come upon, that tale in which the farmer outsmarts Old Nick by planting either a top crop or a root crop? In the German story reprinted here from Grimm's, 'The Peasant and the Devil," the only actors are a wily farmer and the Prince of Lies himself, the crops parsnips and grain. In the Russian version, the peasant outwits a bear. In the Communist Chinese, the farmer tricks his greedy landlord. In the Egyptian, the actors are a wolf and a mouse. In the American slave narrative "Sheer Crops," Brer Rabbit gulls Brer Bear. The crops range from potatoes and corn to taro and wheat, but in any language it is a delightful story: witty, carefully developed, with an ending that is as inevitable as it is satisfying. Every culture seems to treasure the cunning of the underdog.

Tales that are set down and then transported through time on the pages of a book have a slightly different character from those orally transmitted. Not better—different. Often events glossed over or forgotten by the oral tellers are tidied up, made cleaner, elaborated upon, fixed to serve a specific purpose. Even some of our best-known oral transcribers were "guilty" of such a liberal hand. It is no longer a scholarly secret that Sir Walter Scott added verses to the folk ballads he collected or that the Brothers Grimm "helped" their respondents, several of whom were not really German peasants, as the Grimms had implied, but rather middle-class French Huguenots whose sources were most likely Perrault's literary adaptations of old tales. In fact, many newly recovered stories can be traced back to literary sources, and so we reseed and resow our fields of tales. Sometimes, like the crop dividers, we get what is on top and sometimes we take what is below. Yet we must remind ourselves that most transcribers are not violating the tales. Rather, they are well within the tradition of tale telling, which is a tradition of constant and continuing re-creation.

Francis James Child, collector of the Child ballads (and himself not above aiding the process), once suggested that the tradition is abetted by one of three different kind of tellers: the blind beggar, the nurserymaid, and the clerk. The blind beggar sings for his supper and so is constrained to change his story to suit the listening audience, the better to be paid for his tales. The nurserymaid changes stories to suit what she assumes are the appetites and moral needs of her young charges. And the clerk is the literary teller, writing down stories that suit the needs of an audience of one, the self.

Occasionally, of course, a particular transcriber is so able, so effective, so inventive, that the story itself is changed forever. Charles Perrault was such a reworker. He reinvented, among others, "Cinderella" in such a potent form that it is *his* telling and not the five hundred European variants that remains the premier version of the tale (though I have chosen another, less-known version, the Russian "Vasilisa the Beautiful"). In his seventeenth-century retelling, Perrault gave Cinderella a fairy godmother and a midnight warning, two things which up to that time she did not possess. And then—history draws a scrim over the actual events and we can only guess—someone, Perrault or perhaps the English translator of his *Histoires ou contes du temps passé*, made a brilliant mistake. The heroine's fur (*vair*) slipper was misread as glass (*verre*). Thus in Story all mistakes are made true by the telling.

Some stories, though, are born directly onto the page, strange children of an oral father and a literary mother. Such art tales have been made popular for centuries by authors such as Homer, Apuleius, Aesop, Marie de France, Mme. Le Prince de Beaumont, Hans Christian Andersen, Oscar Wilde, Laurence Housman, Isak Dinesen, Isaac Bashevis Singer. Today most stories of this kind are marketed as nursery fare or as genre tales by children's-book authors or science fiction/fantasy writers and exist in a narrow ghetto apart from mainstream literature, much to the reading public's loss. Such stories owe their settings, their archetypal characters, even bits of their magic to the past, but thematically they draw upon the century and the place in which they are written. This should not be surprising. Authors are as rooted in society as their readers. And if they reach back to earlier beliefs upon which to base their tales, perhaps the reason is, as Graham Greene contends, that "man has to resort to some kind of superstition. They are the nails in his boots that keep him on the rock."

Oral, transcribed, or literary tale—what matters is whether it is a good story. In the vast tapestry of Story woven on a literary warp there are threads of the oral and transcribed traditions. Back and forth the shuttle has gone, thoroughly confusing the patterns until only the most assiduous scholar can pick through and trace down any one particular strand. And in doing so, the sorter and picker often misses the beauty of the cloth. In this book, though the emphasis is on stories from the oral tradition, an occasional tale tampered with and tidied up by its original transcriber or literary source has slipped in. The one thing I have tried to avoid is stories that have remained literary tales, no matter how wonderful, whether from the magic-filled *Arabian Nights* collection, Andersen's 150-plus classic tales, Boccaccio's lusty *Decameron*, Washington Irving's Americana, Oscar Wilde's artful fairy stories, the Arthurian faerie of Marie de France, or the shtetl re-creations of Isaac Bashevis Singer. There are many magnificent collections of such art tales, many of them quite folklike; but they are distinguished from the oral stories by their grace of prose, an elegant formality, an appreciation and conscious use of magic as metaphor, extensive descriptive passages, and a literary diction.

This collection comes more directly from the folk archives where tales are basic, with a metaphoric content that must be read *into* the story by sophisticated listeners, where the language has been honed by centuries of tongue-polishing, where the stories are not personal history artfully disguised but are more often, in Roger Abrahams's words, a codification of "hard-won truths" and the dramatization of "the rationale behind traditions." To aid the folklorist *manqué*, however, I have annotated each tale at the end of the book, including those in this Introduction.

III

There is no argument: stories are powerful. Even before literary criticism, psychological interpretation, or the anthropological/sociological/historical schools of folklore analysis were born, the people who told and listened to stories knew it. So tales that warned about speaking out of turn or talking too much or the foolishness of certain kinds of wisdom found their way into the body of folklore.

In Africa, one of the most popular of such stories is told by many different tribes. It also traveled on the slave ships to America, where it became a jocular tale. The following version is from the Nupe of Nigeria:

A hunter goes into the bush. He finds an old human skull. The hunter says: "What brought you here?" The skull answers: "Talking brought me here." The hunter runs off. He runs to the king. He tells the king: "I found a dry human skull in the bush. It asks you how its father and mother are."

The king says: "Never since my mother bore me have I heard that a dead skull can speak." The king summons the Alkali, the Saba, and the Degi and asks them if they have ever heard the like. None of the wise men has heard the like and they decide to send a guard out with the hunter into the bush to find out if his story is true and, if so, to learn the reason for it. The guard accompany the hunter into the bush with the order to kill him on the spot should he have lied. The guard and the hunter come to the skull. The hunter addresses the skull: "Skull, speak." The skull is silent. The hunter asks as before: "What brought you here?" The skull does not answer. The whole day long the hunter begs the skull to speak, but it does not answer. In the evening the guard tell the hunter to make the skull speak, and when he cannot they kill him in accordance with the king's command. When the guard are gone the skull opens its jaws and asks the dead hunter's head: "What brought you here?" The dead hunter's head replies: "Talking brought me here!"

Stories are powerful. They are a journey and a joining. In a tale we meet new places, new people, new ideas. And they become *our* places, *our* people, *our* ideas. As the noted Russian author and literature specialist Kornei Chukovsky has written, storytelling fosters "compassion and humanness, this marvelous ability of man to be disturbed by another's misfortunes, to feel joy at another being's happiness, to experience another's fate as one's own."

Next, the story is history, for each tale carries with it over the miles and through the generations the bruises and blandishments and embraces of the societies in which it has dwelt. "Cinderella" can be traced back to China, where noblewomen had their feet bound as infants. This emphasis on the lotus foot in the tiny slipper that defines the nobility of its wearer can still be seen in a number of the variants. "Red Riding Hood," according to Professor Jack Zipes in his controversial study *Fairy Tales and the Art of Subversion*, began as a warning tale to civilize French girls out of sexual experimentation so effectively that, even when the ending of the story has been changed, the moral is set: Do not go to bed with wolves! Civilizations are made up of

cultures; stories record the aspirations of the people within cultures.
Yet the stories last long past the cradling societies. In Robert Louis
Stevenson's charming poem, we see this clearly:

> *Bright is the ring of words*
> *When the right man rings them,*
> *Fair the fall of songs*
> *When the singer sings them.*
> *Still they are carolled and said—*
> *On wings they are carried—*
> *After the singer is dead*
> *And the maker buried.*

Then, stories are a mystery, giving out clues to open the locked
doors of self. Though the Jungians have been trying different keys
in that lock for some time, not only Jung himself but also his articulate
followers Joseph Campbell and Marie von Franz, it took the Freudian
psychiatrist Bruno Bettelheim to bring word of the psychological
elements to the general public with a best-selling book, *The Uses of
Enchantment* (1976). Bettelheim spoke of the tales lending permission
to the listeners. He said that folk stories were not only a record of
emotions carried through centuries but were actually part of a child's
rehearsals for adult life. (Though it must be noted by any serious
student of the book that the tales he uses as demonstrations were not
originally told in the nursery.) In stories like "The Frog-Prince" he
sees tumescence and detumescence; in "Red Riding Hood," men-
struation; in "Jack and the Beanstalk," the Oedipus complex. The
fairy tale, says Bettelheim, "takes these existential anxieties and di-
lemmas very seriously and addresses itself directly to them: the need
to be loved and the fear that one is thought worthless; the love of
life, and the fear of death." In this view, stories can be homeopathic,
the storyteller a healer.
  Recently I attended a fairy tale conference at Princeton University
where the participants were so busy being academic about the motifs
and morphology of a tale, about the sociological implications of the
endings of Grimm stories, about the bourgeois subsumption of
the female tale teller, about the psychological embellishments and the
validation of emotion, that the words "Once upon a time . . ." were
never spoken. The tale was treated as an anthropological document
or as an archaeological dig or as a prototype of therapy or as a product
of a particular social-economic evolution. No one remembered even

to mention that a story has its own logic, its own meaning, its own integrity, or, in the words of the Maori storyteller:

> *The breath of life,*
> *The spirit of life,*
> *The word of life,*
> *It flies to you and you and you,*
> *Always the word.*

If the story does not have that breath of life, all the journeying, all the history, all the mystery, are for nought. And it is up to the tale teller to make sure that the story speaks.

> *Whenever misfortune threatened the Jews, Rabbi Israel Baal Shem Tov would retreat to the forest, light the fire, say the prayer and the misfortune would be avoided. In the passing of time this task fell to a second rabbi who knew both the place in the forest and the prayer but not how to light the fire. Nevertheless the misfortune was avoided. A third rabbi knew only the place; the prayer and the fire had been forgotten. But this too was enough and the misfortune was avoided. Finally the task fell to Rabbi Israel of Rizhyn who knew neither the place nor the fire nor the prayer. All he could do was tell the story. "And it was sufficient."*

IV

In the United States today there is a renaissance of storytelling. Except for some few backwoods pockets, storytelling in America was moribund by the mid-twentieth century. The corpse was kept minimally animated by librarians who told stories using book illustrations or flannel-board cutouts or hand puppets or assorted props. First radio, then film, and finally television seemed to have delivered a death blow. Listeners relied on entertainers separated from them by mechanics, and the tellers used stories more as jokes or as lead-ins to comedy routines. Only occasionally could one find a teller of note who was not a librarian—at summer camps, perhaps, or at a church function. But the real social activity of storytelling was propped up in the nursery or the children's room in the library, as alive as a limp Raggedy Ann.

Then, out of the folk renascence of the sixties, the same young men and women who were attracted by folk crafts were drawn to the purity of folk songs. These young people were eager to rediscover roots, their own or others. Out of that movement another movement was born. In 1974 an infant-sized festival was launched in a pocket-sized town in Tennessee, more to help revitalize the town than to spark a movement. October in Jonesboro, when the leaves have begun turning on the mountainsides and the nights are often cool and the morning fresh with a heavy dew, seemed a magical backdrop against which to set the first American festival dedicated to Story. Some two hundred participants, mostly curious listeners, came that weekend. Today the October Jonesboro festival attracts closer to three thousand, including tellers, would-be tellers, and listeners. There are also festivals, conferences, workshops, and weekends dedicated to storytelling in over twenty other states, as well as in Canada and England.

Out of that first festival grew an organization, NAPPS, the National Association for the Preservation and Perpetuation of Storytelling. Although there had been one or two storytelling organizations before (such as the National Story League in Pennsylvania), NAPPS has gained national attention.

One might dwell on the irony of having to organize and relearn what was once that most human of activities—storytelling. But in fact, in most cultures where Story was (and is) important, storytelling has been an apprenticed occupation. As Joseph Campbell wrote: "There is a romantic idea that myth comes from the people. It doesn't; it comes from the teacher, the shaman and visionary as the giver and interpreter of myth. The visionary translates what he sees into an art or ritual form." By projection, then, tales—which are the personalizing of the great myths, the bits and pieces of the everyday where the great mythic structures impinge upon humanity—still need a structurer. And that person is the tale teller, who holds culture in the mouth.

The Irish poet-tellers studied their art for 15 years, and had to be wise in philosophy, astronomy, magic, and conversant with 250 prime tales and a hundred subsidiary ones. The shanachies, who told the historical tales, were entrusted with 178 prime stories.

The Greek storytellers learned not only to tell a great body of work, but also to perform on the kithara, which distinguished them from the amateurs who used the lyre.

The Navajo singer recited creation stories that lasted two to three days. Other long prayers and tales to do with the Blessingway ceremonies were in his repertory. Some 30 major ceremonies, each containing hundreds of songs and tales, were committed to memory.

The skalds of the North not only learned scores of tales and songs, but as a vassal to a noble lord, a skald might fight by his master's side and then either recount his lord's great battle deeds or sing his master's death song, adding either—or both—to an already large body of memorized work.

Medieval troubadors were expected to know the current court and countryside favorite tales as well as recite the latest in court scandals, play two instruments well, and further, to be able to repeat the noteworthy theses from the universities.

Irish ollahms and shanachies, African *griots*, Norse skalds, German minnesingers, French troubadors, Anglo-Saxon gleemen, Norman minstrels—these were but some of the professionals in the world of Story. They told long, complex traditional tales to great gatherings and were repaid for their efforts by a particular place in society, money, gifts, property, wives or husbands, supper, ale, or the high king's favor.

And next to the hearth, by the bedside, on the back porch, round the cracker barrel, in the lap, the nonprofessionals kept the small spark alive when the guilds and the gatherings failed. These "lesser" tellers were not trained nor were they picked out for their fabulous memories, but they did manage more often than not to remember the story. What they did not actually remember, they either made up or left out. Mouth to ear, mouth to ear, over and over and over again, grandmother and grandfather, uncle and aunt, mother and father, nanny and nurse were in turn listener and teller.

Storytelling is still part of the everyday lives of many people throughout the world, though too often, what Don Futterman reported about a Moroccan community in the Negev is true: "The younger generations found storytelling to be backward, embarrassing. They were impatient with the elders' foolish ramblings. So the old tellers had stopped telling stories almost completely." When modern cultures clash with traditional ways, too often it is the older and quieter mode that dies. Still, storytelling exists around the world: the Japanese picture showman who holds up illustrations as he talks; the shadow-puppet players in Java; the Brazilian clothesline teller who, like the string tellers among the Lega of Zaire, attaches objects matching each tale in his repertory to the line; the Maître Conte in Haiti who announces a tale with the interrogatory *Cric?* and will not begin unless the audience shouts back *Crac!*; the women of the Walberi in Australia who trace pictures illustrating their stories in the sand; the Inuit who "storyknife," drawing pictures in the snow in winter and the mud in summer with a whalebone knife to accompany their tales. And thanks to the rededication of storytellers in America, stories are once again alive and well across the North American continent.

V

Storytelling is a personal art that makes public what is private and makes private what is public. By choosing this or that story to tell, I reveal much about myself. Wonder tales, transformation stories, romances, stories with ironic twists, and jocular tales appeal to me the most, my preferences being informed by the fact that I am a twentieth-century American eclectic. In choosing stories for this book I had to stretch myself and pick stories that might not have appealed to me before. Those of us who are used to the plot-lines of European tales, where three is a prime magic number and events usually round off after the third adventure or the third task, may find that an American Indian story or an Eskimo tale or a piece from Siberia has a strange feel. It is not just that the names are difficult to pronounce—Celtic names are equally troublesome to the unpracticed tongue—but rather that the time sequences feel odd or the story seems to end in the wrong place. In order to minimize such feelings of strangeness, I have tried to make the stories more accessible by organizing the book into sections, thirteen (that magical number) in all.

Many of the tales included here are ones I have heard particular tellers tell. I cannot read the stories without the sound of their inflections in my ear. Laura Simms tells "The Little Old Woman with Five Cows" with rollicking, tongue-tripping gusto. Odds Botkins tells "Sedna" with guitar and bird-call accompaniment. Barbara Freeman can make an audience fall off its chairs laughing at "Old Dry Frye." Connie Regan brings chills every time she tells "Mr. Fox." But even if the readers of this book never hear these particular tellers, the stories have been chosen because of the felicitous way they speak from the page. I chose tales that I like and would enjoy coming to again and again in print.

Katharine Briggs points out in *British Folktales* that the study of folklore encompasses many disciplines: "Sociology, Anthropology, Literature, Linguistics, Music, Drama, History, Archaeology . . ." But the lover of folktales needs little access to the academic disciplines in order to enjoy these stories—only a listening ear and an open heart, those same attributes the original listeners had. Folk stories touch on all aspects of the human experience, another way of saying "Sociology, Anthropology, Literature, Linguistics . . ." that litany of academe. The best stories are the ones that forsake message or straight historical context and are just whopping good tales.

I am reminded of the encounter William James, the philosopher, supposedly had with an old woman after one of his public lectures on the solar system:

> The ancient beldame came to the front of the hall, leaning on her mahogany walking stick. "You are wrong, Mr. James," she said as she drew near. "The Earth does not revolve around the sun."
>
> "Then, Madame," asked James politely, "what is your theory?"
>
> "Our world is balanced on the back of a giant turtle," she argued.
>
> "And what," asked James politely, "does that turtle stand upon?"
>
> "Why he stands upon the back of a second, larger turtle," the old woman replied.
>
> "And," James continued relentlessly, "on what does that turtle stand?"
>
> The old woman drew herself up and stared James in the eye. "It's no good, Mr. James," she said ringingly. "It's turtles all the way down!"

This, of course, may have been only an apocryphal meeting, a legend-in-the-making, an invented conversation ascribed to a famous personage. "Fakelore," as folklorists Alan Dundes and Richard Dorson like to say. But within the context of literature, the James anecdote is quite appropriate. Literature is not made up of the pieces of periods and genres described by academic inquiry but is rather story resting on the sturdy back of Story. And it's no use, my learned friends: it's story *all the way down.*

That is really the genesis of this volume of tales from around the world: these are great stories for telling and listening, stories resting on stories. You will not find the most famous fairy tales here, for they are easily accessible elsewhere. Not "Cinderella," but interesting other versions—"The Goose Girl" and "Vasilisa the Beautiful." Not "The Frog-Prince," but "The Toad-Bridegroom," a Korean tale that handles some of the same material. Not "Bluebeard," but "Mr. Fox." The thumbprints of the other tales, like the whorls on a turtle's shell, remind us of the historical passage of stories. My notes at the back of the book will detail a few of those curlicues, but the notes are not integrated into the text, because nothing should distract from the important matter—the stories themselves.

Like the hero of the Irish tale that opens the book, "The Man Who Had No Story," a reader may come to this volume thinking he has no tale to tell. But by the end, there will be over 150 stories in his repertory. And if a teller ever gets stuck for a story—or is simply in no mood to recite—there is always a way out. He simply has to start the Japanese "Endless Story" or this round story heard by British collector Katharine Briggs:

> It was a dark and stormy night, and the Captain stood on the bridge, and he said to the Mate, "Tell us a yarn."
>
> And the Mate began, "It was a dark and stormy night, and the Captain stood on the bridge, and he said to the Mate, 'Tell us a yarn.' And the Mate began . . ."

Given that story, the audience will soon enough take care of itself.

WHY WE TELL STORIES
For Linda Foster

1

Because we used to have leaves
and on damp days
our muscles feel a tug,
painful now, from when roots
pulled us into the ground

and because our children believe
they can fly, an instinct retained
from when the bones in our arms
were shaped like zithers and broke
neatly under their feathers

and because before we had lungs
we know how far it was to the bottom
as we floated open-eyed
like painted scarves through the scenery
of dreams, and because we awakened

and learned to speak

2

We sat by the fire in our caves,
and because we were poor, we made up a tale

about a treasure mountain
that would open only for us

and because we were always defeated,
we invented impossible riddles
only we could solve,
monsters only we could kill,
women who could love no one else

and because we had survived
sisters and brothers, daughters and sons,
we discovered bones that rose
from the dark earth and sang
as white birds in the trees

3

Because the story of our life
becomes our life

Because each of us tells
the same story
but tells it differently

and none of us tells it
the same way twice

Because grandmothers looking like spiders
want to enchant the children
and grandfathers need to convince us
what happened happened because of them

and though we listen only
haphazardly, with one ear,
we will begin our story
with the word and

—LISEL MUELLER

TELLING
TALES

Stories about stories are common coin in the world's cultures, for the power of tale telling—and therefore the importance of the storyteller—had to be remarked upon by the tellers themselves, one of the earliest practices in self-promotion.

A popular form of storytelling is the riddle tale in which the unriddler proves his or her worthiness. So widespread are these stories that there have been scholarly treatises on the subject. Riddles are among the earliest and most universal of pre-stories; each is a little metaphor that often includes character and setting as well as a mystery at its core. It is not a long step from there to investing the riddle with a coherent plot structure either surrounding the riddle itself or incorporated within the riddle's body. Thus were riddle stories born. Some are highly elaborated tales, such as the Italian "Catherine, Sly Country Lass," and some are just a tiny step up from the bareboned riddle, like the African "Leopard, Goat, and Yam." But the tradition of riddling is so old and popular in folklore that even Samson's famous "Out of the eater came forth meat, and out of the strong came forth sweetness," in the Old Testament, and Oedipus's contest with the Sphinx who asks, "What goes on four legs in the morning, two legs at noon, and three legs in the evening?" are not the earliest examples of the type. Plutarch wrote of Homer that he died of chagrin when he could not solve a riddle, and in the riddling stories sometimes a man's or woman's life *is* on the line.

Finally, the prevalence of stories about lies, liars, and lying contests is a further extension of the stories-about-stories genre. Actual brag stories or tall tales will be included in the section called "Wonder Tales," but narratives about the liars themselves are included here.

THE MAN WHO HAD NO STORY
Ireland

Well, there was a man down here in Barr an Ghaoith a long time ago and his name was Brian Ó Braonacháin. The trade that he had was cutting rods, making baskets of them, and selling them in Glenties and in Dunloe and in Fintown and everywhere he could get them sold.

But one year he was down here and there wasn't a single rod in the whole of Barr an Ghaoith that he hadn't cut, made baskets of, sold, and then spent the money.

Those were bad times—the English were in power and they wouldn't let the Irish earn a single penny in any way. And Brian didn't know what to do.

But in those days there was a little glen outside of Barr an Ghaoith that they called Alt an Torr and there were remarkably fine rods growing there. But nobody dared cut any rods there, for everyone made out that it was a fairy glen.

But one morning Brian said to his wife that if she made him up a little lunch he would go out and cut the makings of a couple of baskets and perhaps no harm would come to him.

The wife got up and made up a lunch for him. He put it in his pocket and he took a hook and a rope under his arm.

He went out to the glen and he wasn't long in the glen until he had cut two fine bundles of rods.

When he was tying them together so that he could carry them with the rope on his back, a terrible fog started to gather around him. He decided that he would sit down and eat his lunch and perhaps that the fog would clear. He sat down and he ate the lunch he had with him and when he had finished eating it was so dark that he could not see his finger in front of him.

He stood up and he got terribly scared. He looked to the east and he looked to the west and he saw a light. Where there is light there must be people, he thought, and he headed for the light. And he tripped and fell the whole time, but in the end he came up to the light. There was a big long house there. The door was open and there was a fine light coming out of the window and the door.

He put his head in the door and an old woman was sitting in the corner and an old man on the other side of the fire. Both of them saluted Brian Ó Braonacháin from Barr an Ghaoith and wished him welcome, and they asked him to come up and sit in at the fire.

Brian came up and he sat in at the fire between the pair of them. They talked for a while. But he had not been sitting there long when the old man asked him to tell a fairy tale.

"That is something that I never did in all my life," said Brian, "tell a story of any kind. I can't tell Fenian tales or fairy tales of any kind."

"Well," said the old woman, said she, "take that bucket and go down to the well below the house and fetch a bucket of water and do something for your keep."

"I'll do anything," said Brian, "except tell a story."

He took the bucket, went down to the well and filled it with water from the well. He left it standing on the flagstone beside the well, so that the water would run off it, before he brought it in. But a big blast of wind came and he was swept off up into the sky. He was blown east and he was blown west and when he fell to the ground he could see neither the bucket nor the well nor anything at all.

He looked around and he saw a light and he made out that where there was light there must be people and he headed for the light. He tripped and fell the whole time, it was so dark. But at last he came to the light. There was a big long house there, far bigger than the first house, two lights in it and a fine light out of the door.

He put his head in the door, and what was it but a wake-house. There was a row of men sitting by the back wall of the house and a row of men sitting by the front wall of the house and up at the fire there was a girl with curly black hair sitting on a chair. She saluted and welcomed Brian Ó Braonacháin from Barr an Ghaoith and she asked him to come up and sit beside her on the chair.

Brian came up and he sat beside her on the chair and very shy he was, too. But he had not been sitting long when a big man who was in the company stood up.

"It is a very lonely wake we are having here tonight," said he, "a couple of us must go to get a fiddler, so that we can start dancing."

"Oh," said the girl with the curly black hair, "you don't need to go for any fiddler tonight" said she, "you have the best fiddler in Ireland among you here tonight," said she, "Brian Ó Braonacháin from Barr an Ghaoith."

"Oh, that is something I never did in my life," said Brian, "play a tune on a fiddle, and there is no music or singing or fiddling of any kind in my head."

"Oh," said she, "don't make me a liar, you are the very man who can fiddle."

Before Brian knew he had the bow and the fiddle in his hand and he played away and they danced away, and they all said that they had never heard any fiddler playing a tune on a fiddle better than Brian Ó Braonacháin from Barr an Ghaoith.

The big man who was in the company stood up and said that the dancing must stop now. "A couple of us must go for the priest, so that we can say Mass," said he, "for this corpse must go out of here before daybreak."

"Oh," said the girl with the curly dark hair, "there is no need to go for any priest tonight, the best priest in Ireland is sitting here beside me on the chair, Brian Ó Braonacháin from Barr an Ghaoith."

"Oh, I have nothing of a priest's power or holiness," said Brian, "and I do not know anything about a priest's work in any way."

"Come, come," said she, "you will do that just as well as you did the rest."

Before Brian knew he was standing at the altar with two clerks and with the vestments on him.

He started to say Mass and he gave out the prayers after Mass. And the whole congregation that was listening said that they never heard any priest in Ireland giving out prayers better than Brian Ó Braonacháin.

Then the corpse was placed in a coffin outside the door and four men put the coffin on their shoulders. They were three fairly short men and one big tall man and the coffin was terribly shaky.

"One or two of us," said the big man who was in the company, said he, "must go for a doctor so that we can cut a piece off the legs of that big man to make him level with the other three."

"Oh," said the girl with the curly black hair, "you don't need to go for any doctor tonight, the best doctor in Ireland is here among you tonight, Brian Ó Braonacháin from Barr an Ghaoith."

"Oh, that is something I never did in my life," said Brian, "doctoring of any sort. I never got any doctor's schooling at all."

"You'll do that just as well as you did the rest," said she.

The lances were given to Brian and he cut a piece off the big man's legs, under his knees, and he stuck the legs back on, and he made him level with the other three men.

Then they put the coffin on their shoulders and they walked

gently and carefully west, until they came to the graveyard. There was a big stone wall around the graveyard, ten feet high, or maybe twelve. And they had to lift one man up on the wall first and they were going up one by one and going down into the graveyard on the other side. And the last man on top of the wall ready to go down into the graveyard was Brian Ó Braonacháin.

But a big blast of wind came and he was swept off up into the sky. He was blown to the east and he was blown to the west. When he fell down to the ground, he could see neither the graveyard nor the coffin nor the funeral. But where did he fall? He fell down on the flagstone beside the well where he had been at the beginning of the night. He looked at the bucket and the water was hardly dry on the outside of it.

He took the bucket and up he went into the house. And the old man and the old woman were sitting where he had left them at nightfall. He left the bucket by the dresser and he came up and sat in between the pair of them again.

"Now, Brian," said the old man, "can you tell a fairy tale?"

"I can," said he, "I am the man who has got a story to tell."

He began to tell the old woman and the old man what he had gone through since nightfall.

"Well, Brian," said the old man, "wherever you are from now on," said he, "and whenever anybody asks you tell a story, tell them that story, and you are the man who will have a story to tell."

The old woman got up and made Brian a good supper. And when he had had his supper she made up a feather bed for him and he went to bed. And he wasn't in bed long before he fell asleep, for he was tired after all he had gone through since nightfall.

But when he woke in the morning, where was he? He was lying in Alt an Torr outside Barr an Ghaoith with his head on the two bundles of rods. He got up and went home and he never cut a rod from that day to this.

How Spider Obtained
the Sky God's Stories
Africa (Ashanti)

Kwaku Anansi, the spider, once went to Nyankonpon, the sky god, in order to buy the sky god's stories. The sky god said, "What makes you think *you* can buy them?" The spider answered and said, "I know I shall be able." Thereupon the sky god said, "Great and powerful towns like Kokofu, Bekwai, Asumengya, have come, but they were unable to purchase them, and yet you who are but a mere masterless man, you say you will be able?"

The spider said, "What is the price of the stories?" The sky god said, "They cannot be bought for anything except Onini, the python; Osebo, the leopard; Mmoatia, the fairy; and Mmoboro, the hornets." The spider said, "I will bring some of all these things, and, what is more, I'll add my old mother, Nsia, the sixth child, to the lot."

The sky god said, "Go and bring them then." The spider came back, and told his mother all about it, saying, "I wish to buy the stories of the sky god, and the sky god says I must bring Onini, the python; Osebo, the leopard; Mmoatia, the fairy; and Mmoboro, the hornets; and I said I would add you to the lot and give you to the sky god." Now the spider consulted his wife, Aso, saying, "What is to be done that we may get Onini, the python?" Aso said to him, "You go off and cut a branch of a palm tree, and cut some string-creeper as well, and bring them." And the spider came back with them. And Aso said, "Take them to the stream." So Anansi took them; and, as he was going along he said, "It's longer than he is, it's not so long as he; you lie, it's longer than he."

The spider said, "There he is, lying yonder." The python, who had overheard this imaginary conversation, then asked, "What's this all about?" To which the spider replied, "Is it not my wife, Aso, who is arguing with me that this palm branch is longer than you, and I say she is a liar." And Onini, the python, said, "Bring it, and come and measure me." Anansi took the palm branch and laid it along the python's body. Then he said, "Stretch yourself out." And the python stretched himself out, and Anansi took the rope-creeper and wound it and the sound of the tying was *nwenene! nwenene! nwenene!* until he came to the head. Anansi, the spider said, "Fool, I shall take you to the sky god and receive the sky god's tales in exchange." So Anansi took him off to Nyame, the sky god. The sky god then said, "My hand has touched it; there remains what still remains."

The spider returned and came and told his wife what had happened, saying, "There remain the hornets." His wife said, "Look for a gourd, and fill it with water and go off with it." The spider went along through the bush, when he saw a swarm of hornets hanging there, and he poured out some of the water and sprinkled it on them. He then poured the remainder upon himself and cut a leaf of plantain and covered his head with it. And now he addressed the hornets, saying, "As the rain has come, had you not better come and enter this, my gourd, so that the rain will not beat you; don't you see that I have taken a plantain leaf to cover myself?" Then the hornets said, "We thank you, Aku, we thank you, Aku." All the hornets flew, disappearing into the gourd, *fom!*

Father Spider covered the mouth, and exclaimed, "Fools, I have got you, and I am taking you to receive the tales of the sky god in exchange." And he took the hornets to the sky god. The sky god said, "My hand has touched it; what remains still remains."

The spider came back once more, and told his wife, and said, "There remains Osebo, the leopard." Aso said, "Go and dig a hole." Anansi said, "That's enough, I understand." Then the spider went off to look for the leopard's tracks, and, having found them, he dug a very deep pit, covered it over, and came back home. Very early next day, when objects began to be visible, the spider said he would go off, and when he went, lo, a leopard was lying in the pit. Anansi said, "Little father's child, little mother's child, I have told you not to get drunk, and now, just as one would expect of you, you have become intoxicated, and that's why you have fallen into the pit. If I were to say I would get you out, next day, if you saw me, or likewise any of my children, you would go and catch me and them." The leopard said, "O! I could not do such a thing."

Anansi then went and cut two sticks, put one here, and one there, and said, "Put one of your paws here, and one also of your paws here." And the leopard placed them where he was told. As he was about to climb up, Anansi lifted up his knife, and in a flash it descended on his head, *gao!* was the sound it made. The pit received the leopard and *fom!* was the sound of the falling. Anansi got a ladder to descend into the pit to go and get the leopard out. He got the leopard out and came back with it, exclaiming, "Fool, I am taking you to exchange for the stories of the sky god." He lifted up the leopard to go and give to Nyame, the sky god. The sky god said, "My hands have touched it; what remains still remains."

Then the spider came back, carved an Akua's child, a black flat-faced wooden doll, tapped some sticky fluid from a tree and plastered the doll's body with it. Then he made *eto*, pounded yams, and put some in the doll's hand. Again he pounded some more and placed it in a brass basin; he tied string round the doll's waist, and went with it and placed it at the foot of the odum tree, the place where the fairies come to play. And a fairy came along. She said, "Akua, may I eat a little of this mash?" Anansi tugged at the string, and the doll nodded her head. The fairy turned to one of the sisters, saying, "She says I may eat some." She said, "Eat some, then." And she finished eating, and thanked her. But when she thanked her, the doll did not answer. And the fairy said to her sister, "When I thank her, she does not reply." The sister of the first fairy said, "Slap her crying-place." And she slapped it, *pa!* And her hand stuck there. She said to her sister, "My hand has stuck there." She said, "Take the one that remains and slap her crying-place again." And she took it and slapped her, *pa!* and this one, too, stuck fast. And the fairy told her sister, saying, "My two hands have stuck fast." She said, "Push it with your stom-ach." She pushed it and her stomach stuck to it. And Anansi came and tied her up, and he said, "Fool, I have got you, I shall take you to the sky god in exchange for his stories." And he went off home with her.

Now Anansi spoke to his mother, Ya Nsia, the sixth child, saying, "Rise up, let us go, for I am taking you along with the fairy to go and give you to the sky god in exchange for his stories." He lifted them up, and went off there to where the sky god was. Arrived there he said, "Sky god, here is a fairy and my old woman whom I spoke about, here she is, too." Now the sky god called his elders, the Kontire and Akwam chiefs, the Adonten, the Gyase, the Oyoko, Ankobea, and Kyidom. And he put the matter before them, saying, "Very great kings have come and were not able to buy the sky god's stories, but Kwaku Anansi, the spider, has been able to pay the price: I have received from him Osebo, the leopard; I have received from him Onini, the python; and of his own accord, Anansi has added his mother to the lot; all these things lie here." He said, "Sing his praise." "Eee!" they shouted. The sky god said, "Kwaku Anansi, from today and going on forever, I take my sky god's stories and I present them to you, *kose! kose! kose!* my blessing, blessing, blessing! No more shall we call them the stories of the sky god, but we shall call them spider stories."

This, my story, which I have related, if it be sweet, or if it be not sweet, take some elsewhere, and let some come back to me.

HELPING TO LIE
Germany

There once was a nobleman who liked to tell terrible lies, but sometimes he got stuck. Once he wanted to hire a new servant. When one came to offer his services, the nobleman asked him if he could lie. "Well," he said, "if it's got to be!"

"Yes," said the nobleman, "I sometimes get stuck telling lies. Then you will have to help me."

One day they were in an inn, and the nobleman was as usual telling lies: "Once I went hunting and I shot three hares in the air."

"This is not possible," said the others.

"Then you better fetch my coachman," he said, "to bear witness." They fetched him. "Johann, listen, I have just been telling these gentlemen about the three hares I shot in the air. Now you tell them how that was."

"Yes, sir. We were in the meadow, and a hare came jumping through the hedge, and while it was jumping out, you shot and it was dead. Afterward, when it was cut open, there were two young hares inside." Of course the others could say nothing to this.

On their way home the nobleman said that it was well done.

"Well, sir," said Johann, "the next time you tell lies, try to keep out of the air. On firm ground it will be easier for me to help you."

The Ash Lad Who Made the Princess Say "You're a Liar!"
Norway

There was once a king who had a daughter, and she was such a liar that no one could equal her. So he made it known that the one who could lie so that he made her say, "You're a liar!" would get both her and half the kingdom. There were many who tried, for everyone was only too willing to have the princess and half the kingdom, but all of them fared badly.

Then there were three brothers who were bent upon trying their luck. The two eldest set out first, but they fared no better than all the others. So the Ash Lad set out, and he met the princess in the stable.

"Good day!" he said. "It's a pleasure to meet you."

"Good day," she said. "It's nice to meet you, too! You don't have as big a barn as we do," she said, "for, when a shepherd stands at each end and blows on a ram's horn, one can't hear the other!"

"Oh, yes indeed!" said the boy. "Ours is much bigger, for when a cow is got with calf at one end of it, she doesn't bear it before she gets to the other."

"You don't say so!" said the princess. "Well, you haven't such a big ox as we do. There you can see it! When a man sits on each horn, one can't reach the other with a twelve-foot pole!"

"Pooh!" said the boy. "We have an ox so big that, when someone is sitting on each horn blowing a lure, one can't hear the other!"

"Oh indeed?" said the princess. "But you don't have as much milk as we do, all the same," she said, "for we milk into enormous troughs, and carry it in and pour it into big cauldrons, and curdle big cheeses!"

"Oh, we milk into great cauldrons, and cart them in and pour it into huge brewing vats, and curdle cheeses as big as a house. And then we have a grey mare to tread the cheese. But once it foaled in the cheese, and after we had been eating cheese for seven years, we came upon a big grey horse. I was going to drive to the mill with it one day, then its backbone broke; but I knew a remedy for that. I took a spruce tree and put it in for a backbone, and no other back did the horse have as long as we had it. But that tree grew, and became so big that I climbed up to Heaven through it, and when I got there, one of the saints was sitting weaving a bristle rope of barley broth. All at once the spruce broke and I couldn't get down again, but the good saint lowered me down on one of the ropes, and I landed in a fox's den. And there sat my mother and your father patching shoes, and all at once my mother gave your father such a blow that the scurf flew off 'im!"

"You're a liar!" said the princess. "My father's never been scurfy in his life!"

THE PARSON AND THE SEXTON
Norway

There was once a parson who was such a blusterer that whenever he saw anyone come driving towards him on the highway, he would roar from afar: *"Off the road! Off the road! Here comes the parson himself!"*

Once when he was carrying on like this, he met the king.

"Off the road! Off the road!" he shouted a long way off; but the king kept on driving straight ahead. So, for once, the parson had to turn his horse aside. And when the king came alongside he said, "Tomorrow you shall come to the court. And if you can't answer three questions I am going to put to you, you shall lose both frock and collar for the sake of your pride!"

This was quite a different tune from what the parson was used to. Bluster and bellow he could, and carry on worse than bad, too. But question-and-answer was out of his field. So he went to the sexton, who was said to have a better head on his shoulders than the parson, and told him that *he* wasn't keen on going, "for one fool can ask more than ten wise men can answer," he said. And so he got the sexton to go in his place.

Well, the sexton went; and he came to the royal manor dressed in the parson's frock and ruff collar. The king met him out on the porch, wearing both crown and scepter, and looking so grand he fairly shone.

"So you're there, are you?" said the king.

Yes he was . . . that was sure enough.

"Now, tell me first," said the king, "how far is it from east to west?"

"That's a day's journey, that is," said the sexton.

"How so?" asked the king.

"Well, the sun rises in the east and sets in the west, and does it nicely in a day," said the sexton.

"All right," said the king, "but tell me now, what do you think I'm worth, just as you see me here?"

"Let's see, Christ was valued at thirty pieces of silver, so I'd better not set you any higher than . . . twenty-nine," said the sexton.

"Mmmmmmmmmmmm!" said the king. "Well, since you're so wise on all counts, tell me what I'm thinking now!"

"Oh, I suppose you're thinking that it's the parson who's standing here before you. But I'm sorry to say you're wrong, for it's the sexton!"

"Aha! Then go home with you, and *you* be parson and let *him* be sexton!" said the king.

And so it was!

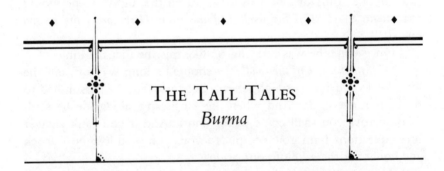

THE TALL TALES
Burma

There once lived three brothers who were known throughout the land for the tall tales they told. They would travel from place to place telling their strange stories to whoever would listen. No one ever believed their tales and all who heard them would cry out with exclamations of disbelief.

One day while traveling very far from home the three brothers came upon a wealthy prince. The prince was dressed very elegantly and bedecked in jewels such as the three men had never seen in their lives. They thought how wonderful it would be to have such possessions so they devised a plan whereby they could use their storytelling ability to trick the prince out of his belongings.

They said to the prince: "Let's tell each other stories of past adventures and if anyone should doubt the truth of what the other is saying then that person must become a slave to the others." Now the brothers had no use for a slave but if they could make the prince their slave then they could take his clothes because they would then belong to them.

The prince agreed to their plan. The brothers were sure they would win because no one had ever heard their stories without uttering cries of disbelief. And so they found a passer-by and asked him to act as judge in the matter. All sat down under the shade of a tree and the storytelling began.

The first brother stood up to tell his tale. With a smile on his face he began to speak: "When I was a young boy I thought it would be fun to hide from my brothers so I climbed the tallest tree in our village and remained there all day while my brothers searched high and low for me. When night fell my brothers gave up the search and returned home. It was then that I realized that I was unable to climb down the tree. But I knew I could get down with the help of a rope, so I went to the nearest cottage and borrowed a rope and was then able to climb down the tree and return home."

When the prince heard this ridiculous story he did not make a comment but merely stood and waited for the next story to begin. The three brothers were quite surprised but were sure that the second story would not be believed by the prince. And so the second brother began his tale: "That day when my brother hid from us I was searching for him in the forest. I saw something run into the bushes and thinking it was my brother I ran in after it. When I got into the bushes I saw that it was not my brother but a huge hungry tiger. He opened his mouth to devour me and I jumped inside and crawled into his belly before he could chew me up. When inside I started jumping up and down and making loud, fierce noises. The beast did not know what was happening and became so frightened that he spit me out with such force that I traveled several hundred feet through the air and landed back in the middle of our village. And so though I was but a young lad I saved our whole village from the fearful tiger, because never again did the beast come near our village."

After this story the prince once again made no comment. He merely asked that the third story begin. The three brothers were quite upset by this and as the last brother began his tale he had quite a frown upon his face. But he was still quite determined to make up a story so absurd that the prince could not this time help but doubt its truthfulness. And so he began his tale: "One day as I was wallking along the banks of the river I saw that all the fishermen seemed quite unhappy. I inquired as to why they seemed so sad. They therefore informed me that they had not caught one fish in a week and their families were going hungry as a result. I told them that I would try and help them. So I dove into the water and was immediately transformed into a fish. I swam around until I saw the source of the problem. A giant fish had eaten all the smaller fish and was himself avoiding the fishermen's nets. When this giant saw me he came toward me and was about to devour me, but I changed back to human form and slashed the fish open with my sword. The fish inside his belly were then able to escape. Many swam right into the waiting nets. When I returned to shore many of the fish were so thankful that I had saved them that they returned with me. When the fishermen saw all these fish jumping onto shore after me they were indeed pleased and rewarded me abundantly."

When this story was finished the prince did not doubt a word of it. The three brothers were quite upset, but at least they knew that they would not doubt the words of the prince. And so the prince began his tale: "I am a prince of great wealth and property. I am on the road in search of three slaves who have escaped from me. I have searched high and low for them as they were very valuable property. I was about to give up the search when I met you three fellows. But now my search is ended because I have found my missing slaves, because you gentlemen are they."

When the brothers heard these words they were shocked. If they agreed to the prince's story then they were admitting that they were his slaves, but if they doubted what he said then they lost the bet and became his slaves anyway. The brothers were so upset by the cleverness of the prince that they said not a word. The passer-by who was judging the contest nevertheless declared that the prince had won the wager.

The prince did not make slaves of these men but instead allowed them to return to their village with the promise that they would never tell tall tales again. And the three brothers were thereafter known throughout the land for their honesty and truthfulness.

CATHERINE, SLY COUNTRY LASS
Italy

One day a farmer hoeing his vineyard struck something hard. He bent over and saw that he had unearthed a fine mortar. He picked it up, rubbed the dirt off, and found the object to be solid gold.

"Only a king could own something like this," he said. "I'll take it to my king, who will most likely give me a handsome present in return!"

At home he found his daughter Catherine waiting for him, and he showed her the mortar, announcing he would present it to the king. Catherine said, "Beyond all doubt, it's as lovely as lovely can be. But if you take it to the king he'll find fault with it, since something is missing, and you'll even end up paying for it."

"And just what is missing? What could even a king find wrong with it, simpleton?"

"You just wait; the king will say:

> *The mortar is big and beautiful,*
> *But where, you dummy, is the pestle?*

The farmer shrugged his shoulders. "The idea of a king talking like that! Do you think he's an ignoramus like you?"

He tucked the mortar under his arm and marched straight to the king's palace. The guards weren't going to let him in, but he told them he was bringing a wonderful gift, so they took him to His Majesty. "Sacred Crown," began the farmer, "in my vineyard I found this solid gold mortar, and I said to myself that the only place fit to display it was your palace. Therefore I am giving it to you, if you will have it."

The king took the mortar and turned it round and round, running his eye over every inch of it. Then he shook his head and spoke:

> *The mortar is big and beautiful,*
> *But where is the pestle?*

Catherine's words exactly, except that the king didn't call him a dummy, since kings are well-bred persons. The farmer slapped his brow and couldn't help but exclaim, "Word for word! She guessed it!"

"Who guessed what?" asked the king.

"I beg your pardon," said the farmer. "My daughter told me the king would say just those words, and I refused to believe her."

"This daughter of yours," said the king, "must be a very clever girl. Let's see just how clever. Take her this flax and tell her to make me shirts for a whole regiment of soldiers. But tell her to do it quickly, since I need the shirts right now."

The farmer was stunned. But you don't argue with a king, so he picked up the bundle (which contained only a few measly strands of flax), bowed to the king, and set out for home, leaving the mortar without receiving a word of thanks, much less anything else.

"My daughter," he said to Catherine, "you are really in for it now." And he told her what the king had ordered.

"You get upset over nothing," replied Catherine. "Give me that bundle." She took the flax and shook it. As you know, there are always scalings in flax, even if it has been carded by an expert. A few scalings dropped on the floor, so tiny you could scarcely see them. Catherine gathered them up and said to her father, "Here. Go right back to the king and tell him for me that I will make him the shirts. But since I have no loom to weave the cloth, tell him to have one made for me out of this handful of scalings, and his order will be carried out to the letter."

The farmer didn't have the nerve to go back to the king, especially with that message; but Catherine nagged him until he finally agreed.

Learning how cunning Catherine was, the king was now eager to see her with her own eyes. He said, "That daughter of yours is a clever girl! Send her to the palace, so that I'll have the pleasure of chatting with her. But mind that she comes to me neither naked nor clothed, on a stomach neither full nor empty, neither in the daytime nor at night, neither on foot nor on horseback. She is to obey me in every single detail, or both your head and hers will roll."

The farmer arrived home in the lowest of spirits. But his daughter merrily said, "I know how, Daddy. Just bring me a fishing net."

In the morning before daybreak, Catherine rose and draped herself with the fishing net (that way she was neither naked nor clothed), ate a lupin (that way her stomach was neither empty nor full), led out the nanny goat and straddled it, with one foot dragging the ground and the other in the air (that way she was neither on foot nor on horseback), and reached the palace just as the sky grew lighter (it was neither day nor night). Taking her for a madwoman in that outlandish get-up, the guards barred the way; but on learning that she was just carrying out the sovereign's order, they escorted her to the royal chambers.

"Majesty, I am here in compliance with your order."

The king split his sides laughing, and said, "Clever Catherine! You're just the girl I was looking for. I am now going to marry you and make you queen. But on one condition, remember: you must never, never poke your nose into my business." (The king had realized that Catherine was smarter than he was.)

When the farmer heard about it, he said, "If the king wants you for his wife, you have no choice but to marry him. But watch your step, for if the king quickly decides what he wants, he can decide just as quickly what he no longer wants. Be sure to leave your workclothes hanging up here on a hook. In case you ever have to come home, you'll find them all ready to put back on."

But Catherine was so happy and excited that she paid little attention to her father's words, and a few days after the wedding was celebrated. There were festivities throughout the kingdom, with a big fair in the capital. The inns were filled to overflow, and many farmers had to sleep in the town squares, which were crowded all the way up to the king's palace.

One farmer, who had brought to town a pregnant cow to sell, found no barn to put the animal in, so an innkeeper told him he could put it under a shed at the inn and tether it to another farmer's cart. Lo and behold, in the night, the cow gave birth to a calf. In the morning the proud owner of the cow was preparing to lead his two animals away when out rushed the owner of the cart, shouting, "That's all right about the cow, she's yours. But hands off the calf, it's mine."

"What do you mean, it's yours? Didn't my cow have it last night?"

"Why wouldn't it be mine?" answered the other farmer. "The cow was tied to the cart, the cart's mine, so the calf belongs to the owner of the cart."

A heated quarrel arose, and in no time they were fighting. They grabbed props from under the cart and struck in blind fury at one another. At the noise, a large crowd gathered around them; then the constables ran up, separated the two men, and marched them straight into the king's court of justice.

It was once the custom in the royal city, mind you, for the king's wife also to express her opinion. But now with Catherine as queen, it happened that every time the king delivered a judgment, she opposed it. Weary of that in no time, the king said to her, "I warned you not to meddle in state business. From now on you'll stay out of the court of justice." And so she did. The farmers therefore appeared before the king alone.

After hearing both sides, the king rendered this decision: "The calf goes with the cart."

The owner of the cow found the decision too unjust for words, but what could he do? The king's judgment was final. Seeing the farmer so upset, the innkeeper advised him to go to the queen, who might find a way out.

The farmer went to the palace and asked a servant, "Could you tell me, my good man, if I might have a word with the queen?"

"That is impossible," replied the servant, "since the king has forbidden her to hear people's cases."

The farmer then went up to the garden wall. Spying the queen, he jumped over the wall and burst into tears as he told how unjust her husband had been to him. The queen said, "My advice is this. The king is going hunting tomorrow in the vicinity of a lake that is always bone-dry at this time of year. Do the following: hang a fish-dipper on your belt, take a net, and go through the motions of fishing. At the sight of someone fishing in that dry lake, the king will laugh and then ask why you're fishing where there's no water. You must answer: 'Majesty, if a cart can give birth to a calf, maybe I can catch a fish in a dry lake.' "

The next morning, with dipper dangling at his side and net in hand, the farmer went off to the dry lake, sat down on the shore, lowered his net, then raised it as though it were full of fish. The king came up with his retinue and saw him. Laughing, he asked the farmer if he had lost his mind. The farmer answered him exactly as the queen had suggested.

At that reply, the king exclaimed, "My good man, somebody else had a finger in this pie. You've been talking to the queen."

The farmer did not deny it, and the king pronounced a new judgment awarding him the calf.

Then he sent for Catherine and said, "You've been meddling again, and you know I forbade that. So now you can go back to your father. Take the thing you like most of all in the palace and go home this very evening and be a farm girl once more."

Humbly, Catherine replied, "I will do as Your Majesty wills. Only, I would ask one favor: let me leave tomorrow. Tonight it would be too embarrassing for you and for me, and your subjects would gossip."

"Very well," said the king. "We'll dine together for the last time, and you will go away tomorrow."

So what did sly Catherine turn around and do but have the cooks prepare roasts and hams and other heavy food that would make a person drowsy and thirsty. She also ordered the best wines brought up from the cellar. At dinner the king ate and ate and ate, while Catherine emptied bottle after bottle into his glass. Soon his vision clouded up, he started stuttering, and at last fell asleep in his armchair, like a pig.

Then Catherine said to the servants, "Pick up the armchair with its contents and follow me. And not a word out of you, or else!" She left the palace, passed through the city gate, and didn't stop until she reached her house, late in the night.

"Open up, Daddy, it's me," she cried.

At the sound of his daughter's voice, the old farmer ran to the window. "Back at this hour of the night? I told you so! I was wise to hold on to your workclothes. They're still here hanging on the hook in your room."

"Come on, let me in," said Catherine, "and don't talk so much!"

The farmer opened the door and saw the servants bearing the armchair with the king in it. Catherine had him carried into her room, undressed, and put into her bed. Then she dismissed the servants and lay down beside the king.

Around midnight the king awakened. The mattress seemed harder than usual, and the sheets rougher. He turned over and felt his wife there beside him. He said, "Catherine, didn't I tell you to go home?"

"Yes, Majesty," she replied, "but it's not day yet. Go back to sleep."

The king went back to sleep. In the morning he woke up to the braying of the donkey and the bleating of the sheep, and saw the sunshine streaming through the window. He shook himself, for he no longer recognized the royal bedchamber. He turned to his wife. "Catherine, where on earth are we?"

She answered, "Didn't you tell me, Majesty, to return home with the thing I liked best of all? I took *you*, and I'm keeping you."

The king laughed, and they made up. They went back to the royal palace, where they still live, and from that day on, the king has never appeared in the court of justice without his wife.

THE WISE LITTLE GIRL
Russia

Two brothers were traveling together: one was poor and the other was rich, and each had a horse, the poor one a mare, and the rich one a gelding. They stopped for the night, one beside the other. The poor man's mare bore a foal during the night, and the foal rolled under the rich man's cart.

In the morning the rich man roused his poor brother, saying, "Get up, brother. During the night my cart bore a foal."

The brother rose and said, "How is it possible for a cart to give birth to a foal? It was my mare who bore the foal!"

The rich brother said, "If your mare were his mother, he would have been found lying beside her."

To settle their quarrel they went to the authorities. The rich man gave the judges money and the poor man presented his case in words.

Finally word of this affair reached the tsar himself. He summoned both brothers before him and proposed to them four riddles: "What is the strongest and swiftest thing in the world? What is the fattest thing in the world? What is the softest thing? And what is the loveliest thing?" He gave them three days' time and said, "On the fourth day come back with your answers."

The rich man thought and thought, remembered his godmother and went to ask her advice. She bade him sit down to table, treated him to food and drink, and then asked, "Why are you so sad, my godson?"

"The sovereign has proposed four riddles to me, and given me only three days to solve them."

"What are the riddles? Tell me."

"Well, godmother, this is the first riddle: 'What is the strongest and swiftest thing in the world?' "

"That's not difficult! My husband has a bare mare; nothing in the world is swifter than she is; if you lash her with a whip she will overtake a hare."

"The second riddle is: 'What is the fattest thing in the world?' "

"We have been feeding a spotted boar for the last two years; he has become so fat that he can barely stand on his legs."

"The third riddle is: 'What is the softest thing in the world?' "

"That's well known. Eider down—you cannot think of anything softer."

"The fourth riddle is: 'What is the loveliest thing in the world?' "

"The loveliest thing in the world is my grandson Ivanushka."

"Thank you, godmother, you have advised me well. I shall be grateful to you for the rest of my life."

As for the poor brother, he shed bitter tears and went home. He was met by his seven-year-old daughter—she was his only child—who said, "Why are you sighing and shedding tears, Father?"

"How can I help sighing and shedding tears? The tsar has proposed four riddles to me, and I shall never be able to solve them."

"Tell me, what are these riddles?"

"Here they are, my little daughter: 'What is the strongest and swiftest thing in the world? What is the fattest thing, what is the softest thing, and what is the loveliest thing?' "

"Father, go to the tsar and tell him that the strongest and fastest thing in the world is the wind; the fattest is the earth, for she feeds everything that grows and lives; the softest of all is the hand, for whatever a man may lie on, he puts his hand under his head; and there is nothing lovelier in the world than sleep."

The two brothers, the poor one and the rich one, came to the tsar. The tsar heard their answers to the riddles, and asked the poor man, "Did you solve these riddles yourself, or did someone solve them for you?"

The poor man answered, "Your Majesty, I have a seven-year-old daughter, and she gave me the answers."

"If your daughter is so wise, here is a silken thread for her; let her weave an embroidered towel for me by tomorrow morning."

The peasant took the silken thread and came home sad and grieving. "We are in trouble," he said to his daughter. "The tsar has ordered you to weave a towel from this thread."

"Grieve not, Father," said the little girl. She broke off a twig from a broom, gave it to her father, and told him, "Go to the tsar and ask him to find a master who can make a loom from this twig; on it I will weave his towel."

The peasant did as his daughter told him. The tsar listened to him and gave him a hundred and fifty eggs, saying, "Give these eggs to your daughter; let her hatch one hundred and fifty chicks by tomorrow."

The peasant returned home, even more sad and grieving than the first time. "Ah, my daughter," he said, "you are barely out of one trouble before another is upon you."

"Grieve not, Father," answered the seven-year-old girl. She baked the eggs for dinner and for supper and sent her father to the king. "Tell him," she said to her father, "that one-day grain is needed to feed the chicks. In one day let a field be plowed and the millet sown, harvested, and threshed; our chickens refuse to peck any other grain."

The tsar listened to this and said, "Since your daughter is so wise, let her appear before me tomorrow morning—and I want her to come neither on foot nor on horseback, neither naked nor dressed, neither with a present nor without a gift."

"Now," thought the peasant, "even my daughter cannot solve such a difficult riddle; we are lost."

"Grieve not," his seven-year-old daughter said to him. "Go to the hunters and buy me a live hare and a live quail." The father bought her a hare and a quail.

Next morning the seven-year-old girl took off her clothes, donned a net, took the quail in her hand, sat upon the hare, and went to the palace. The tsar met her at the gate. She bowed to him, saying, "Here is a little gift for you, Your Majesty," and handed him the quail. The tsar stretched out his hand, but the quail shook her wings and—flap, flap!—was gone.

"Very well," said the tsar, "you have done as I ordered you to do. Now tell me—since your father is so poor, what do you live on?"

"My father catches fish on the shore, and he never puts bait in the water; and I make fish soup in my skirt."

"You are stupid! Fish never live on the shore, fish live in the water."

"And you—are you wise? Who ever saw a cart bear foals? Not a cart but a mare bears foals."

The tsar awarded the foal to the poor peasant and took the daughter into his own palace; when she grew up he married her and she became the tsarina.

CLEVER ANSWERS
Russia

A soldier had served in his regiment for fully twenty-five years without ever having seen the tsar in person. When he returned home and was questioned about the tsar, he did not know what to say. His parents and friends began to taunt him. "You served for twenty-five years," they said, "yet you never saw the tsar."

The soldier felt humiliated, so he made ready and went to have a look at the tsar. He came to the palace.

The tsar asked him, "What have you come for, soldier?"

"Your Majesty, I served you and God for a full twenty-five years, yet I never saw you in person; so I have come to look at you."

"Well, look your fill." The soldier walked around the tsar three times examining him.

The tsar said, "Am I handsome?"

"Yes, Your Majesty," answered the soldier.

"And now, soldier, tell me—is it far from heaven to earth?"

"It is so far that when a noise is made there, we can hear it here."

"And is the earth wide?"

"The sun rises over there and sets over here: that's the width of the earth."

"And is the earth deep?"

"I had a grandfather who died about ninety years ago. He was buried in the earth and since then has never come home; so it must be deep."

Then the tsar sent the soldier to prison, saying, "Keep your eyes open, soldier! I will send you thirty geese; try to pluck a feather out of each one."

"Very well," the soldier said.

The tsar summoned thirty wealthy merchants and proposed the same riddles to them that he had proposed to the soldier. They racked their brains but were unable to answer the questions, and the tsar ordered them to be put in prison.

The soldier asked them, "Honorable merchants, why have you been imprisoned?"

"The tsar asked us how far heaven is from earth, how wide the earth is, and how deep it is, but we are uneducated people and could not find the answers."

"If each one of you will give me a thousand rubles, I will tell you the answers."

"Gladly, brother, only tell us."

The soldier took a thousand rubles from each and told them how to solve the tsar's riddles. Two days later the tsar summoned the merchants and the soldier before him; he proposed the same riddles to the merchants, and as soon as they answered correctly, he let them go. Then he said to the soldier, "Well, have you managed to pluck a feather from each?"

"Yes, Your Majesty, and it was a golden feather, too."

"And how far is it to your home?"

"It cannot be seen from here, so it must be far."

"Here is a thousand rubles for you; God speed you."

The soldier returned home and began to live a carefree and easy life.

A Dispute in Sign Language
Israel

Once there was a wicked priest who hated Jews. One day he summoned the chief rabbi and said to him, "I want to have a dispute with a Jew in the language of signs. I give you thirty dys to prepare yourself, and if nobody appears to take part in the dispute, I shall order that all the Jews be killed."

"What was the rabbi to do? He brought the bad tidings to his people and ordered them to fast and to pray in the synagogue. A week went by, two weeks, three weeks passed, but there was no one with the courage to accept the priest's challenge and the great responsibility. It was already the fourth week, and still there was no one to represent the Jews in the dispute.

Then along came a poultry dealer who had been away, bringing chickens from the nearby villages into the town. He had not heard what was going on there, but he noticed on his arrival that the market was closed, and at home he found his wife and children fasting, praying, and weeping.

"What is the matter?" asked the poultry dealer. His wife replied, "The wicked priest has ordered a Jew to hold a discussion with him in the language of signs. If there is no one who is able to do so, all of us will be killed."

"Is that all the matter?" wondered the poultry dealer in surprise. "Go to the rabbi, and tell him that I am ready to participate."

"What are you talking about? How can you understand the priest? Greater and wiser men than you have not been willing to take upon themselves this task!" cried his wife.

"Why should you worry? In any case we shall all be killed." And off they went together to the rabbi.

"Rabbi," said the man, "I am ready to meet the priest!"

The rabbi blessed him. "May God help you and bring you success."

So the priest was told that a Jew, sent by the rabbi, would hold a discussion with him in sign language.

"You have to understand my signs and to answer them in the same way," explained the priest to the Jew before a great assembly. Then he pointed a finger to him. In reply the Jew pointed two fingers. Then the priest took a piece of white cheese from his pocket. In reply the Jew took out an egg. Then the priest took the seeds of some grain and scattered them on the floor. In reply, the Jew set a hen free from the coop and let it eat up the seeds.

"Well done," exclaimed the priest in amazement. "You answered my questions correctly." And he gave the poultry dealer many gifts and ordered his servant to bathe him and to give him fine garments to wear.

"Now I know that the Jews are wise men, if the most humble among them was able to understand me," admitted the priest.

The town was in great excitement, and the people waited in suspense for the result of the dispute. When they saw the poultry dealer leaving the priest's house in fine garments and with a happy expression on his face, they understood that everything was in order, blessed be the Almighty.

"How did it go? What did the priest ask you?" all the people wanted to know. The rabbi called the poultry dealer to his home and asked him to relate what had happened.

And this is what the poultry dealer related: "The priest pointed with one finger to my eyes, meaning to take out my eye. I pointed with two fingers to imply, I would take out *both* his eyes. Then he took out a piece of cheese to show that I was hungry while he had cheese. So I took out an egg to show that I was not in need of his alms. Then he spilled some wheat grain on the floor. So I fed my hen, knowing it was hungry and thinking what a pity to waste the grain."

At the same time the priest's friends questioned him: "What did you ask the Jew? What did he reply?"

The priest related: "At first I pointed one finger, meaning that there is only one king. He pointed with two fingers, meaning that there are two kings, the King in Heaven and the king on earth. Then I took out a piece of cheese, meaning, Is this cheese from a white or a black goat? In answer he took out an egg, meaning, Is this egg from a white or a brown hen? Finally I scattered some grain on the floor, meaning that the Jews are spread all over the world. Whereupon he freed his hen which ate up all the grain, meaning that the Messiah will come and gather all the Jews from the four corners of the world."

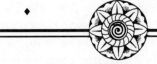

LEOPARD, GOAT, AND YAM
Africa (Hausa)

A certain man was running away from his village, and he was taking with him all his property. This consisted of a leopard, a goat, and a yam. Now in time he came to a river where there was only one canoe. It was so small that it was impossible for him to take more than one part of his property with him at a time. Now how did he succeed in getting it all to the other side? If he left the yam with the goat or the leopard with the goat, the goat would eat the yam or the leopard devour the goat.

The answer is: He took the goat over first and then the yam. He then recrossed the goat and ferried over the leopard, returning a fourth time for the goat.

AN ENDLESS STORY
Japan

Long ago all the rats in Nagasaki got together and decided that since there was nothing left to eat in Nagasaki, they would cross over to Satsuma. They boarded a ship and set out. It happened that on the way they met a ship on which all the rats in Satsuma had gone aboard, intending to go to Nagasaki. They asked one another how things were and discovered that there was nothing to eat in either Satsuma or Nagasaki. There was no use in going to Nagasaki nor any use in going to Satsuma, so they decided to jump into the sea and drown.

The first rat began to cry, *chu chu*, and jumped over with a splash. Then another rat cried, *chu chu*, and jumped over with a splash. Then another cried, *chu chu*, and jumped over with a splash . . .

The
VERY
YOUNG
and the
VERY
OLD

The wisdom of the babe and of the oldest member of a particular society is often celebrated in folklore. They share a kind of innocence and clear-sightedness that translates into sagacity. There seems to be an untapped power in both the baby and the ancient.

The connections between both ends of the age spectrum are most clearly and cleverly revealed in those stories about changelings in which a centuries-old fairy is laid in the cradle disguised as a fretful babe. Especially in Northern Europe—in the Scandinavian countries and in Ireland—are such tales to be found.

GLOOSCAP AND THE BABY
American Indian (Algonquian)

Glooscap, having conquered the Kewawkqu', a race of giants and magicians, and the Medecolin, who were cunning sorcerers, and Pamola, a wicked spirit of the night, besides hosts of fiends, goblins, cannibals, and witches, felt himself great indeed, and boasted to a woman that there was nothing left for him to subdue.

But the woman laughed and said, "Are you quite sure, master? There is still one who remains unconquered, and nothing can overcome him."

In some surprise Glooscap inquired the name of this mighty one.

"He is called Wasis," replied the woman, "but I strongly advise you to have no dealings with him."

Wasis was only a baby, who sat on the floor sucking a piece of maple sugar and crooning a little song to himself. Now Glooscap had never married and was ignorant of how children are managed, but with perfect confidence he smiled at the baby and asked it to come to him. The baby smiled back but never moved, whereupon Glooscap imitated a beautiful birdsong. Wasis, however, paid no attention and went on sucking his maple sugar. Unaccustomed to such treatment, Glooscap lashed himself into a rage and in terrible and threatening accents ordered Wasis to come to him at once. But Wasis burst into dire howls, which quite drowned the god's thundering, and would not budge for any threats.

Glooscap, thoroughly aroused, summoned all his magical resources. He recited the most terrible spells, the most dreadful incantations. He sang the songs which raise the dead, and those which send the Devil scurrying to the nethermost depths. But Wasis merely smiled and looked a trifle bored.

At last Glooscap rushed from the hut in despair, while Wasis, sitting on the floor, cried, "Goo, goo!" And to this day the Indians say that when a baby says "Goo," he remembers the time when he conquered mighty Glooscap.

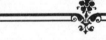

The Brewery of Eggshells
Ireland

Mrs. Sullivan fancied that her youngest child had been exchanged by "fairies' theft," and certainly appearances warranted such a conclusion; for in one night her healthy, blue-eyed boy had become shriveled up into almost nothing, and never ceased squalling and crying. This naturally made poor Mrs. Sullivan very unhapy; and all the neighbors, by way of comforting her, said that her own child was, beyond any kind of doubt, with the Good People, and that one of themselves was put in his place.

Mrs. Sullivan of course could not disbelieve what everyone told her, but she did not wish to hurt the thing; for although its face was so withered, and its body wasted away to a mere skeleton, it had still a strong resemblance to her own boy. She, therefore, could not find it in her heart to roast it alive on the griddle, or to burn its nose off with the red-hot tongs, or to throw it out in the snow on the roadside, notwithstanding these, and several like proceedings, were strongly recommended to her for the recovery of her child.

One day who should Mrs. Sullivan meet but a cunning woman, well known about the country by the name of Ellen Leah (or Grey Ellen). She had the gift, however she got it, of telling where the dead were, and what was good for the rest of their souls; and could charm away warts and wens, and do a great many wonderful things of the same nature.

"You're in grief this morning, Mrs. Sullivan," were the first words of Ellen Leah to her.

"You may say that, Ellen," said Mrs. Sullivan, "and good cause I have to be in grief, for there was my own fine child whipped off from me out of his cradle, without as much as 'by your leave' or 'ask your pardon,' and an ugly dony bit of a shriveled-up fairy put in his place; no wonder, then, that you see me in grief, Ellen."

"Small blame to you, Mrs. Sullivan," said Ellen Leah, "but are you sure 'tis a fairy?"

"Sure!" echoed Mrs. Sullivan, "sure enough I am to my sorrow, and can I doubt my own two eyes? Every mother's soul must feel for me!"

"Will you take an old woman's advice?" said Ellen Leah, fixing her wild and mysterious gaze upon the unhappy mother; and, after a pause, she added, "but maybe you'll call it foolish?"

"Can you get me back my child, my own child, Ellen?" said Mrs. Sullivan with great energy.

"If you do as I bid you," returned Ellen Leah, "you'll know." Mrs. Sullivan was silent in expectation, and Ellen continued. "Put down the big pot, full of water, on the fire, and make it boil like mad; then get a dozen new-laid eggs, break them, and keep the shells, but throw away the rest; when that is done, put the shells in the pot of boiling water, and you will soon know whether it is your own boy or a fairy. If you find that it is a fairy in the cradle, take the red-hot poker and cram it down his ugly throat, and you will not have much trouble with him after that, I promise you."

Home went Mrs. Sullivan, and did as Ellen Leah desired. She put the pot on the fire, and plenty of turf under it and set the water boiling at such a rate, that if ever water was red-hot, it surely was.

The child was lying, for a wonder, quite easy and quiet in the cradle, every now and then cocking his eye, that would twinkle as keen as a star in a frosty night, over at the great fire, and the big pot upon it; and he looked on with great attention at Mrs. Sullivan breaking the eggs and putting down the eggshells to boil. At last he asked, with the voice of a very old man, "What are you doing, Mammy?"

Mrs. Sullivan's heart, as she said herself, was up in her mouth ready to choke her, at hearing the child speak. But she contrived to put the poker in the fire, and to answer, without making any wonder at the words, "I'm brewing, *a vick* [my son]."

"And what are you brewing, Mammy?" said the little imp, whose supernatural gift of speech now proved beyond question that he was a fairy substitute.

"I wish the poker was red," thought Mrs. Sullivan; but it was a large one, and took a long time heating; so she determined to keep him in talk until the poker was in a proper state to thrust down his throat, and therefore repeated the question.

"Is it what I'm brewing, *a vick*," said she, "you want to know?"

"Yes, Mammy: what are you brewing?" returned the fairy.

"Eggshells, *a vick*," said Mrs. Sullivan.

"Oh!" shrieked the imp, starting up in the cradle and clapping his hands together, "I'm fifteen hundred years in the world, and I never saw a brewery of eggshells before!" The poker was by this time quite red, and Mrs. Sullivan, seizing it, ran furiously towards the cradle; but somehow or other her foot slipped, and she fell flat on the floor, and the poker flew out of her hand to the other end of the house. However, she got up without much loss of time and went to the cradle, intending to pitch the wicked thing that was in it into the pot of boiling water, when there she saw her own child in a sweet sleep, one of his soft round arms rested upon the pillow—his features were as placid as if their repose had never been disturbed, save the rosy mouth, which moved with a gentle and regular breathing.

FATHER OF EIGHTEEN ELVES
Iceland

On a farm one summer it happened that everybody was out in the fields except the mistress herself, who stayed at home to mind the house, with her son, who was three or four years old. This boy had grown and thriven well up to this time; he was talking already, was intelligent, and seemed a most promising child. Now, as the woman had various chores to do besides minding her child, she had to turn her back on him for a little while and go down to a stream near the house to wash some churns. She left him in the doorway, and there is nothing to tell until she came back after a brief while. As soon as she spoke to him, he shrieked and howled in a more vicious and ugly way than she ever expected, for up till then he had been a very placid child, affectionate and likeable, but now all she got was squalling and shrieks. This went on for some time; the child never spoke one word, but was so terribly willful and moody that the woman did not know what to do about the change in him; moveover, he stopped growing, and began to look quite like an imbecile.

The mother was very upset over it all, and she decides to go and see a neighbor of hers who was thought to be a wise woman and to know a great deal, and she tells her her troubles. The neighbor questions her closely, asking how long it is since the child began to be so unmanageable, and how she thought the change had begun. The mother tells her just what had happened.

When this wise neighbor had heard the whole story, she says, "Don't you think, my dear, that the child is a changeling? It's my opinion that he was exchanged while you left him alone in the doorway."

"I don't know," says the mother. "Can't you teach me some way to get at the truth?"

"So I can," says the other. "You must leave the child by himself some time, and arrange for something really extraordinary to happen in front of him, and then he will say something when he sees there is no one nearby. But you must listen secretly to know what he says, and if the boy's words seem at all odd or suspicious, whip him unmercifully until something happens."

With this, they broke off their talk, and the mother thanked her neighbor for her good advice, and went home.

As soon as she gets back, she sets down a tiny pot in the middle of the kitchen floor; then she takes several broom handles and ties them end to end until the top end is poking right up the kitchen chimney, and to the bottom end she ties the porridge stirring-stick, and this she sets upright in the little pot. As soon as she had rigged up this contraption in the kitchen, she fetched the child in and left him alone there; then she left the room, but stood listening outside, where she could peep in through the crack of the door.

She had not been long gone when she sees the child start waddling round and round the pot with the porridge stick in it and studying it carefully; and in the end the child says, "I'm old enough now, as my whiskers show, and I'm a father with eighteen children of my own in Elfland, and yet never in my life have I seen so long a pole in so small a pot!"

At that, the woman runs back in with a good birch, seizes the changeling, and beats him long and unmercifully, and then he howls most horribly.

When she had been whipping him for some while, she sees a woman who was a stranger to her coming into the kitchen with a little boy in her arms, and a sweet pretty child he is.

This stranger gives the child a loving look, and says to the mother, "We don't act fairly by one another; I cuddle your child, but you beat my husband."

Saying this, she puts down this child, the housewife's own son, and leaves him there; but she takes her old man off with her, and the two of them disappear. But the boy grew up with his own mother, and turned out a fine man.

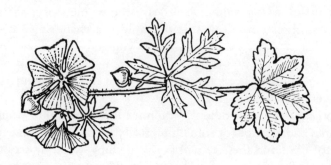

THE FLY
Vietnam

Everyone in the village knew the usurer, a rich and smart man. Having accumulated a fortune over the years, he settled down to a life of leisure in his big house surrounded by an immense garden and guarded by a pack of ferocious dogs. But still unsatisfied with what he had acquired, the man went on making money by lending it to people all over the county at exorbitant rates. The usurer reigned supreme in the area, for numerous were those who were in debt to him.

One day, the rich man set out for the house of one of his peasants. Despite repeated reminders, the poor laborer just could not manage to pay off his longstanding debt. Working himself to a shadow, the peasant barely succeeded in making ends meet. The moneylender was therefore determined that if he could not get his money back this time, he would proceed to confiscate some of his debtor's most valuable belongings. But the rich man found no one at the peasant's house but a small boy of eight or nine playing alone in the dirt yard.

"Child, are your parents home?" the rich man asked.

"No, sir," the boy replied, then went on playing with his sticks and stones, paying no attention whatever to the man.

"Then, where are they?" the rich man asked, somewhat irritated, but the little boy went on playing and did not answer.

When the rich man repeated his query, the boy looked up and answered, with deliberate slowness, "Well, sir, my father has gone to cut living trees and plant dead ones and my mother is at the marketplace selling the wind and buying the moon."

"What? What in heaven are you talking about?" the rich man commanded. "Quick, tell me where they are, or you will see what this stick can do to you!" The bamboo walking stick in the big man's hand looked indeed menacing.

After repeated, questioning, however, the boy only gave the same reply. Exasperated, the rich man told him, "All right, little devil, listen to me! I came here today to take the money your parents owe me. But if you tell me where they really are and what they are doing, I will forget all about the debt. Is that clear to you?"

"Oh, sir, why are you joking with a poor little boy? Do you expect me to believe what you are saying?" For the first time the boy looked interested.

"Well, there is heaven and there is earth to witness my promise," the rich man said, pointing up to the sky and down to the ground.

But the boy only laughed. "Sir, heaven and earth cannot talk and therefore cannot testify. I want some living thing to be our witness."

Catching sight of a fly alighting on a bamboo pole nearby, and laughing inside because he was fooling the boy, the rich man proposed, "There is a fly. He can be our witness. Now, hurry and tell me what you mean when you say that your father is out cutting living trees and planting dead ones, while your mother is at the market selling the wind and buying the moon."

Looking at the fly on the pole, the boy said, "A fly is a good enough witness for me. Well, here it is, sir. My father has simply gone to cut down bamboos and make a fence with them for a man near the river. And my mother . . . oh, sir, you'll keep your promise, won't you? You will free my parents of all their debts? You really mean it?"

"Yes, yes, I do solemnly swear in front of this fly here." The rich man urged the boy to go on.

"Well, my mother, she has gone to the market to sell fans so she can buy oil for our lamps. Isn't that what you would call selling the wind to buy the moon?"

Shaking his head, the rich man had to admit inwardly that the boy was a clever one. However, he thought, the little genius still had much to learn, believing as he did that a fly could be a witness for anybody. Bidding the boy goodbye, the man told him that he would soon return to make good his promise.

A few days had passed when the moneylender returned. This time he found the poor peasant couple at home, for it was late in the evening. A nasty scene ensued, the rich man claiming his money and the poor peasant apologizing and begging for another delay. Their argument awakened the little boy, who ran to his father and told him, "Father, Father, you don't have to pay your debt. This gentleman here has promised me that he would forget all about the money you owe him."

"Nonsense!' The rich man shook his walking stick at both father and son. "Nonsense! Are you going to stand there and listen to a child's inventions? I never spoke a word to this boy. Now, tell me, are you going to pay or are you not?"

The whole affair ended by being brought before the mandarin who governed the county. Not knowing what to believe, all the poor peasant and his wife could do was to bring their son with them when they went to court. The little boy's insistence about the rich man's promise was their only encouragement.

The mandarin began by asking the boy to relate exactly what had happened between himself and the moneylender. Happily, the boy hastened to tell about the explanations he gave the rich man in exchange for the debt.

"Well," the mandarin said to the boy, "if this man here has indeed made such a promise, we have only your word for it. How do we know that you have not invented the whole story yourself? In a case such as this, you need a witness to confirm it, and you have none." The boy remained calm and declared that naturally there was a witness to their conversation.

"Who is that, child?" the mandarin asked.

"A fly, Your Honor."

"A fly? What do you mean, a fly? Watch out, young man, fantasies are not to be tolerated in this place!" The mandarin's benevolent face suddenly became stern.

"Yes, Your Honor, a fly. A fly which was alighting on this gentleman's nose!" The boy leaped from his seat.

"Insolent little devil, that's a pack of lies!" The rich man roared indignantly, his face like a ripe tomato. "The fly was *not* on my nose; *he was on the housepole* . . ." But he stopped dead. It was, however, too late.

The majestic mandarin himself could not help bursting out laughing. Then the audience burst out laughing. The boy's parents too, although timidly, laughed. And the boy, and the rich man himself, also laughed. With one hand on his stomach, the mandarin waved the other hand toward the rich man:

"Now, now, that's all settled. You have indeed made your promises, dear sir, to the child. *Housepole or no housepole, your conversation did happen after all!* The court says you must keep your promise."

And still chuckling, he dismissed all parties.

THE TWO PICKPOCKETS
England

There was a provincial pickpocket who was very successful at his work, and he thought he'd go up to London and see what he could do there. So he went up to London, and he was even more successful.

One day he was busy in Oxford Street when he suddenly found that his own pocketbook had been taken. He looked round and saw a very attractive blond girl walking away. He was sure that she was the one who had picked his pocket, so he followed her and got his pocketbook back from her. He was so much taken by her cleverness in robbing him that he suggested that they should go into partnership together. And so they did, and succeeded brilliantly.

At length the provincial pickpocket thought, "We're the best pickpockets in London. If we married we could breed up a race of the best pickpockets in the world." So he asked the girl, and she was quite agreeable, and they were married, and in due time a beautiful little baby boy was born to them. But the poor little fellow was deformed. His right arm was bent to his chest, and the little fist tightly clenched. And nothing they could do would straighten it.

The poor parents were much distressed. "He'll never make a pickpocket," they said, "with a paralyzed right arm." They took him at once to the doctor, but the doctor said he was too young, they must wait. But they didn't want to wait; they took him to one doctor after another, and at last—because they were very rich by this time—to the best child specialist they could hear of.

The specialist took out his gold watch, and felt the pulse on the little paralyzed arm. "The flow of blood seems normal," he said. "What a bright little fellow he is for his age! He's focusing his eyes on my watch." He took the chain out of his waistcoat, and swung the watch to and fro, and the baby's eyes followed it. Then the little bent arm straightened out towards the watch, the little clenched fingers opened to take it, and down dropped the midwife's gold wedding ring.

THE SEVENTH FATHER
OF THE HOUSE
Norway

There was once a man who was traveling. He came, at last, to a beautiful big farm. It had a manor house so fine that it could easily have been a small castle.

"This will be a good place to rest," he said to himself as he went in through the gate. An old man, with grey hair and beard, was chopping wood nearby.

"Good evening, father," said the traveler. "Can you put me up for the night?"

"I'm not the father of the house," said the old one. "Go into the kitchen and talk to my father."

The traveler went into the kitchen. There he found a man who was even older, down on his knees in front of the hearth, blowing on the fire.

"Good evening, father. Can you put me up for the night?" said the traveler.

"I'm not the father of the house," said the old fellow. "But go in and talk to my father. He's sitting by the table in the parlor."

So the traveler went into the parlor and talked to the man who was sitting by the table. He was much older than both the others, and he sat, shivering and shaking, his teeth chattering, reading from a big book almost like a little child.

"Good evening, father. Will you put me up for the night?" said the man.

"I'm not the father of the house, but talk to my father who's sitting on the settle," said the old man who sat by the table, shivering and shaking, his teeth chattering.

So the traveler went over to the one who was sitting on the settle, and he was busy trying to smoke a pipe of tobacco. But he was so huddled up and his hands shook so that he could hardly hold on to the pipe.

"Good evening, father," said the traveler again. "Can you put me up for the night?"

"I'm not the father of the house," replied the huddled-up old fellow. "But talk to my father who's lying in the bed."

The traveler went over to the bed, and there lay an old, old man in whom there was no sign of life but a pair of big eyes.

"Good evening, father. Can you put me up for the night?" said the traveler.

"I'm not the father of the house, but talk to my father who's lying in the cradle," said the man with the big eyes.

Well, the traveler went over to the cradle. There lay an ancient fellow, so shriveled up that he was no bigger than a baby. And there was no way of telling there was life in him except for a rattle in his throat now and then.

"Good evening, father. Can you put me up for the night?" said the man.

It took a long time before he got an answer, and even longer before the fellow finished it. He said—he like all the others—that he was not the father of the house. "But talk to my father. He's hanging in the horn on the wall."

The traveler stared up along the walls, and at last he caught sight of the horn, too. But when he tried to see the one who was lying in it, there was nothing to be seen but a little ash-white form that had the likeness of a human face.

Then he was so frightened that he cried aloud, "GOOD EVENING, FATHER! WILL YOU PUT ME UP FOR THE NIGHT?"

There was a squeaking sound up in the horn like a tiny titmouse, and it was all he could do to make out that the sound meant "Yes, my child."

Then in came a table decked with the costliest dishes, and with ale and spirits, too. And when the traveler had eaten and drunk, in came a good bed covered with reindeer hides. And he was very glad that at last he had found the true father of the house.

THE KING'S FAVORITE
China

In ancient times the beautiful woman Mi Tzu-hsia was the favorite of the lord of Wei. Now, according to the law of Wei, anyone who rode in the king's carriage without permission would be punished by amputation of the foot. When Mi Tzu-hsia's mother fell ill, someone brought the news to her in the middle of the night. So she took the king's carriage and went out, and the king only praised her for it. "Such filial devotion!" he said. "For her mother's sake she risked the punishment of amputation!"

Another day she was dallying with the lord of Wei in the fruit garden. She took a peach, which she found so sweet that instead of finishing it she handed it to the lord to taste. "How she loves me," said the lord of Wei, "forgetting the pleasure of her own taste to share with me!"

But when Mi Tzu-hsia's beauty began to fade, the king's affection cooled. And when she offended the king, he said, "Didn't she once take my carriage without permission? And didn't she once give me a peach that she had already chewed on?"

WAGGING MY TAIL IN THE MUD
China

The hermit poet Chuang Tzu was angling in the River Pu. The king of Ch'u sent two noblemen to invite Chuang to come before him. "We were hoping you would take on certain affairs of state," they said. Holding his pole steady and without looking at them, Chuang Tzu said, "I hear Ch'u has a sacred tortoise that has been dead three thousand years, and the king has it enshrined in a cushioned box in the ancestral hall. Do you think the tortoise would be happier wagging his tail in the mud than having his shell honored?" "Of course," replied the two noblemen. "Then begone," said Chuang Tzu. "I mean to keep wagging mine in the mud."

WHEN ONE MAN HAS TWO WIVES
Syria

A man had two wives and both loved him, though one was young and the other old. Whenever the man lay down to sleep with his head on the young wife's knees, she would pluck the white hairs from his head so that he should appear youthful. And whenever he rested his head in the older wife's lap and slept, she would pluck out the black hairs from his head so that he should be white-haired like herself. And it was not long before the man was bald.

Such is the origin of the saying "Between Hannah and Bannah, vanished are our beards."

THE OLD MAN AND HIS GRANDSON
Germany

There was once a very old man, whose eyes had become dim, his ears dull of hearing, his knees trembled, and when he sat at table he could hardly hold the spoon, and spilled the broth upon the tablecloth or let it run out of his mouth. His son and his son's wife were disgusted at this, so the old grandfather at last had to sit in the corner behind the stove, and they gave him his food in an earthenware bowl, and not even enough of it. And he used to look towards the table with his eyes full of tears. Once, too, his trembling hands could not hold the bowl, and it fell to the ground and broke. The young wife scolded him, but he said nothing and only sighed. Then they bought him a wooden bowl for a few halfpence, out of which he had to eat.

They were once sitting thus when the little grandson of four years old began to gather together some bits of wood upon the ground. "What are you doing there?" asked the father. "I am making a little trough," answered the child, "for Father and Mother to eat out of when I am big."

The man and his wife looked at each other for a while, and presently began to cry. Then they took the old grandfather to the table, and henceforth always let him eat with them, and likewise said nothing if he did spill a little of anything.

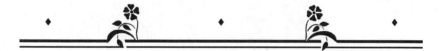

Half a Blanket
Ireland

This son was married and he had a young son himself in the cradle, and the old grandfather, the son's father, was knocking about, not much good then for anything, only eating and smoking. So the son of the old fellow said the old man would have to go; leave—that was the word: take the broad road for it.

Well, his own son, the child was in the cradle. And the wife was pleading with her husband for to give the old man a chance but he wouldn't listen. So she pleaded with her husband to give the old fellow a blanket when he was ready to go.

"Give him a whole blanket," says she.

The son was for giving him half a blanket but he says, "All right. I'll give a whole blanket."

"Do no such'n a thing," says the child in the cradle. "Give him only half a blanket and keep the other half safely by. For I'll need it when I have to give it to you when it's my turn to put you out to the world."

That was from the child that couldn't talk. So the old fellow was let stay, he wouldn't get leave then to go at all, when the son heard what his own child had in store for himself.

TRUE
LOVES
and
FALSE

ove stories in folklore tend to be stark. The audience is told that there is a great love between the man and the woman: "When he entered and saw the maiden he lost consciousness. But he revived and fell in love." The fact of love is simply stated. It is the consequences of that love that are explored in folktales.

In the literary tradition the reasons for love or passion are detailed. In folklore only the simplest and most artless reasons are offered. Sometimes it is physical: "This was a maiden of indescribable beauty." Sometimes it is recalled action: "But of them all, the bravest and most gallant was a Mr. Fox." Sometimes it is the homely virtues that are extolled: "She is quiet and chaste as a dove." But the reasons are never long nor is there usually any development beyond the statement.

In this section fifteen different kinds of love stories appear. Some are tales of magical wooings, as in "The Little Old Woman with Five Cows." Some are stories of long-delayed weddings, as in the Chinese "The Waiting Maid's Parrot." Some are replete with terrifying suitors, as in the Bluebeard variant "Mr. Fox." A few have to do with animal brides or bridegrooms: a cat or a toad. The tales in which a man or woman falls in love with or marries someone from the faerie world often end unhappily. The human partner is left with a longing that no one else can satisfy, and the ache is palpable to the story listener.

No section on true loves can be complete without a few stories about husbands and wives faithful even after death, though more stories about this phenomenon—and the Orphic motif of the underworld search—can also be found in the final two sections of the book, "Ghosts and Revenants" and "Death and the World's End."

How Men and Women Got Together
American Indian (Blood-Piegan)

Old Man had made the world and everything on it. He had done everything well, except that he had put the men in one place and the women in another, quite a distance away. So they lived separately for a while.

Men and women did everything in exactly the same way. Both had buffalo jumps—steep cliffs over which they chased buffalo herds so that the animals fell to their death at the foot of the cliff. Then both the men and the women butchered the dead animals. This meat was their only food; they had not yet discovered other things that were good to eat.

After a while the men learned how to make bows and arrows. The women learned how to tan buffalo hides and make tipis and beautiful robes decorated with porcupine quills.

One day Old Man said to himself, "I think I did everything well, but I made one bad mistake, putting women and men in different places. There's no joy or pleasure in that. Men and women are different from each other, and these different things must be made to unite so that there will be more people. I must make men mate with women. I will put some pleasure, some good feeling into it; otherwise the men won't be keen to do what is necessary. I myself must set an example."

Old Man went over to where the women were living. He traveled for four days and four nights before he saw the women in their camp. He was hiding behind some trees, watching. He said to himself, "Ho, what a good life they're having! They have these fine tipis made of tanned buffalo hide, while we men have only brush shelters or raw, stinking, green hides to cover us. And look what fine clothes they wear, while we have to go around with a few pelts around our loins! Really, I made a mistake putting the women so far away from us. They must live with us and make fine tents and beautiful clothes for us also. I'll go back and ask the other men how they feel about this."

So Old Man went back to his camp and told the men what he

had seen. When they heard about all the useful and beautiful things the women had, the men said, "Let's go over there and get together with these different human beings."

"It's not only those things that are worth having," said Old Man. "There's something else—a very pleasurable thing I plan on creating."

Now, while this was going on in the men's camp, the chief of the women's village had discovered the tracks Old Man had made while prowling around. She sent a young woman to follow them and report back. The young woman arrived near the men's camp, hid herself, and watched for a short while. Then she hurried back to the women as fast as she could and told everybody, "There's a camp over there with human beings living in it. They seem different from us, taller and stronger. Oh, sisters, these beings live very well, better than us. They have a thing shooting sharp sticks, and with these they kill many kinds of game—food that we don't have. They are never hungry."

When they heard this, all the women said, "How we wish that these strange human beings would come here and kill all kinds of food for us!" When the women were finishing their meeting, the men were already over the hill toward them. The women looked at the men and saw how shabbily dressed they were, with just a little bit of rawhide around their loins. They looked at the men's matted hair, smelled the strong smell coming from their unwashed bodies. They looked at their dirty skin. They said to each other, "These beings called men don't know how to live. They have no proper clothes. They're dirty; they smell. We don't want people like these." The woman chief hurled a rock at Old Man, shouting "Go away!" Then all the women threw rocks and shouted "Go away!"

Old Man said, "It was no mistake putting these creatures far away from us. Women are dangerous. I shouldn't have created them." Then Old Man and all the men went back to their own place.

After the men left, the woman chief had second thoughts. "These poor men," she said, "they don't know any better, but we could teach them. We could make clothes for them. Instead of shaming them, maybe we could get them to come back if we dress as poorly as they do, just with a piece of hide or fur around our waist.

And in the men's camp, Old Man said, "Maybe we should try to meet these women creatures once more. Yes, we should give it another chance. See what I did on the sly." He opened his traveling bundle in which he kept his jerk meat and other supplies, and out of it took a resplendent white buckskin outfit. "I managed to steal this when those women weren't looking. It's too small for me, but I'll add on a little buffalo hide here and a little bear fur there, and put a shield over here, where it doesn't come together over my belly. And I'll make myself a feather headdress and paint my face. Then maybe this woman chief will look at me with new eyes. Let me go alone to speak with the women creatures first. You stay back a little and hide until I have straightened things out."

So Old Man dressed up as best he could. He even purified himself in a sweat bath which he thought up for this purpose. He looked at his reflection in the lake waters and exclaimed, "Oh, how beautiful I am! I never knew I was that good-looking! Now that woman chief will surely like me."

Then Old Man led the way back to the women's camp. There was one woman on the lookout, and even though the men were staying back in hiding, she saw them coming. Then she spotted Old Man standing alone on a hilltop overlooking the camp. She hurried to tell the woman chief, who was butchering with most of the other women at the buffalo jump. For this job they wore their poorest outfits: just pieces of rawhide with a hole for the head, or maybe only a strap of rawhide around the waist. What little they had on was stiff with blood and reeked of freshly slaughtered carcasses. Even their faces and hands were streaked with blood.

"We'll meet these men just as we are," said the woman chief. "They will appreciate our being dressed like them."

So the woman chief went up to the hill on which Old Man was standing, and the other women followed her. When he saw the woman chief standing there in her butchering clothes, her flint skinning knife still in her hand, her hair matted and unkempt, he exclaimed, "Hah! Hrumph! This woman chief is ugly. She's dressed in rags covered with blood. She stinks. I want nothing to do with a creature like this. And those other women are just like her. No, I made no mistake putting these beings far away from us men!" And having said this, he turned around and went back the way he had come, with all his men following him.

"It seems we can't do anything right," said the woman chief. "Whatever it is, those male beings misunderstand it. But I still think we should unite with them. I think they have something we haven't got, and we have something they haven't got, and these things must come together. We'll try one last time to get them to understand us. Let's make ourselves beautiful."

The women went into the river and bathed. They washed and combed their hair, braided it, and attached hair strings of bone pipes and shell beads. They put on their finest robes of well-tanned, dazzling white doeskin covered with wonderful designs of porcupine quills more colorful than the rainbow. They placed bone and shell chokers around their necks and shell bracelets around their wrists. On their feet they put full quilled moccasins. Finally the women painted their cheeks with sacred red face paint. Thus wonderfully decked out, they started on their journey to the men's camp.

In the village of male creatures, Old Man was cross and ill-humored. Nothing pleased him. Nothing he ate tasted good. He slept fitfully. He got angry over nothing. And so it was with all the men. "I don't know what's the matter," said Old Man. "I wish women were beautiful instead of ugly, sweet-smelling instead of malodorous, good-tempered instead of coming at us with stones or bloody knives in their hands."

"We wish it too," said all the other men.

Then a lookout came running, telling Old Man, "The women beings are marching over here to our camp. Probably they're coming to kill us. Quick everybody, get your bows and arrows!"

"No, wait!" said Old Man. "Quick! Go to the river. Clean yourselves. Anoint and rub your bodies with fat. Arrange your hair pleasingly. Smoke yourselves up with cedar. Put on your best fur garments. Paint your faces with sacred red paint. Put bright feathers on your heads." Old Man himself dressed in the quilled robe stolen from the women's camp which he had made into a war shirt. He wore his great chief's headdress. He put on his necklace of bear claws. Thus arrayed, the men assembled at the entrance of their camp, awaiting the women's coming.

The women came. They were singing. Their white quilled robes dazzled the men's eyes. Their bodies were fragrant with the good smell of sweet grass. Their cheeks shone with sacred red face paint.

Old Man exclaimed, "Why, these women beings are beautiful! They delight my eyes! Their singing is wonderfully pleasing to my ears. Their bodies are sweet-smelling and alluring!"

"They make our hearts leap," said the other men.

"I'll go talk to their woman chief," said Old Man. "I'll fix things up with her."

The woman chief in the meantime remarked to the other women, "Why, these men beings are really not as uncouth as we thought. Their rawness is a sort of strength. The sight of their arm muscles pleases my eyes. the sound of their deep voices thrills my ears. They are not altogether bad, these men."

Old Man went up to the woman chief and said, "Let's you and I go someplace and talk."

"Yes, let's do that," answered the woman chief. They went someplace. The woman chief looked at Old Man and liked what she saw. Old Man looked at the woman chief and his heart pounded with joy. "Let's try one thing that has never been tried before," he said to the woman chief.

"I always like to try out new, useful things," she answered.

"Maybe one should lie down, trying this," said Old Man.

"Maybe one should," agreed the woman chief. They lay down.

After a while Old Man said, "This is surely the most wonderful thing that ever happened to me. I couldn't ever imagine such a wonderful thing."

"And I," said the woman chief, "I never dreamed I could feel so good. This is much better, even, than eating buffalo tongues. It's too good to be properly described."

"Let's go and tell the others about it," said Old Man.

When Old Man and the woman chief got back to the camp, they found nobody there. All the male creatures and the women beings had already paired off and gone someplace, each pair to their own spot. They didn't need to be told about this new thing; they had already found out.

When the men and women came back from wherever they had gone, they were smiling. Their eyes were smiling. Their mouths were smiling, their whole bodies were smiling, so it seemed.

Then the women moved in with the men. They brought all their things, all their skills to the men's village. Then the women quilled and tanned for the men. Then the men hunted for the women. Then there was love. Then there was happiness. Then there was marriage. Then there were children.

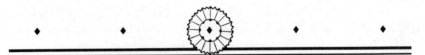

THE LITTLE OLD WOMAN
WITH FIVE COWS
Siberia (Yakut)

One morning a little old woman got up and went to the field containing her five cows. She took from the earth a herb with five sprouts and, without breaking either root or branch, carried it home and wrapped it in a blanket and placed it on her pillow. Then she went out again and sat down to milk her cows. Suddenly she heard tambourine bells jingle and scissors fall, on account of which noise she upset the milk. Having run home and looked, she found that the plant was uninjured. Again she issued forth to milk the cows, and again thought she heard the tambourine bells jingle and scissors fall, and once more she spilled her milk.

Returning to the house, she looked into the bedchamber. There sat a maiden with eyes of chalcedony and lips of dark stone, with a face of light-colored stone and with eyebrows like two dark sables stretching their forefeet toward each other. Her body was visible through her dress; her bones were visible through her body; her nerves spreading this way and that, like mercury, were visible through her bones. The plant had become this maiden of indescribable beauty.

Soon afterwards Kharjit-Bergen, son of the meritorious Khan Kara, went into the dark forest. He saw a grey squirrel sitting on a curved twig, near the house of the little old woman with five cows, and he began to shoot, but as the light was bad, for the sun was already setting, he did not at once succeed in his purpose. At this time one of his arrows fell into the chimney. "Old woman! take the arrow and bring it me!" he cried, but received no answer. His cheeks and forehead grew flushed and he became angry; a wave of arrogance sprang from the back of his neck, and he rushed into the house.

When he entered and saw the maiden, he lost consciousness. But he revived and fell in love. Then he went out and, jumping on his horse, raced home at full gallop. "Parents!" said he, "there is such a beautiful maiden at the house of a little old woman with five cows! Get hold of this maiden and give her to me!"

The father sent nine servants on horseback, and they galloped at full speed to the house of the little old woman with five cows. All the servants became unconscious when they beheld the maiden's beauty. However, they recovered, and all went away except the best one of them. "Little old woman!" said he, "give this girl to the son of the meritorious Khan Kara!" "I will give her," was the answer. They spoke to the maiden. "I will go," she announced. "Now, as the bridegroom's wedding gift," said the old woman, "drive up cattle, and fill my open fields with horses and horned stock!" Immediately the request was uttered and before the agreement was concluded, the man gave an order to collect and drive up the animals as the bridegroom's gift. "Take the maiden and depart!" said the old woman, when the stock of horses and cattle had been given as arranged. The maiden was quickly adorned, and a finely speckled horse that spoke like a human being was led up to her skillfully. They put on it a silver halter, saddled it with a silver saddle, which was placed over an upper silver saddle cloth and a lower silver saddle cloth, and they attached a little silver whip. Then the son-in-law led the bride from the mother's side by the whip, mounted his horse, and took the bride home.

They went along the road, and the young man said, "In the depths of the forest there is a trap for foxes. I will go there. Proceed along this road; it divides into two paths. On the road leading to the east is hanging a sable's skin. But on the road leading to the west there should be the skin of a male bear with the paws and head and with white fur at the neck. Go on the path where the sable's skin is hanging." He pointed out the road and went away.

The girl made her way to the fork in the road, but on coming to it forgot the directions. Going along the path where the bear's skin was hanging, she reached a small iron hut. Suddenly out of the hut came a devil's daughter, dressed in an iron garment above the knee. She had only one leg, and that was twisted; a single bent hand projected from below her breast, and her single furious eye was situated in the middle of her forehead. Having shot forth a fifty-foot iron tongue onto her breast, she pulled the girl from the horse, dropped her to the ground, and tore all the skin from her face and threw it on her own face. She dragged off all the girl's finery and put it on herself. Then mounting, the devil's daughter rode away.

The husband met the devil's daughter when she arrived at the house of the meritorious Khan Kara. Nine youths came to take her horse by the halter; eight maidens did likewise. It is said that the bride wrongly fastened her horse to the willow tree where the old widow from Semyaksin used to tether her spotted ox. The greater part of those who thus received the bride became sorely depressed, and the remainder were disenchanted; sorrow fell on them.

All who met the bride abominated her. Even the red weasels ran away from her, showing she was repugnant to them. Grass had been strewn on the pathway up to her hut, and on this grass she was led by the hand. Having entered, she replenished the fire with the tops of three young larch trees. Then they concealed her behind a curtain, while they themselves ate, drank, and played and laughed and made merry.

But the marriage feast came to an end, and there was a return to ordinary life. The little old woman with five cows, on going into open country to seek her cows, found that the plant with five sprouts was growing better than usual. She dug it up with its roots and, carrying it home, wrapped it up and placed it on her pillow. Then she went back and began to milk the cows, but the tambourine with the bells began to tinkle, and the scissors fell with a noise. Going back to the house, the old woman found the lovely maiden seated and looking more lovely than ever.

"Mother," she said, "my husband took me away from here. My dear husband said, 'I must go away on some business,' but before he went he said, 'Go along the path where the sable's skin is hanging, and do not go where the bear's skin is hanging.' I forgot and went along the second path to a little iron house. A devil's daughter tore the skin from my face and put it on her own face; she dragged off all my fine things and put them on; and next this devil's daughter mounted my horse and set out. She threw away skin and bones, and a grey dog seized my lungs and heart with his teeth and carried them to open country. I grew here as a plant, for it was decreed that I should not die altogether. Perhaps it has seen settled that later I shall bear children. The devil's daughter has affected my fate, for she has married my husband and contaminated his flesh and blood; she has absorbed his flesh and blood. When shall I see him?"

The meritorious Khan Khara came to the field belonging to the little old woman with five cows. The speckled white horse, who was endowed with human speech, knew that his mistress had revived, and he began to speak. He complained to Khan Khara thus:

"The devil's daughter has killed my mistress, torn all the skin from her face, and covered her own face with it; she has dragged away my mistress's finery and clothed herself in it. The devil's daughter has gone to live with Khan Khara's son and become his bride. But my mistress has revived and now lives. If your son does not take this holy girl as his bride, then I will complain to the white Lord God on his seat of white stone, by the lake that has silver waves and golden floating ice, and blocks of silver and black ice. And I will shatter your house and your fire, and will leave you no means of living. A divine man must not take a devil's daughter. Fasten this devil's-daughter bride to the legs of a wild horse. Let a stream of rushing water fall on your son and cleanse him during thirty days, and let the worms and reptiles suck away his contaminated blood. Afterwards draw him from the water and expose him to the wind on the top of a tree for thirty nights, so that breezes from the north and from the south may penetrate his heart and liver, and purify his contaminated flesh and blood. When he is cleansed, let him persuade and retake his wife!"

The khan heard and understood the horse's words; it is said he threw aside tears from both eyes; then he galloped home. On seeing him the bride changed countenance.

"Son!" said Khan Khara, "whence and from whom did you take your wife?" "She is the daughter of the little old woman with five cows." "What was the appearance of the horse on which you brought her? What kind of woman did you bring? Do you know her origin?"

To these questions the son answered, "Beyond the third heaven, in the upper region which has the white stone seat, is the white God. His younger brother collected migratory birds and united them into one society. Seven maidens, his daughters in the form of seven cranes, came to earth and feasted and entered a round field and danced, and an instructress descended to them. She took the best of the seven cranes and said, 'Your mission is to go out to people, to be a Yakut on this middle land. You must not dislike this impure middle land! You are appointed worthy of the son of the meritorious Khan Khara and are to wear a skin made of eight sables. On account of him, you will become human and bear children and bring them up.' After speaking, she cut off the end of the crane's wings. The maiden wept. 'Turn into a mare's-tail grass, and grow!' said the instructress. 'A little old woman with five cows will find the herb and turn it into a maiden and give her in marriage to Khan Khara's son.' I took her according to this direction and as she was described to me, but I accepted a strange being. In reality, as appears to me, I took nothing!"

After his son's reply the khan said, "Having seen and heard, I have come. The speckled horse with the human voice has complained to me. When you bore away your wife, you spoke to her of a forked road. You said, 'On the eastern path there is hanging a sable's skin and on the western path a bear's skin.' You said, 'Do not go on the path with the bear's skin, but go along the path showing a sable's skin!' But she forgot, and passed along the path which had the bear's skin. She reached an iron hut and then a devil's daughter jumped out to meet her, dragged her from her horse and threw her down, tore the whole of the skin from her face, and placed it on her own face. The devil's daughter dressed herself in the girl's finery and silver ornaments and rode hither as a bride. She fastened the horse to the old willow; it is already a mark. 'Attach the devil's daughter to the feet of a wild stallion!' said the horse to me, 'and wash your son in a swift stream for a whole month of thirty nights; let worms and reptiles suck away his contaminated body and blood. Carry him away and expose him to the breeze on the top of a tree during a month of thirty nights. Let the breezes search him from the north and from the south, let it blow through his heart and liver!' said the horse to me. 'Let him go and persuade his wife and take her! But away with this woman! Do not show her! She will devour people and cattle. If you do not get rid of her,' said the horse, 'I will complain to the white God.' "

On hearing this, the son became much ashamed. A workman called Boloruk seized the bride, who was sitting behind a curtain, and dragging her by the foot, fastened her on the legs of a wild horse. The horse kicked the devil's daughter to pieces and to death. Her body and blood were attacked on the ground by worms and reptiles, and became worms and reptiles moving about till the present time. After being placed in a steam of rushing water, the khan's son was placed on a tree, so that the spring breezes coming from the north and from the south blew through him. Thus his contaminated body and blood were purified, and when he was brought home, dried up and scarcely breathing, only his skin and bones remained.

He rode to the region of the wedding gift as before and, having picketed his horse, dismounted at his mother-in-law's house. The little old woman who owned the five cows fluttered out joyfully. She rejoiced as if the dead had come to life and the lost had been found. From the picketing spot to the tent she strewed green grass and spread on the front bed a white horse's skin with hoofs. She killed a milch cow and a large-breasted mare and made a wedding feast.

The girl approached her husband in tears. "Why have you come to me?" she asked. "You spilled my dark blood, you cut my skin deeply. You gave me up as food for dogs and ducks. You gave me to the daughter of an eight-legged devil. After that, how can you seek a wife here? Girls are more numerous than perch, and women than grayling. My heart is wounded and my mind is agitated! I will not come!"

"I did not send you to the daughter of an eight-legged devil, and when I went away on an important matter I pointed out your path. I did not knowingly direct you to a perilous place, and I did not know what would happen when I said to you, 'Go and meet your fate!' The lady instructress and protectress, the creatress, chose you and appointed you for me. Therefore you revived and are alive," he said, "and whatever may happen, good or ill, I shall unfailingly take you!"

The little old woman with five cows wiped away tears from both eyes and sat down between these two children. "How is it that, having met, you do not rejoice when you have returned to life after death, and been found after having been lost? Neither of you must oppose my will!"

The maiden gave her word, but said, "Agreed!" unwillingly. Then the young man sprang up and danced and jumped and embraced and kissed and drew in his breath. The couple played the best games and burst into loud laughter and talked unceasingly. Outside they fastened the speckled horse that spoke like a human being, laid on him the silver saddle cloth, saddled him with the silver saddle, bridled him with the silver bridle, hung on him the silver saddlebags, and attached to him the little silver whip. When the maiden had been dressed and all was complete on her, she was sent off. She and her husband knew as they went along that it was winter by the fine snow that was falling; they knew it was summer by the rain; they knew it was autumn by the fog.

The servants from the nine houses of Khan Khara, the house servants from eight houses and the room attendants from seven houses, and nine lords' sons who came out like nine cranes thought, "How will the bride arrive? Will she march out or will she saunter? And will sables arise from her footsteps?" Thinking thus, they prepared arrows so vigorously that the skin came off their fingers; they attended so closely to their work that their sight became dull. Seven grown-up daughters like seven cranes, born at one time, twisted threads so that the skin came from their knees, and said, "If when the bride comes she blows her nose loudly, dear little kings will be plentiful."

The son arrived with his bride, and two maidens took their horses by the bridle at the picket rope. The son and his bride dismounted and she blew her nose; therefore dear little kings would come! Instantly the women began to weave garments. Sables ran along the place from which the bride stepped forward, and some of the young men hastened into the dark forest to shoot them.

From the foot of the picketing post to the tent the way had been spread with green grass. On arriving, the bride kindled the fire with three branches of larch. Then they hid her behind a curtain. They stretched a strap in nine portions and tied to it ninety white speckled foals. On the right side of the house they thrust into the ground nine posts and fastened to them nine white foals and put on the foals nine friendly sorcerers who drank kumiss. On the left side of the house they set up eight posts.

Wedding festivities were begun in honor of the bride's entry into the home. Warriors collected and experts came together. It is said that nine ancestral spirits came from a higher place and twelve ancestral spirits rose from the ground. It is said that nine tribes came from under the ground and, using whips of dry wood, trotted badly. Those having iron stirrups crowded together, and those having copper stirrups went unsteadily. All had collected from the foreign tribes and from the tents of the nomad villages; there were singers, there were dancers, there were storytellers; there were those who jumped on one foot and there were leapers; there were crowds possessing five-kopeck pieces and there were saunterers.

Then the dwellers on high flew upwards, those dwelling in the lower regions sank into the earth, and inhabitants of the middle region, the earth, separated and walked away. The litter remained till the third day; but before the morrow most of the fragments had been collected, all animals had been enclosed, and children were sporting in the place. Their descendants are said to be alive today.

THE PRAYER THAT
WAS ANSWERED
Tibet

The little room glittered with light from the butter lamps, arranged neatly on a low table in front of the shrine. In the light from the lamps one could pick out the holy objects arranged on the shrine—the sacred books wrapped in cloth, the image of the Buddha, a framed picture of the Dalai Lama, silver offering bowls, and on the wall behind, with incense smoke curling around it, one could see the *thangka* painting of Tibet's patron deity and protector, Chenrezik, the bodhisattva of compassion, with eleven heads and a thousand arms. All around on the walls of the small room were paintings of other deities, all of whom were objects of devotion to the people of Tibet. There was a painting depicting Dolma, the female aspect of compassion, and Jamyang (Manjushri), the bodhisattva of wisdom.

This room, the shrine room, was the richest in the tiny house, for the people of Tibet were a religious people whose lives revolved around the teachings of the Buddha, as expounded by the great gurus and saints who had achieved the ultimate state of enlightenment. The people believed that although the great saints had reached the state of enlightenment they were still concerned for the welfare of all beings, and remained to protect and guide them on their journey through this and future lives.

So believed the old woman who sat in the corner of the shrine room, the beads of her rosary moving through her fingers as slowly she repeated the prayer of Chenrezik, OM MANI PADME HUM. Over and over again the powerful prayer rolled from her lips. The old woman was concerned, for she was a poor widow, without money or land; all she had in the world was an only daughter. The old woman knew that without a dowry to offer, her daughter would not be sought by the rich men of the land, and so would live her life in poverty and hunger. The old woman cared not for her own life, for it was almost over, but she wanted very much for her daughter to be prosperous and happy. It was for this that she prayed.

Now it happened that a poor man from a neighboring village had heard of the old woman's daughter, and when he saw her in the marketplace he was so moved by her beauty that he determined to make her his wife. He knew that the mother would hardly be willing for her daughter to marry a man of such little substance, so he plotted to make the mother believe that he was rich and prosperous.

Concealing himself in the shrine room of the old woman's house, the poor man waited for her to enter, make her offerings of food, and settle down in the corner to pray. The old woman prayed and prayed in earnest, begging for a rich man to come and take her daughter's hand in marriage. The poor man listened and waited for the old woman to finish; then, just as she was about to leave the room, he spoke.

The old woman was startled when she heard the voice; seeing no one in the room she believed it to be the voice of the gods. She heard the voice say how in the morning of the next day a wealthy man would appear on a white horse, and would ask for her daughter's hand in marriage.

The old woman was overjoyed. With her daughter she cleaned the house from top to bottom, making it ready for the rich man the gods were sending as a husband for her daughter. Then she prepared food and told her neighbors to make ready for a big celebration the next day, for her only daughter was to wed a rich man.

The next day the old woman and her daughter awoke early; the birds were singing and the blue of the sky contrasted with the fiery mountain peaks, bathed in the glow of the rising sun. The old woman and the daughter were excited and happy, and they settled themselves outside their tiny house to await the arrival of the man on a white horse.

Soon they caught their first glimpse of the man on the horizon. As he rode toward the house the daughter felt sudden pangs of foreboding. She wondered if he would be handsome and kind, and whether her married life would be joyful and happy as she anticipated. All these questions sprang to her mind; then she remembered this man was a gift from the gods so she need feel no fear.

The poor man, dressed in garments his neighbors had lent him, and riding the white horse which was the only one he owned, stopped in front of the old woman's house, dismounted, smiled at the daughter and took her hand in his. The old woman found it hard to contain her excitement and bade the man the house to take refreshment. This he did, and after they had talked for a little while he asked the old woman if he could take her daughter's hand in marriage.

There was much joy, a celebration was held, and all the neighbors and friends gathered to wish the couple good fortune, for it was felt that here was a match that was truly made in Heaven!

The poor man took the girl, with her few possessions packed in a trunk, and they set off for his humble home in a nearby village. On the journey the poor man began to feel concerned about his deception. He was frightened that the girl would scream and shout when she saw that he was not a rich man at all, but a very humble peasant; he feared too that she would run away and be lost to him forever. The poor man, troubled by these thoughts, decided on a plan. He took the girl's possession out of the trunk and buried them in the earth. Then he ordered the girl into the trunk, telling her that he wished to surprise her when they reached his home. Once the girl was inside the trunk the man locked it and made his way home, leaving the girl in a ditch at the side of a forest path.

When he reached his home the poor man ran to the houses of his nearby neighbors, and telling them that he was bringing home a nervous new bride, warned them not be concerned if they heard screams and shouts during the night. Then he fitted strong new bolts to his door so that the girl would not be able to escape.

While the poor man was away, a rich chieftain passed the spot where the imprisoned girl was lying in the trunk, awaiting the return of her husband. The chieftain ordered his men to open the trunk, and when he saw the girl inside he was so taken by her frail beauty that he took her away with him, leaving a fierce bear in her place inside the trunk.

The poor man returned to fetch his bride, tied a rope around the trunk and dragged it to his home. Inside the house he opened the trunk and was overwhelmed by the fierce bear, made more ferocious by its imprisonment and rough handling. The poor man screamed and shouted for help as the bear attacked him, but the neighbors took no heed of the noise, for they had already been warned.

So the poor man who had plotted and pretended to be a god died at the hands of a savage bear, and the girl lived happily ever after as the wife of a rich chieftain. The old woman's prayers had been answered.

THE MERCHANT'S DAUGHTER
AND THE SLANDERER
Russia

Once there was a merchant who had two children, a daughter and a son. When the merchant was on his deathbed (his wife had been taken to the graveyard before him) he said, "My children, live well with each other, in love and concord, just as I lived with your deceased mother." Then he died. He was buried and prayers were said for the repose of his soul, as is fitting.

Shortly afterward, the merchant's son decided to trade beyond the sea. He rigged up three ships, loaded them with a variety of goods, and said to his sister, "Now, my beloved sister, I am going on a long voyage and leaving you at home all alone. Mind you, behave properly, do not engage in evil things, and do not consort with strangers." Then they exchanged portraits; the sister took her brother's portrait, the brother took his sister's. They wept as they took leave of each other and said farewell.

The merchant's son raised anchor, pushed off from shore, hoisted sail, and reached the open sea. He sailed for one year, he sailed for another year, and in the third year he came to a certain wealthy capital and anchored his ships in the port. As soon as he arrived he took a bowl full of precious stones and rolls of his best velvet, damask, and satin, and took them to the king of those parts as a gift. He came to the palace, gave his gift to the king, and petitioned for leave to trade in his capital.

The precious gift was to the king's liking and he said to the merchant's son, "Your gift is munificent; in all my life I have never received a finer one. In return I grant you the first place on the market. Buy and sell, fear no one, and if anyone injures you, come straight to me. Tomorrow I myself will visit your ship."

Next day the king came to the merchant's son, began to walk on his ship and examine his goods, and in the master's cabin saw a portrait hanging on the wall. He asked the merchant's son, "Whose portrait is that?"

"My sister's, Your Majesty."

"Well, Mr. Merchant, such a beauty I have not seen in all my days. Tell me the truth: what is her character and what are her manners?"

"She is quiet and chaste as a dove."

"Well, if so, she will be a queen; I will take her to wife."

At that time, a certain general who was spiteful and envious was with the king; at the thought that anyone else might find happiness he choked with rage. He heard the king's words and became terribly angry. "Now," he thought, "our wives will have to bow to a woman of the merchant class!" He could not restrain himself and said to the king, "Your Majesty, do not order me to be put to death, order me to speak."

"Speak."

"This merchant's daughter is not a suitable match for you. I met her long ago, and more than once I lay on the bed and played amorous games with her. She is quite a dissolute girl."

"How can you, foreign merchant, say that she is quiet and chaste as a dove, and that she never engages in evil things?"

"Your Majesty, if the general is not lying, let him get my sister's ring from her and find out what is her secret mark."

"Very well," said the king, and he gave the general a furlough. "If you fail to get the ring and tell me the secret mark by such and such a day, your head shall fall by my sword."

The general made ready and went to the town where the merchant's daughter lived; he arrived and did not know what to do. He walked back and forth in the streets, low in spirits and thoughtful. He happened to meet an old woman who begged for alms; he gave her something. She asked, "What are you thinking about?"

"Why should I tell you? You cannot help me in my trouble."

"Who knows? Perhaps I can help you."

"Do you know where such and such a merchant's daughter lives?"

"Of course I do."

"If so, get me her ring and find out what is her secret mark. If you do this for me, I shall reward you with gold."

The old woman hobbled to the merchant's daughter, knocked at her door, said that she was going to the Holy Land, and asked for alms. She spoke so cunningly that the lovely maiden became quite bewitched and did not realize that she had blurted out where her secret mark was; and while all this talk was going on, the old woman slipped the girl's ring from the table and hid it in her sleeve. Then she said farewell to the merchant's daughter and ran to the general. She gave him the ring and said, "Her secret mark is a golden hair under her left arm."

The general rewarded her liberally and set out on his way back. He came to his kingdom and reported to the palace; and the merchant's son was there too. "Well," asked the king, "have you got the ring?"

"Here it is, Your Majesty."

"And what is the merchant's daughter's secret mark?"

"A golden hair under her left arm."

"Is that correct?" asked the king of the merchant's son.

"It is, Your Majesty."

"Then how dared you lie to me? For this I will order you put to death."

"Your Majesty, do not refuse me one favor. Give me leave to write a letter to my sister; let her come and say farewell to me."

"Very well," said the king, "write to her, but I won't wait long." He postponed the execution and in the meantime ordered that the young man be put in chains and thrown into a dungeon.

The merchant's daughter, upon receiving her brother's letter, set out immediately. As she traveled she knitted a golden glove and wept bitterly; her tears fell as diamonds, and she gathered these diamonds and studded the glove with them. She arrived in the capital, rented an apartment in the house of a poor widow, and asked, "What is the news in your city?"

"There is no news except that a foreign merchant is being made to suffer because of his sister. Tomorrow he will be hanged."

Next morning the merchant's daughter arose, hired a carriage, donned a rich garment, and went to the square. There the gallows was ready, troops were standing guard, and a great multitude of people had gathered; and now they led out her brother. She got out of the carriage, went straight to the king, handed him the glove that she had knitted on her way, and said, "Your Majesty, I beg of you, estimate what such a glove is worth."

The king examined it. "Ah," he said, "it is priceless!"

"Well, your general was in my house and stole a glove exactly like it, the other of the pair. Please order that a search be made for it."

The king summoned the general, and said to him, "There is a complaint against you that you stole a precious glove." The general began to swear that he knew nothing about it.

"What do you mean, you don't know?" said the merchant's daughter. "You have been in my house so many times, lain with me on the bed, played amorous games with me."

"But I have never seen you before! I have never been in your house, and not for anything in the world could I say at this moment who you are or whence you have come."

"If so, Your Majesty, why is my brother made to suffer?"

"Which brother?" asked the king.

"The one who is now being led to the gallows."

Thus the truth became known. The king ordered the merchant's son to be released and the general to be hanged; and himself sat in the carriage with the lovely maiden, the merchant's daughter, and drove to the church. They married, made a great feast, began to live in happiness and prosperity, and are still living to this very day.

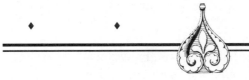

WHAT HAPPENED TO HADJI
Turkey

Hadji was a merchant in the Great Bazaar of Stambul. Being a pious Mohammedan, he was of course a married man, but even so he was not invulnerable to the charms of women. It happened one day that a charming hanum came to his shop to purchase some spices. After the departure of his fair visitor, Hadji, do what he might, could not drive her image from his mind's eye. Furthermore, he was greatly puzzled by a tiny black bag containing twelve grains of wheat, which the hanum had evidently forgotten.

Till a late hour that night did Hadji remain in his shop, in the hope that either the hanum or one of her servants would come for the bag and thus give him the means of seeing her again, or at least of learning where she lived. But Hadji was doomed to disappointment, and, much preoccupied, he returned to his house. There he sat, plunged in thought, unresponsive to his wife's conversation.

Hadji remained downcast day after day, but at last, giving way to his wife's entreaties, he told what had happened and admitted that ever since that fatal day his soul had been in bondage to the fair unknown.

"Oh, husband," replied his wife, "and do you not understand what that black bag containing the twelve grains of wheat means?"

"Alas, no," replied Hadji.

"Why, my husband, it is plain; plain as if it had been told. She lives in the Wheat Market, at house number 12, with a black door."

Much excited, Hadji rushed off and found that there was a number 12 in the Wheat Market, with a black door, so he promptly knocked. The door opened, and whom should he behold but the lady in question! Instead of speaking to him, however, she threw a basin of water out into the street and then shut the door. Hadji did not know what to think of this. Having lingered about the doorway for a time, he at length returned home. He greeted his wife more pleasantly than he had done for many days and told her of his adventure.

"Why," said his wife, "don't you understand what the basin of water thrown out of the door means?"

"Alas, no," said Hadji.

"Veyh! Veyh!" she exclaimed pityingly, "it means that at the back of the house there is a running stream, and that you must go to her that way."

Off rushed Hadji, and found that his wife was right; there *was* a running stream at the back of the house, so he knocked at the back door. The hanum, however, instead of opening it, came to the window, showed a mirror, reversed it, and then disappeared. Hadji lingered at the back of the house for a long time, but, seeing no further sign of life, he returned to his own home much dejected. On his entering the doorway, his wife greeted him with, "Well, was it not as a I told you?"

"Yes," said Hadji. "You are truly a wonderful woman! But I do not know why she came to the window and showed me a mirror, both front and back, instead of opening the door."

"Oh," said his wife, "that is very simple, must go when the face of the moon has rever: o'clock." The hour arrived, Hadji hurried off, the one to see his love, and the other to inform t

Whilst Hadji and his charmer were talking police seized them and carried them both off to p wife, having accomplished her mission, returned h

The next morning she baked a quantity of l taking them to the prison, begged entrance of the mission to distribute those cakes to the prisoners, fc ᴜ⌒e repose of the souls of her dead. This being a request which could not be denied, she was allowed to enter. Finding the cell in which the lady who had attracted her husband was confined, she offered to save her the disgrace of the exposure, provided she would consent never again to cast loving eyes upon Hadji the merchant. Those conditions were gratefully accepted, and Hadji's wife changed places with the prisoner.

When they were brought before the judge, Hadji was thunderstruck to see his wife, but, being a wise man, he held his peace and let her do the talking, which she did most vigorously. Vehemently did she protest against the insult inflicted on both her and her husband. What right had the police to bring them to prison because they chose to converse in a garden, seeing that they were lawfully wedded people? To witness that they were man and wife she called upon the watchman and the priest of the district and several of her neighbors.

Poor Hadji was dumbfounded, as, accompanied by his wife, he soon after left the prison where he had expected to stay at least a year or two. "Truly thou art a wonderful woman!" was all he was able to say.

♦   ♦   ♦   ♦   ♦

MR. FOX
England

Lady Mary was young, and Lady Mary was fair. She had two brothers, and more lovers than she could count. But of them all, the bravest

gallant was a Mr. Fox, whom she met when she was down
father's country house. No one knew who Mr. Fox was; but
was certainly brave, and surely rich, and of all her lovers, Lady
Mary cared for him alone. At last it was agreed upon between them
that they should be married. Lady Mary asked Mr. Fox where they
should live, and he described to her his castle, and where it was, but,
strange to say, did not ask her, or her brothers, to come and see it.

So one day, near the wedding day, when her brothers were out,
and Mr. Fox was away for a day or two on business, as he said, Lady
Mary set out for Mr. Fox's castle. And after many searchings, she
came at last to it, and a fine strong house it was, with high walls and
a deep moat. And when she came up to the gateway, she saw written
on it:

BE BOLD, BE BOLD

But as the gate was open, she went through it, and found no one
there. So she went up to the doorway, and over it she found written:

BE BOLD, BE BOLD, BUT NOT TOO BOLD

Still she went on, till she came to the hall, and went up the broad
stairs till she came to a door in the gallery, over which was written:

BE BOLD, BE BOLD, BUT NOT TOO BOLD,
LEST THAT YOUR HEART'S BLOOD SHOULD RUN COLD

But Lady Mary was a brave one, she was, and she opened the
door, and what do you think she saw? Why, bodies and skeletons of
beautiful young ladies all stained with blood. So Lady Mary thought
it was high time to get out of that horrid place, and she closed the
door, went through the gallery, and was just going down the stairs,
and out of the hall, when who should she see through the window,
but Mr. Fox dragging a beautiful young lady from the gateway to
the door. Lady Mary rushed downstairs, and hid herself behind a
cask, just in time, as Mr. Fox came in with the young lady, who
seemed to have fainted.

Just as he got near Lady Mary, Mr. Fox saw a diamond ring
glittering on the finger of the young lady he was dragging, and he
tried to pull it off. But it was tightly fixed, and would not come off,
so Mr. Fox cursed and swore, and drew his sword, raised it, and
brought it down upon the hand of the poor lady.

The sword cut off the hand, which jumped up into the air, and fell of all places in the world into Lady Mary's lap. Mr. Fox looked about a bit, but did not think of looking behind the cask, so at last he went on dragging the young lady up the stairs into the Bloody Chamber.

As soon as she heard him pass through the gallery, Lady Mary crept out of the door, down through the gateway, and ran home as fast as she could.

Now it happened that the very next day the marriage contract of Lady Mary and Mr. Fox was to be signed, and there was a splendid breakfast before that.

And when Mr. Fox was seated at table opposite Lady Mary, he looked at her. "How pale you are this morning, my dear." "Yes," she said. "I had a bad night's rest last night. I had horrible dreams." "Dreams go by contraries," said Mr. Fox; "but tell us your dream, and your sweet voice will make the time pass till the happy hour comes."

"I dreamed," said Lady Mary, "that I went yestermorn to your castle, and I found it in the woods, with high walls, and a deep moat, and over the gateway was written:

BE BOLD, BE BOLD

"But it is not so, nor it was not so," said Mr. Fox.
"And when I came to the doorway over it was written:

BE BOLD, BE BOLD, BUT NOT TOO BOLD

"It is not so, nor it was not so," said Mr. Fox.
"And then I went upstairs, and came to a gallery, at the end of which was a door, on which was written:

BE BOLD, BE BOLD, BUT NOT TOO BOLD,
LEST THAT YOUR HEART'S BLOOD SHOULD RUN COLD

"It is not so, nor it was not so," said Mr. Fox.
"And then—and then I opened the door, and the room was filled with the bodies and skeletons of poor dead women, all stained with their blood."

"It is not so, nor it was not so, and God forbid it should be so," said Mr. Fox.

"I then dreamed that I rushed down the gallery, and just as I was going down the stairs, I saw you, Mr. Fox, coming up to the hall door, dragging after you a poor young lady, rich and beautiful."

"It is not so, nor it was not so. And God forbid it should be so," said Mr. Fox.

"I rushed downstairs, just in time to hide myself behind a cask, when you, Mr. Fox, came in dragging the young lady by the arm. And, as you passed me, Mr. Fox, I thought I saw you try and get off her diamond ring, and when you could not, Mr. Fox, it seemed to me in my dream, that you out with your sword and hacked off the poor lady's hand to get the ring."

"It is not so, nor it was not so. And God forbid it should be so," said Mr. Fox, and was going to say something else as he rose from his seat, when Lady Mary cried out:

"But it is so, and it was so. Here's hand and ring I have to show," and pulled out the lady's hand from her dress, and pointed it straight at Mr. Fox.

At once her brothers and her friends drew their swords and cut Mr. Fox into a thousand pieces.

THE WAITING MAID'S PARROT
China

A young waiting maid had been taken into a great household of Szechwan province. She was so beautiful and intelligent that the master favored her over all the other servingwomen and kept her apart from them. It happened that a certain official presented the family with a rare parrot, one so cunning and clever that it could speak with a human voice. The master charged his favorite waiting maid with the care and feeding of the bird as her sole duty.

One day when the maid was feeding it, the bird suddenly spoke: "Take good care of me, sister, and you'll deserve a proper husband for it." Abashed, the maid slapped at the bird with her fan, but it did not flinch. From that time the maid would respond with a jest or a scolding whenever the bird had something to say, until the practice of chattering to it became a habit that she was no longer conscious of. For after all, she was alone in a single room with only a bird in a hanging cage. And if the confidences whispered between them made them intimate companions, whose business was it?

One day the maid was in the bath when the bird had just finished bathing. The creature was so tame that she had not locked its cage, and to her surprise it shook its wings and flew out, circling the room. She snatched at it frantically, but the bird punctured the paper window, looped through it, and was gone, leaving the maid watching helplessly.

Terrified of her master, the girl contrived to hide her guilt. She dressed and moved the cage to the eaves outside her room, then went to him and said tearfully, "Your obedient waiting maid forgot and closed her door to bathe, never expecting to be taken advantage of by someone who came in and released the bird. But I gladly bear the blame and would even die without resentment for my offense."

The master, who knew full well that the other maids were jealous of her, accepted her story. He questioned the rest of the household but could not find the culprit, and the investigation was dropped.

Ten days later the master's wife sent the waiting maid on an errand to a matron named Liang. The matron's unmarried son, Liang Hsü, was spending the day reading in his study. Presently a bird flew in and settled itself on his desk. In a human voice it said, "I have been searching for an ideal mate for you. Why don't you go and have a look?" Startled, Hsü put down his book and chased after the talking parrot. It led him out of his room, and he spied an enchanting maid of sixteen, dressed in dark colors except for a red skirt, shyly enter the house. Now the parrot was nowhere to be seen.

Hsü looked into the girl's face and saw that her beauty was truly exceptional. He found an excuse to follow her into the inner hall, where she conversed softly and fluidly with his mother. There he learned that she was a waiting maid in a mighty household. Yet her demure air utterly captivated him. The waiting maid also noticed the highborn youth and glanced at him from time to time. Though they could not exchange a single word, their affections were engaged.

On returning to her house the waiting maid went to her room, where the empty cage sat beside her bed. Perched on top of it was the bird, peacefully resting with eyes shut and talons curled. As happy as if she had found a royal jewel, the waiting maid snatched at the bird, which fluttered away and protested loudly: "Here I am, sister, nearly spent from dashing about on your behalf, and by good fortune I have found a fine husband for you. Why do you still want to lock me up?" Marveling, the maid listened while the bird told its story.

The bird concluded: "Though I cannot carry you two off beyond the compound wall as the heroic slave of fiction did, I can communicate your heart's desire to him, sister, if he is indeed the man you care for."

The waiting maid blushed but made no reply. "Young people in love were ever this way," the parrot scoffed. "But someone may be coming, and I must leave now." With that the bird set its feathers in motion and flew off.

The girl had been deeply attracted to Liang Hsü and felt ashamed to be joining the ranks of the master's concubines. Tossing and turning through the night, she was tormented by these two emotions.

The next day when the bird saw that no one was around, it returned to its original perch. The maid beckoned to it and said, "The master dotes on me and will never surrender me to the Liangs. To him that would be 'using a pearl to shoot down a sparrow.' Then again, young Liang is handsome, talented, and rich. Suppose he *were* attracted to a fresh flower; would he stoop to take a waiting maid for his proper wife? I thank you for your trouble, but I fear such an affair must fail. Nothing can be done."

The bird stirred its wings, swept away, and did not come back until evening. Then under cover of darkness it flew into the room and told the maid, "Young Liang shows his feelings for you in this verse." The parrot recited a poem written by the young man:

> *I care not if your fan be plain,*
> *My love is for your face so fair.*
> *If we could mount the nuptial bird,*
> *We'd soar aloft, a wedded pair.*

The maid rejoiced to hear this and confided her heartfelt wish to the parrot. As morning approached, she set the bird free.

In his lonely study, Liang Hsü had been thinking of the maid night and day. When he rose that morning and saw a hovering bird, it looked to him like the one that had come before. He joked with it, saying, "My good fellow, can you tell me something of the lady of my heart? Certainly you are a bird among birds; we shall have to have a biography of you so that you will be remembered for all eternity!"

The bird flew down and furled its wings, settling upon a painted screen. It told Liang of the maid's affection and the depth of her anxiety. Elated, Hsü asked if the maid could read. "Somewhat," the bird replied, and then and there Hsü wrote a letter revealing his love and vowing to marry her. He sealed the note and set it on the ground. The parrot swooped down, took the paper in its beak, and flew away, leaving Liang Hsü more astonished than ever by the oddness of it all.

For several days the young man did not see the bird. All news of the maid was abruptly cut off, and he was racked by yearning and despair. Then he heard that a maid in the great household where his beloved served had died and been hastily buried. Suspecting the worst, he made inquiries and verified that it was his own heart's love, though he could not discover the cause of her death. So great was his grief that he almost lost his voice from weeping.

What Liang Hsü did not know was that the maid had seen his note and, ashamed of her inability to write, had removed an earring and given it to the bird to carry back to her intended. The bird was to tell him the location of her parents' home and ask him to visit them and make a gift of money. Her freedom could then be redeemed and she could marry Liang Hsü.

The bird took the earring in its beak and flew aloft, but midway in its course a young tough struck it in the cheek with a rock. The talking parrot tumbled lifeless to the ground.

It was not long before disaster struck the maid also. At first the master had favored her because of her beauty, and everyone had expected that she would take her place among the master's concubines. But she had resisted the idea and had grumbled behind the master's back. When she had put the blame for the lost bird on the other maids and servants, they had looked at her askance even though they had escaped a whipping. They feared that she would cause trouble for them once she became the master's favorite concubine, so they soon attacked her in unison. Having heard her talking to the bird in her room during the night, they spread the slander that she was involved with some man. The tale was quickly sowed in the ear of the master, who began to nurse a deep jealousy. Presently he made a search of the maid's room and came across Liang Hsü's love letter. Enraged now, he had the maid interrogated under torture. Since the story of the parrot partook somewhat of the absurd, the maid herself could not give a clear account of it, and so she was beaten until her body was covered with bruises and her breath scarcely came. Though she was near death, the master did not wait but put her alive into a coffin and ordered her buried in the wilds.

After he learned of her death, Liang Hsü treasured the memory of his buried jewel. He sat, wounded in spirit, and dozed off at his desk. Suddenly a woman entered his dreams. Clothed in feathers, she walked with a dancing gait as she came before him and pulled her lapels together in the ceremonial salute traditionally required of women. "I am the parrot," she said, "and my elder sister, your heart's love, is a parrot as well. Thanks to her virtuous conduct in our previous lifetime, she was transformed into a human, and by chance I was reunited with her. I became concerned that she would be humiliated in an unworthy match, so I respectfully made an occasion to introduce her to you. Who would have thought I would die before accomplishing my mission—leaving my sister's virtue to be defiled, a wrong she bore unto death. The pity of it! And yet something of her vital force still remains, though none save you can help her."

In his dream Liang Hsü was overjoyed and rose to question the vision. Pointing a finger, she said, "One hundred paces beyond the city . . . the tomb of the fair one is not far away . . ." The woman fell to the ground, turned into a crane, and soared to the heavens.

Liang Hsü awoke with a start. At once he ordered his horse and rode out beyond the city wall. He knew of a certain hamlet whose name had the same sound as "hundred paces," the hint in the dream. There he found the burial site, although he did not dare open it right away. He took a room in the hamlet, and when night came he paid his servant to accompany him to the dread place and help him open the tomb. It was not very deep, and when they reached the coffin he thought he could hear the sound of breathing. He broke open the lid, and the maid returned to life.

Delirious with joy, Liang Hsü went to a nearby Buddhist convent and humbly knocked at the gates. He related in full his reasons for coming, and the nuns, who took pleasure in acts of charity, agreed to help him lift the maid from the hole. Liang Hsü carried her to the convent on his own back and left her with the nuns. After seeing to the costs, he went home.

It was over a month before the maid regained her strength. Then Liang Hsü asked a nun from the convent to be his matchmaker and explain as forcefully as possible to his mother that his heart belonged to a girl from a poor home.

Hsü's mother went to see the maid whom she remembered meeting once before, and listened sympathetically to the girl's tearful story. Having always treasured her son, the mother would never thwart his wishes. She took his fiancée home from the convent and severed relations with the maid's former household, so that the girl's whereabouts were kept secret. And Liang Hsü remembered the talking parrot's kindness so well that whenever he met someone who had captured one of these birds, he would buy it and free it.

THE WHITE CAT
France

There was once a king who had three sons, all handsome, brave, and noble of heart. Nevertheless, some wicked courtiers made their father believe they were eager to wear his crown before he was ready to resign it. He therefore invented a plan to get them out of the kingdom and prevent their carrying out any undutiful projects.

Sending for them, he conversed with them kindly, and said, "You must realize, my dear children, that my great age prevents me from attending as closely as I have hitherto done to state affairs. I fear this may be injurious to my subjects. I therefore desire to place my crown on the head of one of you; but it is no more than just that, in return for such a present, you should procure me some amusement in my retirement, before I leave the capital forever. I cannot help thinking that a little dog, handsome, faithful, and engaging, would be the very thing to make me happy, so I declare that he who brings me the most perfect little dog shall be my sucessor."

The Princes were much surprised at the fancy of their father to have a little dog, yet they accepted the proposition with pleasure. Accordingly, they set off on their travels, after taking leave of the King, who presented them with abundance of money and jewels, and appointed that day twelvemonth for their return.

Before separating, however, they took some refreshment together in an old palace about three miles out of town. They mutually agreed to meet in the same place on that day twelvemonth, and go all together with their presents to court. They also agreed to change their names and travel incognito.

Each took a different road. But it is intended to relate the adventures of only the youngest, who was the most comely, amiable, and accomplished prince in the world. As he traveled from town to town, he bought all the handsome dogs that fell in his way; and as soon as he saw one that was handsomer than those he had, he made a present of the rest, for twenty servants would scarcely have been sufficient to take care of all the dogs he was continually purchasing.

At length, wandering he knew not whither, he found himself in a forest. Night suddenly came on, and with it a violent storm of thunder, lightning, and rain. To add to his perplexity, he lost his way.

After he had groped about for a long time, he perceived a light, which made him suppose that he was not far from some house. He went toward it, and in a short time found himself at the gates of the most magnificent palace he had ever beheld. The entrance door was of gold, covered with sapphires, which shone so that the strongest eyesight could scarcely bear to look at it. This was the light the Prince had seen from the forest.

The Prince observed a deer's foot fastened to the golden door by a chain of diamonds. He could not help wondering at the magnificence he beheld, and the security in which the inhabitants seemed to live.

"For," said he to himself, "nothing could be easier than for thieves to steal this chain, and as many of the sapphire stones as would make their fortunes."

He pulled the chain and heard a bell, the sound of which was exquisite. In a few moments the door was opened; yet he perceived nothing but twelve hands in the air, each holding a torch.

The Prince felt himself gently pushed on from behind by some other hands. He walked on in great perplexity till he entered a vestibule inlaid with porphyry and lapis stone, where the most melodious voice he had ever heard chanted the following words:

> Welcome, Prince, no danger fear,
> Mirth and love attend you here;
> You shall break the magic spell,
> That on a beauteous lady fell.
> Welcome, Prince, no danger fear,
> Mirth and love attend you here.

The Prince now advanced with confidence, wondering what these words could mean. The hands moved him forward toward a large door of coral, which opened of itself to give him admittance into a splendid apartment built of mother-of-pearl, through which he passed into others, so richly adorned with paintings and jewels, and so resplendently lighted with thousands of lamps, that he imagined he must be in an enchanted palace. When he had passed through sixty apartments, all equally splendid, he was stopped by the hands, and a large easy chair advanced of itself toward the fireplace. Then the hands took off his wet clothes, and supplied their place with the finest linen imaginable, adding a comfortable dressing gown embroidered with gold and pearls.

The hands next brought him an elegant dressing table, and combed his hair so very gently that he scarcely felt their touch. They held before him a beautiful basin, filled with perfumes, for him to wash his face and hands, and afterward took off the dressing gown and dressed him in a suit of clothes of still greater splendor. When his toilet was complete, they conducted him to an apartment he had not yet seen, and which also was magnificently furnished. There was a table spread for supper, and everything upon it was of the purest gold adorned with jewels.

The Prince observed there were two covers set, and was wondering who was to be his companion, when his attention was suddenly caught by a small figure not a foot high which just then entered the room and advanced toward him. It had on a long black veil, and was supported by two cats dressed in mourning and with swords by their sides. They were followed by a numerous retinue of cats, some carrying cages full of rats, and others mousetraps full of mice.

The Prince was at a loss what to think. The little figure now approached, and threw aside her veil. He beheld a most beautiful White Cat. She seemed young and melancholy.

"My Prince," she said, "you are welcome. Your presence affords me the greatest pleasure."

"Madam," replied he, "I would fain thank you for your generosity, nor can I help observing that you must be an extraordinary creature to possess, with your present form, the gift of speech and the most magnificent palace I have ever seen."

"All this is very true," answered the beautiful cat; "but, Prince, I am not fond of talking, and least of all do I like compliments. Let us therefore sit down to supper."

The hands then placed the dishes on the table, and the Prince and White Cat seated themselves at it. The first dish was a pie made of young pigeons, and the next was a fricassee of the fattest mice.

The White Cat, who guessed the Prince's thoughts, assured him that there were certain dishes at table which had been dressed on purpose for him, in which there was not a morsel of either rat or mouse. Accordingly, he ate heartily of such as she recommended.

When supper was over, he perceived that the White Cat had a portrait set in gold hanging to one of her feet. He begged her permission to look at it. To his astonishment, he saw the portrait of a handsome young man who exactly resembled himself! He thought there was something most extraordinary in all this; yet, as the White Cat sighed and looked very sorrowful, he did not venture to ask any questions. He conversed with her on different subjects, and found her extremely well versed in everything that was passing in the world.

When the evening was far advanced, his hostess wished him a good night, and he was conducted by the hands to his bedchamber, which was different from anything he had seen in the palace, being hung with the wings of butterflies mixed with the most curious feathers. His bed was of gauze, festooned with bunches of the gayest ribbons, and the looking glasses reached from the floor to the ceiling.

The Prince slept little, and in the morning was awakened by a confused noise. The hands took him out of bed and put on him a handsome hunting jacket. He looked into the courtyard and perceived more than five hundred cats busily employed in preparing for the hunting field—for this was a day of festival.

Presently the White Cat came to his apartment, and having politely inquired after his health, she invited him to partake of their amusement. The Prince mounted a wooden horse, richly caparisoned, which had been prepared for him. The beautiful White Cat mounted a monkey; she wore a dragoon's cap, which made her look so fierce that all the rats and mice ran away in the utmost terror.

Everything being ready, the horns sounded and away they went. No hunting was ever more agreeable.

When the chase was over, the whole retinue returned to the palace. The White Cat immediately exchanged her dragoon's cap for the veil, and sat down to supper with the Prince, who, being very hungry, ate heartily, and afterward partook with her of the most delicious wines.

He then was conducted to his chamber as before, and wakened in the morning to renew the same sort of life, which day after day became so charming to him that he no longer thought of anything but of pleasing the sweet little creature who received him so courteously. Accordingly, every day was spent in new amusements.

The Prince had almost forgotten his country and relations, and sometimes even regretted that he was not a cat, so great was his affection for his mewing companions.

"Alas!" said he to the White Cat, "how will it afflict me to leave you, whom I have love so much! Either make yourself a lady or make me a cat."

She smiled at the Prince's wish, but offered no reply.

At length the twelvemonth was nearly expired. The White Cat, who knew the very day when the Prince was to reach his father's palace, reminded him that he had but three days longer to look for a perfect little dog. The Prince, astonished at his own forgetfulness, began to grieve.

The cat told him not to be so sorrowful, since she would not only provide him with a little dog, but also with a wooden horse which should convey him safely home in less than twelve hours.

"Look here," said she, showing him an acorn, "this contains what you desire."

The Prince put the acorn to his ear, and heard the barking of a little dog. Transported with joy, he thanked the cat a thousand times, and the next day, bidding her a tender farewell, he set out on his return.

The Prince arrived first at the place of rendezvous, and was soon joined by his brothers. They embraced and began to give an account of their success. The youngest showed them only a little mongrel cur, telling them that he thought it could not fail to please the King, from its extraordinary beauty.

The brothers trod on each other's toes under the table, as much as to say, "We have little to fear from this sorry-looking animal."

The next day they went together to the palace. The dogs of the two elder brothers were lying on cushions, and so curiously wrapped around with embroidered quilts that one would scarcely venture to touch them. The youngest produced his cur, and all wondered how the Prince could hope to receive a crown for such a shabby present.

The King examined the two little dogs of the elder Princes, and declared he thought them so equally beautiful that he knew not to which, with justice, he could give the preference. They accordingly began to dispute, when the youngest Prince, taking his acorn from his pocket, soon ended their contention; for a little dog appeared which could with ease go through the smallest ring, and was besides a miracle of beauty.

The King could not possibly hesitate in declaring his satisfaction; yet, as he was no more inclined than the year before to part with his crown, he told his sons that he was extremely obliged to them for the pains they had taken, and since they had succeeded so well, he wished they would make a second attempt. He therefore begged they would take another year in order to procure a piece of cambric fine enough to be drawn through the eye of a small needle.

The three Princes thought this very hard; yet they set out, in obedience to the King's command. The two eldest took different roads, and the youngest remounted his wooden horse, and in a short time arrived at the palace of his beloved White Cat, who received him with the greatest joy, while the hands helped him to dismount and provided him with immediate refreshment. Afterward the Prince gave the White Cat an account of the admiration which had been bestowed on the beautiful little dog and informed her of the further injunction of his father.

"Make yourself perfectly easy, dear Prince," said she. "I have in my palace some cats who are perfect adepts in making such cambric as the King requires; so you have nothing to do but to give me the pleasure of your company while it is being made and I will procure you all the amusement possible."

She ordered the most curious fireworks to be played off in sight of the window of the apartment in which they were sitting, and nothing but festivity and rejoicing was heard throughout the palace for the Prince's return.

As the White Cat frequently gave proofs of an excellent understanding, the Prince was by no means tired of her company. She talked with him of state affairs, of theaters, of fashions—in short, she was at a loss on no subject whatever.

In this manner the twelvemonth again passed quickly away, but the cat took care to remind the Prince of his duty in proper time.

"For once, my Prince," said she, "I will have the pleasure of equipping you as suits your high rank."

Looking into the courtyard, he saw a superb carriage, ornamented all over with gold, silver, pearls, and diamonds, drawn by twelve horses as white as snow, and harnessed in the most sumptuous trappings. Behind the carriage a thousand guards, richly appareled, were waiting to attend on the Prince's person. The cat then presented him with a nut.

"You will find in it," said she, "the piece of cambric I promised you; do not break the shell till you are in the presence of the King your father." Then, she hastily bade him adieu.

Nothing could exceed the speed with which the snow-white horses conveyed this fortunate Prince to his father's palace, where his brothers had just arrived before him. They embraced each other, and demanded an immediate audience of the King, who received them with the greatest of kindness. The Princes hastened to place at the feet of his majesty the curious present he had required them to procure.

The eldest produced a piece of cambric so extremely fine that his friends had no doubt of its passing through the eye of a needle. But when the King tried to draw the cambric through the eye of the needle it would not pass, though it failed but very little.

Then came the second Prince, who made as sure of obtaining the crown as his brother had done, but, alas! with no better success; for though his piece of cambric was exquisitely fine, yet it could not be drawn through the eye of the needle.

It was now the turn of the youngest Prince, who accordingly advanced, and opening an elegant little box inlaid with jewels, took out a walnut and cracked the shell, imagining he should immediately perceive his piece of cambric. But what was his astonishment to see nothing but a filbert! He did not, however, lose his hopes. He cracked the filbert, and it presented him with a cherry stone. The lords of the court, who had assembled to witness this extraordinary trial, could not, any more than the Princes his brothers, refrain from laughing, to think he should be so silly as to claim the crown on no better pretensions. The Prince, however, cracked the cherry stone, which was filled with a kernel. He divided it, and found in the middle a grain of wheat, and in that a grain of millet seed. He was now absolutely confounded, and could not help muttering between his teeth, "O White Cat, White Cat, thou hast deceived me!" At this instant he felt his hand scratched by the claw of a cat, upon which he again took courage. Opening the grain of millet seed, to the astonishment of all present he drew forth a piece of cambric four hundred yards long, and fine enough to be threaded with perfect ease through the eye of the needle.

When the King found he had no pretext left for refusing the crown to his youngest son, he sighed deeply, and it was easy to be seen that he was sorry for the Prince's success.

"My sons," said he, "it is so gratifying to the heart of a father to receive proofs of his children's love and obedience, that I cannot refuse myself the satisfaction of requiring of you one thing more. You must undertake another expedition. That one of you who, by the end of the year, brings me the most beautiful lady shall marry her and obtain my crown."

So they again took leave of the King and of each other, and set out without delay; and in less than twelve hours our young Prince arrived at the palace of his dear White Cat. Everything went on as before till the end of another year. At length only one day remained of the year.

The White Cat thus addressed him: "Tomorrow, my Prince, you must present yourself at the palace of your father and give him a proof of your obedience. It depends only on yourself to conduct thither the most beautiful princess ever yet beheld, for the time is come when the enchantment by which I am bound may be ended.

You must cut off my head and tail," continued she, "and throw them into the fire."

"I!" said the Prince hastily—"I cut off your head and tail! You surely mean to try my affection, which, believe me, beautiful cat, is truly yours."

"You mistake me, generous Prince," said she. "I do not doubt your regard, but if you wish to see me in any other form than that of a cat you must consent to do as I desire."

The Prince's eyes filled with tears as she spoke, yet he considered himself obliged to undertake the dreadful task. The cat continuing to press him with the greatest eagerness, with a trembling hand he drew his sword, cut off her head and tail, and threw them into the fire. No sooner was this done than the most beautiful lady his eyes had ever seen stood before him. Ere he had sufficiently recovered from his surprise to speak to her, a long train of attendants, who at the same moment as their mistress were changed to their natural shapes, came to offer their congratulations to the Queen and inquire her commands. She received them with the greatest kindness, and ordering them to withdraw, thus addressed the astonished Prince:

"Do not imagine, dear Prince, that I have always been a cat. My father was the monarch of six kingdoms. He tenderly loved my mother, and left her always at liberty to follow her own inclinations. Her prevailing passion was to travel, and a short time before my birth, having heard of some fairies who owned large gardens filled with the most delicious fruits, she had so strong a desire to eat some of them that she set out for the country where they lived. She arrived at their abode, which she found to be a magnificent palace, glittering on all sides with gold and precious stones. She knocked a long time at the gates, but no one came, nor could she perceive the least sign that it had any inhabitant. The difficulty, however, only increased the violence of my mother's longing, for she saw the tops of the trees above the garden walls loaded with the most luscious fruits. The Queen ordered her attendants to place tents close to the door of the palace; but, having waited six weeks without seeing anyone pass the gates, she fell sick of vexation and her life was despaired of.

"One night, as she lay half asleep, she turned herself about, and opening her eyes, perceived a little old woman, very ugly and deformed, seated in the easy chair by her bedside.

"'I and my sister fairies,' said she, 'take it very ill that Your Majesty should so obstinately persist in getting some of our fruit; but since so precious a life is at stake, we consent to give you as much as you can carry away provided you will give us in return what we shall ask.'

" 'Ah, kind fairy!' cried the Queen, 'I will give you anything that I possess, even my very kingdoms, on condition that I eat of your fruit.'

"The old fairy then informed the Queen that what they required was that she should give them her child as soon as it should be born, adding that every possible care should be taken of it, and that it should become the most accomplished princess.

"The Queen replied that however cruel the conditions she must accept them, since nothing but the fruit could save her life.

"In short, dear Prince," continued the lady, "my mother instantly got out of bed, was dressed by her attendants, entered the palace, and satisfied her longing. Having eaten her fill, she ordered four thousand mules to be loaded with the fruit, which had the virtue of continuing all the year round in a state of perfection. Thus provided, she returned to the King my father, who, with the whole court, received her with rejoicings.

"All this time the Queen said nothing to my father of the promise she had made to give her daughter to the fairies. She grew very melancholy. At length, being pressed by the King, she declared the truth. Nothing could exceed his affliction when he heard that his only child was to be given to the fairies. He bore it, however, as well as he could for fear of adding to my mother's grief, and also believing he should find some means of keeping me in a place of safety, which the fairies would not be able to approach.

"As soon as I was born, he had me conveyed to a tower in the palace, to which there were twenty flights of stairs and a door to each, of which my father kept the key, so that none came near me without his consent.

"When the fairies heard of what had been done, they sent first to demand me, and on my father's refusal, they let loose a monstrous dragon, which devoured men, women, and children, and which, by the breath of its nostrils, destroyed everything it came near, so that even the trees and plants began to die.

"The grief of the King was excessive, and, finding that his whole kingdom would in a short time be reduced to famine, he consented to give me into their hands. I was accordingly laid in a cradle of mother-of-pearl, ornamented with gold and jewels, and carried to their palace, when the dragon immediately disappeared. The fairies placed me in a tower, elegantly furnished, but to which there was no door, so that whoever approached was obliged to come by the windows, which were a great height from the ground. In this place was I educated by the fairies, who behaved to me with the greatest kindness. My clothes were splendid, and I was instructed in every kind of accomplishment; in short, Prince, if I had never seen anyone but themselves I should have remained very happy.

"One day, however, as I was talking at the window with my parrot, I perceived a young gentleman listening to our conversation. As I had never seen a man except in pictures, I was not sorry for the opportunity of gratifying my curiosity. I thought him a very pleasing object. At length he bowed in the most respectful manner, without daring to speak, for he knew that I was in the palace of the fairies. When it began to grow dark he went away, and I vainly endeavored to see which road he took.

"I resolved to find some means of escaping from my tower. I begged the fairies to bring me a netting needle, a mesh, and some cord, saying I wished to make some nets to amuse myself with catching birds at my window. This they readily complied with, and in a short time I completed a ladder long enough to reach to the ground.

"All at once the window opened, and the Fairy Violent, mounted on the dragon's back, rushed into the tower. The fairy touched me with her wand and I instantly became a white cat. She conducted me to this palace, which belonged to my father, and gave me a train of cats for my attendants, together with the twelve hands that waited on Your Highness. She then informed me of my birth and the death of my parents, and pronounced that I should not be restored to my natural figure until a young prince should cut off my head and tail. You ended the enchantment. I need not add that I already love you more than my life. Let us therefore hasten to the palace of the King your father, and obtain his approbation to our marriage."

The Prince and Princess accordingly set out side by side, in a carriage of still greater splendor than before, and reached the palace just as the two brothers had arrived with two beautiful princesses.

The King, hearing that each of his sons had succeeded in finding what he had required, again began to think of some new expedient to delay the time of his resigning the crown. But when the King was assembled with the whole court to pass judgment, the Princess who accompanied the youngest, perceiving his thoughts by his countenance, stepped majestically forward and thus addressed him:

"It is a pity that Your Majesty, who is so capable of governing, should think of resigning the crown! I am fortunate enough to have six kingdoms in my possession; permit me to bestow one on each of the eldest Princes, and to enjoy the remaining four in the society of the youngest. And may it please Your Majesty to keep your own kingdom, and make no decision concerning the beauty of three princesses, who, without such a proof of Your Majesty's preference, will no doubt live happily together!"

The air resounded with the applauses of the assembly. The young Prince and Princess embraced the King, and next their brothers and sisters. The three weddings immediately took place, and the kingdoms were divided as the Princess had proposed.

SEDNA
Eskimo

Long ago, there were no seals or walruses for Eskimos to hunt. There were reindeer and birds, bears and wolves, but there were no animals in the sea. There was, at that time, an Eskimo girl called Sedna who lived with her father in an igloo by the seashore. Sedna was beautiful, and she was courted by men from her own village, and by others who came from faraway lands. But none of these men pleased her and she refused to marry.

One day, a handsome young hunter from a strange far-off country paddled his kayak across the shining sea toward the shores of Sedna's home. He wore beautiful clothes and carried an ivory spear.

He paused at the shore's edge, and called to Sedna, "Come with me! Come to the land of the birds, where there is never hunger and where my tent is made of the most beautiful skins. You will rest on soft bearskins, your lamp will always be filled with oil, and you will always have meat."

Sedna at first refused. Again he told her of the home in which they would live, the rich furs and ivory necklaces that he would give her. Sedna could no longer resist. She left her father's home and joined the young hunter.

When they were out at sea, the young man dropped his paddle into the water. Sedna stared with fright as he raised his hands toward the sky, and before her eyes, they were transformed into huge wings—the wings of a loon. He was no man at all, but a spirit bird, with the power to become a human being.

Sedna sat on the loon's back and they flew toward his home. When they landed on an island in the sea, Sedna discovered that the loon had lied to her. Her new home was cold and windy, and she had to eat fish brought to her by the loon and by the other birds that shared their island.

Soon she was lonesome and afraid, and she cried sadly, "Oh Father, if you knew how sad I am, you would come to me and carry me away in your kayak. I am a stranger here. I am cold and miserable. Please come, and take me back."

When a year had passed and the sea was calm, Sedna's father set out to visit her in her far-off land. She greeted him joyfully and begged him to take her back. He lifted her into his boat, and raced across the sea toward home.

When the loon spirit returned, he found his wife gone. The other birds on the island told him that she had fled with her father. He immediately took the shape of a man, and followed in his kayak. When Sedna's father saw him coming, he covered his daughter with the furs he kept in his boat.

Swiftly the loon spirit rushed alongside in his kayak.

"Let me see my wife," he cried.

Sedna's father refused.

"Sedna," he called out, "come back with me! No man could love you as much as I do."

But Sedna's kayak flashed across the water. The loon-man stopped paddling. Sadly, slowly, he raised his hands toward the sky and once again they became wings. He flew over the kayak that carried his Sedna away from him. He hovered over the boat, crying the strange, sad call of the loon. Then he plunged down into the sea.

The moment the loon spirit disappeared, the sea waves began to swell up in fury. The sea gods were angry that Sedna had betrayed her husband. The kayak rose and fell as huge waves lashed against it. Sedna's father was terrified, and to save himself he pushed Sedna overboard. Sedna rose to the surface and her fingers gripped the edge of the kayak. But her father, frenzied with fear that he would be killed by the vengeful sea spirits, pulled out a knife and stabbed her hands.

Then, it is said, an astonishing thing happened, perhaps because the loon spirit or the sea spirits had willed it: the blood that flowed from Sedna's hands congealed in the water, taking different shapes, until suddenly two seals emerged from it. Sedna fell back into the sea, and coming back again, gripped the boat even more tightly. Again her father stabbed her hands and the blood flowed, and this time walruses emerged from the blood-red sea. In desperate fear for his life, he stabbed her hands a third time, and the blood flowed through the water, congealed, and the whales grew out of it.

At last the storm ended. Sedna sank to the bottom of the sea, and all the sea animals that were born from her blood followed her.

Sedna's father, exhausted and bitter, at last arrived home. He entered his igloo and fell into a deep sleep. Outside, Sedna's dog, who had been her friend since childhood, howled as the wind blew across the land.

That night, Sedna commanded the creatures of the sea that emerged from her blood to bring her father and her dog to her. The sea animals swam furiously in front of her father's igloo. The tides ran higher and higher. They washed up the beach until they demolished the igloo, and they carried Sedna's father and her dog down to the depths of the sea. There they joined Sedna, and all three have lived ever since in the land of the waters.

To this day, Eskimo hunters pray to Sedna, goddess of the seas, who commands all the sea animals. She is vengeful and bitter, and men beg her to release the animals that were born of her so that they might eat. By her whim, a man successfully harpoons seals and walruses or is swept away from land by the stormy seas. The spirits of the great medicine men swim down to her home and comb her hair because her hands still hurt. And if they comb her hair well, she releases a seal, a walrus, or a whale.

URASHIMA THE FISHERMAN
Japan

Young Urashima lived in Tango province, in the village of Tsutsu-gawa. One day in the fall of 477 (it was Emperor Yūryaku's reign), he rowed out alone in the sea to fish. After catching nothing for three days and nights, he was surprised to find that he had taken a five-colored turtle. He got the turtle into the boat and lay down to sleep.

When the turtle changed into a dazzlingly lovely girl, the mystified Urashima asked her who she was.

"I saw you here, alone at sea," she answered with a smile, "and I wanted so much to talk to you! I came on the clouds and the wind."

"But where did you come from, then, on the clouds and wind?"

"I'm an Immortal and I live in the sky. Don't doubt me! Oh, be kind and speak to me tenderly!"

When Urashima understood she was divine all his fear of her melted away.

"I'll love you as long as the sky and earth last," she promised him, "as long as there's a sun and a moon! But tell me, will you have me?"

"Your wish is mine," he answered. "How could I not love you?"

"Then lean on your oars, my darling, and take us to my Eternal Mountain!"

She told him to close his eyes. In no time they reached a large island with earth like jade. Watchtowers on it shone darkly, and palaces gleamed like jade. It was a wonder no eye had seen and no ear had ever heard tell of before.

They landed and strolled on hand in hand to a splendid mansion, where she asked him to wait, then opened the gate and went in. Seven young girls soon came out of the gate, telling each other as they passed him that he was Turtle's husband; and eight girls who came after them told each other the same. That was how he learned her name.

He mentioned the girls when she came back out. She said the seven were the seven stars of the Pleiades, and the eight the cluster of Aldebaran. Then she led him inside.

Her father and mother greeted him warmly and invited him to sit down. They explained the difference between the human and the divine worlds, and they let him know how glad this rare meeting between the gods and a man had made them. He tasted a hundred fragrant delicacies and exchanged cups of wine with the girl's brothers and sisters. Young girls with glowing faces flocked to the happy gathering, while the gods sang their songs sweetly and clearly and danced with fluid grace. The feast was a thousand times more beautiful than any ever enjoyed by mortals in their far-off land.

Urashima never noticed the sun going down, but as twilight came on the immortals all slipped away. He and the maiden, now

alone, lay down in each other's arms and made love. They were man and wife at last.

For three years he forgot his old life and lived in Paradise with the immortals. Then one day he felt a pang of longing for the village where he had been born and the parents he had left behind. After that he missed them more each day.

"Darling," said his wife, "you haven't looked yourself lately. Won't you tell me what's wrong?"

"They say the dying fox turns toward his lair and the lesser man longs to go home. I had never believed it, but now I know it's true."

"Do you want to go back?"

"Here I am in the land of the gods, far from all my family and friends. I shouldn't feel this way, I know, but I can't help being homesick for them. I want so much to go back and see my mother and father!"

His wife brushed away her tears. "We gave ourselves to each other forever!" she lamented. "We promised we'd be as true as gold or the rocks of the mountains! How could a little homesickness make you want to leave me?"

They went for a walk hand in hand, sadly talking it all over. Finally they embraced, and when they separated their parting was sealed.

Urashima's parents-in-law were sad to see him go. His wife gave him a jeweled box. "Dearest," she said, "if you don't forget me and find you want to come back, then grip this box hard. But you mustn't open it, ever."

He got into his boat, and they told him to close his eyes. In no time he was at Tsutsugawa, his home. The place looked entirely different. He recognized nothing there at all.

"Where's Urashima's family—Urashima the fisherman?" he asked a villager.

"Who are you?" the villager answered. "Where are you from? Why are you looking for a man who lived long ago? Yes, I've heard old people mention someone named Urashima. He went out alone on the sea and never came back. That was three hundred years ago. What do you want with him now?"

Bewildered, Urashima roamed the village for ten days without finding any sign of family or old friends. At last he stroked the box his divine lady had given him and thought of her; then, forgetting his recent promise, he opened it. Before his eyes her fragrant form, borne by the clouds and the wind, floated up and vanished into the blue sky. He understood he had disobeyed her and would never see her again. All he could do was gaze after her, then pace weeping along the shore.

When he had dried his tears, he sang about her far, cloud-girdled realm. The clouds, he sang, would bring her the message of his love. Her sweet voice answered him, across the vastness of the sky, entreating him never to forget her. Then a last song burst from him as he struggled with his loss: "My love, when after a night of longing day dawns and I stand at my open door, I hear far off waves breaking on the shores of your Paradise!"

If only he hadn't opened that jeweled box, people have said since, he could have been with her again. But the clouds hid her Paradise from him and left him nothing but his grief.

THE SPIRIT OF THE VAN
Wales

Among the mountains of Carmarthen, lies a beautiful and romantic piece of water, named The Van Pools. Tradition relates, that after midnight, on New Year's Eve, there appears on this lake a being named the Spirit of the Van. She is dressed in a white robe, bound by a golden girdle; her hair is long and golden, her face is pale and melancholy; she sits in a golden boat, and manages a golden oar.

Many years ago there lived in the vicinity of this lake a young farmer, who having heard much of the beauty of this spirit, conceived a most ardent desire to behold her and be satisfied of the truth. On the last night of the year, he therefore went to the edge of the lake, which lay calm and bright beneath the rays of the full moon, and waited anxiously for the first hour of the New Year. It came, and then he beheld the object of his wishes gracefully guiding her golden gondola to and fro over the lake. The moon at length sank behind the mountains, the stars grew dim at the approach of dawn, and the fair spirit was on the point of vanishing, when, unable to restrain himself, he called aloud to her to stay and be his wife; but with a faint cry she faded from his view.

Night after night he now might be seen pacing the shores of the lake, but all in vain. His farm was neglected, his person wasted away, and gloom and melancholy were impressed on his features. At length he confided his secret to one of the mountain sages, whose counsel was to assail the fair spirit with gifts of cheese and bread! The counsel was followed; and on Midsummer Eve the enamored swain went down to the lake, and let fall into it a large cheese and a loaf of bread. But all was vain; no spirit rose. Still he fancied that the spot where he had last seen her shone with more than wonted brightness, and that a musical sound vibrated among the rocks. Encouraged by these signs, he night after night threw in loaves and cheese, but still no spirit came.

At length New Year's Eve returned. He dressed himself in his best, took his largest cheese and seven of his whitest loaves, and repaired to the lake. At the turn of midnight, he dropped them slowly one by one into the water, and then remained in silent expectation. The moon was hid behind a cloud, but by the faint light she gave, he saw the magic skiff appear, and direct its course for where he stood. Its owner stepped ashore, and hearkened to the young man's vows, and consented to become his wife. She brought with her as her dower flocks and herds, and other rural wealth. One charge she gave him, never to strike her, for the third time he should do so she would vanish.

They married, and were happy. After three or four years they were invited to a christening, and to the surprise of all present, in the midst of the ceremony, the spirit burst into tears. Her husband gave an angry glance, and asked her why she thus made a fool of herself. She replied, "The poor babe is entering in a world of sin and sorrow, and misery lies before it; why should I rejoice?" He gave her a push. She warned him that he had struck her once.

Again they were, after some time, invited to attend the funeral of that very child. The spirit now laughed, and danced, and sang. Her husband's wrath was excited, and he asked her why she thus made a fool of herself. "The babe," she said, "has left a world of sin and sorrow, and escaped the misery that was before it, and is gone to be good and happy for ever and ever. Why, then, should I weep?" He gave her a push from him, and again she warned him.

Still they lived happily as before. At length they were invited to a wedding where the bride was young and fair, the husband a withered old miser. In the midst of the festivity, the spirit burst into a copious flood of tears, and to her husband's angry demand of why she thus made a fool of herself, she replied in the hearing of all, "Because summer and winter cannot agree. Youth is wedded to age for paltry gold. I see misery here, and tenfold misery hereafter, to be the lot of both. It is the Devil's compact." Forgetful of her warnings, the husband now thrust her from him with real anger. She looked at him tenderly and reproachfully, and said, "You have struck me for the third and last time. Farewell!"

So saying, she left the place. He rushed out after her, and just reached his home in time to see her speeding to the lake, followed by all her flocks and herds. He pursued her, but in vain. His eyes never more beheld her.

THE TOAD-BRIDEGROOM
Korea

Long ago there lived a poor fisherman in a certain village. One day he went fishing in the lake as usual, but found he could not catch as many fish as he was accustomed to. And on each of the following days he found his catch growing smaller and smaller. He tried new baits, and bought new hooks, but all to no avail. At last even the water of the lake began to disappear, until in the end it became too shallow for fishing.

One afternoon in the late summer the bottom of the lake was exposed to view, and a big toad came out from it. The fishermen immediately thought that it must have eaten up all the fish and angrily cursed the *samzog* or three families of the frog, its parents, brothers, wife and children, for it is popularly believed that the toad is a relative of the frog.

Then the toad spoke to him gently, rolling its eyes, "Do not be angry, for one day I shall bring you good fortune. I wish to live in your house, so please let me go with you." But the fisherman was annoyed that a toad should make such a request and hastened home without it.

That evening the toad came to his house. His wife, who had already heard about it from her husband, received it kindly, and made a bed for it in a corner of the kitchen. Then she brought it worms and scraps to eat. The couple had no children of their own, and decided to keep the toad as a pet. It grew to be as big as a boy, and they came to love it as if it were their son.

Nearby there lived a rich man who had three daughters. One day the toad told the fisherman and his wife that it would like to marry one of the three daughters. They were most alarmed at this unreasonable request and earnestly advised it to forget such an impossible ambition. "It is utterly absurd," they said. "How can poor people like us propose marriage to such a great family? And you are not even a human being."

So the toad replied, "I don't care what the rank of the family is. The parents may object, but yet one of the daughters may be willing to accept me. Who knows? Please go and ask, and let me know what answer you receive."

So the fisherman's wife went and called on the mistress of the rich man's house and told her what her toad-son had asked. The lady was greatly displeased and went and told her husband. He was furiously angry at such a preposterous suggestion and ordered his servant to beat the toad's foster-mother. So the poor woman returned home and told the toad of her painful experience.

"I'm very sorry that you have been treated like that, Mother," the toad said to her, "but don't let it worry you too much. Just wait and see what will happen." Then he went out and caught a hawk and brought it home. Late that night he tied a lighted lantern to its foot, and crept stealthily to the rich man's house. He tied a long string to the hawk's foot and then climbed a tall persimmon tree which stood by the house. Then he held the end of the string in his hand and released the hawk to fly over the house. As it flew into the air he solemnly declared in a loud voice, "The master of this house shall listen to my words, for I have been dispatched by the Heavenly King. Today you rejected a proposal of marriage, and now you shall be punished for your arrogance. I shall give you one day to reconsider your decision. I advise you to accept the toad's proposal, for if you do not, you, your brothers, and your children shall be utterly destroyed."

The people in the house were startled by this nocturnal proclamation from the sky, and they opened the windows to see what was going on. When they looked up into the sky they saw a dim light hovering overhead. The master of the house went out into the garden and kneeled humbly on the ground looking up into the sky. Then the toad let go of the string he held in his hand, and the hawk soared skywards with the lantern still tied to its foot. The rich man was now convinced that what he had heard was spoken by a messenger from Heaven, and at once resolved to consent to the toad's marriage to one of his daughters.

Next morning the rich man went and called on the toad's foster-parents, and apologized humbly for his discourteous refusal on the previous day. He said now that he would gladly accept the toad as his son-in-law. Then he returned home and asked his eldest daughter to marry the toad, but she rushed from the room in fury and humiliation. Then he called his second daughter, and suggested that she be the toad's wife, but she too rushed from the room without a word. So he called his youngest daughter and explained to her that if she refused she would place the whole family in a most difficult position indeed, so stern had been the warning from Heaven. But the youngest daughter agreed without the slightest hesitation to marry the toad.

The wedding took place on the following day, and a great crowd of guests attended consumed by curiosity at such an unusual happening. That night, when they retired, the toad asked his bride to bring him a pair of scissors. She went and got a pair, and then he asked her to cut the skin off his back. This strange request startled her greatly, but he insisted that she do so without delay, and so she made a long cut in his back. Then, lo and behold, there stepped forth from the skin a handsome young man.

In the morning the bridegroom put on his toad skin again, so that nobody noticed any difference. Her two sisters sneered contemptuously at the bride with her repulsive husband, but she took no notice of them. At noon all the men of the household went out on horseback with bows and arrows to hunt. The toad accompanied them on foot and unarmed. But the party had no success in the hunt and had to return empty-handed. The bridegroom stripped off his toad skin and became a man when they had gone, and waved his hand in the air. Then a white-haired old man appeared, and he bade him bring one hundred deer. When the deer came he drove them homeward, once more wearing his toad skin. Everyone was most surprised to see all the deer, and then he suddenly stripped off the toad skin and revealed himself as a handsome young man, at which their astonishment knew no bounds. Then he released all the deer and rose up to Heaven, carrying his bride on his back and his parents on his arms.

TAKEN
Ireland

It is not so long ago that a woman of my mother's kin, the O'Sheas, was taken, and when I was young I knew people who had seen her. She was a beautiful girl, and she hadn't been married a year when she fell sick, and she said that she was going to die, and that if she must die she would rather be in the home in which she had spent her life than in a strange house where she had been less than a year. So she went back to her mother's house, and very soon she died and was buried. She hadn't been buried more than a year when her husband married again, and he had two children by his second wife. But one day there came a letter to her people, a letter with a seal on it.

It was from a farmer who lived in the neighborhood of Fermoy. He said that now for some months, when the family would go to bed at night in his farm, if any food were left out they would find it gone in the morning. And at last he said to himself that he would find out what it was that came at night and took the food.

So he sat up in a corner of the kitchen one night, and in the middle of the night the door opened and a woman came in, the most beautiful woman he had ever seen with his eyes, and she came up the kitchen and lifted the bowl of milk they had left out, and drank of it. He came between her and the door, and she turned to him and said that this was what she had wanted.

So he asked her who she was, and she said that she came from the liss at the corner of his farm, where the fairies kept her prisoner. They had carried her off from a place in Ventry parish, and left a changeling in her place, and the changeling had died and been buried in her stead.

She said that the farmer must write to her people and say that she was in the liss with the fairies, and that she had eaten none of the food of the fairies, for if once she ate of their food she must remain with them forever till she died; and when she came near to death they would carry her through the air and put her in the place of another young woman, and carry the young woman back to be in the liss with them, in her stead. And when he wrote to her people, he must ask her mother if she remembered one night when her daughter lay sick, and the mother was sitting by the fire, and, thinking so, she had forgotten everything else, and the edge of her skirt had caught fire and was burning for some time before she noticed it. If she remembered that night it would be a token for her, for on that night her daughter had been carried off, and the fire in her mother's skirt was the last thing she remembered of her life on earth. And when she had said this she went out through the door, and the farmer saw her no more.

So the next day he wrote the letter as she had told him. But her people did nothing, for they feared that if they brought her back there would be trouble because of the new wife and her two children.

And she came again and again to the farmer, and he wrote seven letters with seals, and the neighbors all said it was a shame to them to leave her with the fairies in the liss. And the husband said it was a great wrong to leave his wife in the liss, and, whatever trouble it would bring, they should go and fetch her out of the liss.

So they set out, her own people and her husband, and when they had gone as far as Dingle, they said they would go and ask the advice of the priest.

So they went to the priest that was there that time, and they told him the story from the beginning to the end. And when he had heard the story, he said that it was a hard case, and against the law of the church. And the husband said that, when they had brought the woman out of the liss, he would not bring her back with him to make sandal in the countryside, but would send her to America, and would live with his second wife and her children. But the priest said that even if a man's wife were in America, she was still his wife, and it was against the law of the Pope that a man should have two wives; and, though it was a hard thing, they must leave her in the liss with the fairies, for it was a less evil that she should eat the fairy bread and be always with the fairies in the liss than that God's law should be broken and a man have two wives living in this world.

They found nothing to say against the priest, and they went home sorrowing. And when the woman heard this from the farmer she went back with the fairies to the liss, and ate their bread and remained with them.

THE GIRL AT THE SHIELING
Iceland

There was once a priest in the North Quarter who had brought up a little girl as his own. The summer pastures belonging to his farm were high up in the fells, and he always sent his sheep and cattle there in the summer with the herdsmen, and with a woman to keep house for them. When his foster-daughter grew up, she became the housekeeper at this shieling, and was as good at this as at everything—for she was a skillful girl, and beautiful, and had many accomplishments. Many well-to-do men asked for her hand, for she was thought the best match in the North Quarter, but she refused all offers.

One day the priest spoke seriously to his adopted daughter and urged her to marry, saying he would not always be there to look after her, for he was an old man. She took it very badly, and said she had no fancy for such things, and was very happy as she was, and that there was no luck in marriage. So they said no more about it, for the time being.

As that winter wore on, people thought the girl was getting rather plump below the belt, and the plumpness grew more and more marked as time went on. In spring her foster-father spoke to her again, and urged her to tell him how things were with her, and said she must surely be with child, and should not go up to the shieling that summer. She strongly denied that she was pregnant, and said there was nothing the matter with her, and that she would see to her housekeeping that summer just as before. When the pastor saw he was getting nowhere, he let her have her way, but he told the men who were to be in the shieling never to go out at any time leaving her quite alone, and this they promised faithfully. So then they all moved up to the shieling, and the girl was as merry as could be.

So time passed, and nothing noteworthy happened. The men at the shieling kept strict watch on their housekeeper and never left her alone.

One evening it happened that a shepherd found that all the sheep and cows were missing, and so every living soul left the shieling except the housekeeper, who stayed behind alone. The search party searched very late and did not find the beasts till almost morning, for it was very misty. When they came home, the housekeeper was up and about, and she was brisker in her movements and lighter on her feet than she had usually been. The men also saw, as time went by, that her plumpness had lessened, though they could not tell how, and so they thought that it must have been some other kind of swelling, and not pregnancy.

So home they went from the shieling in autumn, the whole company of men and beasts. The priest saw then that the housekeeper was far slimmer in the waist than she had been the previous winter, so then he went to the men who had been at the shieling and asked whether they had disobeyed his orders and left the girl quite alone. They told him the truth, that they had once all left her to go out searching for their beasts, as these had all gone missing. The pastor grew angry, and wished bad luck on all who had disregarded his orders, for he said he had suspected as much as soon as the girl went off to the shieling in spring.

Next winter a man came to ask the hand of the priest's foster-daughter, and she was not at all pleased about it, but the priest told her she would not avoid marrying him, for he was a fine man and everyone spoke well of him. He had inherited his father's farm that spring, and his mother ran the house for him. So this marriage was settled, whether the girl liked or not, and their wedding was held next spring at the priest's house.

But before the woman put her bridal dress on, she said to her betrothed, "Before you go ahead and marry me against my wishes, I lay down one condition—that you never take strangers in to lodge for the winter without first telling me, or else things will go wrong for you." And this the man promised.

So the wedding feast was held, and she went home with her husband and took over the running of his home, but her heart was not in it, for she was never cheerful or happy-looking, though her husband pampered her and would not have her working her fingers to the bone.

Every summer she used to stay at home when the others were out haymaking, and her mother-in-law would stay to keep her company and to see to the housekeeping with her. Between whiles they would sit knitting or spinning, and the older woman would tell her stories to amuse her. One day when the old woman had ended a story, she told her daughter-in-law that she ought to tell a story now. But she said that she did not know any. The other pressed her hard, and so she promised to tell her the only one she knew, and so she began her tale:

"There was once a girl on a farm who was housekeeper at the shieling. Not far from the shieling there were great rocky scarps, and she often went walking near them. There was a man of the Hidden Folk who lived inside these scarps, and they soon got acquainted and grew to love one another dearly. He was so good and kind to the girl that he would refuse her nothing, and would follow her wishes in everything. But the upshot was that when some time had gone by the girl became pregnant; the head of her houshold accused her of it when she was about to go to the shieling the following summer, but the girl denied it, and went to the shieling as usual. But he ordered the others who were to be at the shieling never to go off and leave her alone, and they promised. They did all leave her, however, to search for their cattle, and then the pangs of childbirth came on her. The man who had been her lover came then, and sat beside her, and he cut the cord and washed the baby and swaddled it. Then, before he went off with the child, he gave her a drink from a flask, and it was the sweetest drink which I ever—" at that moment the ball of knitting wool slipped from her hand, so she bent down for it, and corrected herself—"which *she* had ever tasted, that's what I meant to say, and so she was well again in a moment, after all her pains. From that hour they never saw one another again, she and the man of the Hidden Folk; but she was married off to another man, much against her will, for she pined bitterly for her first lover, and from that time she never knew one happy day. And so ends this story."

The mother-in-law thanked her for the story, and took good care to remember it. And so things went on for some time, and nothing notable happened, an the woman went on being sad, in her usual way, but was good to her husband all the same.

One summer when the mowing was almost done, two men came up to the farmer; one was tall, the other short, and both wore broad-brimmed hats so that one could hardly see their faces. The taller one spoke up, asking the farmer to take them in for the winter. He said he never took anyone in without his wife knowing, and that he would go and speak to her before promising them lodgings. The tall one said this was a ridiculous thing to say, that such a fine, masterful man was so henpecked that he couldn't make up his mind on a little matter like giving two men bed and board for one winter. So they settled the matter, and the farmer promised these men their winter quarters without asking his wife's leave.

That evening the strangers arrive at the farmer's house, and he assigns them their quarters in a building on the outskirts of the farm, and tells them to stay there. Then he goes to his wife, and tells her how matters stand. She took it very badly, saying that this had been the first favor she had ever asked him, and it would probably be the last, and that as he had taken them in on his own, he could see to everything they might need all winter on his own; and so the conversation ended.

Now all was quiet until one day that autumn, when the farmer and his wife were meaning to go to Holy Communion. It was the custom in those days, as it long was in some parts of Iceland, that those who mean to go to Communion should go to all the people in the house, kiss them and beg their forgiveness if they had offended them. Up till then, the mistress of the house had always avoided the lodgers and not let them see her, and so on this occasion likewise she did not go to greet them.

She and her husband set out, but as soon as they were beyond the fence, he said to her, "You did of course greet our lodgers, didn't you?"

She said no.

He told her not to commit such a sin as to go off without greeting them.

"You show me in many ways that you care nothing for me," said she. "First by the fact that you took these men in without my leave, and now again when you want to force me to kiss them. All the same, I will obey; but you'll be sorry for it, for my life is at stake, and yours too, very likely."

Now she turns back homewards, and is a very long time gone. Now the farmer too goes back home, and goes to where he expects the lodgers to be, and there he finds them, in their own quarters. He sees the taller lodger and the mistress of the house both lying on the floor dead, in one another's arms, and they had died of grief. The other was standing by them, weeping, when the farmer came in, but he soon disappeared, and nobody knew where he went.

From the story which the wife had told her mother-in-law, people felt sure that the tall stranger must have been the elf she had made love with in the shieling, and the small one who disappeared, her son and his.

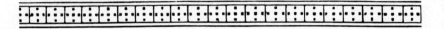

DEER HUNTER AND WHITE CORN MAIDEN

American Indian (Tewa)

Long ago in the ancient home of the San Juan people, in a village whose ruins can be seen across the river from present-day San Juan, lived two magically gifted young people. The youth was called Deer Hunter because even as a boy, he was the only one who never returned empty-handed from the hunt. The girl, whose name was White Corn Maiden, made the finest pottery and embroidered clothing with the most beautiful designs of any woman in the village. These two were the handsomest couple in the village, and it was no surprise to their parents that they always sought one another's company. Seeing that they were favored by the gods, the villagers assumed that they were destined to marry.

And in time they did, and contrary to their elders' expectations, they began to spend even more time with one another. White Corn Maiden began to ignore her pottery making and embroidery, while Deer Hunter gave up hunting, at a time when he could have saved many of his people from hunger. They even began to forget their religious obligations. At the request of the pair's worried parents, the tribal elders called a council. This young couple was ignoring all the traditions by which the tribe had lived and prospered, and the people feared that angry gods might bring famine, flood, sickness, or some other disaster upon the village.

But Deer Hunter and White Corn Maiden ignored the council's pleas and drew closer together, swearing that nothing would ever part them. A sense of doom pervaded the village, even though it was late spring and all nature had unfolded in new life.

Then suddenly White Corn Maiden became ill, and within three days she died. Deer Hunter's grief had no bounds. He refused to speak or eat, preferring to keep watch beside his wife's body until she was buried early the next day.

For four days after death, every soul wanders in and around its village and seeks forgiveness from those whom it may have wronged in life. It is a time of unease for the living, since the soul may appear in the form of a wind, a disembodied voice, a dream, or even in human shape. To prevent such a visitation, the villagers go to the dead person before burial and utter a soft prayer of forgiveness. And on the fourth day after death, the relatives gather to perform a ceremony releasing the soul into the spirit world, from which it will never return.

But Deer Hunter was unable to accept his wife's death. Knowing that he might see her during the four-day interlude, he began to wander around the edge of the village. Soon he drifted farther out into the fields, and it was here at sundown of the fourth day, even while his relatives were gathering for the ceremony of release, that he spotted a small fire near a clump of bushes.

Deer Hunter drew closer and found his wife, as beautiful as she was in life and dressed in all her finery, combing her long hair with a cactus brush in preparation for the last journey. He fell weeping at her feet, imploring her not to leave but to return with him to the village before the releasing rite was consummated. White Corn Maiden begged her husband to let her go, because she no longer belonged to the world of the living. Her return would anger the spirits, she said, and anyhow, soon she would no longer be beautiful, and Deer Hunter would shun her.

He brushed her pleas aside by pledging his undying love and promising that he would let nothing part them. Eventually she relented, saying that she would hold him to his promise. They entered the village just as their relatives were marching to the shrine with the food offering that would release the soul of White Corn Maiden. They were horrified when they saw her, and again they and the village elders begged Deer Hunter to let her go. He ignored them, and an air of grim expectancy settled over the village.

The couple returned to their home, but before many days had passed, Deer Hunter noticed that his wife was beginning to have an unpleasant odor. Then he saw that her beautiful face had grown ashen and her skin dry. At first he only turned his back on her as they slept. Later he began to sit up on the roof all night, but White Corn Maiden always joined him. In time the villagers became used to the sight of Deer Hunter racing among the houses and through the fields with White Corn Maiden, now not much more than skin and bones, in hot pursuit.

Things continued in this way, until one misty morning a tall and imposing figure apeared in the small dance court at the center of the village. He was dressed in spotless white buckskin robes and carried the biggest bow anyone had ever seen. On his back was slung a great quiver with the two largest arrows anyone had ever seen. He remained standing at the center of the village and called, in a voice that carried into every home, for Deer Hunter and White Corn Maiden. Such was its authority that the couple stepped forward meekly and stood facing him.

The awe-inspiring figure told the couple that he had been sent from the spirit world because they, Deer Hunter and White Corn Maiden, had violated their people's traditions and angered the spirits; that because they had been so selfish, they had brought grief and near-disaster to the village. "Since you insist on being together," he said, "you shall have your wish. You will chase one another forever across the sky, as visible reminders that your people must live according to tradition if they are to survive." With this he set Deer Hunter on one arrow and shot him low into the western sky. Putting White Corn Maiden on the other arrow, he placed her just behind her husband.

That evening the villagers saw two new stars in the west. The first, large and very bright, began to move east across the heavens. The second, a smaller, flickering star, followed close behind. So it is to this day, according to the Tewa; the brighter one is Deer Hunter, placed there in the prime of his life. The dimmer star is White Corn Maiden, set there after she had died; yet she will forever chase her husband across the heavens.

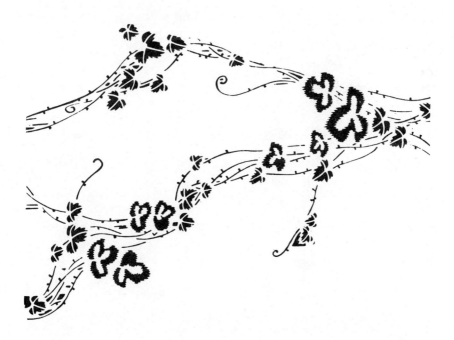

TRICKSTERS,
ROGUES,
and
CHEATS

The figure of the trickster can be found in every folklore tradition. The trickster as hero or as god plays an important role: Anansi in Africa is sometimes heroic, sometimes foolish, with definite supernatural powers. Likewise his famous Native American counterparts, Coyote and Rabbit, act as both fooler and fooled. The trickster as wise man finds his way into Near Eastern tradition, especially in the Jewish stories of resourceful rabbis and the Turkish tales of the Hodja. In Mexico the trickster supreme is Quevedo, who in history was Don Francisco de Quevedo y Villegas, a seventeenth-century Spanish poet and satirist who became a legendary figure starring in a cycle of stories well known throughout the Spanish-speaking world. The German Tyll Ulenspiegel, a popular peasant jester, actually lived in the fourteenth century, but within another two centuries had become a legend around whose name volumes of anecdotes and jests had accumulated. Many of the stories told about these particular tricksters or culture heroes harken back to other tales and other times.

Whether the trickster is an animal such as Brer Rabbit or Raven or the wily fox, or supremely human like the German master thief, he plays his tricks out to the end. And sometimes it is a bloody and awful ending. Anansi dies in "Being Greedy Chokes Anansi" after first having dispatched any number of unnamed animals. The thief must cut off his partner's head in "Crack and Crook." If we dwell on such gory abominations, however, we miss the point of these tricksters: they represent chaos in the ordered life. As Alan Garner writes in *The Guizer*, the trickster is "the advocate of uncertainty." The very amorality of the trickster—who recognizes neither good nor evil—re-emphasizes our own cherished morality. The trickster can also poke fun at our illusions: the desire for a handsome son-in-law is upended in the Japanese tale "The Ugly Son." The wish to live forever is given its due in two stories carrying the same motif: "Peik" and "The Story of Campriano."

Sometimes the trickster himself is tricked, either dying in the end like Anansi or being tied up in a sack like a fox in "The King's Son Goes Bear Hunting." Sometimes he wins himself life ("The Rabbi and the Inquisitor") or the king's daughter ("Peik"). But win or lose, the stories always make us smile at the ingenuity of the hero or shake our heads fondly at his *chutzpah*, that sly gutsiness of the trickster who has outwitted us all in the end.

TYLL ULENSPIEGEL'S MERRY PRANK
Germany

When Tyll was in Poland, King Casimir ruled, and a merry monarch he was. Instead of having one court jester, he had two, and when he heard Tyll was in the land he invited him also to his palace.

Now, the king was proud of his jesters and knew a trick or three himself. Often they argued, and Tyll was always ready with a quick answer, particularly when it came to answering the jesters. So one day the king decided to test which was the cleverest of the three.

There was a great gathering of nobles in the court when the king offered twenty gold pieces and a fine new coat to the one of the three who could make the greatest wish. All the court applauded the generosity of their ruler.

"And," added he, "the wish must be made right now before me and all the court."

Said the first jester, "I wish the heaven above us were nothing but paper and the sea nothing but ink so that I could write the figures of how much money should be mine."

Spoke the second, "I want as many towers and castles as there are stars in heaven so that I might keep all the money that my fellow court jesters here would have."

It was now Tyll's turn. He opened his mouth and spoke, "I would want the two here to make out their wills, leaving their money to me, and that you, Your Majesty, would order them to the gallows right after."

The king and all his court laughed merrily at this, and Tyll won the coat and the money.

Now you know how a quick and merry answer can bring one fame and fortune.

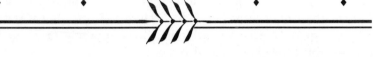

THE HODJA AND THE CAULDRON
Turkey

Being once in need of a cauldron, the Hodja went to one of his neighbors and borrowed a large copper cauldron, which answered his requirements so well that he had no wish to part with it. Instead of returning the borrowed utensil on the promised day, he went to his neighbor and handed him in a somewhat dejected manner a much smaller cauldron resembling in shape the one which he had borrowed.

The owner looked at it suspiciously and asked, "What is this?" Whereupon the Hodja answered, "Your cauldron has given birth to a little one and is far too unwell for me to return it today. Take its offspring instead, I beseech you."

The owner of the cauldron was much surprised, but he was at the same time not a little gratified at this unexpected fertility, and when his wife soundly abused him for having thus allowed himself to be put upon, he testily advised the good dame to have patience and not to ask any questions for a day or two.

The Hodja's need of the cauldron having come to an end, he brought it back and said, "Here, take your cauldron back again, for now it is quite well." The neighbor and his family rejoiced, and the fame of the Hodja was much increased.

Some days later the Hodja again required the cauldron, and this time his neighbor was so pleased to lend it to him that he even helped to carry it to the Hodja's house. After a considerable time had elapsed without any baby cauldron appearing on the scene, the neighbor called on Nasr-ed-Din Hodja to inquire when he might expect his cauldron to return. He as polite and profusely apologetic, but he said that his wife wanted it.

The Hodja seemed very much surprised that his neighbor had not heard the news—the sad news that the cauldron had died. The manner and tone of the obliging neighbor now underwent an instant change, and he remonstrated loudly. Indeed, he created such an uproar that a crowd speedily assembled round the house; but, so far as the Hodja was concerned, the large cauldron was dead for all time, and he advised his neighbor to return home quietly, and break the news to the baby cauldron which he had claimed as his. "For it stands to reason," quoth Nasr-ed-Din Hodja, "that anything or anyone that can give birth to young can also die."

The crowd agreed and said that verily he spake well and truly. It was *hak* [just].

BEING GREEDY CHOKES ANANSI
Jamaica

One time, Anansi lived in a country that had a queen who was also a witch. And she decreed that whoever used the word *five* would fall down dead, because that was her secret name, and she didn't want anyone using it.

Now, Buh Anansi was a clever fellow, and a hungry one too. Things were especially bad because there was a famine, so Anansi made a little house for himself by the side of the river near where everyone came to get water. And when anybody came to get water, he would call out to them, "I beg you to tell me how many yam hills I have here. I can't count very well." So, one by one he thought they would come up and say, "One, two, three, four, *five*," and they would fall down dead. Then Anansi would take them and corn them in his barrel and eat them, and that way he would have lots of food in hungry times and in times of plenty.

So, time went on and he got his house built and his yams planted, and along came Guinea Fowl. Anansi said, "I beg you, missus, tell me how many yam hills I have here." So Guinea Fowl went and sat on one of those hills and said, "One, two, three, four, and the one I'm sitting on!" Anansi said, *"Cho!"* [sucking his teeth], "you can't count right." And Guinea Fowl moved to another hill and said, "One, two, three, four, and the one I'm sitting on!" *"Cho!* you don't count right at all!" "How do you count, then?" Guinea Fowl said, a little vexed at Anansi. "Why this way: one, two, three, four, FIVE!" He fell dead. And Guinea Fowl ate him up.

This story shows that what they say is right: "Being greedy chokes the puppy."

QUEVEDO AND THE KING
Mexico

While Quevedo was in France, the king received notice of the complaints against him, that he was very obscene in his ways. So he called him and said, "Either you leave my country or I'll have you hanged, because the things you have been doing here are not polite."

"No, Majesty, I will try to behave. Please give me another chance."

He says, "Very well, look. I will give you another chance just to show you I am a conscientious king. I give you license to play a trick on me, any trick that you wish, as long as your apology is grosser than the trick. I give you a period of three days. If within those three days you do not play a trick on me and excuse it with an apology grosser than the trick itself, you must leave the country or hang."

"Very well, Majesty. Give me those three days, and I will be here."

The first day passed, the second, and the third. And he couldn't find a solution for the fix he was in. Finally he has to come to the king's reception hall, and he still hasn't thought of a trick to play on the king and what apology to give, so he could stay longer in France, because he liked it there very much.

He hid behind some curtains. The moment arrived when the

king gave audience, to receive all the notables of the town, listen to complaints or give advice or so many things of those times. When the king was passing by the curtains, Quevedo sticks out his hand and grabs him by the private parts.

Then the king says, astonished, "Quevedo! What are you doing?"

Quevedo says, "Pardon, Majesty. I thought it was the queen."

WHY THE HARE RUNS AWAY
Africa (Ewe)

This is a story of the hare and the other animals.

The dry weather was drying up the earth into hardness. There was no dew. Even the creatures of the water suffered from thirst. Famine soon followed, and the animals, having nothing to eat, assembled in council.

"What shall we do," said they, "to keep ourselves from dying of hunger and thirst?" And they deliberated a long time.

At last it was decided that each animal should cut off the tips of its ears, and extract the fat from them. Then all the fat would be collected and sold, and with the money they would get for it, they would buy a hoe and dig a well, so as to get some water.

And all cried, "It is well. Let us cut off the tips of our ears."

They did so, but when it came the hare's turn he refused.

The other animals were astonished, but they said nothing. They took up the ears, extracted the fat, went and sold all, and bought a hoe with the money.

They brought back the hoe and began to dig a well in the dry bed of a lagoon, until at last they found water. They said, "Ha! At last we can slake our thirst a little."

The hare was not there, but when the sun was in the middle of the sky, he took a calabash and went towards the well.

As he walked along, the calabash dragged on the ground and made a great noise. It said, *"Chan-gañ-gañ-gañ, chan-gañ-gañ-gañ."*

The animals, who were watching by the lagoon, heard this terrible noise and were frightened. They asked each other, "What is it?" Then, as the noise kept coming nearer, they ran away. Reaching home, they said something terrible at the lagoon had put them to flight.

When all the animals were gone, the hare could draw up water from the lagoon without interference. Then he went down into the well and bathed, so that the water was muddied.

When the next day came, all the animals ran to get water, and they found it muddied.

"Oh," they cried, "who has spoiled our well?"

Saying this, they went and took a dummy-image. They made birdlime and spread it over the image.

Then, when the sun was again in the middle of the sky, all the animals went and hid in the bush near the well.

Soon the hare came, his calabash crying, *"Chan-gañ-gañ-gañ, chan-gañ-gañ-gañ."* He approached the image. He never suspected that all the animals were hidden in the bush.

The hare saluted the image. The image said nothing. He saluted again, and still the image said nothing.

"Take care," said the hare, "or I will give you slap."

He gave it a slap, and his right hand was stuck fast in the birdlime. He slapped with his left hand, and that was held fast, too.

"Oh! oh!" cried he, "I'll kick with my feet," and he did, but his feet became fixed, and he could not get away.

Then the animals ran out of the bush and came to see the hare and his calabash.

""Shame, shame, oh, hare!" they cried together. "Did you not agree with us to cut off the tips of your ears, and, when it came to your turn, did you not refuse? What! You refused, and yet you come to muddy our water?"

They took whips, they fell upon the hare, and they beat him. They beat him so that they nearly killed him.

"We ought to kill you, accursed hare," they said. "But no—run."

They let him go, and the hare fled. Since then, he does not leave the grass.

COYOTE FIGHTS A LUMP OF PITCH
American Indian (Apache)

Even long ago, when our tribe and animals and birds lived together near white people, Coyote was always in trouble. He would visit among the camps, staying in one for a while and then moving on, and when he stayed at Bear's camp, he used to go over at night to a white man's field and steal the ears off the wheat.

When the white man who owned the farm found out what Coyote was up to, he trailed him long enough to locate his path into the field. Then he called all the white men to a council, and they made a figure of pitch just like a man and placed it in Coyote's path.

That night when Coyote went back to steal wheat again, he saw the pitch man standing there. Thinking it was a real person, he said, "Gray eyes"—he always talked like a Chiricahua Apache—"Get to one side and let me by. I just want a little wheat. Get over, I tell you." The pitch man stayed where he was. "If you don't move," Coyote said, "you'll get my fist in your face. Wherever I go on this earth, if I hit a man with my fist, it kills him." The pitch man never stirred. "All right, then I'm going to hit you." Coyote struck out, but his fist stuck fast in the pitch, clear to his elbow.

"What's the matter?" Coyote cried. "Why have you caught my hand? Turn loose or you'll get my other fist. If I hit a man with that one, it knocks all his wits out!" Then Coyote punched with his other fist, and this arm got stuck in the pitch also. Now he was standing on his two hind legs.

"I'm going to kick you if you keep holding me, and it'll knock you over." Coyote delivered a powerful kick, and his leg went into the pitch and stuck. "This other leg is worse still, and you're going to get it!" he said. He kicked, and his leg stuck into the pitch.

Now Coyote's legs were fast in the pitch; only his tail was free. "If I whip you with my tail, it will cut you in two. So turn me loose!" But the pitch man just stood there. Coyote lashed the pitch with his tail and got it stuck also. Only his head was free, and he was still talking with it. "Why do you hold me this way? I'll bite you in the neck and kill you, so you'd better turn me loose." When the pitch did nothing, Coyote bit it and got his mouth stuck, and there he was.

In the morning, the farmer put a chain around Coyote's neck, took him out of the pitch, and led him to the house. "This is the one who has been stealing from me," he said to his family. The white people held a meeting to discuss what they should do with Coyote. They decided to put him into a pot of boiling water and scald him, so they set the water on to heat and tied Coyote up at the side of the house.

Pretty soon Coyote saw Gray Fox coming along, loafing around the farmer's yard, looking for something to steal from the white man. Coyote called him over. "My cousin," he said, "there are lots of things cooking for me in that pot," though of course the pot was only heating water to scald him in. "There are potatoes, coffee, bread, and all kinds of food for me. It'll soon be done, and the white people are going to bring them to me. You and I can eat them together, but you must help me first. Can you put this chain around your neck while I go and urinate behind that bush?" Fox agreed and, taking the chain off Coyote, put it on his own neck. As soon as Coyote was out of sight behind the bush, he ran off.

After a while the water was good and hot, and the white men came out to Gray Fox. "He seems so little! What happened? He must have shrunk, I guess," they said. They lifted him up and threw him into the pot. Now the hot water boiled his hair right off, leaving Gray Fox bright red and hairless. They took off the chain and threw him under a tree, where he lay motionless until evening. When it got dark and cold, he woke up and started off.

After a while Gray Fox came to Bear's camp and asked, "Where is Coyote?" Bear replied that Coyote always went for his water to some spring above Bear's camp at midnight. So Gray Fox ran off to the springs and hid himself.

Now at midnight Coyote came as usual to the spring, but when he put his head to the water to drink, Gray Fox jumped him. "Now I'm going to kill you and eat you," the fox said. The moon was shining from the sky down into the water, and Coyote, pointing to its reflection, replied, "Don't talk like that, when we can both eat this delicious 'ash bread' down there. All we have to do is drink all the water, and we can take the bread out and have a feast."

They both started to lap up the water, but soon Coyote was merely pretending to drink. Gray Fox drank lots, and when he was full, he got cold. Then Coyote said, 'My cousin, some white people left a camp over here, and I'm going to look for some old rags or quilts to wrap you up in. Wait for me." So Coyote started off, and as soon as he was out of sight, he ran away.

CRACK AND CROOK
Italy

In a distant town there was a famous thief known as Crack, whom nobody had ever been able to catch. The main ambition of this Crack was to meet Crook, another notorious thief, and form a partnership with him. One day as Crack was eating lunch at the tavern across the table from a stranger, he went to look at his watch and found it missing. The only person in the world who could have taken it without my knowing, he thought, is Crook. So what did Crack do but turn right around and steal Crook's purse. When the stranger got ready to pay for his lunch, he found his purse gone and said to his table companion, "Well, well, you must be Crack."

"And you must be Crook."

"Right."

"Fine, we'll work together."

They went to the city and made for the king's treasury, which was completely surrounded by guards. The thieves therefore dug an underground tunnel into the treasury and stole everything. Surveying his loss, the king had no idea how he might catch the robbers. He went to a man named Snare, who had been put in prison for stealing, and said, "If you can tell me who committed this robbery, I'll set you free and make you a marquis."

Snare replied, "It can be none other than Crack or Crook, or both of them together, since they are the most notorious thieves alive. But I'll tell you how you can catch them. Have the price of meat raised to one hundred dollars a pound. The person who pays that much for it will be your thief."

The king had the price of meat raised to one hundred dollars a pound, and everybody stopped buying meat. Finally it was reported that a friar had gone to a certain butcher and bought meat. Snare said, "That had to be Crack or Crook in disguise. I'll now disguise myself and go around to the houses begging. If anybody gives me meat, I'll make a red mark on the front door, and your guards can go and arrest the thieves."

But when he made a red mark on Crack's house, the thief saw it and went and marked all the other doors in the city with red, so there was no telling in the end where Crack and Crook lived.

Snare said to the king, "Didn't I tell you they were foxy? But there's someone else foxier than they are. Here's the next thing to do: put a tub of boiling pitch at the bottom of the treasury steps. Whoever goes down to steal will fall right into it, and his dead body will give him away."

Crack and Crook had run out of money in the meantime and decided to go back to the treasury for more. Crook went in first, but it was dark, and he fell into the tub. Crack came along and tried to pull his friend's body out of the pitch, but it stuck fast in the tub. He then cut off the head and carried it away.

The next day the king went to see if he had caught the thief. "This time we got him! We got him!" But the corpse had no head, so they were none the wiser about the thief or any accomplices he might have had.

Snare said, "There's one more thing we can do: have the dead man dragged through the city by two horses. The house where you hear somebody weeping has to be the thief's house."

In effect, when Crook's wife looked out the window and saw her husband's body being dragged through the street, she began screaming and crying. But Crack was there and knew right away that would be their undoing. He therefore starting smashing dishes right and left and thrashing the poor woman at the same time. Attracted by all that screaming, the guards came in and found a man beating his wife for breaking up all the dishes in the house.

The king then had a decree posted on every street corner that he would pardon the thief who had robbed him, if the thief now managed to steal the sheets out from under him at night. Crack came forward and said he could do it.

That night the king undressed and went to bed with his gun to wait for the thief. Crack got a dead body from a gravedigger, dressed it in his own clothes, and carried it to the roof of the royal palace. At midnight the cadaver, held by a rope, was dangling before the king's windows. Thinking it was Crack, the king fired one shot and watched him fall, cord and all. He ran downstairs to see if he was dead. While the king was gone, Crack slipped into his room and stole the sheets. He was therefore pardoned, and so that he wouldn't have to steal any longer, the king married his daughter to him.

THE MASTER THIEF
Germany

One day an old man and his wife were sitting in front of a miserable house resting a while from their work. Suddenly a splendid carriage with four black horses came driving up, and a richly dressed man descended from it.

The peasant stood up, went to the great man, and asked what he wanted, and in what way he could serve him.

The stranger stretched out his hand to the old man, and said, "I want nothing but to enjoy for once a country dish. Cook me some potatoes, in the way you always have them, and then I will sit down at your table and eat them with pleasure."

The peasant smiled and said, "You are a count or a prince, or perhaps even a duke. Noble gentlemen often have such fancies, but you shall have your wish."

The wife went into the kitchen, and began to wash and rub the potatoes and to make them into balls, as they are eaten by the country folks. Whilst she was busy with this work, the peasant said to the stranger, "Come into my garden with me for a while. I have still something to do there." He had dug some holes in the garden, and now wanted to plant trees in them.

"Have you no children," asked the stranger, "who could help you with your work?"

"No," answered the peasant. "I had a son, it is true, but it is long since he went out into the world. He was a ne'er-do-well; clever and knowing, but he would learn nothing and was full of bad tricks. At last he ran away from me, and since then I have heard nothing of him."

The old man took a young tree, put it in a hole, drove in a post beside it, and when he had shoveled in some earth and had trampled it firmly down, he tied the stem of the tree above, below, and in the middle, fast to the post by a rope of straw.

"But tell me," said the stranger, "why you don't tie that crooked knotted tree, which is lying in the corner there, bent down almost to the ground, to a post also that it may grow straight, as well as these?"

The old man smiled and said, "Sir, you speak according to your knowledge. It is easy to see that you are not familiar with gardening. That tree there is old and misshapen; no one can make it straight now. Trees must be trained while they are young."

"That is how it was with your son," said the stranger. "If you had trained him while he was still young, he would not have run away. Now he too must have grown hard and misshapen."

"Truly it is a long time since he went away," replied the old man. "He must have changed."

"Would you know him again if he were to come to you?" asked the stranger.

"Hardly by his face," replied the peasant, "but he has a mark about him, a birthmark on his shoulder, that looks like a bean."

When he had said that the stranger pulled off his coat, bared his shoulder, and showed the peasant the bean.

"Good God!" cried the old man, "you are really my son!" and love for his child stirred in his heart. "But," he added, "how can you be my son. You have become a great lord and live in wealth and luxury. How have you contrived to to that?"

"Ah, Father," answered the son, "the young tree was bound to no post and has grown crooked. Now it is too old, it will never be straight again. How come I come by all this? I have become a thief, but do not be alarmed. I am a master thief. For me there are neither locks nor bolts; whatsoever I desire is mine. Do not imagine that I steal like a common thief. I only take some of the superfluity of the rich. Poor people are safe. I would rather give to them than take anything from them. It is the same with anything which I can have without trouble, cunning, and dexterity—I never touch it."

"Alas, my son," said the father, "it still does not please me. A thief is still a thief. I tell you it will end badly." He took him to his mother, and when she heard that he was her son, she wept for joy, but when he told her that he had become a master thief, two streams flowed down over her face. At length she said, "Even if he has become a thief, he is still my son, and my eyes have beheld him once more."

They sat down to table, and once again he ate with his parents the wretched food which he had not eaten for so long. The father said, "If our lord, the count up there in the castle, learns who you are, and what trade you follow, he will not take you in his arms and cradle you in them as he did when he held you at the font, but will cause you to swing from a halter."

"Be easy, Father, he will do me no harm, for I understand my trade. I will go to him myself this very day."

When evening drew near, the master thief seated himself in his carriage, and drove to the castle. The count received him civilly, for he took him for a distinguished man. When, however, the stranger made himself known, the count turned pale and was quite silent for some time. At length he said, "You are my godson, and on that account mercy shall take the place of justice, and I will deal leniently with you. Since you pride yourself on being a master thief, I will put your art to the proof, but if you do not stand the test, you must marry the ropemaker's daughter, and the croaking of the raven must be your music on the occasion."

"Lord Count," answered the master thief, "think of three things, as difficult as you like, and if I do not perform your tasks, do with me what you will."

The count reflected for some minutes, and then said, "Well, then, in the first place, you shall steal the horse I keep for my own riding, out of the stable; in the next, you shall steal the sheet from beneath the bodies of my wife and myself when we are asleep, without our observing it, and the wedding ring of my wife as well; thirdly and lastly, you shall steal away out of the church the parson and the clerk. Mark what I am saying, for your life depends on it."

The master thief went to the nearest town; there he bought the clothes of an old peasant woman, and put them on. He stained his face brown, and painted wrinkles on it as well, so that no one could have recognized him. Then he filled a small cask with old Hungary wine in which was mixed a powerful sleeping drink. He put the cask in a basket, which he took on his back, and walked with slow and tottering steps to the count's castle. It was already dark when he arrived. He sat down on a stone in the courtyard and began to cough, like an asthmatic old woman, and to rub his hands as if he were cold.

In front of the door of the stable some soldiers were lying round a fire. One of them observed the woman, and called out to her, "Come nearer, old mother, and warm yourself beside us. After all, you have no bed for the night, and must take one where you can find it."

The old woman tottered up to them, begged them to lift the basket from her back, and sat down beside them at the fire.

"What have you got in your little cask, old hag?" asked one.

"A good mouthful of wine," she answered. "I live by trade. For money and fair words I am quite ready to let you have a glass."

"Let us have it here, then," said the soldier, and when he had tasted one glass he said, "When wine is good, I like another glass," and had another poured out for himself, and the rest followed his example.

"Hallo, comrades," cried one of them to those who were in the stable, "here is an old girl who has wine that is as old as herself. Take a draught, it will warm your stomachs far better than our fire."

The old woman carried her cask into the stable. One of the soldiers had seated himself on the saddled riding horse, another held its bridle in his hand, a third had laid hold of its tail. She poured out as much as they wanted until the spring ran dry. It was not long before the bridle fell from the hand of the one, and he fell down and began to snore; the other left hold of the tail, lay down, and snored still louder. The one who was sitting in the saddle did remain sitting, but bent his head almost down to the horse's neck, and slept and blew with his mouth like the bellows of a forge. The soldiers outside had already been asleep for a long time, and were lying on the ground motionless, as if dead.

When the master thief saw that he had succeeded, he gave the first a rope in his hand instead of the bridle, and the other who had been holding the tail, a wisp of straw, but what was he to do with the one who was sitting on the horse's back? He did not want to throw him down, for he might have awakened and have uttered a cry. He had a good idea: he unbuckled the girths of the saddle, tied a couple of ropes which were hanging to a ring on the wall fast to the saddle, and drew the sleeping rider up into the air on it, then he twisted the rope round the posts and made it fast. He soon unloosed the horse from the chain, but if he had ridden over the stony pavement of the yard they would have heard the noise in the castle. So he wrapped the horse's hoofs in old rags, led him carefully out, leaped upon him, and galloped off.

When day broke, the master thief galloped to the castle on the stolen horse. The count had just got up, and was looking out of the window. "Good morning, Sir Count," he cried to him, "here is the horse, which I have got safely out of the stable! Just look, how beautifully your soldiers are lying there sleeping; and if you will but go into the stable, you will see how comfortable your watchers have made it for themselves."

The count could not help laughing. Then he said, "For once you have succeeded, but things won't go so well the second time, and I warn you that if you come before me as a thief, I will handle you as I would a thief."

When the countess went to bed that night, she closed her hand with the wedding ring tightly together, and the count said, "All the doors are locked and bolted. I will keep awake and wait for the thief, but if he gets in by the window, I will shoot him."

The master thief, however, went in the dark to the gallows, cut a poor sinner who was hanging there down from the halter, and carried him on his back to the castle. Then he set a ladder up to the bedroom, put the dead body on his shoulders, and began to climb up. When he had got so high that the head of the dead man showed at the window, the count, who was watching in his bed, fired a pistol at him, and immediately the thief let the poor sinner fall down, descended the ladder, and hid himself in one corner. The night was sufficiently lighted by the moon for the thief to see distinctly how the count got out of the window onto the ladder, came down, carried the dead body into the garden, and began to dig a hole in which to lay it.

"Now," though the master thief, "the favorable moment has come." He stole nimbly out of his corner and climbed up the ladder straight into the countess's bedroom. "Dear wife," he began in the count's voice, "the thief is dead, but, after all, he is my godson, and has been more of a scapegrace than a villain. I will not put him to open shame. Besides, I am sorry for the parents. I will bury him myself before daybreak in the garden, that the thing may not be known. So give me the sheet. I will wrap up the body in it, and not bury him like a dog." The countess gave him the sheet. "I tell you what," continued the thief, "I have a fit of magnanimity. Give me the ring too—the unhappy man risked his life for it, so he may take it with him into his grave."

She would not gainsay the count, and although she did it unwillingly, she drew the ring from her finger and gave it to him. The thief made off with both these things, and reached home safely before the count in the garden had finished his work of burying.

What a long face the count did pull when the master thief came next morning, and brought him the sheet and the ring. "Are you a wizard?" said he. "Who has fetched you out of the grave in which I myself laid you, and brought you to life again?"

"You did not bury me," said the thief, "but the poor sinner on the gallows," and he told him exactly how everything had happened, and the count was forced to own to him that he was a clever, crafty thief. "But you have not reached the end yet," he added, "you have still to perform the third task, and if you do not succeed in that, all is of no use. The thief smiled and returned no answer.

When night had fallen he went with a long sack on his back, a bundle under his arms, and a lantern in his hand to the village church. In the sack he had some crabs, and in the bundle short wax candles. He sat down in the churchyard, took out a crab, and stuck a wax candle on his back. Then he lighted the little light, put the crab on the ground, and let it creep about. He took a second out of the sack, and treated it in the same way, and so on until the last was out of the sack. Hereupon he put on a long black garment that looked like a monk's cowl, and stuck a grey beard on his chin. When at last he was quite unrecognizable, he took the sack in which the crabs had been, went into the church, and ascended the pulpit.

The clock in the tower was just striking twelve; when the last stroke had sounded, he cried with a loud and piercing voice: "Hearken, sinful men, the end of all things has come! The last day is at hand! Hearken! Hearken! Whosoever wishes to go to Heaven with me must creep into the sack. I am Peter, who opens and shuts the gate of Heaven. Behold how the dead outside there in the churchyard are wandering about collecting their bones. Come, come, and creep into the sack. The world is about to be destroyed!"

The cry echoed through the whole village. The parson and the clerk, who lived nearest to the church, heard it first, and when they saw the lights moving about the churchyard, they observed that something unusual was going on and went into the church. They listened to the sermon for a while, and then the clerk nudged the parson and said, "It would not be amiss if we were to use the opportunity together, and before the dawning of the last day, find an easy way of getting to Heaven."

"To tell the truth," answered the parson, "that is what I myself have been thinking, so if you are inclined, we will set out on our way."

"Yes," answered the clerk, "but you, the pastor, have the precedence. I will follow." So the parson went first, and ascended the pulpit, where the master thief opened his sack. The parson crept in first, and then the clerk. The thief immediately tied up the sack tightly, seized it by the middle, and dragged it down the pulpit steps, and whenever the heads of the two fools bumped against the steps, he cried, "We are going over the mountains." Then he drew them through the village in the same way, and when they were passing through puddles, he cried, 'Now we are going through wet clouds," and when at last he was dragging them up the steps of the castle, he cried, "Now we are on the steps of Heaven, and will soon be in the outer court." When he had got to the top, he pushed the sack into the pigeon house, and when the pigeons fluttered about, he said, "Hark how glad the angels are, and how they are flapping their wings!" Then he bolted the door upon them, and went away.

Next morning he went to the count, and told him that he had performed the third task also, and had carried the parson and clerk out of the church.

"Where have you left them?" asked the lord.

"They are lying upstairs in a sack in the pigeon house, and imagine that they are in Heaven."

The count went up himself, and convinced himself that the master thief had told the truth. When he had delivered the parson and clerk from their captivity, he said, "You are an arch-thief, and have won your wager. For once you escape with a whole skin, but see that you leave my land, for if ever you set foot on it again, you may count on your elevation to the gallows."

The arch-thief took leave of his parents, once more went forth into the wide world, and no one has ever heard of him since.

PEIK
Norway

There was once on a time a man and a woman; they had a son and a daughter who were twins, and they were so like each other that you could not tell the one from the other, except by their clothes.

The boy they called Peik. He was of little use on the farm while the parents lived, for he did not care for anything else but playing tricks upon people, and he was so full of tricks and pranks that no one was left in peace for him. But when the parents died he grew worse and worse—he would not do anything; he only did his best to make an end of what there was left after them, and to quarrel with everybody. The sister worked and toiled all she could, but it was of little help, and so she told him how wrong it was that he would not do anything useful, and asked him:

"What do you think we shall live upon, when you have finished everything?"

"Oh, I'll go and play a trick upon somebody," said Peik.

"Yes, you are always ready and willing when you are bent upon that," said his sister.

"Well, I'll try my best," said Peik.

So when he had made an end of everything, and there was nothing more in the house, he set out on his journey, and walked and walked till he came to the king's palace.

The king was standing at the door, and when he saw the lad he said, "Where are you off to today, Peik?"

"Oh, I am off to see if I cannot play a trick upon somebody," said Peik.

"Can't you play a trick upon me, then?" said the king.

"No, I don't think I can, because I have left my trickery-sticks at home," said Peik.

"Can't you go and fetch them?" said the king. "I should like to see if you are such a clever trickster as folks make you out to be."

"I am not able to walk so far now," said Peik.

"I'll lend you a horse and saddle," said the king.

"I don't think I am able to ride either," said Peik.

"We'll lift you up," said the king, "and I suppose you'll be able to stick on to the horse."

Well, Peik rubbed and scratched his head, as if he was going to pull all his hair off, but he let himself be lifted on top of the horse at last. There he sat, and swung backwards and forwards and sideways as long as the king could see him, and the king laughed till the tears came into his eyes, for he had never seen such a sorry horseman before. But as soon as Peik came into the wood behind the hill, where the king could see him no longer, he sat straight and steady as if he was nailed to the horse and started off as if he had stolen both horse and bridle, and when he came to the town he sold them both.

In the meantime the king walked up and down and waited for Peik. He longed to see him coming back with his trickery-sticks. He could not help laughing when he called to mind how pitiable Peik looked, as he sat rolling to and fro on the horse like a haybag which didn't know which side to fall off on. But hours went and hours came, and no Peik came. So the king guessed at last that he had been played a trick and done out of his horse and saddle as well, although Peik did not have his trickery-sticks with him. But then things took another turn, for the king got in a rage and made up his mind to take Peik's life.

But Peik got to know the day when he was coming, and told his sister to put the porridge pot on the fire with some water in it. But just before the king came in he took the pot off the fire and put it on the chopping block and began making the porridge on the block.

The king wondered at this, and was so taken up with the wonderful pot that he forgot what he had come there for.

"What do you want for that pot?" said he.

"I can't spare it very well," said Peik.

"Why can't you spare it?" said the king. "I'll make it worth your while to sell it."

"Well, it saves me both money and trouble, chopping and carrying," said Peik.

"Never mind, I'll give you a hundred dollars for it," said the king. "You did me out of horse and saddle the other day, and the bridle too, but I'll let bygones be bygones if I get the pot."

"Well, I suppose you must have it, then," said Peik.

When the king came back to the palace he sent out invitations to a great feast, but the meat was to be boiled in the new pot, which was put in the middle of the floor.

The guests thought the king was out of his mind, and went about nudging each other and laughing at him. But he walked round the pot and cackled and chuckled to himself, saying all the time, "All right, all right! wait a bit! it will boil directly." But there was no sign of any boiling.

So the king guessed that Peik had been playing a trick upon him again, and he set out to kill him.

When the king came to his place Peik was standing by the barn.

"Wouldn't it boil?" he said.

"No, it would not," said the king. "But now you shall suffer for it," he said, and was going to get his knife ready.

"I believe you there," said Peik, "for you did not have the block."

"I shouldn't wonder if you are telling a lie again," said the king.

"It's all for the want of the block," said Peik. "The pot won't boil without it."

Well, what was he going to have for it?

It was worth three hundred dollars at least, but for his sake it should go for two, said Peik.

So the king got the block, and set off for home. He invited guests again to a feast and put the pot on the block in the middle of the room. The guests thought the king was gone sheer mad, and went about making game of him. He cackled and chuckled round the pot, saying all the time, "Wait a bit, it will boil soon—it will boil directly." But there was no more chance of its boiling on the block than on the floor.

So the king guessed that he had been tricked by Peik that time as well. He tore his hair, and would not rest till he set out to kill him. He should not spare him this time, whether he had got anything to say for himself or not.

But Peik was prepared to receive him again. He killed a wether and took the bladder and filled it with the blood of the slaughtered animal. He then put the bladder in his sister's bosom and told her what she should say when the king came.

"Where is Peik?" shouted the king. He was in such a rage that his voice trembled.

"He is so poorly that he is not able to move," answered his sister, "and so he thought he would try and get some sleep."

"You must wake him up!" said the king.

No, she dared not do it; he was so hasty.

"Well, I am still more hasty," said the king, "and if you don't wake him I'll—" and with that he put his hand to his side for his knife.

No, no! she would rather wake him. But Peik turned round in his bed in a great rage, pulled out his knife, and stabbed her in the bosom. The knife hit the bladder, a stream of blood gushed out, and she fell down on the floor as if she were dead.

"What a villain you are, Peik," said the king. "You have stabbed your own sister, and that while the king stands by and looks at it."

"Oh, there isn't much danger, as long as I have got breath in my nostrils," said Peik, and took a ram's horn, which he began blowing; and when he had blown a wedding march on it he put the horn to his sister's nostrils and blew life into her again, and she rose up as if nothing had been the matter with her.

"Why, bless me, Peik! Can you kill people and blow life into them again?" said the king.

"Well, yes, what would become of me if I couldn't?" said Peik. "You see, I am so hasty and I can't help killing everyone who comes near me and annoys me."

"I am also very hasty," said the king, "and I must have that horn. I'll give you a hundred dollars for it, and I'll forgive you besides for doing me out of the horse and cheating me on the pot and block business and all the rest."

Peik could not very well spare the horn, but for his sake he should have it, and so the king got it, and set out home as fast as he could.

He had no sooner come home before he must try the horn. He began quarreling and scolding the queen and his eldest daughter, and they scolded him again, but before they knew a word about it he pulled out his knife and stabbed them both so they fell down stone dead, and all who were in the room ran out, they were so afraid.

The king walked up and down the floor for some time and kept on saying there was no danger so long as there was breath in his nostrils, and a great deal more nonsense which had flowed out of Peik's mouth. He then took the horn and began blowing, but although he blew all he could that day and the day after as well, he could not blow life into the bodies. They were dead, and dead they remained, both the queen and his daughter, and so he had to bury them, and to give a grand funeral in the bargain.

When this was done the king set out to settle with Peik and to take his life, but Peik had everything prepared, for he knew the king was coming, and he said to his sister, "You must change clothes with me and be off! You may take all we have with you."

Yes, she changed clothes with him, packed up her things, and started off as fast as she could, while Peik sat all by himself in his sister's clothes.

"Where is that Peik?" said the king, as he came in a great rage through the door.

"He's gone away," said he who sat in the sister's clothes.

"Well, had he been at home now he wouldn't have had long to live," said the king. "It's no use sparing the life of such a scamp."

"He knew Your Majesty was coming to punish him for having played so many tricks upon you, and so he ran away and left me behind here both without food or money," said Peik, trying to appear like a shy bashful maiden.

"Come along with me to the palace, and you shall get enough to live on. There is little use in sitting in the cottage here and starving," said the king.

Yes, he would willingly do that, and so the king took him and let him learn everything, and kept him as one of his own daughters. In fact, the king felt now as if he had all his three daughters again, for Peik stitched and sewed and sang and played with them, and was in their company early and late.

Some time afterwards a prince came to the palace to woo one of the princesses.

"Yes, I have three daughters," said the king. "You have only to say which one you will have."

So the prince got leave to go up in their bower and get acquainted with them. In the end he liked Peik best, and threw a silk handkerchief into his lap, and so they began getting everything ready for the wedding, and shortly the prince's relations arrived at the palace, and the wedding festivities commenced in earnest with feasting and drinking. But on the wedding day, as night was coming on, Peik dared not remain any longer, and he stole out of the palace and ran across the fields, and there was no bride to be found.

And worse remains to be told, for the two princesses were suddenly taken ill, and all the guests had to break up and take their departure just as they were in the middle of all the fun and feasting.

The king was both enraged and sorrowful at these misfortunes, and began to wonder what could really be the cause of them.

So he mounted his horse and rode out, for he thought it was so lonely to stay alone by himself at home. But when he came out in the fields he saw Peik sitting there on a stone, playing a jew's-harp.

"Halloh! are you sitting there, Peik?" asked the king.

"Of course I am," said Peik. "I can't sit in two places at once."

"Well, you have played such vile tricks on me time after time," said the king, "that you will have to come with me and get your deserts."

"Well, I suppose there's no help for it," said Peik, "so I may as well jump into it as creep into it."

When they came to the palace the king gave orders to get ready a barrel, which Peik was to be put in, and when it was ready they carted it up on a high mountain, where he was to lie in the barrel for three days to think on all that he had done, before they rolled the barrel down the mountain into the sea.

On the third day a rich man came past as Peik lay in the barrel singing—

> To Paradise, to Paradise I am bound,
> Safe in my barrel as it turns round and round.

When the man heard this, he asked Peik what he would take to let him take his place.

"I ought to be well paid for that," said Peik, "for there isn't much a chance every day to go straight to Paradise."

The man was willing to give him all he possessed, and so he

knocked out the bottom of the barrel and crept into it instead of Peik.

In the evening the king came to roll the barrel down the mountain.

"A safe journey to you!" said the king; he thought it was Peik who was in it. "You'll roll faster into the sea than if you were drawn by the swiftest reindeer, and now there will be an end both to you and your tricks."

Before the barrel was halfway down the mountain there wasn't a whole stave or bit of it left, nor of the man who was inside. But when the king came home to the palace, Peik was there before him. He sat on the steps and played upon the jew's-harp.

"What! are you sitting here, Peik?" said the king.

"Of course I am," said Peik. "I suppose I may have lodgings and shelter for all my horses, my cattle, and my money."

"Where did I roll you to, that you got all these riches?" asked the king.

"Oh, you rolled me into the sea," said Peik, "and when I came to the bottom there was more than enough to take both of horses and cattle, of gold and goods. They went about in flocks, and the gold lay in heaps as big as houses."

"What will you take to roll me the same way?" said the king.

"Oh, that shan't cost you much," said Peik. "Since you didn't take anything of me, I won't take anything of you either."

So he put the king into a barrel and rolled him down the mountain; and when he thus had got the king out of the way, he went home to the palace and married the youngest princess and had a grand wedding. Afterwards he ruled his land and kingdom well and wisely, but he left off playing tricks upon people and he was never spoken of as Peik any more, but as His Royal Majesty the King!

THE MONKEY AND THE CROCODILE
India

A monkey lived in a great tree on a riverbank. In the river there were many crocodiles.

A crocodile watched the monkeys for a long time, and one day she said to her son, "My son, get one of those monkeys for me. I want the heart of a monkey to eat."

"How am I catch a monkey?" asked the little crocodile. "I do not travel on land, and the monkey does not go into the water."

"Put your wits to work, and you'll find a way," said the mother.

And the little crocodile thought and thought.

At last he said to himself, "I know what I'll do. I'll get that monkey that lives in a big tree on the riverbank. He wishes to go across the river to the island where the fruit is so ripe."

So the crocodile swam to the tree where the monkey lived. But he was a stupid crocodile.

"Oh, monkey," he called, "come with me over to the island where the fruit is so ripe."

"How can I go with you?" asked the monkey. "I do not swim."

"No—but I do. I will take you over on my back,' said the crocodile.

The monkey was greedy, and wanted the ripe fruit, so he jumped down on the crocodile's back.

"Off we go!" said the crocodile.

"This is a fine ride you are giving me!" said the monkey.

"Do you think so? Well, how do you like this?" asked the crocodile, diving.

"Oh, don't!" cried the monkey, as he went under the water. He was afraid to let go, and he did not know what to do under the water.

When the crocodile came up, the monkey sputtered and choked. "Why did you take me under water, crocodile?" he asked.

"I am going to kill you by keeping you under water," answered the crocodile. "My mother wants monkey heart to eat, and I'm going to take yours to her."

"I wish you had told me you wanted my heart," said the monkey, "then I might have brought it with me."

"How queer!" said the stupid crocodile. "Do you mean to say that you left your heart back there in the tree?"

"That is what I mean," said the monkey. "If you want my heart, we must go back to the tree and get it. But we are so near the island where the ripe fruit is, please take me there first."

"No, monkey," said the crocodile, "I'll take you straight back to your tree. Never mind the ripe fruit. Get your heart and bring it to me at once. Then we'll see about going to the island."

"Very well," said the monkey.

"But no sooner had he jumped onto the bank of the river than—whisk! he ran into the tree.

From the topmost branches he called down to the crocodile in the water below:

"My heart is way up here! If you want it, come for it, come for it!"

THE RACE BETWEEN TOAD AND DONKEY
Jamaica

One day, Master King decided to have a race and he would give a big prize to whoever won. Both Toad and Donkey decided to enter, but Toad got Donkey angry with all his boasting about how he'd win.

Now, the race was to be for twenty miles. So when Donkey looked at Toad he wondered out loud how any animal so small and powerless could hope to keep up with him. "I have very long legs, you know, as well as long ears and tail. Just measure our legs, and you'll see why you can't possibly hope to win this race." But Toad was stubborn—and he was smart, too—and he said that he was going to win the race. That just got Donkey more vexed.

So Donkey told the king that he was ready to start, but the king said that he had to make the rules first. At each mile every racer had to sing out to indicate he had gotten that far—for the king wanted to know what was happening in the race, you know.

Now Toad is a smart little fellow, and he said to the king that he needed a little time to take care of business, so would he let him have a day or two. And the king said to the two of them, "You must come here first thing tomorrow." Donkey objected, for he knew that Toad was a very trickifying creature, but the king wouldn't listen.

Now the toad had twenty children, and they all looked exactly alike. And while Donkey was sleeping, Toad took his twenty children along the racing ground, and at every milepost Toad left one of them. He told them that they must listen for Mr. Donkey, and whenever they heard him cry out, they should do so too. And Toad hid one of his children there behind each of those mileposts.

So the race began the next day. Donkey looked around, and he was so sure in his heart that he was going to beat Toad that he sucked his teeth, *Tche*, to show everyone there how little he thought of Toad. "That little bit of a fellow Toad can't keep up with me. I'll even have a little time to eat some grass along the way. *Tche*."

So he just went a little way down the road and he stopped and ate some grass. He poked his head through the fence where he saw some good-looking sweet-potato tops and had a taste of some gungo peas. He took more than an hour to get to the first milepost. And as he got there, he bawled out, "Ha, ha, I'm better than Toad." And the first child heard this, and he called, like all toads do:

Jin-ko-ro-ro, Jin-kok-kok-kok.

The sound really surprised Donkey, who of course thought he had gotten there first. Then he thought, "I delayed too long eating that grass. I must run quicker this next mile." So he set off with greater speed, this time stopping only for a minute to drink some water along the way. And as he got to the next post, he bawled out:

Ha! Ha! Ha! I'm better than Toad.

And then the second child called out:

Jin-ko-ro-ro, Jin-kok-kok-kok.

And Donkey said, "Lord, Toad can really move, for sure. Never mind, there are a lot more miles." So he started, and when he reached the third milepost, he bawled:

Ha! Ha! Ha! I'm better than Toad.

And the third child sang:

Jin-ko-ro-ro, Jin-kok-kok-kok.

Now the jackass got very angry when he heard Toad answer him, and he started to smash the toad, but Toad, being a little fellow, hid himself in the grass.

Donkey was then determined to get to the next milepost before Toad, and he took his tail and he switched it like a horsewhip and he began to gallop. And he got to the fourth milepost and he bawled:

Ha! Ha! Ha! I'm better than Toad.

And out came the answer from the fourth child.

When he heard that, he stood up right there and began to tremble, and he said, "My goodness, what am I going to do? I'm going to have to run so fast I really kick that hard, hard dirt." And he galloped off faster than he ever had before, until he reached the fifth milepost. And now he was very tired, and out of breath. He just barely had enough wind to bawl:

Ha! Ha! Ha! I'm better than Toad.

And then he heard:

Jin-ko-ro-ro, Jin-kok-kok-kok.

This time he was really angry, and he raced on harder than ever. But at each milepost he bawled out the same thing, and at each he heard the same answer. And Donkey got so sad in his mind that he just gave up after a while, sad because he knew he had lost that race.

So through Toad's smartness, Donkey can never be a racer again. Jack Mandora me no choose one.

THE KING'S SON GOES BEAR HUNTING
Finland

Once a peasant, while toiling at the plow, became angry with his horse and cried out, "May a bear devour you!"

It happened that a bear overheard these words and said, "Very well, give me your horse; I will eat him."

The man grieved and begged for delay till his work should be completed. The bear indulged the man's wish.

A fox who chanced to approach the peasant inquired why he was so downcast.

"Unfortunately," answered the man, "I promised in a foolish moment to give my horse to be devoured by a bear, who now demands it."

The fox offered, in return for a reward, to assist the peasant and to deliver the bear to him. The man promised her the gift of several chickens.

"I will fasten a small bell to my neck," said the fox, "and will bound along in the forest from stone to stone. When the bear comes up and remarks, 'What is that noise?' you must answer, 'It is the king's son bear hunting.' "

The fox entered the forest, and having fixed a small bell to her neck, jumped noisily from stone to stone.

The bear approached the peasant and said, "What is that noise."

"It is the king's son bear hunting," answered the peasant.

"If you do not betray me, little brother," implored the bear, "I will not eat your horse!" The peasant promised not to surrender the bear to the hunters.

Then the fox went out to the edge of the forest and shouted, "What is that dark shape near you?"

"Say it is the stump of a tree," said the bear, in a low voice.

"It is a stump," cried the peasant.

The fox shouted, "If it is a stump, why not fell it?"

"Throw me down," said the bear; and the peasant pushed him so that he fell.

"You are a fool," shouted the fox. "If it is a stump, why do you not put it on the sleigh?"

"Put me on the sleigh as if I were a stump," begged the bear; and the peasant lifted him onto the sleigh.

"You are a fool," shouted the fox a third time. "Why do you not fasten it? It will roll off."

"Pretend to fasten me," said the bear, "but not firmly." The peasant fastened the bear securely.

"You will never grow wise, however long you talk," shouted the fox. "Most people put an axe into a sleigh along with a stump."

The bear begged that the axe should not be taken into the sleigh, but the peasant took up the weapon and used it to strike his enemy on the head and kill him.

The fox came out of the forest and the pair set forth to the peasant's house. But before reaching it the man turned to the fox and said, "Wait here till I bring you the chickens; if my children see you they will be frightened."

After going away the peasant returned with an empty bag. "Climb in here," he said to the fox, "and seize the chickens. If I let them out they will escape."

The fox crawled into the bag, whereupon the peasant fastened up the opening and dashed the fox heavily against the ground.

"That is my reward for kindness!" exclaimed the fox.

JOHN BRODISON AND THE POLICEMAN
Ireland

There was a famous character in our country. He lived at Bellanaleck; he was the name of John Brodison.

He was a famous liar.

Aye, he was a famous liar. I knew him. I was often talking to him. He was a kind of a smart old boy, you know: quick-witted.

He was coming out of Enniskillen one night with the ass and

the cart. And the law was: ye had to have a light after a cer~ on a cart, do you see, when it was dark. Ye had to have a light.

So the policeman was standing at Bellanaleck Cross, and Brodison knew that the police would be *there* at the time.

So he got out of the cart.

And he took the donkey out of the cart, and he tied it *behind*.

And he got into the shafts, and he started to pull the cart, and the donkey walking behind him anyway.

And when he came to the Cross, the policeman says, "Brodison," he says, "Ye have no light. *Where's your light*, Brodison?"

"*Ask the driver*," he says.

Aye. "Ask the driver."

Well, that was the sort of a boy he was.

Ah, he had great bids in him.

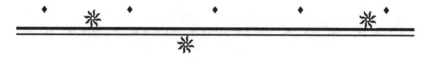

The Rabbi and the Inquisitor
Jewish

The city of Seville was seething with excitement. A Christian boy had been found dead, and the Jews were falsely accused by their enemies of having murdered him in order to use his blood ritually in the baking of matzos for Passover. So the rabbi was brought before the Grand Inquisitor to stand trial as head of the Jewish community.

The Grand Inquisitor hated the rabbi, but, despite all his efforts to prove that the crime had been committed by the Jews, the rabbi succeeded in disproving the charge. Seeing that he had been bested in argument, the inquisitor turned his eyes piously to Heaven and said:

"We will leave the judgment of this matter to God. Let there be a drawing of lots. I shall deposit two pieces of paper in a box. On one I shall write the word 'guilty'—the other will have no writing on it. If the Jew draws the first, it will be a sign from Heaven that the Jews are guilty, and we'll have him burned at the stake. If he

which there is no writing, it will be divine
nocence, so we'll let him go."

d Inquisitor was a cunning fellow. He was anxious
nd since he knew that no one would ever find out
ided to write the word "guilty" on both pieces of
bi suspected he was going to do just this. Therefore,
his hand into the box and drew forth a piece of paper
put it into his mouth and swallowed it.

t is the meaning of this, Jew?" raged the inquisitor. "How
do you *xpect* us to know which paper you drew now that you've
swallowed it?"

"Very simple," replied the rabbi. "You have only to look at the
paper in the box."

So they took out the piece of paper still in the box.

"There!" cried the rabbi triumphantly. "This paper says 'guilty,'
therefore the one I swallowed must have been blank. Now, you must
release me!"

And they had to let him go.

THE UGLY SON
Japan

Long ago a gambler had a son whose eyes and nose looked as though
they had been squashed together by main force. This made the young
man outstandingly ugly. His parents were wondering how on earth
they were to get him married when they heard that a rich man was
seeking a handsome bridegroom for his beloved daughter. They let
the rich man know that the "fairest youth in all the land" wanted to
marry the girl. The rich man accepted the match and set the date for
the betrothal.

On the couple's first night the brotherhood of gamblers gathered
in borrowed finery and escorted the young man to his bride, doing
their best to hide their faces under a brilliant moon. The groom looked

quite presentable among them. This was how he began his nightly visits to the girl, in accordance with custom.

But all too soon came the dreaded night (the one that would seal the marriage forever) when the young man would have to lie with his betrothed right through dawn and into day. Undaunted, the gamblers thought up a plan.

One of them got up over the ceiling of the couple's room, trod the boards till they creaked and groaned, and bellowed in a terrible voice, "Fairest youth in all the land!"

The household quaked to hear him, for they recalled countless stories of supernatural visitations that had started exactly this way. The terrified groom called back, "I hear I'm the one people call fairest youth in the land. What do you want?" Three times the voice over the ceiling roared, and three times the groom replied.

The family wanted to know why he answered at all. "I couldn't help myself," he explained.

"The daughter of this house," the demon bellowed, "has been mine for three years, and I want to know what you think you're doing sleeping with her."

"But—but—" stammered the groom, "I had no idea! I didn't know! Please don't hurt me!"

"You nasty sneak!" the demon roared. "I'll ask you just one thing before I go. Which do you cherish most, your life or your looks?"

"How can I answer that?" protested the bridegroom.

His mother and father-in-law whispered frantically to him that he shouldn't mind his looks as long as he kept his life. "Tell him your looks!" they said.

He obeyed.

The demon replied with a horrid sort of sucking noise. The groom screamed, buried his face in his arms, and collapsed. The demon left.

What had happened to the groom's face? A lamp was brought in, and by its light they saw that his eyes and nose looked as though they had been jammed together. "Oh, if only I'd told him my life!" he sobbed. "How can I live among people with a face like this? And to think that you never once saw me as I used to be! What an awful mistake it was to get involved with a girl claimed by a horrible demon!"

Moved by this complaint, the girl's father promised him his fortune in compensation. In fact, to the young man's entire satisfaction his father-in-law took excellent care of him and even built a separate house for him, on the pretext that the present one's possibly faulty location might have had something to do with the calamity. The young man lived a very pleasant life indeed.

DIVIDING THE GOOSE
Russia

Once there was a poor peasant who had many children, but no possessions except one goose. He saved this goose for a long time; but hunger is nothing to be trifled with—and things had reached such a point that he had nothing to eat. So the peasant killed the goose, roasted it, and put it on the table. So far, so good; but he had no bread and not a grain of salt. He said to his wife, "How can we eat the goose without bread or salt? Perhaps I should take the goose to the baron as a gift and ask him for bread."

"Well, go with God," said his wife.

The peasant came to the baron and said, "I have brought you a goose as a gift. You are welcome to all I have. Do not disdain it, little father."

"Thanks, peasant, thanks. Now divide the goose among us, without doing wrong to anyone."

Now this baron had a wife, two sons and two daughters—all in all there were six in his family. The peasant was given a knife and he began to carve and divide the goose. he cut off the head and gave it to the baron. "You are the head of the house," he said, "so it is fitting that you should have the head." He cut off the pope's nose and gave it to the baron's wife, saying, "Your business is to sit in the house and take care of it, so here is the pope's nose for you." He cut off the legs and gave them to the sons, saying, "Here is a leg for each of you, to trample your father's paths with." And to each daughter he gave a wing. "You won't stay long with your father and mother; when you grow up, off you will fly. And I," he said, "I'm just a stupid peasant, so I'll take what is left." Thus he got most of the goose. The baron laughed, gave the peasant wine to drink, rewarded him with bread, and sent him home.

A rich peasant heard about this, envied the poor one, roasted five geese, and took them to the baron.

"What do you want, peasant?" asked the baron.

"I have brought Your Grace five geese as a gift."

"Thanks, brother! Now apportion them among us without doing wrong to anyone."

The peasant tried this and that, but saw no way of dividing the geese equally. He just stood there scratching his head.

The baron sent for the poor peasant and told him to divide the geese. He took one goose, gave it to the baron and his wife, and said, "Now you are three." He gave another goose to the two sons and a third one to the two daughters, saying, "Now you also are threes." The last pair of geese he took for himself, saying, "Now I and the geese are another three."

The baron said, "You are a clever fellow; you have managed to give everyone an equal share and you have not forgotten yourself either." He rewarded the poor peasant with money and drove out the rich one.

THE MEN WHO WOULDN'T STAY DEAD
France

Gentlemen, if you choose to listen, I will recount to you an adventure which once happened in a castle that stood on the bank of a river, near a bridge, and at a short distance from a town, of which I forget the name, but which we may suppose to be Douai. The master of this castle was humpbacked. Nature had exhausted her ingenuity in the formation of his whimsical figure. In place of understanding, she had given him an immense head, which, nevertheless, was lost between his two shoulders; he had thick hair, a short neck, and a horrible visage. Spite of his deformity, this bugbear bethought himself of falling love with a beautiful young woman, the daughter of a poor but respectable burgess of Douai. He sought her in marriage, and, as he was the richest person in the district, the poor girl was delivered up to him. After the nuptials he was as much to pity as she, for, being devoured by jealousy, he had not tranquillity night or day, but went prying and rambling everywhere, and suffered no stranger to enter his castle.

One day during the Christmas festival, while standing sentinel at his gate, he was accosted by three humpbacked minstrels. They saluted him as a brother and as such asked for refreshment. Contrary to expectation, he led them to his kitchen, gave them a capon with peas, and to each a piece of money. Before they departed, however, he warned them never to return, on pain of being thrown into the river. At this threat of the chatelain the minstrels laughed heartily, and took the road to the town, singing in full chorus, and dancing in grotesque derision. He, on his part, without paying any further attention to them, went to walk in the fields.

The lady, who saw her husband cross the bridge, and had heard the minstrels, called them back to amuse her. They had not been long returned to the castle when her husband knocked at the gate, by which she and the minstrels were equally alarmed. Fortunately the lady perceived, on a bedstead in a neighboring room, three empty coffers. Into each of them she stuffed a minstrel, shut the covers, and then opened the gate to her husband. He had only come back to spy the conduct of his wife, as usual, and after a short stay went out anew, at which you may believe his wife was not dissatisfied. She instantly ran to the coffers to release the minstrels, for night was approaching, and her husband would not probably be long absent. But what was her dismay when she found them all three suffocated! Lamentation, however, was useless. The main object now was to get rid of the dead bodies, and she had not a moment to lose. She ran then to the gate and, seeing a peasant go by, offered him a reward of thirty livres, and leading him into the castle, she took him to one of the coffers and, showing him its contents, told him he must throw the dead body into the river. He asked for a sack, put the carcass into it, pitched it over the bridge into the stream, and then returned quite out of breath to claim the promised reward. "I certainly intended to satisfy you," said the lady, "but you ought first to fulfill the conditions of your bargain; you have agreed to rid me of the dead body, have you not? There, however, it is still"; saying this, she showed him the other coffer, in which the second hunchback had expired. At this sight the clown was perfectly confounded, saying, "How the devil! come back! a sorcerer!" He then stuffed the body into the sack, and threw it, like the other, over the bridge, taking care to put the head down and to observe that it sank.

Meanwhile the lady had again changed the position of the coffers, so that the third was now in the place which had been successively occupied by the two others. When the peasant returned she showed him the remaining body. "You are right, friend," said she, "he must be a magician, for there he is again." The rustic gnashed his teeth with rage. "What the devil! Am I to do nothing but carry about this accursed hunchback?" He then lifted him up, with dreadful imprecations, and, having tied a stone round the neck, threw him into the middle of the current, threatening, if he came out a third time, to dispatch him with a cudgel. The first object that presented itself to the clown on his way back for the reward was the hunchbacked master of the castle returning from his evening walk and making toward the gate. At this sight the peasant could no longer restrain his fury. "Dog of a hunchback, are you there again?" So saying, he sprang on the chatelain, stuffed him into a sack, and threw him headlong into the river after the minstrels. "I'll venture a wager you have not seen him this last time," said the peasant, entering the room where the lady was seated. She answered that she had not. "Yet you were not far from it," replied he. "The sorcerer was already at the gate, but I have taken care of him. Be at your ease, he will not come back now." The lady instantly understood what had happened and repaid the peasant to his satisfaction.

The Story of Campriano
Italy

There was once a man, a tiller of the soil, named Campriano. He had a wife and a mule. Yokels from backward Ciciorana sometimes passed through the field he was working and called to him, "Hey, Campriano, what are you doing?" They would ask him if he was ready to go home, and frequently he and his mule would walk a little way with them.

One morning Campriano slipped a few gold pieces he had saved into his mule's rear end. When the yokels from Ciciorana came by, Campriano said, "Wait for me, I'm going home, too." He loaded his things onto the mule and joined the group in conversation. It was springtime and the fresh grass relished by animals abounded, so the mule, which had eaten his fill, soon cut loose and dropped the money his owner had hidden in him.

The yokels from Ciciorana exclaimed, "Why, Campriano, your mule makes droppings of money!"

"That's right," replied Campriano. "Without him, I'd never manage. He's my fortune."

Right off the bat they said, "Campriano, you must sell him to us! You must!"

"I'm not selling him."

"But if you did, what would you ask for him? A whole lot?"

"I wouldn't sell him for all the money in the world. You'd have to offer me . . . no less than three hundred crowns."

The yokels of Ciciorana dug into their pockets and all together came up with three hundred crowns. They led the mule away, and the minute they got home they told their wives to spread sheets in the stable to catch all the gold that would be dropped during the night.

In the morning they ran to the stable and found the sheets loaded with manure. "Campriano has cheated us! We'll kill him!" With that, they grabbed up pitchforks and shovels and marched off to Campriano's house.

His wife answered the door. "Campriano isn't here, he's out in the vineyard!"

"We'll get him out of the vineyard!" they shouted, and marched on. At the vineyard, they called to him, "Come out, Campriano! We are going to kill you!"

Campriano emerged from the rows of vines. "Why?"

"You sold us the mule, and he doesn't turn out any money!"

"Let me ask how you treated him," said Campriano.

"We treated him fine. He had sweet broth to drink and fresh grass to eat!"

"Poor animal! If he's not dead by now, he will be shortly! He's accustomed to eating roughage that shapes into durable coins, don't you see? Wait a minute, and I'll come and look at him. If he's still all right, I'll take him back. If not, you'll keep him and hold your peace. But first, I have to stop by my house a minute."

"All right! Go ahead, but come straight back. We'll wait here."

Campriano ran to his wife and said, "Put on a pot of beans to boil. But when we return, pretend to pull it out of the cupboard while they boil. Is that clear?"

Campriano accompanied the Ciciorana yokels to the stable and found the mule standing in the middle of the dung-laden sheets. "It's a wonder he's still alive," he said. "This animal is no good for work any more. But how could you! If I'd only known you'd break him down that way! Poor thing!"

The yokels were puzzled. "What do we do now?"

"What do you do now? I have nothing more to say, and you shouldn't either!"

"You have a point!"

"It was just one of those things. Come to my house to dinner, and let's forget the whole business once and for all."

They got to Campriano's and found the door closed. Campriano knocked, and his wife emerged from the barn, pretending to finish her chores and enter the house only at that moment.

The fire was out in the kitchen. Campriano said, "What! You've not cooked my dinner yet?"

"I just got back from the field," she replied. "But I'll scrape up something right away."

She set the table for everybody, then opened the cupboard, where the pot of beans boiled.

"What!" exclaimed the yokels of Ciciorana. "A pot that boils all by itself in the cupboard? How does it do that without any fire underneath it?"

"Goodness knows what we'd do without that pot!" replied Campriano. "How could my wife and I go out together to work if we weren't sure of finding the soup ready and waiting when we got back?"

"Campriano," said the yokels, "you must sell it to us."

"Not for all the money in the world.!"

"Campriano, things didn't work out with the mule. To make up for it, you have to sell us the pot. We'll give you three hundred crowns." Campriano sold the pot for three hundred crowns, and they left.

His wife said to him, "They were ready to kill you over the mule. How will you get out of this one?"

"Leave everything to me," said Campriano. He went to a butcher, bought an ox-bladder, and filled it with raw blood. He said to his wife, "Here, put this bladder in your bosom, and don't be afraid when I throw a knife at you."

The yokels of Ciciorana arrived carrying clubs and stakes. "We want your head! Give us back our money, or we'll kill you!"

"Now, now, calm down! Let's hear what it is this time."

"You told us that pot boiled without fire. We went out to work with our wives, and when we came back, the beans were as raw as ever!"

"Easy, now, easy! It must be the fault of that confounded wife of mine. I'm going to ask her if she didn't switch pots on me . . ."

He called his wife and asked, "Honestly, did you switch pots on these men?"

"Of course I did. You go and give things away without asking me anything. Then I have to do the work! I don't want to part with that pot!"

Campriano let out a yell. "You wretch!" He grabbed a knife, flung it at her, striking the bladder hidden in her bosom, and blood squirted all over the place. Down fell the woman in a whole pool of it.

The two yokels of Ciciorana turned as pale as ghosts. "You mean you'd kill a woman, Campriano, over a pot?"

Glancing at his wife all covered with blood, Campriano pretended to be sorry. "Poor thing, we'll just have to revive her!" He pulled a straw from his pocket, placed it in the woman's mouth, blew three times into it, and the woman rose as sound and fresh as ever.

The two yokels were wide-eyed. "Campriano," they said, "you must give us that straw."

"No, indeed," replied Campriano. "I'm often overcome with the urge to kill my wife. If I didn't have that straw, I couldn't revive her afterward."

They begged and pleaded with him and ended up giving him another three hundred crowns, so Campriano let them have the straw. They went home, picked a fight with their wives, and knifed them. They were apprehended while still blowing into the straw, and imprisoned for life.

The
FOOL:
NUMBSKULLS
and
NOODLEHEADS

The numbskull, noodlehead, idiot, bumpkin, silly—in other words, the fool—is the butt of jocular or droll stories the world around.

A few of the fools have names by which they are famous for their foolishness, like Lazy Jack and Nasr-ed-Din Hodja (who wavers between being the fool and being the rogue). Sometimes the population of a particular country, city, or locality bears the stigma of being peculiarly stupid: the inhabitants of Chelm in Jewish tales, the men of Gotham in England; the Biellese in Italy, the Irish and Poles during certain periods in America, the hillbillies in the American South. Often the stories are interchangeable, from one culture to another, only the name of the fool varying according to the teller.

Some cultures, such as that of the Pueblo Indians of the Southwest, have sacred clowns, and it is the nature of these clowns to insert ribald jokes, foolish actions, and even gross remarks in between the more solemn parts of the religious rituals. They are, as Richard Erdoes and Alfonso Ortiz explain in *American Indian Myths and Legends*, "the comic counterpart of solemnity, the underscoring of the duality of life."

That same underscoring can be seen in the long-valued tradition of the fool in Indo-European cultures. There are mentions of madmen with both poetic and prophetic powers in early Muslim sources: for example, the jester Bahlul in the ninth-century court of Harun al-Rashid. In Imperial Rome fools were kept by wealthy Romans, who also included deformed or imbecilic slaves in their retinues. The clergy in medieval France celebrated a "Feast of Fools" in which ecclesiastical ritual was parodied.

Weaving in and out of this tradition of the fool are the popular stories, jests, songs, narratives, and ballads about fools and foolish behavior. These are supposed to point out, in reverse, just how wise humans *might* be. But, as Alan Garner comments in the introduction to his book *The Guizer*: "The element I think marks us most is that of the Fool. It is where our humanity lies."

THE THREE SILLIES
England

Once upon a time there was a farmer and his wife who had one daughter, and she was courted by a gentleman. Every evening he used to come and see her, and stop to supper at the farmhouse, and the daughter used to be sent down into the cellar to draw the beer for supper.

So one evening she had gone down to draw the beer, and she happened to look up at the ceiling while she was drawing, and she saw a mallet stuck in one of the beams. It must have been there a long, long time, but somehow or other she had never noticed it before, and she began a-thinking. And she thought it was very dangerous to have that mallet there, for she said to herself, "Suppose him and me was to be married, and we was to have a son, and he was to grow up to be a man, and come down into the cellar to draw the beer, like I'm doing now, and the mallet was to fall on his head and kill him, what a dreadful thing it would be!" And she put down the candle and the jug, and sat herself down and began a-crying.

Well, they began to wonder upstairs how it was that she was so long drawing the beer, and her mother went down to see after her, and she found her sitting on the settle crying, and the beer running over the floor. "Why, what ever is the matter?" said her mother.

"Oh, Mother!" says she, "look at that horrid mallet! Suppose we was to be married, and was to have a son, and he was to grow up, and was to come down into the cellar to draw the beer, and the mallet was to fall on his head and kill him, what a dreadful thing it would be."

"Dear, dear! What a dreadful thing it would be!" said the mother, and she sat down aside of the daughter, and started a-crying too.

Then after a bit the father began to wonder that they didn't come back, and he went down into the cellar to look after them himself, and there they two sat a-crying, and the beer running all over the floor. "What ever is the matter?" says he.

"Why," says the mother, "look at that horrid mallet. Just suppose, if our daughter and her sweetheart was to be married, and was to have a son, and he was to grow up, and was to come down into the cellar to draw the beer, and the mallet was to fall on his head and kill him, what a dreadful thing it would be!"

"Dear, dear, dear! so it would!" said the father, and he sat himself down aside of the other two, and started a-crying.

Now the gentleman got tired of stopping up in the kitchen by himself, and at last he went down into the cellar too, to see what they were after; and there they three sat a-crying side by side, and the beer running all over the floor.

And he ran straight and turned the tap. Then he said, "What ever are you three doing, sitting there crying, and letting the beer run all over the floor?"

"Oh," says the father, "look at that horrid mallet! Suppose you and our daughter was to be married, and was to have a son, and he was to grow up, and was to come down into the cellar to draw the beer, and the mallet was to fall on his head and kill him!" And then they all started a-crying worse than before.

But the gentleman burst out a-laughing, and reached up and pulled out the mallet, and then he said, "I've traveled many miles, and I never met three such big sillies as you three before; and now I shall start out on my travels again, and when I can find three bigger sillies than you three, then I'll come back and marry your daughter." So he wished them goodbye, and started off on his travels, and left them all crying because the girl had lost her sweetheart.

Well, he set out, and he traveled a long way, and at last he came to a woman's cottage that had some grass growing on the roof. And the woman was trying to get her cow to go up a ladder to the grass, and the poor thing durst not go. So the gentleman asked the woman what she was doing.

"Why, lookye," she said, "look at all that beautiful grass. I'm going to get the cow onto the roof to eat it. She'll be quite safe, for I shall tie a string round her neck and pass it down the chimney, and tie it to my wrist as I go about the house, so she can't fall off without my knowing it."

"Oh, you poor silly!" said the gentleman, "you should cut the grass and throw it down to the cow!"

But the woman thought it was easier to get the cow up the ladder than to get the grass down, so she pushed her and coaxed her and got her up, and tied a string round her neck, and passed it down the chimney, and fastened it to her own wrist. And the gentleman went on his way, but he hadn't gone far when the cow tumbled off the roof, and hung by the string tied round her neck, and it strangled her. And the weight of the cow tied to her wrist pulled the woman up the chimney, and she stuck fast halfway, and was smothered in the soot.

Well, that was one big silly.

And the gentleman went on and on, and he went to an inn to stop the night, and they were so full at the inn that they had to put him in a double-bedded room, and another traveler was to sleep in the other bed. The other man was a very pleasant fellow, and they got very friendly together; but in the morning, when they were both getting up, the gentleman was surprised to see the other hang his trousers on the knobs of the chest of drawers and run across the room and try to jump into them, and he tried over and over again, and he couldn't manage it; and the gentleman wondered what ever he was doing it for. At last he stopped and wiped his face with his handkerchief. "Oh dear," he says, "I do think trousers are the most awkwardest kind of clothes that ever were. I can't think who could have invented such things. It takes me the best part of an hour to get into mine every morning, and I get so hot! How do you manage yours?"

So the gentleman burst out a-laughing, and showed him how to put them on; and he was very much obliged to him, and said he should never have thought of doing it that way.

So that was another big silly.

Then the gentleman went on his travels again; and he came to a village, and outside the village there was a pond, and round the pond was a crowd of people: And they had got rakes, and brooms, and pitchforks, reaching into the pond; and the gentleman asked what was the matter.

"Why," they say, "matter enough! Moon's tumbled into the pond, and we can't rake her out anyhow!"

So the gentleman burst out a-laughing, and told them to look up into the sky, and that it was only the shadow in the water. But they wouldn't listen to him, and abused him shamefully, and he got away as quick as he could.

So there was a whole lot of sillies bigger than them three sillies at home.

So the gentleman turned back home again, and married the farmer's daughter, and if they don't live happy forever after, that's nothing to do with you or me.

NASR-ED-DIN HODJA IN THE PULPIT
Turkey

Nasr-ed-Din Hodja one day addressed his congregation from the pulpit in the following words: "I beseech you to tell me truly, O brethren! O true believers! if what I am going to say to you is already known to you."

And the answer came, as in one voice, from his congregation, that they did not know, and that it was not possible for them to know, what the Hodja was going to say to them. "Then," quoth the preacher, "of what use to you or to me is an unknown subject?" And he descended from the pulpit and left the mosque.

On the following Friday his congregation, instead of having decreased, had greatly increased, and their anxiety to hear what he was going to say was felt in the very atmosphere.

The Hodja ascended the pulpit and said, "O brethren! O true believers! I beseech you to tell me truly if what I am going to say to you is already known to you."

The answer that came to the Hodja was so spontaneous as to suggest prearrangement. They all shouted, "Yes, Hodja, we do know what you are going to say to us."

"That being the case," quoth the Hodja, "there is no need either of you wasting your time or of me wasting my time." And, descending from the pulpit, he left the mosque. His congregation, having prayed, also left gradually, one by one and in groups.

On the following Friday Nasr-ed-Din Hodja again mounted the pulpit, and saw that his mosque was so crowded that not a nook or corner in it was empty. He addressed his congregation in exactly the same manner. "O brethren! O true believers!" said he, "I ask you to tell me truly if what I am going to say is already known to you?"

And again the answer of his numerous congregation had evidently been prepared beforehand, for one half of them rose and said, "Yes, Hodja, we do know what you are going to say to us," and the other half rose and said, "O Hodja effendi, how could we poor ignorant people know what you intend to say to us?"

The Hodja answered, "It is well said; and now if the half that knows what I am going to say would explain to the other half what it is, I would be deeply grateful, for, of course, it will be unnecessary for me to say anything."

Whereupon he descended from the pulpit and left the mosque.

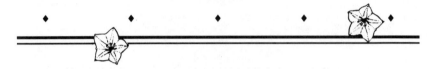

LAZY JACK
England

Once upon a time there was a boy whose name was Jack, and he lived with his mother on a dreary common. They were very poor, and the old woman got her living by spinning, but Jack was so lazy that he would do nothing but bask in the sun in the hot weather, and sit by the corner of the hearth in the wintertime. His mother could not persuade him to do anything for her, and was obliged at last to tell him that if he did not begin to work for his porridge, she would turn him out to get his living as he could.

This threat at length roused Jack, and he went out and hired himself for the day to a neighboring farmer for a penny; but as he was coming home, never having had any money in his possession before, he lost it in passing over a brook. "You stupid boy," said his mother, "you should have put it in your pocket." "I'll do so another time," replied Jack.

The next day Jack went out again, and hired himself to a cow keeper, who gave him a jar of milk for his day's work. Jack took the jar and put it into the large pocket of his jacket, spilling it all, long before he got home. "Dear me!" said the old woman. "You should have carried it on your head." "I'll do so another time," replied Jack.

The following day Jack hired himself again to a farmer, who agreed to give him a cream cheese for his services. In the evening,

Jack took the cheese, and went home with it on his head. By the time he got home the cheese was completely spilled, part of it being lost, and part matted with his hair. "You stupid lout," said his mother, "you should have carried it very carefully in your hands." "I'll do so another time," replied Jack.

The day after this Jack again went out, and hired himself to a baker who would give him nothing for his work but a large tomcat. Jack took the cat, and began carrying it very carefully in his hands, but in a short time pussy scratched him so much that he was compelled to let it go. When he got home, his mother said to him, "You silly fellow, you should have tied it with a string, and dragged it along after you." "I'll do so another time," said Jack.

The next day Jack hired himself to a butcher, who rewarded his labors by the handsome present of a shoulder of mutton. Jack took the mutton, tied it to a string, and trailed it along after him in the dirt, so that by the time he had got home the meat was completely spoiled. His mother was this time quite out of patience with him, for the next day was Sunday, and she was obliged to content herself with cabbage for her dinner. "You ninnyhammer," said she to her son, "you should have carried it on your shoulder." "I'll do so another time," replied Jack.

On the Monday Jack went once more, and hired himself to a cattle keeper, who gave him a donkey for his trouble. Although Jack was very strong, he found some difficulty in hoisting the donkey on his shoulders, but at last he accomplished it and began walking slowly home with his prize. Now it happened that in the course of his journey there lived a rich man with his only daughter, a beautiful girl, but unfortunately deaf and dumb; she had never laughed in her life, and the doctors said she would never recover till somebody made her laugh. Many tried without success, and at last the father, in despair, offered her in marriage to the first man who could make her laugh. This young lady happened to be looking out of the window, when Jack was passing with the donkey on his shoulders, the legs sticking up in the air; and the sight was so comical and strange, that she burst out into a great fit of laughter, and immediately recovered her speech and hearing. Her father was overjoyed, and fulfilled his promise by marrying her to Jack, who was thus made a rich gentleman. They lived in a large house, and Jack's mother lived with them in great happiness until she died.

CHELM JUSTICE
Jewish

A great calamity befell Chelm one day. The town cobbler murdered one of his customers. So he was brought before the judge, who sentenced him to die by hanging.

When the verdict was read a townsman arose and cried out, "If Your Honor pleases—you have sentenced to death the town cobbler! He's the only one we've got. If you hang him who will mend our shoes?"

"Who? Who?" cried all the people of Chelm with one voice.

The judge nodded in agreement and reconsidered his verdict.

"Good people of Chelm," he said, "What you say is true. Since we have only one cobbler it would be a great wrong against the community to let him die. As there are two roofers in the town, let one of them be hanged instead!"

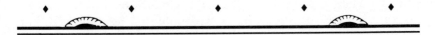

THOSE STUBBORN SOULS, THE BIELLESE
Italy

A farmer was on his way down to Biella one day. The weather was so stormy that it was next to impossible to get over the roads. But the farmer had important business and pushed onward in the face of the driving rain.

He met an old man, who said to him, "A good day to you! Where are you going, my good man, in such haste?"

"To Biella," answered the farmer, without slowing down.

"You might at least say, 'God willing.' "

The farmer stopped, looked the old man in the eye, and snapped, "God willing, I'm on my way to Biella. But even if God isn't willing, I still have to go there all the same."

Now the old man happened to be the Lord. "In that case you'll go to Biella in seven years," he said. "In the meantime, jump into this swamp and stay there for seven years."

Suddenly the farmer changed into a frog and jumped into the swamp.

Seven years went by. The farmer came out of the swamp, turned back into a man, clapped his hat on his hat, and continued on his way to market.

After a short distance he met the old man again. "And where are you going, my good man?"

"To Biella."

"You might say, 'God willing.' "

"If God wills it, fine. If not, I know the consequence and can now go into the swamp unassisted."

Nor for the life of him would he say one word more.

THE DROVERS WHO LOST THEIR FEET
Mexico

This is how the people from Lagos are. There were five drovers traveling together. They were tired. They sat down against a tree, and all of them stretched out their legs. They said, "What are we going to do? We won't be able to get up any more. We are no longer able to tell which of those feet belong to which. What are we going to do? We'll just have to stay here."

Whoo! There they were, pretty hungry and thirsty there, and they couldn't get up.

A man passed by, and he says, "What are you doing there?"

"Well, here we are. We can't get up."

"Why?"

"Because we don't know which feet belong to which."

"For goodness' sake! How much will you give me if I tell you?"

"Well, we'll give you something, as long as you tell us which of those feet belong to which."

He took a big pack needle and began to stick them with it. He stuck one of them.

"Ouch!"

"That's yours. Pull it in."

He stuck another one of them.

"Ouch!"

"That's yours. That one. Pull it in."

And he stuck all of them the same way until he had the very last one on his feet.

THE OLD MAN AND WOMAN
WHO SWITCHED JOBS
Sweden

Once there was an old man, just like any other old man. This old man worked in the forest, chopping wood, and burning charcoal, while his old woman stayed at home spinning, cooking, and taking care of the house. In this way their days passed one after another. But the old man always complained that he had to labor and toil all day long to support both of them while the old woman merely sat at home cooking porridge, eating, and enjoying herself. Even though the old woman told him that there was plenty to do at home as well and that the old man would be badly fed and clothed if she did not look after the house, the old man turned a deaf ear; he was convinced that he alone was pulling their entire load.

One day, after they'd bickered longer than usual, the old woman said, "Have it your way! Tomorrow we'll switch jobs. I'll go to the forest and cut wood for the fire, and you'll stay home and do my chores."

This suited the old man just fine. "I'll take good care of the house," he said. "But how you'll fare in the woods is another story."

Early the next morning the old woman said, "Don't forget to bake the bread, churn the butter, watch the cow, and cook the greens for dinner."

These were all mere trifles, thought the old man, and so they parted. The old woman took the old man's axe and went off to the forest while the old man began to build a fire under the oven and make the dough. When he thought it was ready, he began to bake it. But what sort of bread it was going to be was hard to say, for he forgot the yeast and put the loaves into the oven without first sweeping away the ashes.

The old man thought he'd managed the baking very well, and the thought of fresh bread awakened his appetite.

"Fresh bread is fine," he said to himself, "but if you have some bacon to go along with it, it tastes even better!"

So the next moment he went to the storehouse to fetch their last piece of bacon. But since the bacon was salty, he wanted something to drink with it. He put the bacon on the cellar steps and went downstairs.

Just as he was taking the plug out of the beer barrel, a dog came by and grabbed the bacon. The old man certainly didn't want to lose it, so he jumped up and ran off after the dog. But as he was running he discovered that he still had the plug in his hand, and he abandoned the bacon and ran back so that he could at least save the beer.

But it was too late. The barrel was empty and all the good beer had run out. This made him very unhappy, but he comforted himself with the thought that the old woman probably wasn't doing any better in the forest. Even if he had to do without bacon and beer, at least he still had the nice fresh-baked bread. With bread to eat, life is complete! as the saying goes.

But his comfort was short-lived. When he got inside the hut he found the bread burned to a crisp. Not a single bite was left for him to taste. It was a terrible state of affairs.

"This is no good at all," he moaned. "If only I'd let mother stay at home! If I'm doing this badly, how might she be doing in the forest? By now she may have chopped off both arms and legs!"

But there was no time for thinking. The sun was already high in the sky, and he had to cook greens for dinner. For greens one must have something green, the old man said to himself, and as he couldn't find anything else green, he took the old woman's new homespun jacket, chopped it into little bits, and put the pieces in the pot.

He realized that he couldn't cook greens without water, but the spring was so far away. And besides, he also had to churn butter! How on earth was he going to manage it all?

"If I put the churn on my back and shake it while I'm running to the spring, it'll probably turn to butter by the time I get back," he thought.

And that is what he did. But in his haste he forgot to put the lid on, and when he bent to haul up the water bucket, the cream poured over his shoulders and head and down into the spring.

Disheartened, he returned with the soupy, creamy water.

Now he had to tend to the cow, and since he couldn't be both inside and outside at the same time, how was he going to manage? On top of the house's sod roof, the grass shone a bright green in the sunshine; *there* was a juicy pasture! He tied a long rope around the cow's neck and pulled her up onto the roof, then threw the other end of the rope down the chimney.

Feeling a little happier, he went back inside the cottage and tied the tether hanging down through the chimney around his own waist so that the cow wouldn't get away from him. Then he started blowing on the fire under the pot. But while he was occupied blowing, the cow fell off the roof and pulled him up into the chimney!

At that very moment the old woman came home with a big bundle of firewood on her back. When she saw the cow hanging alongside the cottage wall, she hurried as fast as she could and cut the rope. Then she went inside. There on the floor lay the old man, smoked, burned, and half suffocated.

"God preserve us!" she exclaimed. "Is this how you've been managing at home?"

The poor old man couldn't utter a word; he just moaned and groaned. But it didn't take the old woman long to see how he'd managed: the bacon was gone, the beer run out, the bread burned to coal. The cream was in the spring and her jacket chopped up in the pot. The cow was hanged and the old man himself badly bruised and burned.

What happened later is not hard to guess. The old woman was allowed to care for her house in peace and quiet while the old man went off to the forest. Never again was he heard to complain of his lot.

THE TWO OLD WOMEN'S BET
United States

One time there were two old women got to talkin' about the men-folks: how foolish they could act and what was the craziest fool thing their husbands had ever done. And they got to arguin', so finally they made a bet which one could make the biggest fool of her husband.

So one of 'em said to her man when he come in from work that evenin', says, "Old man, do you feel all right?"

"Yes," he says, "I feel fine."

"Well," she told him, "you sure do look awful puny."

Next mornin' she woke him up, says, "Stick out your tongue, old man." He stuck his tongue out, and she looked at it hard, says, "Law me! you better stay in the bed today. You must be real sick from the look of your tongue."

Went and reached up on the fireboard, got down all the bottles of medicine and tonic was there and dosed the old man out of every bottle. Made him stay in the bed several days, and she kept on talkin' to him about how sick he must be. Dosed him every few minutes and wouldn't feed him nothin' but mush.

Came in one mornin', sat down by the bed, and looked at him real pitiful, started in snifflin' and wipin' her eyes on her apron, says, "Well, honey, I'll sure miss ye when you're gone." Sniffed some more, says, "I done had your coffin made."

And in a few days she had 'em bring the coffin right on in beside the old man's bed. Talked at the old man till she had him thinkin' he was sure 'nough dead. And finally they laid him out, and got everything fixed for the buryin'.

Well, the day that old woman had started a-talkin' her old man into his coffin, the other'n she had gone on to her house and about the time her old man came in from work she had got out her spinnin' wheel and went to whirlin' it. There wasn't a scrap of wool on the spindle, and the old man he finally looked over there and took notice of her, says, "What in the world are ye doin', old woman?"

"Spinnin'," she told him, and 'fore he could say anything she says, "Yes, the finest thread I ever spun. It's wool from virgin sheep, and they tell me anybody that's been tellin' his wife any lies can't see the thread."

So the old man he come on over there and looked at the spindle, says, "Yes, indeed, hit surely is mighty fine thread."

Well, the old woman she'd be there at her wheel every time her old man come in from the field—spin and wind, spin and wind, and every now and then take the shuck off the spindle like it was full of thread and lay it in a box. Then one day the old man come in and she was foolin' with her loom, says, "Got it all warped off today. Just got done threadin' it on the loom." And directly she sat down and started in weavin'—step on the treadles, throwin' the shuttle and it empty. The old man he'd come and look and tell her what fine cloth it was, and the old woman she'd weave right on. Made him think she was workin' day and night. Then one evenin' she took hold on the beam and made the old man help her unwind the cloth.

"Lay it on the table, old man—Look out! You're a-lettin' it drag the floor."

Then she took her scissors and went to cuttin'.

"What you makin', old woman?"

"Makin' you the finest suit of clothes you ever had."

Got out a needle directly and sat down like she was sewin'. And there she was, every time the old man got back to the house, workin' that needle back and forth. So he come in one evenin' and she says to him, "Try on the britches, old man. Here." The old man he shucked off his overalls and made like he was puttin' on the new britches.

"Here's your new shirt," she told him, and he pulled off his old one and did his arms this-a-way and that-a-way gettin' into his fine new shirt. "Button it up, old man." And he put his fingers up to his throat and fiddled 'em right on down.

"Now," she says, "Let's see does the coat fit ye." And she come at him with her hands up like she was holdin' out his coat for him, so he backed up to her and stuck his arms in his fine new coat.

"Stand off there now, and let me see is it all right—Yes, it's just fine. You sure do look good."

And the old man stood there with nothin' on but his shoes and his hat and his long underwear.

Well, about that time the other old man's funeral was appointed and everybody in the settlement started for the buryin' ground. The grave was all dug and the preacher was there, and here came the coffin in a wagon, and finally the crowd started gatherin'. And pretty soon that old man with the fine new suit of clothes came in sight. Well, everybody's eyes popped open, and they didn't know whether they ought to laugh or not, but the kids went to gigglin' and about the time that old man got fairly close, one feller laughed right out, and then they all throwed their heads back and laughed good. And the old man he'd try to tell somebody about his fine new suit of clothes, and then the preacher busted out laughin' and slappin' his knee—and everybody got to laughin' and hollerin' so hard the dead man sat up to see what was goin' on. Some of 'em broke and ran when the corpse rose up like that, but they saw him start in laughin'—laughed so hard he nearly fell out the coffin—so they all came back to find out what-'n-all was goin' on.

The two old women had started in quarrelin' about which one had won the bet, and the man in the coffin heard 'em, and when he could stop laughin' long enough, he told 'em, says, "Don't lay it on me, ladies! He's got me beat a mile!"

A Stroke of Luck
Hungary

He went plowing. He was a poor man. The plow cut a furrow and turned up a lot of money. When he set eyes on it, he began to speculate about what to say to his wife. He feared that she might blurt it out to the neighbors, and they would be served a summons to appear before the magistrate.

He went and bought a hare and a fish.

When she brought him his midday meal, he said to her after he had dined, "Let's fry a fish."

She said, "What do you think! How could we catch a fish here in the field?"

"Come on, woman, I've just seen a couple of them, when I was plowing around the blackthorn shrub." He led her to the blackthorn shrub.

Says the woman, "Look, old man, there's a fish."

"Haven't I told you so?" And he flung the ox goad at the shrub so that the fish turned out at once.

Then he said, "Let's catch a hare."

"Don't be kidding me. You haven't got a gun."

"Never mind. I'll knock it off with the ox goad."

They were going along when she cried out, "Look! there's a hare on the tree yonder there."

The man flung his goad at the tree and the hare fell down.

They were working till the day drew to a close, and in the evening they made their way home. When they went past the church, they heard an ass braying.

The man said to the woman, "You know what the ass is braying? He is saying, 'The priest says in his sermon that soon a comet will appear and that will be the end of the world!' "

They went on. When they passed the city hall, the ass uttered another loud bray. The man said, "The ass says, 'The magistrate and the town clerk have just been caught embezzling public funds.' "

As time wore on they were making good use of their money.

The neighbors kept asking them, "Where did that lot of money come from?"

Then she said to one of the neighbor women, "I wouldn't mind telling you, but you mustn't pass it on to anyone." And she told her that they had found the money. Their neighbor reported it to the magistrate, and they were summoned to appear before him. And when he was questioned about the money, the man denied it. By no means did they find any money. Not a penny had been found by them.

The magistrate then said, "Your wife will tell me."

"What's the use asking her. She's just a silly woman," he said.

The woman flew into a temper and began to shout at him, "Don't you dare say that again. Didn't we find the money when we caught the fish under the blackthorn bush?"

"Now Your Honor may hear for yourself. Catching a fish in a bush. What next!"

"Can't you remember how you shot down a hare from the tree with the ox goad?"

"Well, haven't I told Your Honor? It's no use asking that fool of a woman."

"A fool you are yourself. Have you forgotten that on our way home we heard an ass braying when we passed the church, and you said that the priest was preaching that a comet would appear and that would be the end of the world?"

"Now wasn't I right, Your Honor? It would be better to leave her alone, or she might give offense with her silly talk."

The woman flew into a rage and said, "Don't you remember that when we were passing the city hall and the ass uttered a loud bray you were telling me that the magistrate and the town clerk had been just caught out . . . ."

The magistrate jumped to his feet and said to the man, "Take her home, my good man. She seems to have lost her wits."

THE SAUSAGE
Sweden

There was once an old woman, who was all alone one evening in her cottage, occupied with her household affairs. While she was waiting for her husband, who was away at work over in the forest, and while she was bustling about, a fine, grand lady came in, and so the woman began to curtsey and curtsey, for she had never seen such a grand person before.

"I should be so much obliged if you would lend me your brewing pan," said the lady, "for my daughter is going to be married, and I expect guests from all parts."

Oh dear, yes! That she might have, said the woman, although she could not remember whether she had ever seen her before, and so she went to fetch the pan.

The lady took it, and thanked the woman, saying that she would pay her well for the loan of it, and so she went her way.

Two days afterwards the lady came back with it, and this time she also found the woman alone.

"Many thanks for the loan," said the lady, "and now in return you shall have three wishes."

And with this the lady left, and vanished so quickly that the old woman had not even time to ask her name or where she lived. But that did not matter, she thought, for now she had three wishes, and she began to think what she should wish for. She expected her husband back soon, and she thought it would be best to wait till he came home and could have a say in the matter. But the least they could wish for must be a fine big farm—the best in the parish, and a box full of money, and just fancy how happy and comfortable they would be then, for they had worked so hard all their days! Ah, yes, then the neighbors would have something to wonder at, for you may guess how they would stare at all the fine things she would have.

But since they were now so rich it was really a shame that there should be nothing but some blue, sour milk and some hard crusts of bread in the cupboard for her husband when he came home tired and weary, he who was fond of hot food. She had just been to her neighbor's, and there she had seen a fine big sausage, which they were going to have for supper.

"Ah, deary me, I wish I had that sausage here!" sighed the old woman; and the next moment a big sausage lay on the table right before her.

She was just going to put it in the pan when her husband came in.

"Father, father!" cried the woman, "it's all over with our troubles and hard work now. I lent my brewing pan to a fine lady, and when she brought it back she promised we should have three wishes. And now you must help me to wish for something really good, for you're so clever at hitting upon the right thing—and it's all true, for just look at the sausage, which I got the moment I wished for it!"

"What do you mean, you silly old woman?" shouted the husband, who became angry. "Have you been wishing for such a paltry thing as a sausage, when you might have had anything you liked in the world? I wish the sausage were sticking to your nose, since you haven't any better sense."

All at once the woman gave a cry, for sure enough there was the sausage sticking to her nose; and she began tearing and pulling away at it, but the more she pulled the firmer it seemed to stick. She was not able to get it off.

"Oh dear, oh dear!" sobbed the woman. "You don't seem to have any more sense than I, since you can wish me such ill-luck. I only wanted something nice for you, and then—oh dear, oh dear!" and the old woman went on crying and sobbing.

The husband tried, of course, to help his wife to get rid of the sausage; but for all he pulled and tugged away at it he did not succeed, and he was nearly pulling his wife's head off her body.

But they had one wish left, and what were they now to wish?

Yes, what were they to wish? They might, of course, wish for something fine and grand; but what could they do with all the finery in the world, as long as the mistress of the house had a long sausage sticking to the end of her nose? She would never be able to show herself anywhere!

"You wish for something," said the woman in the midst of her crying.

"No, you wish," said the husband, who also began crying when he saw the state his wife was in, and saw the terrible sausage hanging down her face.

So he thought he would make the best use he could of the last wish, and said:

"I wish my wife was rid of that sausage."

And the next moment it was gone!

They both became so glad that they jumped up and danced round the room in great glee—for you must know that although a sausage may be ever so nice when you have it in your mouth, it is quite a different thing to having one sticking to your nose all your life.

Nail Soup
Sweden

There was once a tramp, who went plodding his way through a forest. The distance between the houses was so great that he had little hope of finding a shelter before the night set in. But all of a sudden he saw some lights between the trees. He then discovered a cottage, where there was a fire burning on the hearth. How nice it would be to roast one's self before that fire, and to get a bite of something, he thought; and so he dragged himself towards the cottage.

Just then an old woman came towards him.

"Good evening, and well met!" said the tramp.

"Good evening," said the woman. "Where do you come from?"

"South of the sun, and east of the moon," said the tramp; "and now I am on the way home again, for I have been all over the world with the exception of this parish," he said.

"You must be a great traveler, then," said the woman. "What may be your business here?"

"Oh, I want a shelter for the night," he said.

"I thought as much," said the woman; "but you may as well get away from here at once, for my husband is not at home, and my place is not an inn," she said.

"My good woman," said the tramp, "you must not be so cross and hard-hearted, for we are both human beings, and should help one another, it is written."

"Help one another?" said the woman. "Help? Did you ever hear such a thing? Who'll help me, do you think? I haven't got a morsel in the house! No, you'll have to look for quarters elsewhere," she said.

But the tramp was like the rest of his kind; he did not consider himself beaten at the first rebuff. Although the old woman grumbled and complained as much as she could, he was just as persistent as ever, and went on begging and praying like a starved dog, until at last she gave in, and he got permission to lie on the floor for the night.

That was very kind, he thought, and he thanked her for it.

"Better on the floor without sleep, than suffer cold in the forest deep," he said, for he was a merry fellow, this tramp, and was always ready with a rhyme.

When he came into the room he could see that the woman was not so badly off as she had pretended; but she was a greedy and stingy woman of the worst sort, and was always complaining and grumbling.

He now made himself very agreeable, of course, and asked her in his most insinuating manner for something to eat.

"Where am I to get it from?" said the woman. "I haven't tasted a morsel myself the whole day."

But the tramp was a cunning fellow, he was.

"Poor old granny, you must be starving," he said. "Well, well, I suppose I shall have to ask you to have something with me, then."

"Have something with you!" said the woman. "You don't look as if you could ask any one to have anything! What have you got to offer one, I should like to know?"

"He who far and wide does roam sees many things not known at home, and he who many things has seen has wits about him and senses keen," said the tramp. "Better dead than lose one's head! Lend me a pot, granny!"

The old woman now became very inquisitive, as you may guess, and so she let him have a pot.

He filled it with water and put it on the fire, and then he blew with all his might till the fire was burning fiercely all round it. Then he took a four-inch nail from his pocket, turned it three times in his hand, and put it into the pot.

The woman stared with all her might.

"What's this going to be?" she asked.

"Nail broth," said the tramp, and began to stir the water with the porridge stick.

"Nail broth?" asked the woman.

"Yes, nail broth," said the tramp.

The old woman had seen and heard a good deal in her time, but that anybody could have made broth with a nail, well, she had never heard the like before.

"That's something for poor people to know," she said, "and I should like to learn how to make it."

"That which is not worth having, will always go a-begging," said the tramp.

But if she wanted to learn how to make it she had only to watch him, he said, and went on stirring the broth.

The old woman squatted on the ground, her hands clasping her knees, and her eyes following his hand as he stirred the broth.

"This generally makes good broth," he said, "but this time it will very likely be rather thin, for I have been making broth the whole week with the same nail. If one only had a handful of sifted oatmeal to put in, that would make it all right," he said. "But what one has to go without, it's no use thinking more about," and so he stirred the broth again.

"Well, I think I have a scrap of flour somewhere," said the old woman, and went out to fetch some, and it was both good and fine.

The tramp began putting the flour into the broth, and went on stirring, while the woman sat staring now at him and then at the pot until her eyes nearly burst their sockets.

"This broth would be good enough for company," he said, putting in one handful of flour after another. "If I had only a bit of salted beef and a few potatoes to put in, it would be fit for gentlefolks, however particular they might be," he said. "But what one has to go without, it's no use thinking more about."

When the old woman really began to think it over, she thought she had some potatoes, and perhaps a bit of beef as well; and these she gave the tramp, who went on stirring, while she sat and stared as hard as ever.

"This will be grand enough for the best in the land," he said.

"Well, I never!" said the woman; "and just fancy—all with a nail!"

He was really a wonderful man, that tramp! He could do more than drink a sup and turn the tankard up, he could.

"If one had only a little barley and a drop of milk, we could ask the king himself to have some of it," he said, "for this is what he has every blessed evening—that I know, for I have been in service under the king's cook," he said.

"Dear me! Ask the king to have some! Well, I never!" exclaimed the woman, slapping her knees. She was quite awestruck at the tramp and his grand connections.

"But what one has to go without, it's no use thinking more about," said the tramp.

And then she remembered she had a little barley; and as for milk, well, she wasn't quite out of that, she said, for her best cow had just calved. And then she went to fetch both the one and the other.

The tramp went on stirring, and the woman sat staring, one moment at him and the next at the pot.

Then all at once the tramp took out the nail.

"Now it's ready, and now we'll have a real good feast," he said. "But to this kind of soup the king and the queen always take a dram or two, and one sandwich at least. And then they always have a cloth on the table when they eat," he said. "But what one has to go without, it's no use thinking more about."

But by this time the old woman herself had begun to feel quite grand and fine, I can tell you; and if that was all that was wanted to make it just as the king had it, she thought it would be nice to have it just the same way for once, and play at being king and queen with the tramp. She went straight to a cupboard and brought out the brandy bottle, dram glasses, butter and cheese, smoked beef and veal, until at last the table looked as if it were decked out for company.

Never in her life had the old woman had such a grand feast, and never had she tasted such broth, and just fancy, made only with a nail!

She was in such a good and merry humor at having learned such an economical way of making broth that she did not know how to make enough of the tramp who had taught her such a useful thing.

So they ate and drank, and drank and ate, until they became both tired and sleepy.

The tramp was now going to lie down on the floor. But that would never do, thought the old woman; no, that was impossible. "Such a grand person must have a bed to lie in," she said.

He did not need much pressing. "It's just like the sweet Christmas time," he said, "and a nicer woman I never came across. Ah, well! Happy are they who meet with such good people," said he; and he lay down on the bed and went asleep.

And next morning when he woke the first thing he got was coffee and a dram.

When he was going the old woman gave him a bright dollar piece.

"And thanks, many thanks, for what you have taught me," she said. "Now I shall live in comfort, since I have learned how to make broth with a nail."

"Well it isn't very difficult, if one only has something good to add to it," said the tramp as he went his way.

The woman stood at the door staring after him.

"Such people don't grow on every bush," she said.

Old Dry Frye
United States

One time there was an old man named Dry Frye. He was a preacher but all he preached for was revival collections and all the fried chicken he could eat. And one time he stayed for supper and he was eatin' fried chicken so fast he got a chicken bone stuck in his throat. Choked him to death. Well, the man of the house he was scared. "Law me!" he says, "they'll find old Dry Frye here and they'll hang me for murder sure!" So he took old Dry Frye to a house down the road a piece and propped him up against the door. Somebody went to go out the door directly old Dry Frye fell in the house. "Law me!" says the man of the house. "It's old Dry Frye!" (Everybody knew old Dry Frye.) "We got to get shed of him quick or we're liable to be hung for murder!"

So he took old Dry Frye and propped him up in the bresh 'side
the road. And way up in the night some men come along, thought
it was a highway robber layin' for 'em. So they chunked rocks at
him, knocked him down, and when they seen who it was (everybody
knew old Dry Frye) they thought they'd killed him, and they got
scared they'd be hung for murder 'cause they'd passed several people
on the road who'd 'a knowed who was along there that night.

Well, they took old Dry Frye and propped him up against a
man's cornhouse. And that man he went out early the next mornin';
and he'd been missin' corn—so when he seen there was somebody
over there at his cornhouse he ran and got his gun. Slipped around,
hollered, "Get away from there or I'll shoot!"

And when old Dry Frye never moved he shot and Dry Frye
tumbled over and hit the ground.

"Law me!" says the man. "I belive that was old Dry Frye."
(Everybody knew old Dry Frye.) "Now I've done killed him and I'll
sure get hung for murder."

So he went and saw it *was* him and seen how dead he was, and
went to studyin' up some way to get shed of him. Well, he throwed
him in the cornhouse to hide him, and that night he took old Dry
Frye down to a baptizin' place 'side a bend in the river where they
were fixin' to have a big baptizin' the next day, propped him up on
a stump on the riverbank—over a right deep place where the bank
was pretty high—propped his elbows on his knees and his chin in his
hands. Made him look awful natural. Left him there, went on home
and slept sound.

So early the next mornin', 'fore anybody else, a little old feisty
boy came down there foolin' around the baptizin' place. Saw old Dry
Frye, hollered, "Howdy, Mr. Frye."

Went over closer.

"Howdy, Mr. Dry Frye."

Old Dry Frye sat right on.

"I said Howdy, Dry Frye."

Old Dry Frye kept on sittin'. That boy, now he was just as feisty
as he could be. He didn't care how he spoke to nobody.

"Look-a-here, Old Dry Frye, if you don't answer me Howdy
I'm goin' to knock your elbows out from under you—Howdy, Mr.
Frye!"

So that feisty boy he reached over and swiped old Dry Frye a
lick and over in the river the old man went, right down the bank
into that deep water, sunk clean out of sight. Then that boy thought
sure he'd drownded Dry Frye. He got scared about bein' hung for

murder but he couldn't do nothin' about it right then 'cause he'd seen folks comin' down the road for the baptizin'. So he hung around and directly everybody gathered for the baptizin', and they waited and waited for old Dry Frye to come and preach, but he didn't come and didn't come and when they got to askin' who'd seen old Dry Frye, one man said he'd left his place right after supper, and another man said why, no, he'd not seen old Dry Frye since last meetin'. And that feisty boy he let out a giggle where he was sittin' on one of the benches in the back, and the other boys asked him what he was laughin' at, but he'd just get tickled again and not tell 'em nothin'. So finally the folks sung a few hymns and took up a collection. So meetin' broke and everybody went on home, and that boy he went on home, too.

Then 'way along late that night he went down and hooked old Dry Frye out of the river and put him in a sack. Got his shoulder under it and started down the road to hide him somewhere. Well, there were a couple of rogues comin' along that same night, had stole a couple of hogs and had 'em sacked up carryin' 'em on their shoulders. Them rogues came over a little rise in the road, saw that boy, and they got scared, dropped their sacks and run back lickety-split and hid in the bresh. The boy he never saw the two rogues so he came on, saw them two sacks and set old Dry Frye down to see what was in the other sacks. Then he left old Dry Frye layin' there, picked up one of the hogs and went on back home.

So the two rogues they slipped out directly and when they saw the two sacks still layin' there, they picked 'em up and kept on goin'. Got on home and hung the sacks up in the meathouse. Then the next mornin' the old woman got up to cook breakfast, went out to the smokehouse to cut some meat. Ripped open one of them sacks and there hung old Dry Frye. Well, she hollered and dropped her butcher knife and she got away from there in such a hurry she tore down one side of the smokehouse, broke out two posts on the back porch, and knocked the kitchen door clean off the hinges. She was sorta scared. She hollered and squalled and the men come runnin' in their shirt-tails and finally looked out in the smokehouse, saw old Dry Frye hangin' up there in the place of a hog.

"Law me!" says one of 'em. "It's old Dry Frye?" (Everybody knew old Dry Frye.) "We'll sure be hung for murder if we don't get shed of him some way or other."

Well, they had some wild horses in a wilderness out on the mountain. So they rounded up one of 'em, got him in the barn. Then they put an old no-'count saddle on him and an old piece of bridle, and put old Dry Frye on. Stropped his legs to the bellyhand, tied his hands to the saddlehorn and pulled the reins through, stuck his old hat on his head; and then they slipped out and opened all the gates. Opened the barn door and let the horse go. He shot out of there and down the road he went with that old preacher-man a-bouncin' first one side and then the other. And them rogues run out and went to shootin' and hollerin', "He's stole our horse! Stop him! Somebody stop him yonder! Horse thief! Horse thief!"

Everybody down the road come runnin' out their houses a-shoutin' and hollerin' and a-shootin' around, but that horse had done jumped the fence and took out up the mountain and it looked like he was headed for Kentucky.

And as far as I know old Dry Frye is over there yet a-tearin' around through the wilderness on that wild horse.

"BYE-BYE"
Haiti

All the birds were flying from Haiti to New York. But Turtle could not go, for he had no wings.

Pigeon felt sorry for Turtle and said, "Turtle, I'll take you with me. This is what we'll do. I'll hold in my mouth one end of a piece of wood and you hold on to the other end. But you must not let go. No matter what happens, do not let go or you'll fall into the water."

Pigeon took one end of a piece of wood and Turtle the other end. Up into the air Pigeon flew and Turtle with him, across the land and toward the sea.

As they came near the ocean, Turtle and Pigeon saw on the shore a group of animals who had gathered together to wave goodbye to the birds who were leaving. They were waving steadily until they noticed Turtle and Pigeon. Turtle? They stopped waving and a great hubbub broke out.

"Look!" they cried to each other. "Turtle is going to New York. Even Turtle is going to New York!"

And Turtle was so pleased to hear everyone talking about him that he called out the one English word he knew:

"Bye-bye!"

Oh-oh. Turtle had opened his mouth, and in opening his mouth to speak, he let go of the piece of wood and fell into the sea.

For that reason there are many Pigeons in New York, but Turtle is still in Haiti.

THE BARN IS BURNING
Afro-American (North Carolina)

During slavery time, there was a rich old master in Brunswick County that owned more than three hundred slaves. Among them was one very smart slave named Tom. What I mean by smart is that he was a smooth operator—he knew what was happening. He came to be so smart because he would crawl under the master's house every night and listen to the master tell his wife what kind of work he was going to have the slaves do the next day. When the master would come out of the house the next morning and begin to tell the slaves what kind of work he wanted them to do that day, Old Tom would say, "Wait just a minute, Master. I know exactly what you're going to have us do." So the master would stop talking and let Old Tom tell the slaves what he had in mind for them to do that day. Old Tom could always tell the slaves exactly what the master wanted them to do, too; and the master was very surprised, because he didn't know how Old Tom was getting his information.

Old Tom wanted to prove to his master that he was the smartest slave on the plantation, because the smartest slave always got the easiest work—and Old Tom was tired of working so hard. Sometimes the masters let their smart slaves sleep in a bed in the big house, too; so Old Tom had been dreaming about how, one day maybe, he would get to sleep in a real bed instead of on an old quilt on his cabin floor. And it wasn't long before his dreams came to be true, because the next week after Old Tom had started prophesying what work the slaves were supposed to do that day, Old Master told his wife that he thought he was going to bring Old Tom to live in the house with them. And he did, and he gave him a room to sleep in with a big old bed and everything. Old Tom was so tickled he didn't know what to do with himself—just think, living in the same house with Old Master.

One winter night, when the master and his wife were seated around the fire, the master called Old Tom in to test his smartness. He pointed to the fire and said, "Tom, what is that?"

"That's a fire, Old Master," said Tom.

"No, it isn't either," replied Old Master. "That's a flame of evaporation."

Just then a cat passed in front of the fire, and Old Master said, "Tom, do you know what that was that just passed by in front of the fireplace?"

"That's a cat, sir," replied Tom.

Then Old Master said, "No, it's not either. That's a high-ball-a-sooner."

Old Tom was getting tired of answering questions by this time, so he went over to the window and started looking out. The old master walked over to the window where Tom was and said, "Tom, what is that you're looking at through the window?"

"I'm looking at a haystack," said Tom.

Then Old Master said, "That's not a haystack, that's a high tower."

Then Old Tom sat down in a chair and started getting ready to go to his room in the attic to go to bed for the night. He didn't want to get the carpet all spotted up with dirt in the living room, so he started unbuckling his shoes and taking them off. When the old man looked and saw Tom taking off his shoes, he said, "What are those, Tom?"

And Tom said, "Those are my shoes."

"No, they aren't either," said Old Master. "Those are your tramp-tramps."

Then the old master pointed through the archway to where a bed could be seen in his bedroom, sand said, "What's that I'm pointing to in there, Tom?"

"That's a bed," said Old Tom,.

"No, it's not either," said Old Master. "That's a flowery bed of ease, and I'm going right now and get in it because we've all got a hard day's work coming up tomorrow."

So the old master and the old missus went into their bedroom and went to bed. Then Old Tom went on up to the attic room where they had him sleeping and he got in his big old bed. But just then the cat ran through the fire in the fireplace and caught on fire and started raising a howl. So Tom jumped out of bed and looked, and saw the cat run out to the haystack and set it on fire. Old Tom was there at the window, and when he saw the cat on fire and the haystack on fire, he started yelling as loud as he could, "Master, Master, you better get up out of your flowery bed of ease and put on your tramp-tramps because your high-ball-a-sooner has run through your flame of evaporation and set your high tower on fire."

Old Master didn't move a peg—he just chuckled to his wife and said, "Listen to that high-class slave up there using all that Latin."

Then once more Old Tom yelled out, "Master, Master, I said that you better get out of your flowery bed of ease, and put on your tramp-tramps, because your high-ball-a-sooner has run through your flame of evaporation and set your high tower on fire."

But Old Master just chuckled to his wife again, and said, "That sure is a smart slave, that Tom, isn't he? Just listen to him talking all that Latin up there again."

Old Tom went on yelling like this about five more times. But when he saw that Old Master wasn't getting out of bed, he yelled, "Master, you better get up out of that bed and put on your shoes and go out there and put out that haystack fire that your cat started, or else your whole damn farm's going to burn up!" I guess that got Old Master up pretty quick!

HEROES:
LIKELY
and
UNLIKELY

Joseph Campbell sums up the monomyth of the hero in his monumental work *The Hero with a Thousand Faces*: "A hero ventures forth from the world of common day into a region of supernatural wonder: fabulous forces are there encountered and a decisive victory is won: the hero comes back from this mysterious adventure with the power to bestow boons on his fellow man."

However, in the small bits and fragments of the great hero myths, which we call folktales, the hero or heroine may take on a much more modest role. Whether these heroes are culture heroes like Ireland's Finn MacCumhail in "The Birth of Finn MacCumhail," unlikely heroes like the young bondmaid in "Li Chi Slays the Serpent," or humble ones like Long Arrow in "The Orphan Boy and the Elk Dog," they appeal to us because they manage to outwit, outfight, and outmaneuver dragons, ogres, witches, warlocks, or angry fathers.

This is just a sampling of heroes and hero types, because hero tales are scattered throughout the other sections of the book. "The Man Who Had No Story," with its unlikely hero, is in the "Telling Tales" section; the hero of "Vasilisa the Beautiful," is certainly as brave and strong as any, and her story is in the section called "Not Quite Human."

But a hero is a hero only if he or she has some fear, some moment of wariness. That is what the boy in "The Story of the Youth Who Went Forth to Learn What Fear Was" seems to perceive when he says, "That, too must be an art of which I understand nothing." So he undergoes rigorous testing, that encountering of fabulous forces of which Campbell reminds us. He even wins the king's daughter. All unknown to himself, he has been a hero, and he learns to shudder by a homely trick at the very end.

THE BIRTH OF FINN MACCUMHAIL
Ireland

Cumhal MacArt was a great champion in the West of Erin, and it was prophesied of him that if he ever married he would meet death in the next battle he fought.

For this reason he had no wife, and knew no woman for a long time; till one day he saw the king's daughter, who was so beautiful that he forgot all fear and married her in secret.

Next day after the marriage, news came that a battle had to be fought.

Now a Druid had told the king that his daughter's son would take the kingdom for him. So he made up his mind to look after the daughter, and not let any man come near her.

Before he went to the battle, Cumhal told his mother everything— told her of his relations with the king's daughter.

He said, "I shall be killed in battle today, according to the prophecy of the Druid, and I'm afraid if his daughter has a son the king will kill the child, for the prophecy is that he will lose the kingdom by the son of his own daughter. Now, if the king's daughter has a son do you hide and rear him, if you can. You will be his only hope and stay."

Cumhal was killed in the battle, and within that year the king's daughter had a son.

By command of his grandfather, the boy was thrown out of the castle window into a lough, to be drowned, on the day of his birth.

The boy sank from sight. But after remaining awhile under the water, he rose again to the surface, and came to land holding a live salmon in his hand.

The grandmother of the boy, Cumhal's mother, stood watching on the shore, and said to herself as she saw this, "He is my grandson, the true son of my own child," and seizing the boy, she rushed away with him, and vanished, before the king's people could stop her.

When the king heard that the old woman had escaped with his daughter's son, he fell into a terrible rage, and ordered all the male children born that day in the kingdom to be put to death, hoping in this way to kill his own grandson, and save the crown for himself.

After she had disappeared from the bank of the lough, the old woman, Cumhal's mother, made her way to a thick forest, where she spent that night as best she could. Next day she came to a great oak tree. Then she hired a man to cut out a chamber in the tree.

When all was finished, and there was a nice room in the oak for herself and her grandson, and a whelp of the same age as the boy, and which she had brought with her from the castle, she said to the man, "Give me the axe which you have in your hand, there is something here that I want to fix."

The man gave the axe into her hand, and that minute she swept the head off him, saying, "You'll never tell any man about this place now."

One day the whelp ate some of the fine chippings (*bran*) left cut by the carpenter from the inside of the tree. The old woman said, "You'll be called Bran from this out."

All three lived in the tree together, and the old woman did not take her grandson out till the end of five years; and then he couldn't walk, he had been sitting so long inside.

When the old grandmother had taught the boy to walk, she brought him one day to the brow of a hill from which there was a long slope. She took a switch and said, "Now, run down this place. I will follow and strike you with this switch, and coming up I will run ahead, and you strike me as often as you can."

The first time they ran down, his grandmother struck him many times. In coming up the first time, he did not strike her at all. Every time they ran down she struck him less, and every time they ran up he struck her more.

They ran up and down for three days. And at the end of that time she could not strike him once, and he struck her at every step he took. He had now become a great runner.

When he was fifteen years of age, the old woman went with him to a hurling match between the forces of his grandfather and those of a neighboring king. Both sides were equal in skill; and neither was able to win, till the youth opposed his grandfather's people. Then, he won every game. When the ball was thrown in the air, he struck it coming down, and so again and again—never letting the ball touch the ground till he had driven it through the barrier.

The old king, who was very angry and greatly mortified at the defeat of his people, exclaimed, as he saw the youth, who was very fair and had white hair, "Who is that *finn cumhal* [white cap]?"

"Ah, that is it. Finn will be his name, and Finn MacCumhail he is," said the old woman.

The king ordered his people to seize and put the young man to death, on the spot. The old woman hurried to the side of her grandson. They slipped from the crowd and away they went, a hill at a leap, a glen at a step, and thirty-two miles at a running leap. They ran a long distance, till Finn grew tired. Then the old grandmother took him on her back, putting his feet into two pockets which were in her dress, one on each side, and ran on with the same swiftness as before, a hill at a leap, a glen at a step, and thirty-two miles at a running leap.

After a time, the old woman felt the approach of pursuit, and said to Finn, "Look behind, and tell me what you see."

"I see," said he, "a white horse with a champion on his back."

"Oh, no fear," said she. "A white horse has no endurance. He can never catch us, we are safe from him." And on they sped. A second time she felt the approach of pursuit, and again she said, "Look back, and see who is coming."

Finn looked back, and said, "I see a warrior riding on a brown horse."

"Never fear," said the old woman. "There is never a brown horse but is giddy, he cannot overtake us." She rushed on as before. A third time she said, "Look around, and see who is coming now."

Finn looked, and said, "I see a black warrior on a black horse, following fast."

"There is no horse so tough as a black horse," said the grandmother. "There is no escape from this one. My grandson, one or both of us must die. I am old, my time has nearly come. I will die, and you and Bran save yourselves. (Bran had been with them all the time.) Right ahead is a deep bog. You jump off my back, and escape as best you can. I'll jump into the bog up to my neck. And when the king's men come, I'll say that you are in the bog before me, sunk out of sight, and I'm trying to find you. As my hair and yours are the same color, they will think my head good enough to carry back. They will cut it off, and take it in place of yours, and show it to the king. That will satisfy his anger."

Finn slipped down, took farewell of his grandmother, and hurried on with Bran. The old woman came to the bog, jumped in, and sank to her neck. The king's men were soon at the edge of the bog, and the black rider called out to the old woman, "Where is Finn?"

"He is here in the bog before me, and I'm trying can I find him."

As the horsemen could not find Finn, and thought the old woman's head would do to carry back, they cut it off, and took it with them, saying, "This will satisfy the king."

Finn and Bran went on till they came to a great cave, in which they found a herd of goats. At the further end of the cave was a smoldering fire. The two lay down to rest.

A couple of hours later, in came a giant with a salmon in his hand. This giant was of awful height, he had but one eye, and that in the middle of his forehead, as large as the sun in heaven.

When he saw Finn, he called out, "Here, take this salmon and roast it. But be careful, for if you raise a single blister on it I'll cut the head off you. I've followed this salmon for three days and three nights without stopping, and I never let it out of my sight, for it is the most wonderful salmon in the world."

The giant lay down to sleep in the middle of the cave. Finn spitted the salmon, and held it over the fire.

The minute the giant closed the one eye in his head, he began to snore. Every time he drew a breath into his body, he dragged Finn, the spit, the salmon, Bran, and all the goats to his mouth. And every time he drove a breath out of himself, he threw them back to the places they were in before. Finn was drawn time after time to the mouth of the giant with such force, that he was in dread of going down his throat.

When partly cooked, a blister rose on the salmon. Finn pressed the place with his thumb, to know could he break the blister, and hide from the giant the harm that was done. But he burned his thumb, and, to ease the pain, put it between his teeth, and gnawed the skin to the flesh, the flesh to the bone, the bone to the marrow. And when he had tasted the marrow, he received the knowledge of all things. Next moment, he was drawn by the breath of the giant right up to his face, and, knowing from his thumb what to do, he plunged the hot spit into the sleeping eye of the giant and destroyed it.

That instant the giant with a single bound was at the low entrance of the cave, and, standing with his back to the wall and a foot on each side of the opening, roared out, "You'll not leave this place alive."

Now Finn killed the largest goat, skinned him as quickly as he could, then putting the skin on himself he drove the herd to where the giant stood; the goats passed out one by one between his legs. When the great goat came the giant took him by the horns. Finn slipped from the skin, and ran out.

"Oh, you've escaped," said the giant, "but before we part let me make you a present."

"I'm afraid to go near you," said Finn. "If you wish to give me a present, put it out this way, and then go back."

The giant placed a ring on the ground, then went back, Finn took the ring and put it on the end of his little finger above the first joint. It clung so firmly that no man in the world could have taken it off.

The giant then called out, "Where are you?"

"On Finn's finger," cried the ring. That instant the giant sprang at Finn and almost came down on his head, thinking in this way to crush him to bits. Finn sprang to a distance. Again the giant asked, "Where are you?"

"On Finn's finger," answered the ring.

Again the giant made a leap, coming down just in front of Finn. Many times he called and many times almost caught Finn, who could not escape with the ring on his finger. While in this terrible struggle, not knowing how to escape, Bran ran up and asked:

"Why don't you chew your thumb?"

Finn bit his thumb to the marrow, and then knew what to do. He took the knife with which he had skinned the goat, cut off his finger at the first joint, and threw it, with the ring still on, into a deeper bog near by.

Again the giant called out, "Where are you?" and the ring answered, "On Finn's finger."

Straightaway the giant sprang towards the voice, sank to his shoulders in the bog, and stayed there.

Finn with Bran now went on his way, and traveled till he reached a deep and thick wood, where a thousand horses were drawing timber, and men felling and preparing it.

"What is this?" asked Finn of the overseer of the workmen.

"Oh, we are building a dun for the king. We build one every day, and every night it is burned to the ground. Our king has an only daughter. He will give her to any man who will save the dun, and he'll leave him the kingdom at his death. If any man undertakes to save the dun and fails, his life must pay for it. The king will cut his head off. The best champions in Erin have tried and failed; they are now in the king's dungeons, a whole army of them, waiting the king's pleasure. He's going to cut the heads off them all in one day."

"Why don't you chew your thumb?" asked Bran.

Finn chewed his thumb to the marrow, and then knew that on the eastern side of the world there lived an old hag with her three sons, and every evening at nightfall she sent the youngest of these to burn the king's dun.

"I will save the king's dun." said Finn.

"Well," said the overseer, "better men than you have tried and lost their lives."

"Oh," said Finn, "I'm not afraid. I'll try for the sake of the king's daughter."

Now Finn, followed by Bran, went with the overseer to the king. "I hear you will give your daughter to the man who saves your dun," said Finn.

"I will," said the king. "But if he fails I must have his head."

"Well," said Finn, "I'll risk my head for the sake of your daughter. If I fail I'm satisfied." The king gave Finn food and drink; he supped, and after supper went to the dun.

"Why don't you chew your thumb?" said Bran. "Then you'll know what to do." He did. Then Bran took her place on the roof, waiting for the old woman's son. Now the old woman in the east told her youngest son to hurry on with his torches, burn the dun, and come back without delay; for the stirabout was boiling and he must not be too late for supper.

He took the torches, and shot off through the air with a wonderful speed. Soon he was in sight of the king's dun, threw the torches upon the thatched roof and set it on fire as usual.

That moment Bran gave the torches such a push with her shoulders, that they fell into the stream which ran around the dun, and were put out. "Who is this," cried the youngest son of the old hag, "who has dared to put out my lights, and interfere with my hereditary right?"

"I," said Finn, who stood in front of him. Then began a terrible battle between Finn and the old woman's son. Bran came down from the dun to help Finn. She bit and tore his enemy's back, stripping the skin and flesh from his head and heels.

After a terrible struggle such as had not been in the world before that night, Finn cut the head off his enemy. But for Bran, Finn could never have conquered.

The time for the return of her son had passed; supper was ready. The old woman, impatient and angry, said to the second son, "You take torches and hurrry on, see why your brother loiters. I'll pay him for this when he comes home! But be careful and don't do like him, or you'll have your pay too. Hurry back, for the stirabout is boiling and ready for supper."

He started off, was met and killed exactly as his brother, except that he was stronger and the battle fiercer. But for Bran, Finn would have lost his life that night.

The old woman was raging at the delay, and spoke to her eldest son, who had not been out of the house for years. (It was only in case of the greatest need that she sent him. He had a cat's head, and was called Pus an Chuine, "Puss of the Corner"; he was the eldest and strongest of all the brothers.) "Now take torches, go and see what delays your brothers. I'll pay them for this when they come home."

The eldest brother shot off through the air, came to the king's dun, and threw his torches upon the roof. They had just singed the straw a little, when Bran pushed them off with such force that they fell into the stream and were quenched.

"Who is this," screamed Cat-Head, "who dares to interfere with my ancestral right?"

"I," shouted Finn. Then the struggle began fiercer than with the second brother. Bran helped from behind, tearing the flesh from his head to his heels. But at length Cat-Head fastened his teeth into Finn's breast, biting and gnawing till Finn cut the head off. The body fell to the ground, but the head lived, gnawing as terribly as before. Do what they could it was impossible to kill it. Finn hacked and cut, but could neither kill nor pull it off. When nearly exhausted, Bran said:

"Why don't you chew your thumb?"

Finn chewed his thumb and reaching the marrow knew that the old woman in the east was ready to start with torches to find her sons, and burn the dun herself, and that she had a vial of liquid with which she could bring the sons to life; and that nothing could free him from Cat-Head but the old woman's blood.

After midnight the old hag, enraged at the delay of her sons, started and shot through the air like lightning, more swiftly than her sons. She threw her torches from afar upon the roof of the dun. But Bran as before hurled them into the stream.

Now the old woman circled around in the air looking for her sons. Finn was getting very weak from pain and loss of blood, for Cat-Head was biting at his breast all the time.

Bran called out, "Rouse yourself, O Finn. Use all your power or we are lost! If the old hag gets a drop from the vial upon the bodies of her sons, they will come to life, and then we're done for."

Thus roused, Finn with one spring reached the old woman in the air, and swept the bottle from her grasp; which falling upon the ground was emptied.

The old hag gave a scream which was heard all over the world, came to the ground, and closed with Finn. Then followed a battle greater than the world had ever known before that night, or has ever seen since. Water sprang out of grey rocks, cows cast their calves even when they had none, and hard rushes grew soft in the remotest corner of Erin, so desperate was the fighting and so awful, between Finn and the old hag. Finn would have died that night but for Bran.

Just as daylight was coming Finn swept the head off the old woman, caught some of her blood, and rubbed it around Cat-Head, who fell off dead.

He rubbed his own wounds with the blood and was cured; then rubbed some on Bran, who had been singed with the torches, and she was as well as ever. Finn, exhausted with fighting, dropped down and fell asleep.

While he was sleeping the chief steward of the king came to the dun, found it standing safe and sound, and seeing Finn lying there asleep knew that he had saved it. Bran tried to waken Finn, pulled and tugged, but could not rouse him.

The steward went to the king, and said, "I have saved the dun, and I claim the reward."

"It shall be given you," answered the king. And straightaway the steward was recognized as the king's son-in-law, and orders were given to make ready for the wedding.

Bran had listened to what was going on, and when her master woke, exactly at midday, she told him of all that was taking place in the castle of the king.

Finn went to the king, and said, "I have saved your dun, and I claim the reward."

"Oh," said the king, "my steward claimed the reward, and it has been given to him."

"He had nothing to do with saving the dun. I saved it," said Finn.

"Well," answered the king, "he is the first man who told me of its safety and claimed the reward."

"Bring him here. Let me look at him," said Finn.

He was sent for, and came. "Did you save the king's dun?" asked Finn. "I did," said the steward.

"You did not, and take that for your lies," said Finn; and striking him with the edge of his open hand swept the head off his body, dashing it against the other side of the room, flattening it like paste on the wall.

"You are the man," said the king to Finn, "who saved the dun; yours is the reward. All the champions, and there is many a man of them, who have failed to save it are in the dungeons of my fortress; their heads must be cut off before the wedding takes place."

"Will you let me see them?" asked Finn.

"I will," said the king.

Finn went down to the men, and found the first champions of Erin in the dungeons. "Will you obey me in all things if I save you from death?" said Finn. "We will," said they. Then he went back to the king and asked:

"Will you give me the lives of these champions of Erin, in place of your daughter's hand?"

"I will," said the king.

All the champions were liberated, and left the king's castle that day. Ever after they followed the orders of Finn, and these were the beginning of his forces and the first of the Fenians of Erin.

Li Chi Slays the Serpent
China

In Fukien, in the ancient state of Yüeh, stands the Yung mountain range, whose peaks sometimes reach a height of many miles. To the northwest there is a cleft in the mountains once inhabited by a giant serpent seventy or eighty feet long and wider than the span of ten hands. It kept the local people in a state of a constant terror and had already killed many commandants from the capital city and many magistrates and officers of nearby towns. Offerings of oxen and sheep did not appease the monster. By entering men's dreams and making its wishes known through mediums, it demanded young girls of twelve or thirteen to feast on.

Helpless, the commandant and the magistrates selected daughters of bondmaids or criminals and kept them until the appointed dates. One day in the eighth month of every year, they would deliver a girl to the mouth of the monster's cave, and the serpent would come out and swallow the victim. This continued for nine years until nine girls had been devoured.

In the tenth year the officials had again begun to look for a girl to hold in readiness for the appointed time. A man of Chianglo county, Li Tan, had raised six daughters and no sons. Chi, his youngest girl, responded to the search for a victim by volunteering. Her parents refused to allow it, but she said, "Dear parents, you have no one to depend on, for having brought forth six daughters and not a single son, it is as if you were childless. I could never compare with Ti Jung of the Han Dynasty, who offered herself as a bondmaid to the emperor in exchange for her father's life. I cannot take care of you in your old age; I only waste your food and clothes. Since I'm no use to you alive, why shouldn't I give up my life a little sooner? What could be wrong in selling me to gain a bit of money for yourselves?" But the father and mother loved her too much to consent, so she went in secret.

The volunteer then asked the authorities for a sharp sword and a snake-hunting dog. When the appointed day of the eighth month arrived, she seated herself in the temple, clutching the sword and leading the dog. First she took several pecks of rice balls moistened with malt sugar and placed them at the mouth of the serpent's cave,

The serpent appeared. Its head was a large as a rice barrel; its eyes were like mirrors two feet across. Smelling the fragrance of the rice balls, it opened its mouth to eat them. Then Li Chi unleashed the snake-hunting dog, which bit hard into the serpent. Li Chi herself came up from behind and scored the serpent with several deep cuts. The wounds hurt so terribly that the monster leaped into the open and died.

Li Chi went into the serpent's cave and recovered the skulls of the nine victims. She sighed as she brought them out, saying, "For your timidity you were devoured. How pitiful!" Slowly she made her way homeward.

The king of Yüeh learned of these events and made Li Chi his queen. He appointed her father magistrate of Chianglo county, and her mother and elder sisters were given riches. From that time forth, the district was free of monsters. Ballads celebrating Li Chi survive to this day.

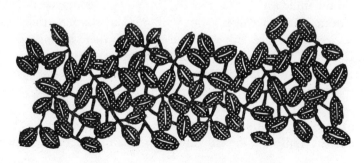

THE DEVIL WITH THE
THREE GOLDEN HAIRS
Germany

There was once a poor woman who gave birth to a little son; and as he came into the world with a caul on, it was predicted that in his fourteenth year he would have the king's daughter for his wife. It happened that soon afterwards the king came into the village, and no one knew that he was the king, and when he asked the people what news there was, they answered, "A child has just been born with a caul on; whatever anyone so born undertakes turns out well. It is prophesied, too, that in his fourteenth year he will have the king's daughter for his wife."

The king, who had a bad heart, and was angry about the prophecy, went to the parents, and, seeming quite friendly, said, "You poor people, let me have your child, and I will take care of it." At first they refused, but when the stranger offered them a large amount of gold for it and when they thought, "It is a child of good fortune, and everything must turn out well for it," they at last consented and gave him the child.

The king put it in a box and rode away with it until he came to a deep piece of water. Then he threw the box into it and thought, "I have freed my daughter from her undesired suitor."

The box, however, did not sink, but floated like a boat, and not a drop of water made its way into it. And it floated to within two miles of the king's chief city, where there was a mill, and it came to a halt at the milldam. A miller's boy, who by good luck was standing there, noticed it and pulled it out with a hook, thinking that he had found a great treasure, but when he opened it there lay a pretty boy inside, quite fresh and lively. He took him to the miller and his wife, and as they had no children they were glad and said, "God has given him to us." They took great care of the foundling, and he grew up in all goodness.

It happened that once in a storm the king went into the mill, and he asked the millfolk if the tall youth were their son. "No," answered they, "he's a foundling. Fourteen years ago he floated down to the milldam in a box, and the miller's boy pulled him out of the water."

Then the king knew that it was none other than the child of good fortune which he had thrown into the water, and he said, "My good people, could not the youth take a letter to the queen? I will give him two gold pieces as a reward."

"Just as the king commands," answered they, and they told the boy to hold himself in readiness. Then the king wrote a letter to the queen, wherein he said, "As soon as the boy arrives with this letter, let him be killed and buried, and all must be done before I come home."

The boy set out with this letter; but he lost his way, and in the evening came to a large forest. In the darkness he saw a small light; he went towards it and reached a cottage. When he went in, an old woman was sitting by the fire quite alone. She started when she saw the boy, and said; "Whence do you come, and whither are you going?"

"I come from the mill," he answered, "and wish to go to the queen, to whom I am taking a letter; but as I have lost my way in the forest I should like to stay here overnight."

"You poor boy," said the woman, "you have come into a den of thieves, and when they come home they will kill you."

"Let them come," said the boy, "I am not afraid. But I am so tired that I cannot go any farther." And he stretched himself upon a bench and fell asleep.

Soon afterwards the robbers came and angrily asked what strange boy was lying there. "Ah," said the old woman, "it is an innocent child who has lost himself in the forest, and out of pity I have let him come in. He has to take a letter to the queen."

The robbers opened the letter and read it, and in it was written that the boy as soon as he arrived should be put to death. Then the hard-hearted robbers felt pity, and their leader tore up the letter and wrote another, saying, that as soon as the boy came, he should be married at once to the king's daughter. Then they let him lie quietly on the bench until the next morning, and when he awoke they gave him the letter and showed him the right way.

And the queen, when she had received the letter and read it, did as was written in it, and had a splendid wedding feast prepared, and the king's daughter was married to the child of good fortune. And as the youth was handsome and friendly, she lived with him in joy and contentment.

After some time the king returned to his palace and saw that the prophecy was fulfilled, and the child married to his daughter. "How has that come to pass?" said he. "I gave quite another order in my letter."

So the queen gave him the letter and said that he might see for himself what was written in it. The king read the letter and saw quite well that it had been exchanged for the other. He asked the youth what had become of the letter entrusted to him and why he had brought another instead of it.

"I know nothing about it," answered he. "It must have been changed in the night, when I slept in the forest."

The king said in a passion, "You shall not have everything quite so much your own way. Whosoever marries my daughter must fetch me from Hell three golden hairs from the head of the Devil. Bring me what I want, and you shall keep my daughter." In this way the king hoped to be rid of him forever.

But the child of good fortune answered, "I will fetch the golden hairs. I am not afraid of the Devil." Whereupon he took leave of them and began his journey.

The road led him to a large town, where the watchman by the gates asked him what his trade was and what he knew. "I know everything," answered the child of good fortune.

"Then you can do us a favor," said the watchman, "if you will tell us why our market fountain, which once flowed with wine, has become dry and no longer gives even water."

"That you shall know," answered he. "Only wait until I come back."

Then he went farther and came to another town, and there also the gatekeeper asked him what was his trade and what he knew.

"I know everything," answered he.

"Then you can do us a favor and tell us why a tree in our town which once bore golden apples now does not even put forth leaves."

"You shall know that," answered he. "Only wait until I come back."

Then he went on and came to a wide river over which he must cross. The ferryman asked him what his trade was and what he knew.

"I know everything," answered he.

"Then you can do me a favor," said the ferryman, "and tell me why I must always be rowing backwards and forwards and am never set free."

"You shall know that," answered he. "Only wait until I come back."

When he had crossed the water he found the entrance to Hell.

It was black and sooty within, and the Devil was not at home, but his grandmother was sitting in a large armchair.

"What do you want?" said she to him, but she did not look so very wicked.

"I should like to have three golden hairs from the Devil's head," answered he, "else I cannot keep my wife."

"That is a good deal to ask for," said she. "If the Devil comes home and finds you, it will cost you your life; but as I pity you, I will see if I cannot help you."

She changed him into an ant and said, "Creep into the folds of my dress, you will be safe there."

"Yes," answered he, "so far, so good. But there are three things besides that I want to know: why a fountain which once flowed with wine has become dry and no longer gives even water; why a tree which once bore golden apples does not even put forth leaves; and why a ferryman must always be going backwards and forwards and is never set free."

"Those are difficult questions," answered she, "but just be silent and quiet and pay attention to what the Devil says when I pull out the three golden hairs."

As the evening came on, the Devil returned home. No sooner had he entered than he noticed that the air was not pure. "I smell man's flesh," said he. "All is not right here." Then he pried into every corner, and searched, but could not find anything. His grandmother scolded him. "It has just been swept," said she, "and everything put in order, and now you are upsetting it again. You have always got man's flesh in your nose. Sit down and eat your supper."

When he had eaten and drunk he was tired, and laid his head in his grandmother's lap and told her she should louse him a little. It was not long before he was fast asleep, snoring and breathing heavily. Then the old woman took hold of a golden hair, pulled it out, and laid it down beside her.

"Oh!" cried the Devil, "what are you doing?"

"I have had a bad dream," answered the grandmother, "so I seized hold of your hair."

"What did you dream then?" said the Devil.

"I dreamt that a fountain in a marketplace from which wine once flowed was dried up, and not even water would flow out of it. What is the cause of it?"

"Oh, ho! if they did but know it," answered the Devil, "there is a toad sitting under a stone in the well; if they killed it, the wine would flow again."

The grandmother loused him again until he went to sleep and snored so that the windows shook. Then she pulled the second hair out.

"Ha! what are you doing?" cried the Devil angrily.

"Do not take it ill," said she, "I did it in a dream."

"What have you dreamt this time?" asked he.

"I dreamt that in a certain kingdom there stood an apple tree which had once borne golden apples, but now would not even bear leaves. What, think you, was the reason?"

"Oh! if they did but know," answered the Devil. "A mouse is gnawing at the root; if they killed it they would have golden apples again, but if it gnaws much longer the tree will wither altogether. But I have had enough of your dreams. If you disturb me in my sleep again you will get a box on the ear."

The grandmother spoke gently to him and picked his lice once more until he fell asleep and snored. Then she took hold of the third golden hair and pulled it out. The Devil jumped up, roared out, and would have treated her ill is she had not quieted him again and said, "Who can help bad dreams?"

"What was the dream, then?" asked he, and was quite curious.

"I dreamt of a ferryman who complained that he must always ferry from one side to the other, and was never released. What is the cause of it?"

"Ah! the fool," answered the Devil. "When anyone comes and wants to go across he must put the oar in his hand, and the other man will have to ferry and he will be free."

As the grandmother had plucked out the three golden hairs, and the three questions were answered, she let the old Devil alone, and he slept until daybreak.

When the Devil had gone out again the old woman took the ant out of the folds of her dress, and gave the child of good fortune his human shape again. "There are the three golden hairs for you," said she. "What the Devil said to your three questions, I suppose you heard?"

"Yes," answered he, "I heard, and will take care to remember."

"You have what you want," said she, "and now you can go your way."

He thanked the old woman for helping him in his need, and left Hell well content that everything had turned out so fortunately.

When he came to the ferryman he was expected to give the promised answer. "Ferry me across first," said the child of good fortune, "and then I will tell you how you can be set free," and when he had reached the opposite shore, he gave him the Devil's advice: "Next time anyone comes who wants to be ferried over, just put the oar in his hand."

He went on and came to the town wherein stood the unfruitful tree, and there too the watchman wanted an answer. So he told him what he had heard from the Devil: "Kill the mouse which is gnawing at its root, and it will again bear golden apples." Then the watchman thanked him, and gave him as a reward two asses laden with gold, which followed him.

Finally, he came to the town whose well was dry. He told the watchman what the Devil had said: "A toad is in the well beneath a stone; you must find it and kill it, and the well will again give wine in plenty." The watchman thanked him, and also gave him two asses laden with gold.

At last the child of good fortune got home to his wife, who was heartily glad to see him again and to hear how well he had prospered in everything. To the king he took what he had asked for, the Devil's three golden hairs, and when the king saw the four asses laden with gold he was quite content, and said, "Now all the conditions are fulfilled, and you can keep my daughter. But tell me, dear son-in-law, where did all that gold come from? This is tremendous wealth!"

"I was rowed across a river," answered he, "and got it there. It lies on the shore instead of sand."

"Can I too fetch some of it?" said the king, and he was quite eager about it.

"As much as you like," answered he. "There is a ferryman on the river; let him ferry you over, and you can fill your sacks on the other side."

The greedy king set out in all haste, and when he came to the river he beckoned to the ferryman to put him across. The ferryman came and bade him get in, and when they got to the other shore he put the oar in his hand and sprang out. But from this time forth the king had to ferry as a punishment for his sins. Perhaps he is ferrying still? If he is, it is because no one has taken the oar from him.

THE LONGWITTON DRAGON
England

In a wood not far from the village of Longwitton are three wells which have been famous for many years. Long ago people used to travel from far and near to drink the water from the wells, for it was as sweet as wine and had great healing powers. Many a shepherd whose bones ached after the long, wet winter on the hills came to drink and ease his pains, and many a sickly child found new health there. The people of Longwitton were justly proud of their wells, for there seemed to be magic in them.

One day, however, a plowman, going to quench his thirst, was alarmed to find a huge dragon there. It had coiled its tail round one of the trees, and pushed its long black tongue into the well, and was lapping the water like a dog. When it heard him approach it vanished; but the plowman knew that it had only made itself invisible, for he heard its claws in the dead leaves, and felt its hot breath on his face. He fled from it in terror, and only escaped by zigzagging through the trees.

From that day no pilgrim dared visit the magic wells, for the dragon haunted them. It was a fearsome monster, with a skin as warty as a toad's and a long tail like a big lizard's. It tore up the ground with its claws, and scraped the bark from the trees as it brushed past them. But few people caught sight of it, for when anyone drew near it made itself invisible, and nothing could be seen except the leaves trembling before its breath and the flowers being crushed beneath its feet. It did little harm, and seemed content to live alone in the wood and drink from the wells; but whenever the men of Longwitton set out to attack it, it was infuriated, and the trees shook round about it as if a whirlwind had suddenly struck the wood. It seemed to have claimed the wells and would not give them up to anyone. The wells grew overgrown and untidy, while the shepherds had to nurse their aches as best they could.

But one day there came riding by Longwitton a knight in search of adventure.

"We have here a jealous dragon, sir," said the people of Long-witton to him, "which we would gladly be rid of, but it has the power of making itself invisible, and no man can get near enough to strike a blow at it."

"I will overcome that difficulty," said the knight. "I will stay here tonight, and give battle to the dragon tomorrow."

So the next morning he annointed his eyes with a magic ointment which he had been given on his travels, and rode to the wood. The dragon was lying sleeping near one of the wells, but when it heard the sound of the horse's hoofs in the dry leaves its ears pricked up, and the spines on its back rose. Then, trusting to its invisibility, it charged. The knight was ready. The dragon, overcareless, struck wildly with its claws, and the knight plunged his sword into its side. The dragon roared with pain, for the wound was severe, but it backed quickly, until it stood defending the well, and prepared to attack again. But no matter how dreadful a wound the knight inflicted, the dragon seemed to keep its strength, and the wounds healed as quickly as they were received. For hours they fought, the dragon with its clumsy movements being no match for the nimbler man; but at last the knight, worn out and arm-weary, rode away.

He was almost ashamed to confess his failure to the villagers, but he was not easily dismayed.

"I will fight the dragon again tomorrow," he said.

But the next day, although he delivered enough blows to kill a thousand dragons, the beast was as strong at the end of the day as at the beginning, and the knight was forced to retire again.

"I will try a third time," he said. "This dragon must possess some other magical power which I have not noticed. Tomorrow I will use my eyes more and my arm less."

So he went out the third day, and for the third time attacked the dragon. But this time, as he laid about him, he kept his eyes wide open, and at last he noticed that, no matter how fiercely he drove against the dragon, it would not stir from the well; and then looking more clearly he observed that it always lay so that the tip of its tail dipped into the water.

"Ah! That is the secret," he said. And he dismounted from his horse, and led it a little into the wood. Then he approached the dragon on foot, and pierced it lightly here and there till, enraged, it roared wildly and leapt at him. Then he retreated, fighting faintly and de-luding the monster into thinking that he was exhausted and beaten. Step by step he fell back until he had lured it from the well. Then, suddenly leaping onto his horse, he rode round the dragon, and placed himself between it and the well. The dragon, perceiving how it had been tricked, roared like a mad bull and fought desperately to get back to the well. But this knight, knowing now that he had mastered it, dealt it blow on blow, and this time every wound weakened it more and more. The blood dripped from its side and burned the grass beneath it; it grew feebler and feebler until it fell heavily and lay still.

The next day the people of Longwitton buried it. Then they tidied the wells, and sent out news that the monster was dead, and there was rejoicing that night in every cottage for twenty miles round.

THE ORPHAN BOY AND THE ELK DOG
American Indian (Blackfoot)

In the days when people had only dogs to carry their bundles, two orphan children, a boy and his sister, were having a hard time. The boy was deaf, and because he could not understand what people said, they thought him foolish and dull-witted. Even his relatives wanted nothing to do with him. The name he had been given at birth, while his parents still lived, was Long Arrow. Now he was like a beaten, mangy dog, the kind who hungrily roams outside a camp, circling it from afar, smelling the good meat boiling in the kettles but never coming close for fear of being kicked. Only his sister, who was bright and beautiful, loved him.

Then the sister was adopted by a family from another camp, people who were attracted by her good looks and pleasing ways. Though they wanted her for a daughter, they certainly did not want the awkward, stupid boy. And so they took away the only person who cared about him, and the orphan boy was left to fend for himself. He lived on scraps thrown to the dogs and things he found on the refuse heaps. He dressed in remnants of skins and frayed robes discarded by the poorest people. At night he bedded down in a grass-lined dugout, like an animal in its den.

Eventually the game was hunted out near the camp that the boy regarded as his, and the people decided to move. The lodges were taken down, belongings were packed into rawhide bags and put on dog travois, and the village departed. "Stay here," they told the boy. "We don't want your kind coming with us."

For two or three days the boy fed on scraps the people had left behind, but he knew he would starve if he stayed. He had to join his people, whether they liked it or not. He followed their tracks, frantic that he would lose them, and crying at the same time. Soon the sweat was running down his skinny body. As he was stumbling, running, panting, something suddenly snapped in his left ear with a sound like a small crack, and a wormlike substance came out of that ear. All at once on his left side he could hear birdsongs for the first time. He took this wormlike thing in his left hand and hurried on. Then there was a snap in his right ear and a wormlike thing came out of it, and on his right side he could hear the rushing waters of a stream. His hearing was restored! And it was razor-sharp—he could make out the rustling of a tiny mouse in dry leaves a good distance away. The orphan boy laughed and was happy for the first time in his life. With renewed courage he followed the trail his people had made.

In the meantime the village had settled into its new place. Men were already out hunting. Thus the boy came upon Good Running, a kindly old chief, butchering a fat buffalo cow he had just killed. When the chief saw the boy, he said to himself, "Here comes that poor good-for-nothing boy. It was wrong to abandon him." To the boy Good Running said "Rest here, grandson, you're sweaty and covered with dust. Here, have some tripe."

The boy wolfed down the meat. He was not used to hearing and talking yet, but his eyes were alert and Good Running also noticed a change in his manner. "This boy," the chief said to himself, "is neither stupid nor crazy." He gave the orphan a piece of the hump meat, then a piece of liver, then a piece of raw kidney, and at last the very best kind of meat—a slice of tongue. The more the old man looked at the boy, the more he liked him. On the spur of the moment he said, "Grandson, I'm going to adopt you; there's a place for you in my tipi. And I'm going to make you into a good hunter and warrior." The boy wept, this time for joy. Good Running said, "They called you a stupid, crazy boy, but now that I think of it, the name you were given at birth is Long Arrow. I'll see that people call you by your right name. Now come along."

The chief's wife was not pleased. "Why do you put this burden on me," she said, "bringing into our lodge this good-for-nothing, this slow-witted crazy boy? Maybe you're a little slow-witted and crazy yourself!"

"Woman, keep talking like that and I'll beat you! This boy isn't slow or crazy; he's a good boy, and I have taken him for my grandson. Look—he's barefooted. Hurry up, and make a pair of moccasins for him, and if you don't do it well I'll take a stick to you."

Good Running's wife grumbled but did as she was told. Her husband was a kind man, but when aroused, his anger was great.

So a new life began for Long Arrow. He had to learn to speak and to understand well, and to catch up on all the things a boy should know. He was a fast learner and soon surpassed other boys his age in knowledge and skills. At last even Good Running's wife accepted him.

He grew up into a fine young hunter, tall and good-looking in the quilled buckskin outfit the chief's wife made for him. He helped his grandfather in everything and became a staff for Good Running to lean on. But he was lonely, for most people in the camp could not forget that Long Arrow had once been an outcast. "Grandfather," he said one day, "I want to do something to make you proud and show people that you were wise to adopt me. What can I do?"

Good Running answered, "Someday you will be a chief and do great things."

"But what's a great thing I could do now, Grandfather?"

The chief thought for a long time. "Maybe I shouldn't tell you this," he said. "I love you and don't want to lose you. But on winter nights, men talk of powerful spirit people living at the bottom of a faraway lake. Down in that lake the spirit people keep mystery animals who do their work for them. These animals are larger than a great elk, but they carry the burdens of the spirit people like dogs. So they're called Pono-Kamita—Elk Dogs. They are said to be swift, strong, gentle, and beautiful beyond imagination. Every fourth generation, one of our young warriors has gone to find these spirit folk and bring back an Elk Dog for us. But none of our brave young men has ever returned."

"Grandfather, I'm not afraid. I'll go and find the Elk Dog."

"Grandson, first learn to be a man. Learn the right prayers and ceremonies. Be brave. Be generous and open-handed. Pity the old and the fatherless, and let the holy men of the tribe find a medicine for you which will protect you on your dangerous journey. We will begin by purifying you in the sweat bath."

So Long Arrow was purified with the white steam of the sweat lodge. He was taught how to use the pipe, and how to pray to the Great Mystery Power. The tribe's holy men gave him a medicine and made for him a shield with designs on it to ward off danger.

Then one morning, without telling anybody, Good Running loaded his best travois dog with all the things Long Arrow would need for traveling. The chief gave him his medicine, his shield, and his own fine bow and, just as the sun came up, went with his grandson to the edge of the camp to purify him with sweet-smelling cedar smoke. Long Arrow left unheard and unseen by anyone else. After a while some people noticed that he was gone, but no one except his grandfather knew where and for what purpose.

Following Good Running's advice, Long Arrow wandered southward. On the fourth day of his journey he came to a small pond, where a strange man was standing as if waiting for him. "Why have you come here?" the stranger asked.

"I have come to find the mysterious Elk Dog."

"Ah, there I cannot help you," said the man, who was the spirit of the pond. "But if you travel further south, four-times-four days, you might chance upon a bigger lake and there meet one of my uncles. Possibly he might talk to you; then again, he might not. That's all I can tell you."

Long Arrow thanked the man, who went down to the bottom of the pond, where he lived.

Long Arrow wandered on, walking for long hours and taking little time for rest. Through deep canyons and over high mountains he went, wearing out his moccasins and enduring cold and heat, hunger and thirst.

Finally Long Arrow approached a big lake surrounded by steep pine-covered hills. There he came face to face with a tall man, fierce and scowling and twice the height of most humans. This stranger carried a long lance with a heavy spearpoint made of shining flint. "Young one," he growled, "why did you come here?"

"I came to find the mysterious Elk Dog."

The stranger, who was the spirit of the lake, stuck his face right into Long Arrow's and shook his mighty lance. "Little one, aren't you afraid of me?" he snarled.

"No, I am not," answered Long Arrow, smiling.

The tall spirit man gave a hideous grin, which was his way of being friendly. "I like small humans who aren't afraid," he said, "but I can't help you. Perhaps our grandfather will take the trouble to listen to you. More likely he won't. Walk south for four-times-four days, and maybe you'll find him. But probably you won't." With that the tall spirit turned his back on Long Arrow and went to the bottom of the lake, where he lived.

Long Arrow walked on for another four-times-four days, sleeping and resting little. By now he staggered and stumbled in his weakness, and his dog was not much better off. At last he came to the biggest lake he had ever seen, surrounded by towering snow-capped peaks and waterfalls of ice. This time there was nobody to receive him. As a matter of fact, there seemed to be no living thing around. "This must be the Great Mystery Lake," thought Long Arrow. Exhausted, he fell down upon the shortgrass meadow by the lake, fell down among the wild flowers, and went to sleep with his tired dog curled up at his feet.

When Long Arrow awoke, the sun was already high. He opened his eyes and saw a beautiful child standing before him, a boy in a dazzling white buckskin robe decorated with porcupine quills of many colors. The boy said, "We have been expecting you for a long time. My grandfather invites you to his lodge. Follow me."

Telling his dog to wait, Long Arrow took his medicine shield and his grandfather's bow and went with the wonderful child. They came to the edge of the lake. The spirit boy pointed to the water and said, "My grandfather's lodge is down there. Come!" The child turned himself into a kingfisher and dove straight to the bottom.

Afraid, Long Arrow thought, "How can I follow him and not be drowned?" But then he said to himself, "I knew all the time that this would not be easy. In setting out to find the Elk Dog, I already threw my life away." And he boldly jumped into the water. To his surprise, he found it did not make him wet, that it parted before him, that he could breathe and see. He touched the lake's sandy bottom. It sloped down, down toward a center point.

Long Arrow descended this slope until he came to a small flat valley. In the middle of it stood a large tipi of tanned buffalo hide. The images of two strange animals were drawn on it in sacred vermilion paint. A kingfisher perched high on the top of the tipi flew down and turned again into the beautiful boy, who said, "Welcome. Enter my grandfather's lodge."

Long Arrow followed the spirit boy inside. In the back at the seat of honor sat a black-robed old man with flowing white hair and such power emanating from him that Long Arrow felt himself in the presence of a truly Great One. The holy man welcomed Long Arrow and offered him food. The man's wife came in bringing dishes of buffalo hump, liver, tongues, delicious chunks of deer meat, the roasted flesh of strange, tasty water birds, and meat pounded together with berries, chokecherries, and kidney fat. Famished after his long journey, Long Arrow ate with relish. Yet he still looked around to admire the furnishings of the tipi, the painted inner curtain, the many medi-

cine shields, wonderfully wrought weapons, shirts and robes decorated with porcupine quills in rainbow colors, beautifully painted
rawhide containers filled with wonderful things, and much else that
dazzled him.

After Long Arrow had stilled his hunger, the old spirit chief
filled the pipe and passed it to his guest. They smoked, praying
silently. After a while the old man said, "Some came before you from
time to time, but they were always afraid of the deep water, and so
they went away with empty hands. But you, grandson, were brave
enough to plunge in, and therefore you are chosen to receive a wonderful gift to carry back to your people. Now, go outside with my
grandson."

The beautiful boy took Long Arrow to a meadow on which
some strange animals, unlike any the young man had ever seen, were
galloping and gamboling, neighing and nickering. They were truly
wonderful to look at, with their glossy coats fine as a maiden's hair,
their long manes and tails streaming in the wind. Now rearing, now
nuzzling, they looked at Long Arrow with gentle eyes which belied
their fiery appearance.

"At last," thought Long Arrow, "here they are before my own
eyes, the Pono-Kamita, the Elk Dogs!"

"Watch me," said the mystery boy, "so that you learn to do
what I am doing." Gracefully and without effort, the boy swung
himself onto the back of a jet-black Elk Dog with a high, arched
neck. Larger than any elk Long Arrow had ever come across, the
animal carried the boy all over the meadow swiftly as the wind. Then
the boy returned, jumped off his mount, and said, "Now you try
it." A little timidly Long Arrow climbed up on the beautiful Elk
Dog's back. Seemingly regarding him as feather-light, it took off like
a flying arrow. The young man felt himself soaring through the air
as a bird does, and experienced a happiness greater even than the joy
he had felt when Good Running had adopted him as a grandson.

When they had finished riding the Elk Dogs, the spirit boy said
to Long Arrow, "Young hunter from the land above the waters, I
want you to have what you have come for. Listen to me. You may
have noticed that my grandfather wears a black medicine robe as long
as a woman's dress, and that he is always trying to hide his feet. Try
to get a glimpse of them, for if you do, he can refuse you nothing.
He will then tell you to ask him for a gift, and you must ask for these
three things: his rainbow-colored quilled belt, his black medicine
robe, and a herd of these animals which you seem to like."

Long Arrow thanked him and vowed to follow his advice. For

four days the young man stayed in the spirit chief's lodge, where he ate well and often went out riding on the Elk Dogs. But try as he would, he could never get a look at the old man's feet. The spirit chief always kept them carefully covered. Then on the morning of the fourth day, the old one was walking out of the tipi when his medicine robe caught in the entrance flap. As the robe opened, Long Arrow caught a glimpse of a leg and one foot. He was awed to see that it was not a human limb at all, but the glossy leg and firm hoof of an Elk Dog! He could not stifle a cry of surprise, and the old man looked over his shoulder and saw that his leg and hoof were exposed. The chief seemed a little embarrassed, but shrugged and said, "I tried to hide this, but you must have been fated to see it. Look, both of my feet are those of an Elk Dog. You may as well ask me for a gift. Don't be timid; tell me what you want."

Long Arrow spoke boldly: "I want three things: your belt of rainbow colors, you black medicine robe, and your herd of Elk Dogs."

"Well, so you're really not timid at all!" said the old man. "You ask for a lot, and I'll give it to you, except that you cannot have all my Elk Dogs; I'll give you half of them. Now I must tell you that my black medicine robe and my many-colored belt have Elk Dog magic in them. Always wear the robe when you try to catch Elk Dogs; then they can't get away from you. On quiet nights, if you listen closely to the belt, you will hear the Elk Dog dance song and Elk Dog prayers. You must learn them. And I will give you one more magic gift: this long rope woven from the hair of a white buffalo bull. With it you will never fail to catch whichever Elk Dog you want."

The spirit chief presented him with the gifts and said, "Now you must leave. At first the Elk Dogs will not follow you. Keep the medicine robe and the magic belt on at all times, and walk for four days toward the north. Never look back—always look to the north. On the fourth day the Elk Dogs will come up beside you on the left. Still don't look back. But after they have overtaken you, catch one with the rope of white buffalo hair and ride him home. Don't lose the black robe, or you will lose the Elk Dogs and never catch them again."

Long Arrow listened carefully so that he would remember. Then the old spirit chief had his wife make up a big pack of food, almost too heavy for Long Arrow to carry, and the young man took leave of his generous spirit host. The mysterious boy once again turned himself into a kingfisher and led Long Arrow to the surface of the lake, where his faithful dog greeted him joyfully. Long Arrow fed the dog, put his pack of food on the travois, and started walking north.

On the fourth day the Elk Dogs came up on his left side, as the spirit chief had foretold. Long Arrow snared the black one with the arched neck to ride, and he caught another to carry the pack of food. They galloped swiftly on, the dog barking at the big Elk Dogs' heels.

When Long Arrow arrived at last in his village, the people were afraid and hid. They did not recognize him astride his beautiful Elk Dog but took him for a monster, half man and half animal. Long Arrow kept calling, "Grandfather Good Running, it's your grandson. I've come back bringing Elk Dogs!"

Recognizing the voice, Good Running came out of hiding and wept for joy, because he had given Long Arrow up for lost. Then all the others emerged from their hiding places to admire the wonderful new animals.

Long Arrow said, "My grandfather and grandmother who adopted me, I can never repay you for your kindness. Accept these wonderful Elk Dogs as my gift. Now we no longer need to be humble foot-sloggers, because these animals will carry us swiftly everywhere we want to go. Now buffalo hunting will be easy. Now our tipis will be larger, our possessions will be greater, because an Elk Dog travois can carry a load ten times bigger than that of a dog. Take them, my grandparents. I shall keep for myself only this black male and this black female, which will grow into a fine herd."

"You have indeed done something great, grandson," said Good Running, and he spoke true. The people became the bold riders of the Plains and soon could hardly imagine how they had existed without these wonderful animals.

After some time Good Running, rich and honored by all, said to Long Arrow, "Grandson, lead us to the Great Mystery Lake so we can camp by its shores. Let's visit the spirt chief and the wondrous boy; maybe they will give us more of their power and magic gifts."

Long Arrow led the people southward and again found the Great Mystery Lake. But the waters would no longer part for him, nor would any of the kingfishers they saw turn into a boy. Nor, gazing down into the crystal-clear water, could they discover people, Elk Dogs, or a tipi. There was nothing in the lake but a few fish.

MOLLY WHUPPIE
England

Once upon a time there was a man and a wife had too many children, and they could not get meat for them, so they took the three youngest and left them in a wood. They traveled and traveled and could see never a house. It began to be dark, and they were hungry. At last they saw a light and made for it; it turned out to be a house. They knocked at the door, and a woman came to it, who said, "What do you want?"

They said, "Please let us in and give us something to eat."

The woman said, "I can't do that, as my man is a giant, and he would kill you if he comes home."

They begged hard. "Let us stop for a little while," said they, "and we will go away before he comes." So she took them in, and set them down before the fire, and gave them milk and bread; but just as they had begun to eat, a great knock came to the door, and a dreadful voice said:

> *Fee, fie, fo, fum,*
> *I smell the blood of some earthly one.*

"Who have you there, wife?"

"Eh," said the wife, "it's three poor lassies cold and hungry, and they will go away. Ye won't touch 'em, man."

He said nothing, but ate up a big supper, and ordered them to stay all night.

Now he had three lassies of his own, and they were to sleep in the same bed with the three strangers. The youngest of the three strange lassies was called Molly Whuppie, and she was very clever. She noticed that before they went to bed the giant put straw ropes round her neck and her sisters', and round his own lassies' necks, he put gold chains. So Molly took care and did not fall asleep, but waited till she was sure everyone was sleeping sound. Then she slipped out of the bed, and took the straw ropes off her own and her sisters' necks, and took the gold chains off the giant's lassies. She then put the straw ropes on the giant's lassies and the gold on herself and her sisters, and lay down. And in the middle of the night up rose the giant, armed with a great club, and felt for the necks with the straw. It was dark. He took his own lassies out of bed on to the floor, and battered them until they were dead, and then lay down again, thinking he had managed finely.

Molly thought it time she and her sisters were off and away, so she wakened them and told them to be quiet, and they slipped out of the house. They all got out safe, and they ran and ran, and never stopped until morning, when they saw a grand house before them. It turned out to be a king's house: so Molly went in, and told her story to the king.

He said, "Well, Molly, you are a clever girl, and you have managed well, but, if you would manage better, and go back and steal the giant's sword that hangs on the back of his bed, I would give your eldest sister my eldest son to marry."

Molly said she would try. So she went back, and managed to slip into the giant's house, and crept in below the bed. The giant came home, and ate up a great supper, and went to bed. Molly waited until he was snoring, and she crept out, and reached over the giant and got down the sword; but just as she got it out over the bed it gave a rattle, and up jumped the giant, and Molly ran out at the door and the sword with her; and she ran, and he ran, till they came to the "Bridge of one hair," and she got over, but he couldn't, and he says, "Woe worth ye, Molly Whuppie! never ye come again."

And she says, "Twice yet, carle," quoth she, "I'll come to Spain." So Molly took the sword to the king, and her sister was married to his son.

Well, the king he says, "Ye've managed well, Molly, but if ye would manage better, and steal the purse that lies below the giant's pillow, I would marry your second sister to my second son."

And Molly said she would try. So she set out for the giant's house, and slipped in, and hid again below the bed, and waited till the giant had eaten his supper, and was snoring sound asleep. She slipped out and slipped her hand below the pillow, and got out the purse; but just as she was going out the giant awakened, and ran after her; and she ran, and he ran, till they came to the "Bridge of one hair," and she got over, but he couldn't, and he said, "Woe worth ye, Molly Whuppie! never you come again."

"Once yet, carle," quoth she, "I'll come to Spain." So Molly took the purse to the king, and her second sister was married to the king's second son.

After that the king says to Molly, "Molly, you are a clever girl, but if you would do better yet, and steal the giant's ring that he wears on his finger, I will give you my youngest son for yourself."

Molly said she would try. So back she goes to the giant's house, and hides herself below the bed. The giant wasn't long ere he came home, and, after he had eaten a great big supper, he went to his bed, and shortly was snoring loud. Molly crept out and reached over the bed, and got hold of the giant's hand, and she pulled and she pulled until she got off the ring; but just as she got it off the giant got up, and gripped her by the hand and he says, "Now I have caught you, Molly Whuppie, and, if I had done as much ill to you as ye have done to me, what would ye do to me?"

Molly says, "I would put you into a sack, and I'd put the cat inside wi' you, and the dog aside you, and a needle and thread and a shears, and I'd hang you up upon the wall, and I'd go to the wood, and choose the thickest stick I could get, and I would come home, and take you down, and bang you till you were dead."

"Well, Molly," says the giant, "I'll just do that to you."

So he gets a sack, and puts Molly into it, and the cat and the dog beside her, and needle and thread and shears, and hangs her upon the wall, and goes to the wood to choose a stick.

Molly she sings out, "Oh, if ye saw what I see."

"Oh," says the giant's wife, "what do ye see, Molly?"

But Molly never said a word but, "Oh, if ye saw what I see!"

The giant's wife begged that Molly would take her up into the sack till she would see what Molly saw. So Molly took the shears and cut a hole in the sack, and took out the needle and thread with her, and jumped down and helped the giant's wife up into the sack, and sewed up the hole.

The giant's wife saw nothing, and began to ask to get down again; but Molly never minded, but hid herself at the back of the door. Home came the giant, and a great big tree in his hand, and he took down the sack, and began to batter it.

His wife cried, "It's me, man," but the dog barked and the cat mewed, and he did not know his wife's voice.

But Molly came out from the back of the door, and the giant saw her and he after her; and he ran, and she ran, till they came to the "Bridge of one hair," and she got over but he couldn't; and he said, "Woe worth you, Molly Whuppie! never you come again."

"Never more, carle," quoth she, "will I come again to Spain."

So Molly took the ring to the king, and she was married to his youngest son, and she never saw the giant again.

THE BEGINNING OF THE NARRAN LAKE
Australia (Aboriginal)

Old Baiame said to his two young wives, Birra-nulu and Kunnan-beili, "I have stuck a white feather between the hind legs of a bee, and am going to let it go and then follow it to its nest, that I may get honey. While I go for the honey, go you two out and get frogs and yams, then meet me at Coorigil Spring, where we will camp, for sweet and clear is the water there."

The wives, taking their goolays, or net bags, and yam sticks, went out as he told them. Having gone far, and dug out many yams and frogs, they were tired when they reached Coorigil, and seeing the cool, fresh water they longed to bathe. But first they built a bough shade, and there left the goolays holding their food, and the yams and frogs they had found.

When their camp was ready for the coming of Baiame, who having wooed his wives with a nulla-nulla kept them obedient by fear of the same weapon, then went the girls to the spring to bathe. Gladly they plunged in, having first divested themselves of their goomillas, or string belts, which they were still young enough to wear, and which they left on the ground near the spring.

Scarcely were they enjoying the cool rest the water gave their hot, tired limbs, when they were seized and swallowed by two Kurrias, or crocodiles.

Having swallowed the girls the Kurrias dived into an opening in the side of the spring, which was the entrance to an underground watercourse leading to the Narran River. Through this passage they went, taking all the water from the spring with them into the Narran, whose course they also dried as they went along.

Meantime Baiame, unwitting the fate of his wives, was honey

hunting. He had followed the bee with the white feather on it for some distance; then the bee flew on to some boodha, or saltbush flowers, and would move no farther.

Baiame said, "Something has happened, or the bee would not stay here and refuse to be moved on towards its nest. I must go to Coorigil Spring and see if my wives are safe. Something terrible has surely happened."

And Baiame turned in haste towards the spring.

When he reached there he saw the bough shed his wives had made, he saw the yams they had dug from the ground, and he saw the frogs, but Birra-nulu and Kunnan-beili he saw not.

He called aloud for them. But no answer. He went towards the spring; on the edge of it he saw the goomillas of his wives. He looked into the spring and, seeing it dry, he said, "It is the work of the Kurrias; they have opened the underground passage and gone with my wives to the river, and opening the passage has dried the spring. Well do I know where the passage joins the Narran, and there will I swiftly go."

Arming himself with spears and woggaras, he started in pursuit.

He soon reached the deep hole where the underground channel of the Coorigil joined the Narran. There he saw what he had never seen before, namely, this deep hole gone dry. And he said, "They have emptied the holes as they went along, taking the water with them. But well know I the deep holes of the river. I will not follow the bend, thus trebling the distance I have to go, but I will cut across from big hole to big hole, and by so doing I may yet get ahead of the Kurrias."

Swiftly on sped Baiame, making short cuts from big hole to big hole, and his track is still marked by the morillas, or pebbly ridges, that stretch down the Narran, pointing in towards the deep holes.

Every hole as he came to it he found dry, until at last he reached the end of the Narran; the hole there was still quite wet and muddy. Then he knew he was near his enemies, and soon he saw them.

He managed to get, unseen, a little way ahead of the Kurrias. He hid himself behind a big dheal tree. As the Kurrias came near they separated, one turning to go in another direction. Quickly Baiame hurled one spear after another, wounding both Kurrias, who writhed with pain and lashed their tails furiously, making great hollows in the ground, which the water they had brought with them quickly filled. Thinking they might again escape him, Baiame drove them from the water with his spears, and then, at close quarters, he killed them with his woggaras.

And ever afterwards, at floodtime, the Narran flowed into this hollow which the Kurrias in their writhings had made.

When Baiame saw that the Kurrias were quite dead, he cut them open and took out the bodies of his wives. They were covered with wet slime and seemed quite lifeless, but he carried them and laid them on two nests of red ants. Then he sat down at some little distance and watched them. The ants quickly covered the bodies, cleaned them rapidly of the wet slime, and soon Baiame noticed the muscles of the girls twitching.

"Ah," he said, "there is life, they feel the sting of the ants."

Almost as he spoke came a sound as a thunderclap, but the sound seemed to come from the ears of the girls. And as the echo was dying away, slowly the girls rose to their feet. For a moment they stood apart, a dazed expression on their faces. Then they clung together, shaking as if stricken with a deadly fear. But Baiame came to them and explained how they had been rescued from the Kurrias by him. He bade them to beware of ever bathing in the deep holes of the Narran, lest such holes be the haunt of Kurrias.

Then he bade them look at the water now at Boogira, and said, "Soon will the black swans find their way here, the pelicans and the ducks; where there was dry land and stones in the past, in the future there will be water and waterfowl. From henceforth, when the Narran runs it will run into this hole, and by the spreading of its waters will a big lake be made."

And what Baiame said has come to pass, as the Narran Lake shows, with its large sheet of water, spreading for miles, the home of thousands of wildfowl.

THE FLYING HEAD
American Indian (Iroquois)

In days long past, evil monsters and spirits preyed upon humans. As long as the sun was shining, the monsters hid unseen in deep caves, but on stormy nights they came out of their dens and prowled the earth. The most terrible of all was the great Flying Head. Though only a scowling, snarling head without a body, it was four times as tall as the tallest man. Its skin was so thick and matted with hair that no weapon could penetrate it. Two huge bird wings grew from either side of its cheeks, and with them it could soar into the sky or dive down, floating, like a buzzard. Instead of teeth, the Flying Head had a mouth full of huge, piercing fangs with which it seized and devoured its prey. And everything was prey to this monster, every living being, including people.

One dark night a young woman alone with her baby was sitting in a long house. Everybody had fled and hidden, because someone had seen the great Flying Head darting among the treetops of the forest. The young mother had not run away because, as she said to herself, "Someone must make a stand against this monster. It might as well be me." So she sat by the hearth, building a big fire, heating in the flames a number of large, red-hot, glowing stones.

She sat waiting and watching, until suddenly the Flying Head appeared in the door. Grinning horribly, it looked into the longhouse, but she pretended not to see it and acted as if she were cooking a meal. She made believe that she was eating some of the red-hot rocks, picking them up with a forked stick and seeming to put them into her mouth. (In reality she passed them behind her face and dropped them on the ground.) All the while she was smacking her lips, exclaiming, "Ah, how good this is! What wonderful food! Never has anyone feasted on meat like this!"

Hearing her, the monster could not restrain itself. It thrust its head deep inside the lodge, opened its jaws wide, and seized and swallowed in one mighty gulp the whole heap of glowing, hissing rocks. As soon as it had swallowed, the monster uttered a terrible cry which echoed throughout the land. With wings flapping the great Flying Head fled screaming, screaming, screaming over mountains, streams, and forest, screaming so that the biggest trees were shaking, screaming until the earth trembled, screaming until the leaves fell from the branches. At last the screams were fading away in the distance, fading, fading, until at last they could no longer be heard. Then the people everywhere could take their hands from their ears and breathe safely. After that the Flying Head was never seen again, and nobody knows what became of it.

THE STORY OF THE YOUTH WHO WENT FORTH TO LEARN WHAT FEAR WAS
Germany

A certain father had two sons, the elder of whom was smart and sensible, and could do everything; but the younger was stupid and could neither learn nor understand anything, and when people saw him they said, "There's a fellow who will give his father some trouble!" When anything had to be done, it was always the elder who was forced to do it; but if his father bade him fetch anything when it was late, or in the nighttime, and the way led through the churchyard, or any other dismal place, he answered, "Oh, no, Father, I'll not go there, it makes me shudder!" for he was afraid. Or when stories were told by the fire at night which made the flesh creep, the listeners sometimes said, "Oh, it makes us shudder!" The younger sat in a corner and listened with the rest of them, and could not imagine what they could mean. "They are always saying, 'It makes me shudder, it makes me shudder!' It does not make me shudder," thought he. "That, too, must be an art of which I understand nothing!"

Now it came to pass that his father said to him one day, "Hearken to me, you fellow in the corner there, you are growing tall and strong, and you too must learn something by which you can earn your bread. Look how your brother works, but you do not even earn your salt."

"Well, Father," he replied, "I am quite willing to learn something—indeed, if it could but be managed, I should like to learn how to shudder. I don't understand that at all yet."

The elder brother smiled when he heard that, and thought to himself, "Good God, what a blockhead that brother of mine is! He will never be good for anything as long as he lives! He who wants to be a sickle must bend himself betimes."

The father sighed, and answered him, "You shall soon learn what it is to shudder, but you will not earn your bread by that."

Soon after this the sexton came to the house on a visit, and the father bewailed his trouble, and told him how his younger son was so backward in every respect that he knew nothing and learned nothing. "Just think," said he, "when I asked him how he was going to earn his bread, he actually wanted to learn to shudder."

"If that be all," replied the sexton, "he can learn that with me. Send him to me, and I will soon polish him."

The father was glad to do it, for he thought, "It will train boy a little." The sexton therefore took the boy into his house, and he had to ring the church bell. After a day or two, the sexton awoke him at midnight, and bade him arise and go up into the church tower and ring the bell. "You shall soon learn what shuddering is," thought he, and secretly went there before him; and when the boy was at the top of the tower and turned round, and was just going to take hold of the bell rope, he saw a white figure standing on the stairs opposite the sounding hole.

"Who is there?" cried he, but the figure made no reply, and did not move or stir. "Give an answer," cried the boy, "or take yourself off. You have no business here at night."

The sexton, however, remained standing motionless so that the boy might think he was a ghost.

The boy cried a second time, "What do you want here?—speak if you are an honest fellow, or I will throw you down the steps!"

The sexton thought, "He can't mean to be as bad as his words," uttered no sound, and stood as if he were made of stone. Then the boy called to him for the third time, and as that was also to no purpose, he ran against him and pushed the ghost down the stairs, so that it fell down ten steps and remained lying there in a corner. Thereupon he rang the bell, went home, and without saying a word went to bed, and fell asleep.

The sexton's wife waited a long time for her husband, but he did not come back. At length she became uneasy, and wakened the boy, and asked, "Do you not know where my husband is? He climbed up the tower before you did."

"No, I don't know," replied the boy, "but someone was standing by the sounding hole on the other side of the steps, and as he would neither give an answer nor go away, I took him for a scoundrel and threw him downstairs. Just go there, and you will see if it was he. I should be sorry if it were." The woman ran away and found her husband, who was lying moaning in the corner, and had broken his leg.

She carried him down, and then with loud screams she hastened to the boy's father. "Your boy," cried she, "has been the cause of a great misfortune! He has thrown my husband down the steps so that he broke his leg. Take the good-for-nothing fellow out of our house."

The father was terrified, and ran thither and scolded the boy.

"What wicked tricks are these?" said he, "the Devil must have put them into your head."

"Father," he replied, "do listen to me. I am quite innocent. He was standing there by night like one intent on doing evil. I did not know who it was, and I entreated him three times either to speak or to go away."

"Ah," said the father, "I have nothing but unhappiness with you. Go out of my sight. I will see you no more."

"Yes, Father, right willingly, wait only until it is day. Then will I go forth and learn how to shudder, and then I shall, at any rate, understand one art which will support me."

"Learn what you will," spoke the father, "it is all the same to me. Here are fifty talers for you. Take these and go into the wide world, and tell no one from whence you come, and who is your father, for I have reason to be ashamed of you."

"Yes, Father, it shall be as you will. If you desire nothing more than that, I can easily keep it in mind."

When day dawned, therefore, the boy put his fifty talers into his pocket, and went forth on the great highway, and continually said to himself, "If I could but shudder! If I could but shudder!"

Then a man approached who heard this conversation which the youth was holding with himself and when they had walked a little farther to where they could see the gallows, the man said to him, "Look, there is the tree where seven men have married the rope-maker's daughter, and are now learning how to fly. Sit down beneath it, and wait till night comes, and you will soon learn how to shudder."

"If that is all that is wanted," answered the youth, "it is easily done; but if I learn how to shudder as fast as that, you shall have my fifty talers. Just come back to me early in the morning." Then the youth went to the gallows, sat down beneath it, and waited till evening came. And as he was cold, he lighted himself a fire, but at midnight the wind blew so sharply that in spite of his fire, he could not get warm. And as the wind knocked the hanged men against each other, and they moved backwards and forwards, he thought to himself, "If you shiver below by the fire, how those up above must freeze and suffer!" And as he felt pity for them, he raised the ladder and climbed up, unbound one of them after the other, and brought down all seven. Then he stoked the fire, blew it, and set them all round it to warm themselves.

But they sat there and did not stir, and the fire caught their clothes. So he said, "Take care, or I will hang you up again." The dead men, however, did not hear, but were quite silent, and let their rags go on burning. At this he grew angry, and said, "If you will not take care, I cannot help you, I will not be burned with you," and he hung them up again each in his turn! Then he sat down by his fire and fell asleep.

The next morning the man came to him and wanted to have the fifty talers, and said, "Well, do you know how to shudder?"

"No," answered he, "how should I know? Those fellows up there did not open their mouths, and were so stupid that they let the few old rags which they had on their bodies get burnt."

Then the man saw that he would not get the fifty talers that day, and went away saying, "Such a youth has never come my way before."

The youth likewise went his way, and once more began to mutter to himself: "Ah, if I could but shudder! Ah, if I could but shudder!"

A wagoner who was striding behind him heard this and asked, "Who are you?"

"I don't know," answered the youth.

Then the wagoner asked, "From whence do you come?"

"I know not."

"Who is your father?"

"That I may not tell you."

"What is it that you are always muttering between your teeth?"

"Ah," replied the youth, "I do so wish I could shudder, but no one can teach me how."

"Enough of your foolish chatter," said the wagoner. "Come, go with me, I will see about a place for you."

The youth went with the wagoner, and in the evening they arrived at an inn where they wished to pass the night. Then at the entrance of the parlor the youth again said quite loudly, 'If I could but shudder! If I could but shudder!"

The host, who heard this, laughed and said, "If that is your desire, there ought to be a good opportunity for you here."

"Ah, be silent," and the hostess. "So many prying persons have already lost their lives, it would be a pity and a shame if such beautiful eyes as these should never see the daylight again."

But the youth said, "However difficult it may be, I will learn it. For this purpose indeed have I journeyed forth." He let the host have no rest, until the latter told him that not far from thence stood a haunted castle where any one could very easily learn what shuddering was, if he would but watch in it for three nights. The king had promised that he who would venture should have his daughter to wife, and she was the most beautiful maiden the sun shone on. Likewise in the castle lay great treasures, which were guarded by evil spirits, and these treasures would then be freed, and would make a poor man rich enough. Already many men had gone into the castle, but as yet none had come out again. Then the youth went next morning to the king, and said, "If it be allowed, I will willingly watch three nights in the haunted castle."

The king looked at him, and as the youth pleased him, he said, "You may ask for three things to take into the castle with you, but they must be things without life."

Then he answered, "Then I ask for a fire, a turning lathe, and a cutting board with a knife."

The king had these things carried into the castle for him during the day. When night was drawing near, the youth went up and made himself a bright fire in one of the rooms, placed the cutting board and knife beside it, and seated himself by the turning lathe. "Ah, if I could but shudder!" said he, "but I shall not learn it here either."

Towards midnight he was about to poke his fire, and as he was blowing it, something cried suddenly from one corner, "Au, miau! how cold we are!"

"You fools!" cried he, "what are you crying about? If you are cold, come and take a seat by the fire and warm yourselves." And when he had said that, two great black cats came with one tremendous leap and sat down on each side of him, and looked savagely at him with their fiery eyes. After a short time, when they had warmed themselves, they said, "Comrade, shall we have a game of cards?"

"Why not?" he replied, "but just show me your paws." Then they stretched out their claws. "Oh," said he, "what long nails you have! Wait, I must first cut them for you." Thereupon he seized them by the throats, put them on the cutting board and screwed their feet fast. "I have looked at your fingers," said he, "and my fancy for card-playing has gone," and he struck them dead and threw them out into the water.

But when he had made away with these two, and was about to sit down again by his fire, out from every hole and corner came black cats and black dogs with red-hot chains, and more and more of them came until he could no longer move, and they yelled horribly, and got on his fire, pulled it to pieces, and tried to put it out. He watched them for a while quietly, but at last when they were going too far, he seized his cutting knife, and cried, "Away with you, vermin," and began to cut them down. Some of them ran away, the others he killed, and threw out into the fishpond.

When he came back he fanned the embers of his fire again and warmed himself. And as he thus sat, his eyes would keep open no longer, and he felt a desire to sleep. Then he looked round and saw a great bed in the corner. "That is the very thing for me," said he, and got into it. When he was just going to shut his eyes, however, the bed began to move of its own accord, and went over the whole of the castle. "That's right," said he, "but go faster." Then the bed rolled on as if six horses were harnessed to it, up and down, over thresholds and stairs, but suddenly hop, hop, it turned over upside down, and lay on him like a mountain. But he threw quilts and pillows up in the air, got out and said, "Now anyone who likes may drive," and lay down by his fire, and slept till it was day.

In the morning the king came, and when he saw him lying there on the ground, he thought the evil spirits had killed him and he was dead. Then said he, "After all it is a pity—for so handsome a man."

The youth heard it, got up, and said, "It has not come to that yet."

Then the king was astonished, but very glad, and asked how he had fared. "Very well indeed," answered he. "One night is past, the two others will pass likewise." Then he went to the innkeeper, who opened his eyes very wide, and said, "I never expected to see you alive again! Have you learned how to shudder yet?"

"No," said he, "it is all in vain. If someone would but tell me!"

The second night he again went up into the old castle, sat down by the fire, and once more began his old song: "If I could but shudder!" When midnight came, an uproar and noise of tumbling about was heard; at first it was low, but it grew louder and louder. Then it was quiet for a while, and at length with a loud scream, half a man came down the chimney and fell before him. "Hullo!" cried he, "another half belongs to this. This is not enough!" Then the uproar began again, there was a roaring and howling, and the other half fell down likewise. "Wait," said he, "I will just stoke up the fire a little for you." When he had done that and looked round again, the two pieces were joined together, and a hideous man was sitting in his place. "That is no part of our bargain," said the youth, "the bench is mine." The man wanted to push him away; the youth, however, would not allow that, but thrust him off with all his strength, and seated himself again in his own place. Then still more men fell down, one after the other; they brought nine dead men's legs and two skulls, and set them up and played at ninepins with them. The youth also wanted to play and said, "Listen you, can I join you?"

"Yes, if you have any money."

"Money enough," replied he, "but your balls are not quite round."

Then he took the skulls and put them in the lathe and turned them till they were round. "There, now they will roll better!" said he. "Hurrah! now we'll have fun!" He played with them and lost some of his money, but when it struck twelve, everything vanished from his sight. He lay down and quietly fell asleep.

Next morning the king came to inquire after him. "How has it fared with you this time?" asked he.

"I have been playing at ninepins," he answered, "and have lost a couple of farthings."

"Have you not shuddered then?"

"What?" said he. "I have had a wonderful time! If I did but know what it was to shudder!"

The third night he sat down again on his bench and said quite sadly, "If I could but shudder." When it grew late, six tall men came in and brought a coffin. Then said he, "Ha, ha, that is certainly my little cousin, who died only a few days ago," and he beckoned with his finger, and cried, "Come, little cousin, come." They placed the coffin on the ground, but he went to it and took the lid off, and a dead man lay therein. He felt his face, but it was cold as ice. "Wait," said he, "I will warm you a little," and went to the fire and warmed his hand and laid it on the dead man's face, but he remained cold. Then he took him out, and sat down by the fire and laid him on his breast and rubbed his arms that the blood might circulate again. As this also did no good, he thought to himself, "When two people lie in bed together, they warm each other," and carried him to the bed, covered him over, and lay down by him. After a short time the dead man became warm too, and began to move. Then said the youth, "See, little cousin, have I not warmed you?"

The dead man, however, got up and cried, "Now will I strangle you."

"What!" said he, "is that the way you think me? You shall at once go into your coffin again," and he took him up, threw him into it, and shut the lid. Then came the six men and carried him away again. "I cannot manage to shudder," said he. "I shall never learn it here as long as I live."

Then a man entered who was taller than all others, and looked terrible. He was old, however, and had a long white beard. "You wretch," cried he, "you shall soon learn what it is to shudder, for you shall die."

"Not so fast," replied the youth. "If I am to die, I shall have to have a say in it."

"I will soon seize you," said the fiend.

"Softly, softly, do not talk so big. I am as strong as you are, and perhaps even stronger."

"We shall see," said the old man. "If you are stronger, I will let you go—come, we will try." Then he led him by dark passages to a smith's forge, took an axe, and with one blow struck an anvil into the ground.

"I can do better than that," said the youth, and went to the other anvil. The old man placed himself near and wanted to look on, and his white beard hung down. Then the youth seized the axe, split the anvil with one blow, and in it caught the old man's beard. "Now I have you," said the youth. "Now it is your turn to die." Then he seized an iron bar and beat the old man till he moaned and entreated him to stop, when he would give him great riches. The youth drew out the axe and let him go.

The old man led him back into the castle, and in a cellar showed him three chests full of gold. "Of these," said he, "one part is for the poor, the other for the king, the third yours." In the meantime it struck twelve, and the spirit disappeared, so that the youth stood in darkness. "I shall still be able to find my way out," said he, and felt about, found the way into the room, and slept there by his fire.

Next morning the king came and said, "Now you must have learned what shuddering is?"

"No," he answered. "What can it be? My dead cousin was here, and a bearded man came and showed me a great deal of money down below, but no one told me what it was to shudder."

"Then," said the king, "you have saved the castle, and shall marry my daughter."

"That is all very well," said he, "but still I do not know what it is to shudder!"

Then the gold was brought up and the wedding celebrated. But howsoever much the young king loved his wife, and however happy he was, he still said always, "If I could but shudder—if I could but shudder." And this at last angered her.

Her waiting maid said, "I will find a cure for him; he shall soon learn what it is to shudder." She went out to the stream which flowed through the garden, and had a whole bucketful of gudgeons brought to her. At night when the young king was sleeping, his wife was to draw the clothes off him and empty the bucketful of cold water with the gudgeons in it over him, so that the little fishes would sprawl about him. Then he woke up and cried, "Oh, what makes me shudder so?—what makes me shudder so, dear wife? Ah! now I know what it is to shudder!"

WONDER TALES, TALL TALES, and BRAG

Baron Munchausen, that consummate liar and braggart invented in the eighteenth century by Rudolf Erich Raspe in volumes that were both satirical and libelous, always assured his listeners: "Having heard, for the first time, that my adventures have been doubted, and looked upon as jokes, I feel bound to come forward and vindicate my character *for veracity*, by paying three shillings at the Mansion House of this great city for the affidavits, hereto appended." However, as one of the affidavits, signed by those truth tellers Gulliver, Sinbad, and Aladdin, says: "As we have been believed, whose adventures are tenfold more wonderful, *so* do we hope all true believers will give him their full faith and credence."

So, too, the wonder tales and braggadocio, romantic embellishments, and outright lies that follow should be believed, as they say in the Appalachians, by "considering the source." Whether it is a German taradiddle about a goose girl who talks to the head of her late lamented horse which is hanging on the wall (and it talks back!), or the quick magic of the miracle-making priest who teaches a farmer a lesson in "The Magic Pear Tree," these tales are all filled with one kind of wonder or another.

TALK
Africa (Ashanti)

Once, not far from the city of Accra on the Gulf of Guinea, a country man went out to his garden to dig up some yams to take to market. While he was digging, one of the yams said to him, "Well, at last you're here. You never weeded me, but now you come around with your digging stick. Go away and leave me alone!"

The farmer turned around and looked at his cow in amazement. The cow was chewing her cud and looking at him.

"Did you say something?" he asked.

The cow kept on chewing and said nothing, but the man's dog spoke up. "It wasn't the cow who spoke to you," the dog said. "It was the yam. The yam says leave him alone."

The man became angry, because his dog had never talked before, and he didn't like his tone besides. So he took his knife and cut a branch from a palm tree to whip his dog. Just then the palm tree said, "Put that branch down!"

The man was getting very upset about the way things were going, and he started to throw the palm branch away, but the palm branch said, "Man, put me down softly!"

He put the branch down gently on a stone, and the stone said, "Hey, take that thing off me!"

This was enough, and the frightened farmer started to run for his village. On the way he met a fisherman going the other way with a fish trap on his head.

"What's the hurry?" the fisherman asked.

"My yam said, 'Leave me alone!' Then the dog said, 'Listen to what the yam says!' When I went to whip the dog with a palm branch the tree said, 'Put that branch down!' Then the palm branch said, 'Do it softly!' Then the stone said, 'Take that thing off me!' "

"Is that all?" the man with the fish trap asked. "Is that so frightening?"

"Well," the man's fish trap said, "did he take it off the stone?"

"Wah!" the fisherman shouted. He threw the fish trap on the ground and began to run with the farmer, and on the trail they met a weaver with a bundle of cloth on his head.

"Where are you going in such a rush?" he asked them.

"My yam said, 'Leave me alone!' " the farmer said. "The dog said, 'Listen to what the yam says!' The tree said, 'Put that branch down!' The branch said, 'Do it softly!' And the stone said, 'Take that thing off me!' "

"And then," the fisherman continued, "the fish trap said, 'Did he take it off?' "

"That's nothing to get excited about," the weaver said. "No reason at all."

"Oh, yes it is," his bundle of cloth said. "If it happened to you you'd run too!"

"Wah!" the weaver shouted. He threw his bundle on the trail and started running with the other men.

They came panting to the ford in the river and found a man bathing. "Are you chasing a gazelle?" he asked them.

The first man said breathlessly, "My yam talked at me, and it said, 'Leave me alone!' And my dog said, 'Listen to your yam!' And when I cut myself a branch the tree said, 'Put that branch down!' And the branch said, 'Do it softly!' And the stone said, 'Take that thing off me!' "

The fisherman panted. "And my trap said, 'Did he?' "

The weaver wheezed. "And my bundle of cloth said, 'You'd run too!' "

"Is that why you're running?" the man in the river asked.

"Well, wouldn't you run if you were in their position?" the river said.

The man jumped out of the water and began to run with the others. They ran down the main street of the village to the house of the chief. The chief's servant brought his stool out, and he came and sat on it to listen to their complaints. The men began to recite their troubles.

"I went out to my garden to dig yams," the farmer said, waving his arms. "Then everything began to talk! My yam said, 'Leave me alone!' My dog said, 'Pay attention to your yam!' The tree said, 'Put that branch down!' The branch said, 'Do it softly!' And the stone said, 'Take it off me!' "

"And my fish trap said, 'Well, did he take it off?' " the fisherman said.

"And my cloth said, 'You'd run too!' " the weaver said.

"And the river said the same," the bather said hoarsely, his eyes bulging.

The chief listened to them patiently, but he couldn't refrain from scowling. "Now this is really a wild story," he said at last. "You'd better all go back to your work before I punish you for disturbing the peace."

So the men went away, and the chief shook his head and mumbled to himself, "Nonsense like that upsets the community."

"Fantastic, isn't it?" his stool said. "Imagine, a talking yam!"

THE KING OF IRELAND'S SON
Ireland

Once upon a time, and a very good time it was too, when the streets were paved with penny loaves and houses were whitewashed with buttermilk and the pigs ran round with knives and forks in their snouts shouting: "Eat me, eat me!" there lived a King of Ireland and he had three sons named Art, Neart and Ceart. Art is a man's name simply, Neart means strength and Ceart means right or justice. Well, Art was his father's favorite and the other two boys were very jealous of him. At one particular time, you could hear, all around the country, heavenly music coming from somewhere, and the King wanted to know where it was coming from. So he said to his three sons: "Go out and whichever of you finds out where the heavenly music is coming from, can have half my kingdom."

So the three of them set off out until they came to a big hole and from this big hole they could hear the sound of the music coming. Neart and Ceart said to Art: "Will you go down? You're the lightest and the youngest and we'll let you down into this hole on a rope. You can see where the music is coming from and then we'll pull you up again," hoping never to see him again.

Art said: "Certainly, I will. I think that's a good idea."

Down on the end of a rope he was lowered and he went along

a cave like a long tunnel, along and along and along until it got very dark. He walked for hours until it must have been nighttime, for in the tunnel he couldn't tell night from day. In the end and when his feet were falling off him, he saw a light. Over to the light he went and he met an old man and he said to the old man that was there: "Could you tell me where the heavenly music is coming from?"

"No, then," said the old man, "I can't. But I tell you what you can do. You can stop the night and tomorrow you can walk—it's a day's journey—on to my father's place and he might be able to tell you."

So the old man put him up for the night and gave him the best of food. They had rashers and eggs with black pudding and white pudding and a Cork drisheen, three Hafner's sausages each, the best of homemade wholemeal bread, all washed down with lashings of strong tea, and after that they both went to bed, as well they might after such a feed.

The next morning Art woke up and started on his journey for another day's traveling along the tunnel, until he came to another light and he went in and met an old, old man and he said to him: "Are you the father of the other old man that I saw back along there?"

"That's not an old man," said the second old man, "he's only a hundred."

"Well," said Art, "I'd like to know where the heavenly music is coming from and he said you might be able to help me."

"Well," said the second old man, "that I can't help you. But my father that lives further up might be able to. Come in anyway and I'll feed you for the night and you can get up in the morning and go up and ask my father."

So Art went in and the old, old man gave him a great meal. They had bowls of stirabout, followed by huge plates of the best Limerick ham with spring cabbage and lovely potatoes, that were like balls of flour melting in your mouth, and with all this they drank three pints each of the freshest buttermilk Art had ever tasted. I can tell you he slept soundly that night.

And the next morning he got up and after saying goodbye to the old, old man, he walked for another whole day along the tunnel until he came to another light and there was an old, old, old man. So Art said to him: "Are you the father of the old, old man back there along the tunnel?"

"Well, I am," said the old, old, old man, "but that fellow's not as old as he makes out; he's only a hundred and fifty and he eats all them new-fangled foods, as you probably found out."

"Well," said Art, "he did me very well. But what I wanted to know was if you can tell me where the heavenly music comes from?"

"Well, now," said the old, old, old man, "we'll talk about that in the morning. Come on in now and have a bit to eat and rest yourself. You must be famished after that day's walking."

So in Art went and the old, old, old man got some food ready. They started off with two great bowls of yellow buck porridge each and after that, they had four crubeens apiece with fresh soda bread and homemade butter and they had three pints of the creamiest porter Art had ever drunk to go with it all.

The next morning, he got up and he said to the old man: "Now can you tell me where the heavenly music is coming from?"

"Well, no," said the old, old, old man, "but I know that there's nobody else living at the end of this tunnel except a terrible fierce man, a giant, and," he said, "I wouldn't go near him if I were you. But if you do decide to go up to him, he lives a terrible far distance away at the very end. You'll find, however," he said, "a little stallion when you go a couple of miles up the road there and, if you get up on him, he'll carry you to where the heavenly music comes from. But," he said, "you'll want to be very wary of that giant."

Art went along and he came up to where, sure enough, there was a stallion and there was light with more light further on. So the stallion said to him: "Do you want a lift?"

"I do," said Art, "but I'm going up to where the heavenly music is."

"Well, that's all right," said the stallion "no offense given and no offense taken. Jump up there on me back and I'll take you."

So up on the stallion's back he jumped and the stallion galloped away for nearly a whole day, until he came to one of the most beautiful gardens Art had ever seen. "This," said the stallion, "is the nearest I can take you to where the heavenly music comes from."

Art went up through the garden, wondering at every more marvelous thing that he saw. Nearer and nearer came the heavenly music and at last Art came to a house and the music was coming from there. Into the house Art went and there was the most beautiful girl he had ever seen. And she was singing and making the heavenly music.

"Good morning," said Art and then he said quickly, "don't let me interrupt your song which is the loveliest I've ever heard."

"Oh!" she answered him, "I'm glad you've interrupted it. I have to make music here for an old giant that captured me. I'm the King of Greece's daughter," she said, "and I've been here for a year and a day and I can't get away from this old fellow until someone comes to rescue me. But," she said, "I'd sooner you went away for he's a very big man and very very fierce."

"I'm not afraid of him," said Art, "what can he do?"

"Well," she said, "he'll ask you a number of riddles. He has to hide for three nights and you have to hide for three nights . . . "

Before she could finish, or before Art could say whether he was going to stay or go, he heard a deep voice saying: "Who is this I see in here?" In comes this huge giant and caught poor Art by the throat. "What are you doing here?" he roared.

"I came to find the heavenly music," said Art.

"Well, now you've found it," said the giant, "and much good may it do you. And I'll tell you something," he said, "I'm going to hide for three days and, if you don't find me before the three days are up, I'll cut your head off, skin you, cook you and eat you. And after that," he roared, "if you have found me, you'll hide for three days and if I find you, I'll still kill, skin, cook and eat you."

So poor Art didn't know what to say but, "Well, I'd like to go back and see to my little stallion."

"Right," said the giant, "but we'll start in the morning."

"This is an awful thing," said Art to the stallion when he got back, "what am I going to do—how do I know where he's going to hide?"

"That's all right," said the stallion, "it's getting late at night so we'll want to eat something for, honest to God, my belly thinks my throat is cut. Sit down there now," said the stallion, "and put your left hand into my right ear and you'll find a tablecloth. Spread out the tablecloth," he said, and Art did as he was told. "Now," said the stallion, "put your right hand into my left ear and take out what you'll find there." Art did that and took out the best of fine food and the finest of old drink. "Now," said the stallion, "you take that for yourself and stick your right hand into my left ear again." So Art did that and pulled out a bucket of water and a truss of hay. And Art ate the best of fine food and the finest of old drink and the stallion had the hay and the water. "Now," said the stallion when they were finished, "spread yourself out under my legs and we'll go to sleep for the night." So they went to sleep for the night.

The next morning when they woke up, they could hear the giant shouting: "Now come and find me if you can."

"I can tell you where he is," the little stallion said to Art, "he's at the top of the tree." So Art climbed to the top of the tree and there, right enough, was the giant who comes down very highly annoyed. "Aah!" he roared, "you found me today, but you won't find me tomorrow."

After this, Art had great confidence in the stallion; and that night, he again had a feed of the best of fine food and the finest of old drink, and the stallion had a truss of hay and a bucket of clear water, and they carried on a learned discussion until it was time to go to bed.

Next morning when they got up, the stallion said: "Now go on in through the house and out into the back garden and there you'll see a football. Give the football a good kick."

"All right," said Art and off he went and, in the back garden, he gave the football a terrific kick and out spun the giant.

"Well," said the giant very nastily, "you got me this time, but you won't get me tomorrow for I've got a trick up my sleeve yet."

Art went back to the stallion and told him what had happened and said: "What will we do now?"

"Well," said the stallion, "first of all, we'll have a feed." They ate again all kinds of lovely foods and talked until it was time to go to sleep.

In the morning, Art said: "What will I do now? Where is he hiding?"

"I'll tell you what to do," said the stallion. "When you go inside, ask the girl where he is. But," he said, "without the giant understanding you. Just signal to her, where is he?"

So Art goes and sees the daughter of the King of Greece and she is singing away there and he makes signs to ask where is the giant. The girl pointed to a ring on her finger and, at first, Art didn't understand. But she motioned him to take the ring off, which he did. He looked at it and made signs to show that he didn't believe that the giant could fit in such a small ring. But the girl kept singing away and pointed to him to throw it in the fire. So he did that and there was an enormous screech: "Oh! I'm burnt! I'm burnt!" and out jumped the giant. "Now," he roared, "you caught me the three times, but now it's your turn."

"All right," said Art, "I'll hide tomorrow."

"Well, now," said Art to the stallion when he went back, "we're in a right fix now. Where am I going to hide? Sure I'm a stranger here and don't know the place at all."

"That's all right," said the stallion, "I'll tell you in the morning. In the meantime, put your hands into my two ears and take out the grub." So they had a feed and then Art got under the stallion's legs and slept there for the night.

When he woke up: "Now," said the stallion, "the first thing you do is to take a hair out of my tail and, the hole it leaves, get up into that." So Art took the hair out of the stallion's tail, got up into the hole and stopped there. And the giant searched all round and couldn't find Art all day and nearly went tearing mad. Art came out that night and the giant said: "I didn't find you today but I'll find you tomorrow and eat you."

So that night Art said to the stallion: "Where am I going to hide tomorrow?"

"That's all right," said the stallion, "put your hands into my two ears and take out the food and we'll have a feed first. Then you can stretch out under my legs and have a sleep and we'll talk about the matter in the morning."

In the morning Art said: "Now, where am I going to hide?"

"Take a nail out of my hoof," said the stallion, "get up into the hole and draw the nail up after you." So Art did that and stayed there all day, while the giant went round roaring and swearing.

At night, the giant went back to his house and Art came out of the hole and said: "So you didn't find me."

"No," said the giant, "but I will tomorrow and then I'll kill, skin, cook, and eat you."

Then Art said to the stallion: "Where will I hide tomorrow?" and the stallion said: "One thing at a time. Get out the grub there and we'll have a feed and we'll see about the other matter in the morning."

"Now," said the stallion in the morning, when they woke up fresh and early, "pull out one of my teeth, get up into the hole and draw the tooth up after you." The giant came rampaging around the place and couldn't find Art and, to cut a long story short, he nearly went demented.

In the evening, Art came out and went into the house and there was the King of Greece's daughter. The music was stopped but she looked happier than ever and she said: "You have broken the spell. I had to wait for a stranger to come and beat the giant six times."

"We've done that," said Art, "now I'll take you away from here."

"All right," she said, "although I'm the daughter of the King of Greece."

"Well," said Art, "that's nothing. I'm the King of Ireland's son." So she jumped up on the back of the stallion behind Art and they rode out of the tunnel and back to his father's palace. The King of Greece's daughter then sang some of the heavenly music for the King of Ireland and the King gave Art half his kingdom. The two brothers were banished and Art and the King of Greece's daughter got married and they had a wedding and everybody ate and drank, and wasn't I at the wedding as well as everybody else and I got a present of a pair of paper boots and a pair of stockings made of buttermilk; and that's the end of my story and all I'm going to tell you.

THE GOOSE GIRL
Germany

There was once upon a time an old queen whose husband had been dead for many years, and she had a beautiful daughter. When the princess grew up she was betrothed to a prince who lived at a great distance. When the time came for her to be married, and she had to journey forth into the distant kingdom, the aged queen packed up for her many costly vessels of silver and gold, and trinkets also of gold and silver; and cups and jewels, in short, everything which appertained to a royal dowry, for she loved her child with all her heart. She likewise sent her maid-in-waiting, who was to ride with her, and hand her over to the bridegroom, and each had a horse for the journey, but the horse of the king's daughter was called Falada, and could speak. So when the hour of parting had come, the aged mother went into her bedroom, took a small knife and cut her finger with it until it bled. Then she held a white handkerchief to it into which she let three drops of blood fall, gave it to her daughter and said, "Dear child, preserve this carefully. It will be of service to you on your way."

So they took a sorrowful leave of each other; the princess put the piece of cloth in her bosom, mounted her horse, and then went away to her bridegroom. After she had ridden for a while she felt a burning thirst, and said to her waiting maid, "Dismount, and take my cup which you have brought with you for me, and get me some water from the stream, for I should like to drink."

"If you are thirsty," said the waiting maid, "get off your horse yourself, and lie down and drink out of the water, I don't choose to be your servant."

So in her great thirst the princess alighted, bent down over the water in the stream and drank, and was not allowed to drink out of the golden cup. Then she said, "Ah, Heaven!" and the three drops of blood answered, "If this your mother knew, her heart would break in two." But the king's daughter was humble, said nothing, and mounted her horse again. She rode some miles further, but the day was warm, the sun scorched her, and she was thirsty once more, and when they came to a stream of water, she again cried to her waiting maid, "Dismount, and give me some water in my golden cup," for she had long ago forgotten the girl's ill words.

But the waiting maid said still more haughtily, "If you wish to drink, get it yourself, I don't choose to be your maid."

Then in her great thirst the king's daughter alighted, bent over the flowing stream, wept and said, "Ah, Heaven!" and the drops of blood again replied, "If this your mother knew, her heart would break in two." And as she was thus drinking and leaning right over the stream, the handkerchief with the three drops of blood fell out of her bosom, and floated away with the water without her observing it, so great was her trouble.

The waiting maid, however, had seen it, and she rejoiced to think that she had now power over the bride, for since the princess had lost the drops of blood, she had become weak and powerless. So now when she wanted to mount her horse again, the one that was called Falada, the waiting maid said, "Falada is more suitable for me, and my nag will do for you," and the princess had to be content with that. Then the waiting maid, with many hard words, bade the princess exchange her royal apparel for her own shabby clothes; and at length she was compelled to swear by the clear sky above her, that she would not say one word of this to anyone at the royal court, and if she had not taken this oath she would have been killed on the spot. But Falada saw all this, and observed it well.

The waiting maid now mounted Falada, and the true bride the bad horse, and thus they traveled onwards, until at length they entered the royal palace. There were great rejoicings over her arrival, and the prince sprang forward to meet her, lifted the waiting maid from her horse, and thought she was his consort. She was conducted upstairs, but the real princess was left standing below.

Then the old king looked out of the window and saw her standing in the courtyard, and noticed how dainty and delicate and beautiful she was, and instantly went to the royal apartment, and asked the bride about the girl she had with her who was standing down below in the courtyard, and who she was. "I picked her up on my way for a companion. Give the girl something to work at, that she may not stand idle."

But the old king had no work for her, and knew of none, so he said, "I have a little boy who tends the geese, she may help him." The boy was called Conrad, and the true bride had to help him to tend the geese.

Soon afterwards the false bride said to the young king, "Dearest husband, I beg you to do me a favor."

He answered, "I will do so most willingly."

"Then send for the knacker, and have the head of the horse on which I rode here cut off, for it vexed me on the way." In reality, she was afraid that the horse might tell how she had behaved to the king's daughter.

Then she succeeded in making the king promise that it should be done, and the faithful Falada was to die. This came to the ears of the real princess, and she secretly promised to pay the knacker a piece of gold if he would perform a small service for her. There was a great dark-looking gateway in the town, through which morning and evening she had to pass with the geese: would he be so good as to nail up Falada's head on it, so that she might see him again, more than once. The knacker's man promised to do that, and cut off the head, and nailed it fast beneath the dark gateway.

Early in the morning, when she and Conrad drove out their flock beneath this gateway, she said in passing:

Alas, Falada, hanging there!

Then the head answered:

Alas, young queen, how ill you fare!
If this your mother knew,
Her heart would break in two.

Then they went still further out of the town, and drove their geese into the country. And when they had come to the meadow, she sat down and unbound her hair which was like pure gold, and Conrad saw it and delighted in its brightness, and wanted to pluck out a few hairs. Then she said:

Blow, blow, thou gentle wind, I say,
Blow Conrad's little hat away,
And make him chase it here and there,
Until I have braided all my hair,
And bound it up again.

And there came such a violent wind that it blew Conrad's hat far away across country, and he was forced to run after it. When he came back she had finished combing her hair and was putting it up again, and he could not get any of it. Then Conrad was angry, and would not speak to her, and thus they watched the geese until the evening, and then they went home.

Next day when they were driving the geese out through the dark gateway, the maiden said:

Alas, Falada, hanging there!

Falada answered:

Alas, young queen, how ill you fare!
If this your mother knew,
Her heart would break in two.

And she sat down again in the field and began to comb out her hair, and Conrad ran and tried to clutch it, so she said in haste:

Blow, blow, thou gentle wind, I say,
Blow Conrad's little hat away,
And make him chase it here and there,
Until I have braided all my hair,
And bound it up again.

Then the wind blew, and blew his little hat off his head and far away, and Conrad was forced to run after it, and when he came back, her hair had been put up a long time, and he could get none of it, and so they looked after their geese till evening came.

But in the evening after they had got home, Conrad went to the old king, and said, "I won't tend the geese with that girl any longer!"

"Why not?" inquired the aged king.

"Oh, because she vexes me the whole day long."

Then the aged king commanded him to relate what it was that she did to him. And Conrad said, "In the morning when we pass beneath the dark gateway with the flock, there is a horse's head on the wall, and she says to it:

> *Alas, Falada, hanging there!*

And the head replies:

> *Alas, young queen, how ill you fare!*
> *If this your mother knew,*
> *Her heart would break in two.*

And Conrad went on to relate what happened on the goose pasture, and how when there he had to chase his hat.

The aged king commanded him to drive his flock out again next day, and as soon as morning came, he placed himself behind the dark gateway, and heard how the maiden spoke to the head of Falada, and then he too went into the country, and hid himself in the thicket in the meadow. There he soon saw with his own eyes the goose girl and the goose boy bringing their flock, and how after a while she sat down and unplaited her hair, which shone with radiance. And soon she said:

> *Blow, blow, thou gentle wind, I say,*
> *Blow Conrad's little hat away,*
> *And make him chase it here and there,*
> *Until I have braided all my hair,*
> *And bound it up again.*

Then came a blast of wind and carried off Conrad's hat, so that he had to run far away, while the maiden quietly went on combing and plaiting her hair, all of which the king observed. Then, quite unseen, he went away and when the goose girl came home in the evening, he called her aside, and asked why she did all these things. "I may not tell that, and I dare not lament my sorrows to any human being, for I have sworn not to do so by the heaven which is above me. If I had not done that, I should have lost my life."

He urged her and left her no peace, but he could draw nothing from her.

Then said he, "If you will not tell me anything, tell your sorrows to the iron stove there," and he went away. Then she crept into the iron stove, and began to weep and lament, and emptied her whole heart, and said, "Here am I deserted by the whole world, and yet I am a king's daughter, and a false waiting maid has by force brought me to such a pass that I have been compelled to put off my royal apparel, and she has taken my place with my bridegroom, and I have to perform menial service as a goose girl. If this my mother knew, her heart would break in two."

The aged king, however, was standing outside by the pipe of the stove, and was listening to what she said, and heard it. Then he came back again, and bade her come out of the stove. And royal garments were placed on her, and it was marvelous how beautiful she was!

The aged king summoned his son, and revealed to him that he had got the false bride who was only a waiting maid, but that the true one was standing there, as the former goose girl. The young king rejoiced with all his heart when he saw her beauty and youth, and a great feast was made ready to which all the people and all good friends were invited.

At the head of the table sat the bridegroom with the king's daughter at one side of him, and the waiting maid on the other, but the waiting maid was blinded, and did not recognize the princess in her dazzling array. When they had eaten and drunk, and were merry, the aged king asked the waiting maid, as a riddle, what punishment a person deserved who had behaved in such and such a way to her master, and at the same time related the whole story, and asked what sentence such a person merited.

Then the false bride said, "She deserves no better fate than to be stripped entirely naked, and put in a barrel which is studded inside with pointed nails, and two white horses should be harnessed to it, which will drag her along through one street after another, till she is dead."

"It is you," said the aged king, "and you have pronounced your own sentence, and thus shall it be done unto you." And when the sentence had been carried out, the young king married his true bride, and both of them reigned over their kingdom in peace and happiness.

THE PRINCESS ON THE GLASS HILL
Norway

Once on a time there was a man who had a meadow, which lay high up on the hillside, and in the meadow was a barn, which he had built to keep his hay in. Now, I must tell you there hadn't been much in the barn for the last year or two, for every Saint John's Eve, when the grass stood greenest and deepest, the meadow was eaten down to the very ground the next morning, just as if a whole drove of sheep had been there feeding on it overnight. This happened once, and it happened twice; so at last the man grew weary of losing his crop of hay, and said to his sons—for he had three of them, and the youngest was nicknamed Boots—that now one of them must just go and sleep in the barn in the outlying field when Saint John's Eve came, for it was too good a joke that his grass should be eaten, root and blade, this year, as it had been the last two years. So whichever of them went must keep a sharp lookout—that was what their father said.

Well, the eldest son was ready to go and watch the meadow; trust him for looking after the grass! It shouldn't be his fault if man or beast, or the Fiend himself, got a blade of grass. So, when evening came, he set off to the barn, and lay down to sleep; but a little on in the night came such a clatter, and such an earthquake that walls and roof shook, and groaned, and creaked. Then up jumped the lad, and took to his heels as fast as ever he could; nor dared he once look round till he reached home; and as for the hay, why, it was eaten up this year just as it had been twice before.

The next Saint John's Eve, the man said again it would never do to lose all the grass in the outlying field year after year in this way, so one of his sons must just trudge off to watch it, and watch it well too. Well, the next oldest son was ready to try his luck, so he set off, and lay down to sleep in the barn as his brother had done before him; but as night wore on there came on a rumbling and quaking of the earth, worse even than on the last Saint John's Eve, and when the lad heard it he got frightened, and took to his heels as though he were running a race.

Next year the turn came to Boots, but when he made ready to go, the other two began to laugh and to make game of him, saying—

"You're just the man to watch the hay, that you are, you who have done nothing all your life but sit in the ashes and toast yourself by the fire."

But Boots did not care a pin for their chattering and stumped away, as evening drew on, up the hillside to the outlying field. There he went inside the barn and lay down; but in about an hour's time the barn began to groan and creak, so that it was dreadful to hear.

"Well," said Boots to himself, "if it isn't worse than this, I can stand it well enough."

A little while after came another creak and an earthquake, so that the litter in the barn flew about the lad's ears.

"Oh!" said Boots to himself, "if it isn't worse than this, I daresay I can stand it out."

But just then came a third rumbling, and a third earthquake, so that the lad thought walls and roof were coming down on his head, but it passed off, and all was still as death about him.

"It'll come again, I'll be bound," thought Boots; but no, it did not come again; still it was and still it stayed; but after he had lain a little while he heard a noise as if a horse were standing just outside the barn door, and cropping the grass. He stole to the door, and peeped through a chink, and there stood a horse feeding away. So big and fat and grand a horse, Boots had never set eyes on; by his side on the grass lay a saddle and bridle, and a full set of armor for a knight, all of brass, so bright that the light gleamed from it.

"Ho, ho!" thought the lad. "It's you, is it, that eats up our hay? I'll soon put a spoke in your wheel, just see if I don't."

So he lost no time, but took the steel out of his tinderbox, and threw it over the horse. Then it had no power to stir from the spot, and became so tame that the lad could do what he liked with it. So he got on its back, and rode off with it to a place which no one knew of, and there he put up the horse. When he got home his brothers laughed, and asked how he fared.

"You didn't lie long in the barn, even if you had the heart to go so far as the field."

"Well," said Boots, "all I can say is, I lay in the barn till the sun rose, and neither saw nor heard anything. I can't think what there was in the barn to make you both so afraid."

"A pretty story!" said his brothers. "But we'll soon see how you have watched the meadow." So they set off; but when they reached it, there stood the grass as deep and thick as it had been overnight.

Well, the next Saint John's Eve it was the same story over again: neither of the elder brothers dared to go out to the outlying field to watch the crop; but Boots, he had the heart to go, and everything happened just as it had happened the year before. First a clatter and an earthquake, then a greater clatter and another earthquake, and so on a third time; only this year the earthquakes were far worse than the year before. Than all at once everything was as still as death, and the lad heard how something was cropping the grass outside the barn door, so he stole to the door, and peeped through a chink, and what do you think he saw? Why, another horse standing right up against the wall, chewing and champing with might and main. It was far finer and fatter than that which came the year before, and it had a saddle on its back and a bridle on its neck, and a full suit of mail for a knight lay by its side, all of silver, and as grand as you would wish to see.

"Ho, ho!" said Boots to himself. "It's you that gobbles up our hay, is it? I'll soon put a spoke in your wheel," and with that he took the steel out of his tinderbox and threw it over the horse's crest, which stood as still as a lamb. Well, the lad rode this horse, too, to the hiding place where he kept the other one, and after that he went home.

"I suppose you'll tell us," said one of the brothers, "there's a fine crop this year too, up in the hayfield."

"Well, so there is," said Boots; and off the other to see, and there stood the grass thick and deep, as it was the year before; but they didn't give Boots softer words for all that.

Now, the third Saint John's Eve came, the two elder still hadn't the heart to lie out in the barn and watch the grass, for they had got so scared at heart the night they lay there before, that they couldn't get over the fright. But Boots, he dared to go, and, to make a long story short, the very same thing happened this time as had happened twice before. Three earthquakes came, one after the other, each worse than the one which went before, and when the last came, the lad danced about with the shock from one barn wall to the other, and after that, all at once, it was still as death. Now when he had lain a little while he heard something tugging away at the grass outside the barn, so he stole again to the door chink, and peeped out, and there stood a horse close outside—far, far bigger and fatter than the two he had taken before.

"Ho, ho!" said the lad to himself. "It's you, is it, that comes here eating up our hay? I'll soon stop that—I'll soon put a spoke in your wheel." So he caught up his steel and threw it over the horse's neck, and in a trice it stood as if it were nailed to the ground, and Boots could do as he pleased with it. Then he rode off with it to the hiding place where he kept the other two, and then went home. When he got home his two brothers made game of him as they had done before, saying they could see he had watched the grass well, for he looked for all the world as if he were walking in his sleep, and many other spiteful things they said, but Boots gave no heed to them, only asking them to go and see for themselves; and when they went, there stood the grass as fine and deep this time as it had been twice before.

Now, you must know that the king of the country where Boots lived had a daughter, whom he would only give to the man who could ride up over a hill of glass, for there was a high, high hill, all of glass, as smooth and slippery as ice, close by the king's palace. Upon the tip-top of the hill the king's daughter was to sit, with three golden apples in her lap, and the man who could ride up and carry off the three golden apples was to have half the kingdom and the princess to wife. This the king had stuck up on all the church doors in his realm, and had given it out in many other kingdoms besides. Now, this princess was so lovely that all who set eyes on her fell over head and ears in love with her whether they would or no. So I needn't tell you how all the princes and knights who heard of her were eager to win her to wife, and half the kingdom beside, and how they came riding from all parts of the world on high prancing horses, and clad in the grandest clothes, for there wasn't one of them who hadn't made up his mind that he, and he alone, was to win the princess.

So when the day of trial came which the king had fixed, there was such a crowd of princes and knights under the glass hill, that it made one's head whirl to look at them, and everyone in the country who could even crawl along was off to the hill, for they all were eager to see the man who was to win the princess. So the two elder brothers set off with the rest; but as for Boots, they said outright he shouldn't go with them, for if they were seen with such a dirty changeling, all begrimed with smut from cleaning their shoes and sifting cinders in the dusthole, they said folk would make game of them.

"Very well," said Boots, "it's all one to me. I can go alone, and stand or fall by myself."

Now when the two brothers came to the hill of glass, the knights and princes were all hard at it, riding their horses till they were all in a foam; but it was no good, by my troth, for as soon as ever the horses set foot on the hill, down they slipped, and there wasn't one who could get a yard or two up; and no wonder, for the hill was as smooth as a sheet of glass, and as steep as a house wall. But all were eager to have the princess and half the kingdom, so they rode and slipped, and slipped and rode, and still it was the same story over again. At last all their horses were so weary that they could scarce lift a leg, and in such a sweat that the lather dripped from them, and so the knights had to give up trying any more. So the king was just thinking that he would proclaim a new trial for the next day, to see if they would have better luck, when all at once a knight came riding up on so brave a steed that no one had even seen the like of it in his born days, and the knight had mail of brass, and the horse a brass bit in his mouth, so bright that the sunbeams shone from it. Then all the others called out to him he might just as well spare himself the trouble of riding at the hill, for it would lead to no good; but he gave no heed to them, and put his horse at the hill, and went up it like nothing for a good way, about a third of the height; and when he had got so far, he turned his horse round and rode down again. So lovely a knight the princess thought she had never yet seen, and while he was riding, she sat and thought to herself—

"Would to Heaven he might only come up, and down the other side."

And when she saw him turning back, she threw down one of the golden apples after him, and it rolled down into his shoe. But when he got to the bottom of the hill he rode off so fast that no one could tell what had become of him. That evening all the knights and princes were to go before the king, that he who had ridden so far up the hill might show the apple which the princess had thrown, but there was no one who had anything to show. One after the other they all came, but not a man of them could show the apple.

At even the brothers of Boots came home too, and had such a long story to tell about the riding up the hill.

"First of all," they said, "there was not one of the whole lot who could get so much as a stride up. But at last came one who had a suit of brass mail, and brass bridle and saddle, all so bright that the sun shone from them a mile off. He was a chap to ride, just! He rode a third of the way up the hill of glass, and he could easily have ridden the whole way up if he chose, but he turned round and rode down, thinking, maybe, that was enough for once."

"Oh! I should so like to have seen him, that I should," said Boots who sat by the fireside and stuck his feet into the cinders as was his wont.

"Oh!" said his brothers, "you would, would you? You look fit to keep company with such high lords, nasty beast that you are sitting there among the ashes."

Next day the brothers were all for setting off again, and Boots begged them this time, too, to let him go with them and see the riding; but no, they wouldn't have him at any price, he was too ugly and nasty, they said.

"Well, well!" said Boots. "If I go at all, I must go by myself. I'm not afraid."

So when the brothers got to the hill of glass, all the princes and knights began to ride again, and you may fancy they had taken care to shoe their horses sharp; but it was no good—they rode and slipped, and slipped and rode, just as they had done the day before, and there was no one who could get so far as a yard up the hill. And when they had worn out their horses, so that they could not stir a leg, they were all forced to give it up as a bad job. So the king thought he might as well proclaim that the riding should take place the day after for the last time, just to give them one chance more; but all at once it came across his mind that he might as well wait a little longer, to see if the knight in brass mail would come this day too. Well, they saw nothing of him; but all at once came one riding on a steed, far, far, braver and finer than that on which the knight in brass had ridden, and he had silver mail, and a silver saddle and bridle, all so bright that the sunbeams gleamed and glanced from them far away. Then the others shouted out to him again, saying he might as well hold hard and not try to ride up the hill, for all his trouble would be thrown away; but the knight paid no heed to them, and rode straight at the hill, and right up it, till he had gone two-thirds of the way, and then he wheeled his horse round and rode down again. To tell the truth, the princess liked him still better than the knight in brass, and sat and wished he might only be able to come right up to the top and down the other side; but when she saw him turning back, she threw the second apple after him, and it rolled down and fell into his shoe. But as soon as ever he had come down from the hill of glass, he rode off so fast that no one could see what had become of him.

At even, when all were to go in before the king and the princess, that he who had the golden apple might show it, in they went, one after the other; but there was no one who had any apple to show, and the two brothers, as they had done on the former day, went home and told how things had gone, and how all had ridden at the hill and none got up.

"But, last of all," they said, "came one in a silver suit, and his horse had a silver saddle and a silver bridle. He was just a chap to ride, and he got two-thirds up the hill, and then turned back. He was a fine fellow and no mistake, and the princess threw the second gold apple to him."

"Oh!" said Boots, "I should so like to have seen him too, that I should."

"A pretty story!" they said. "Perhaps you think his coat of mail was as bright as the ashes you are always poking about, and sifting, you nasty dirty beast."

The third day everything happened as it had happened the two days before. Boots begged him to go and see the sight, but the two wouldn't hear of his going with them. When they got to the hill there was no one who could get so much as a yard up it; and now all waited for the knight in silver mail, but they neither saw nor heard of him. At last came one riding on a steed, so brave that no one had ever seen his match; and the knight had a suit of golden mail, and a golden saddle and bridle, so wondrous bright that the sunbeams gleamed from them a mile off. The other knights and princes could not find time to call out to him not to try his luck, for they amazed to see how grand he was. So he rode right at the hill and tore up it like nothing, so that the princess hadn't even time to wish that he might get up the whole way. As soon as ever he reached the top, he took the third golden apple from the princess's lap, and then turned his horse and rode down again. As soon as he got down, he rode off at full speed and was out of sight in no time.

Now, when the brothers got home at even, you may fancy what long stories they told, how the riding had gone off that day; and among other things, they had a deal to say about the knight in golden mail.

"He just was a chap to ride!" they said. "So grand a knight isn't to be found in the wide world."

"Oh!" said Boots, "I should so like to have seen him, that I should."

"Ah!" said his brothers, "his mail shone a deal brighter than the glowing coals which you are always poking and digging at, nasty dirty beast that you are."

Next day all the knights and princes were to pass before the king and the princess—it was too late to do so the night before, I suppose—that he who had the gold apple might bring it forth; but one came after another, first the princes and then the knights, and still no one could show the gold apple.

"Well," said the king, "someone must have it, for it was something that we all saw with our own eyes, how a man came and rode up and bore it off."

So he commanded that everyone who was in the kingdom should come up to the palace and see if they could show the apple. Well, they all came, one after another, but no one had the golden apple, and after a long time the two brothers of Boots came. They were the last of all, so the king asked them if there was no one else in the kingdom who hadn't come.

"Oh, yes," said they. "We have a brother, but he never carried off the golden apple. He hasn't stirred out of the dusthole on any of the three days."

"Never mind that," said the king. "He may as well come up to the palace to rest."

So Boots had to go to the palace.

"How, now," said the king, "have you got the golden apple? Speak out!"

"Yes, I have," said Boots. "Here is the first, and here is the second, and here is the third too," and with that he pulled all three golden apples out of his pockets, and at the same time threw off his sooty rags and stood before them in his gleaming golden mail.

"Yes!" said the king. "You shall have my daughter and half my kingdom, for you well deserve both her and it."

So they got ready for the wedding, and Boots got the princess to wife, and there was great merrymaking at the bridal feast, you may fancy, for they could all be merry though they couldn't ride up the hill of glass; and all I can say is, if they haven't left off their merrymaking yet, they're still at it.

The Promises of the Three Sisters
Egypt

Once there was a king. He wanted to see if his subjects loved him or not. He said to his vizier, "Vizier, send criers throughout my country to tell people not to have any lights on tonight."

The vizier carried out the king's order.

That night the king said to the vizier, "Let's go out and see who loves me and who does not."

They disguised themselves as merchants, wearing merchants' clothes, and went through town. It was very dark in town, for nobody had lights on.

The vizier said to the king, "Now you can be sure that everybody loves you." And they started back to the palace.

At the edge of town, they saw a very faint light coming from a small distant hut. The king was very upset and said to his vizier, "Let's go and see what's the matter with those who have disobeyed my order."

When they arrived at the hut, they found three girls weaving inside. The eldest girl was pretty, the middle girl was prettier, but the youngest girl was the prettiest. The king and the vizier listened to them talk as they wove.

The first one said, "If the king were to marry me, I would bake him a cake that would be enough for him and his army."

The second girl said, "If the king were to marry me, I would weave him a carpet that would seat him and his army."

The third one said, "If the king were to marry me, I would bear him Sitt el-Husn [mistress of beauty] and Clever Muhammad. Their hair would be of gold and silver; for every golden hair there would be a silver hair."

The king listened to what they said and went home. In the morning he sent for them. When they came he asked them, "Why did you disobey my orders? Didn't you know that I ordered that no lights would be lit last night?"

The girls replied, "We knew, king."

"Then why did you disobey my orders?" asked the king.

They answered, "We are orphans, and we have to weave all night so that we can sell what we weave in the morning for three piasters. If we didn't weave, we would die of hunger."

The king said, "I forgive you," and he gave each of them a present and said to the eldest, "Will you marry me?"

"Yes!" Of course the girl agreed.

The day following the wedding night, the king said to her, "Now bake me a cake that will be enough for me and my army."

The girl laughed and said, "Did you believe this? 'Night talk is covered with butter; it melts when the sun rises.' "

The king divorced her and married the middle sister.

Again on the day following the wedding night the king said to her, "Now weave me the rug that will seat me and my army."

The girl laughed and said, "Did you believe this? 'Night talk is covered with butter; it melts when the sun rises.' "

The king divorced her and married the youngest sister.

God was kind to her, and on the day following the wedding night, she was pregnant. After nine months she gave birth to twins, a baby girl and a baby boy. Her sisters, who were living in the palace as servants, had fires of jealousy ignited inside them. They agreed with the midwife to substitute a puppy and a kitten for the boy and the girl. They put the infants in a box and nailed down the lid and threw it in the river.

When they told the king, "Your wife gave birth to a puppy and a kitten," the king was sad, but he replied, "God's grant is always good. Take the children to her, and let her feed them."

He sent her off with her sisters and stayed alone sadly.

Now we go back to the box. It drifted with the current until it got caught in the weeds. A fisherman who had nobody but himself and his wife was fishing nearby. God had been sending him two fish a day, one for himself and one for his wife. He saw the box, picked it out of the water, and ran home to his wife.

His wife said to him, "Take it back to where you found it, for it is either money that we don't need or evil that we don't want at this old age. We are seeking only a good end."

Her husband said to her, "Woman, this was sent to us by God, and we have to accept it."

They opened the box and found the two beautiful babies. The girl had her thumb in the boy's mouth and the boy had his thumb in the girl's mouth. They were suckling each other. They took them in and called the boy Clever Muhammad and the girl Sitt el-Husn.

The woman immediately had milk in her breasts, and that day the fisherman caught four fish.

Folktales' children grow quickly. The boy and girl loved each other very much. When the girl cried, it rained, and her brother, wherever he was, would know that she was unhappy. When she smiled, the sun shone, and her brother would know she was happy.

One day the fisherman called his son and said, "Son, I will die on such-and-such a day. Under my pillow you will find two hairs from a horse's mane. If you need anything, just rub them."

The boy went out fishing in his father's place that day. After a while it started raining, and he realized that his sister was crying and that his father had died. He went back and did what needed to be done and buried his father.

The following day when he was out, the mother called the girl and said to her, "Daughter, I'm going to die on Friday. Under my pillow you will find a purse. Every morning when you open it, you will find ten pounds in it."

A few days later, when the boy was out fishing, it started raining, and again the boy knew that his sister was crying and that his mother had died. He went home and did what needed to be done. He called an old woman who was there: "Mother, won't you help us wash my mother!" And he buried her.

The boy and his sister left the hut and went to town. With every sunrise the girl found ten pounds in the purse. She saved all the money she found and finally bought a plot of land opposite the king's palace. She got builders and said to them, "I want you to build a palace exactly like that of the king."

One day the king was passing by and saw the new palace. He asked, "Whose palace is this?"

People answered him, "Clever Muhammad and his sister Sitt el-Husn's."

The king met Clever Muhammad and found him to be very generous and polite. He liked him very much, and they spent most of their time together. They ate together, drank together, sat together, did everything together.

Now the boy's maternal aunts, his mother's sisters, recognized him because of his gold and silver hair. They kept on inquiring about him and learned also about his sister. Now they said, "Surely they are the two babies that we had thrown in the river."

They went to visit this sister. They said to her, "Sweetheart, your palace is beautiful, and it is complete except for one thing."

She asked, "What is it?"

They answered (they were mischievous), "It is very hard to get, and your brother would not be willing to get it for you."

She said, "Just tell me, and my brother will get it for me."

They said to her, "Your palace lacks the dancing bamboo."

While her brother was sitting with the king, it started raining. He realized that his sister was crying. He asked the king's permission and left. When he got home he asked her, "Why are you crying, sister?"

She told him, "I want the dancing bamboo."

Clever Muhammad said to her, "Don't worry; you will have it."

They prepared rations for him, and he set out "from God's countries to God's peoples" asking about the dancing bamboo.

One old woman told him, "Between you and the dancing bamboo is three years' travel. It is in the garden of Father Ogre. The ogre sleeps for seven years and is awake for seven years. Hurry, may God will that you catch him during his sleep, the seven years of his sleep."

Clever Muhammad went in the direction that the old woman showed him; he finally got to the ogre's garden. He heard neither sound nor word. He climbed the walls, and inside the garden he saw the bamboo, dancing just like humans, even better. When he got close, the bamboo started dancing very hard. The birds started screaming, and the roses shouted, "A stranger! A stranger! A thief!"

He quickly pulled out a bunch of bamboo, wrapped the roots in his mantle, and fled. Meanwhile, it was time for Father Ogre to wake up. The noise and the shouting awakened him, and he came out to look. He saw Clever Muhammad escaping. But before he could do anything, Clever Muhammad was gone. He went back to where he came.

When his sister Sitt el-Husn saw the bamboo, she became very happy. They planted the bunch in the garden. It grew and prospered and kept on dancing.

Her two maternal aunts came and saw the bamboo that dances. They knew that Clever Muhammad had returned safely. They said to Sitt el-Husn, "That bamboo is nothing! Still your garden lacks the singing water!" And they left.

Sitt el-Husn cried, and it rained. Her brother saw it and came back in a hurry. "What is the matter, sister?"

She answered in tears, "I want the singing water!"

He said, "Never worry. I will get it for you."

Like the first time, they prepared rations, and he set out "from God's countries to God's peoples." He took the same road that he had taken before and came to the same old woman. She said to him, "Clever Muhammad! Now what?"

He answered, "I need to get the singing water."

The old woman said to him, "Between you and the singing water is seven years' journey. It is in the garden of Mother Ogress. She is like her son and sleeps for seven years and is awake for seven years. Take this road."

Clever Muhammad took the road which she showed him. He kept on traveling until he came to a beautiful palace with walls as high as ten men's height. He climbed the walls and got in. What happened in the garden of Father Ogre happened in the garden of Mother Ogress. The water started shouting, "A stranger! A thief!" and so did the birds and the roses and the fruits, everything.

He filled a bottle which he had with him, and before the ogress woke up, he was on his way home. He returned to his sister, and they put the water in a fountain. It started singing! Now they had two wonders in their garden, the dancing bamboo and the singing water.

Their two aunts came to visit Sitt el-Husn. Of course they had thought that Clever Muhammad was gone—that he had died, or a beast had eaten him or something—but when they heard that he had returned, they thought of another disaster into which to throw him and his sister Sitt el-Husn.

They went to Sitt el-Husn and said to her, "Now your garden will be perfect, perfect if only you get the talking lark."

They left, and Sitt el-Husn cried. Her brother came. She said to him, "Our palace—is lacking—the talking lark. I want it."

He said to her, "Never mind. I'll get it for you."

He set out with his rations and took the same road which he had taken before. He got to the old woman. She said to him, "Now, Clever Muhammad, what next?"

He said to her, "I need the talking lark!"

The old woman said to him, "All but that! Someone wants you destroyed. You go back home and settle down, for no one knows where the land of the talking lark is."

Clever Muhammad did not know what to do. While he was sitting and thinking, he remembered the two hairs his father had given to him. He rubbed them, and there in front of him he found a horse; this horse was the son of the king of the jinn.

The horse said to him, "I'm at your command. Order and you will find."

Clever Muhammad told him the story. The son of the king of

the jinn said, "Between you and the talking lark there are a thousand years. It is in the garden of the palace of Um-ishi-Aoor, the long-haired lady. I can only take you there, but I can't go in with you. When you get there, you will find sheep grazing there. Take one and cut it in four pieces. In front of her palace you will find two lions. Give each one a sheep quarter. They will say to you, 'Hello, Clever Muhammad. You have honored us.' Do not answer them at all, because if you do, you will find yourself changed into stone. At the second gate of the palace, you will find two dogs. Give each one a sheep quarter. They will say to you, 'Hello, Clever Muhummad. You have honored us.' Do not answer them at all, because if you do, they will tear you apart. Inside the garden you will find Lady Um-ishi-Aoor. She will say to you, 'Hello, Clever Muhammad. I love you, Clever Muhammad. You are predestined for me, Clever Muhammad.' Do not dare to answer her or to utter a word. If you were to speak, she would transform you into stone."

Clever Muhammad did as the son of the king of the jinn told him. As he entered the garden, trees spoke to him: "Hello, Clever Muhammad." And roses spoke to him: "Welcome, Clever Muhammad." And finally he found the long-haired lady before him. There were many stone people all around him; they had wanted to get the lark but had not kept silent. Wherever he looked, there were stone people.

The long-haired lady said to him, "I love you, Clever Muhammad. I know why you are here, Clever Muhammad. I know what your mother's sisters have done to you and to your sister." But he did not pay any attention to what she said. He walked to the middle of the garden and found a golden cage on a marble pedestal. The talking lark was sitting outside of its open door. The lark kept on saying, "Clever Muhammad, you whose father is a king—you who—you who—"

Clever Muhammad did not utter a word. Finally, when the lark got tired of talking, it said, "I am tired! Isn't there someone who will say to me, 'Rest!' Isn't there someone who will say to me, 'Sleep!' Isn't there someone—isn't there someone—"

Finally Clever Muhammad shouted at it, "Why don't you be quiet! Why don't you sleep, brother, and get it over with?" Immediately he was turned to stone.

Now, to whom shall we go back with our tale? To his sister, Sitt el-Husn. His sister's heart felt that her brother was in danger. She put on men's clothing and prepared rations and left. She kept on going—one country carries her and one country puts her down. She finally saw a huge dust cloud reaching to the sky; it kept on coming nearer to her, and finally she saw herself in front of an ogre. Before the ogre could say anything, she said to him, "Peace be upon you, Father Ogre."

The ogre replied, "Had your greeting not preceded your speech, I would have munched on your flesh before your bones. What brings you here?"

She said, "I am looking for the talking lark."

He said to her (he didn't know that she was a woman), "Son, why don't you go back. You are too young to die."

She said, "I must go on."

He said to her, "Keep on going this way; you will find my brother. He is one day older and one year more knowledgeable than myself."

She kept on going until she met the brother of the ogre. She said to him, "Peace be upon you, Father Ogre."

He said to her, "Had your greeting not preceded your speech, I would have munched on your flesh before your bones. What do you want?"

She said, "I want to go to the country of the talking lark."

He said to her, like the first one, "Go back" and all that.

She said, "I must go on."

He said to her, "Keep on going. You will meet our eldest brother. He is one day older and one year more knowledgeable than myself or my younger brother whom you have met."

She kept on going until she finally came to the third ogre. He was the biggest of them all. She said to him, "Peace be upon you."

He answered, "Had your greeting not preceded your speech, I would have munched on your flesh before your bones. What do you want?"

She said, "I want to go to the country of the talking lark."

He said to her, "It must be very important to you. Take this ball and this racket. Hit the ball with the racket and follow it. It will take you there in no time."

She took the ball and the racket and kept on hitting the ball with the racket and following it until she finally found herself in front of the palace of the long-haired lady. She did as her brother did. She killed a sheep and gave each lion a quarter. They let her pass through the gate. When she met the two dogs, she gave each one of them a quarter and found herself inside the garden.

She looked around, and there were whole nations of people petrified, nations upon nations of people. She came to the lark and found that he was standing outside his cage with her brother, a stone, right next to him. The lark kept on saying, "You, Sitt el-Husn, whose father is the king and whose mother is such and such and such and such—"

She did not say a word. Finally the lark did to her exactly what he had done to her brother. The lark started saying, "Oh, I am tired. Isn't there somebody who will say to me, 'Rest!' Isn't there somebody—isn't there somebody—"

She was more clever than her brother. She did not say a word. Finally the lark entered his cage. Immediately, she closed the door after him and picked him up. At this very moment, as soon as she closed the cage, all the people who were stone came back to life. They went to their homes. Her brother did not recognize her. She was dressed in men's clothing then. He said to her, "Thank you, brother," thinking she was a man like himself.

She answered, "I am your sister. What made you this way? Why did you speak to the lark?"

He answered, "God's command."

Together they went outside the palace from whence they came. They found the horse, the jinni, in the same place where her brother had left it before. Her brother mounted it, and she mounted behind him, and in the blink of an eye they were back home.

The lark said, "I want you to give a party for the king. Ask the king to invite all of his ministers, all of his army, all of his people, and ask him not to forget his dog and cat children and also the midwife and his two previous wives."

They all came. The king had the dog and the cat all dressed in silk and seated on golden chairs. When everybody was there, the king asked Clever Muhammad, "What is the party for?"

Clever Muhammad answered, "For this lark."

The king wondered. "A party for a bird? It is only a bird."

The lark spoke to the king, "Peace be upon you, king."

The king was amazed. "And upon you be peace, lark."

The lark said, pointing to the cat and the dog, "What is this, king?"

The king replied, "It is God's grant, lark. Whatever God grants must be good."

The lark said, "Is there a king who would beget dogs and cats, king?"

The king replied, "It is God's will, lark."

The lark said, "Bring the midwife."

They brought her. She came trembling, with her face as blue as indigo. As soon as she saw the children, she immediately shouted, "I didn't do it! It was their maternal aunts! Their maternal aunts said to me, 'Give us the children, and we will give you the dog and the cat to put in their place.' "

Now, everyone in the kingdom was there, and everyone heard. The king said to his people, "He who loves the Chosen Prophet should set fire to the midwife and the aunts." And they burned them. The king restored his wife.

And they lived in stability and prosperity and begat boys and girls.

THE MAGIC MIRROR OF RABBI ADAM
Jewish

Now Rabbi Adam possessed a magic mirror that had once belonged to King David, which permitted him to see things that took place all over the world, and he made it his task to watch over his fellow Jews in that mirror. One day Rabbi Adam looked into this magic mirror and saw that a Jew in a certain city was in mortal danger, although he had done nothing to deserve the fate that awaited him. When he saw this, Rabbi Adam resolved to do something to help this Jew, and he mounted his horse and pronounced a spell, so that the hooves of the horse flew along the ground without touching it, and before an hour had passed Rabbi Adam had arrived in the city of the Jew who was in danger.

As soon as he arrived, Rabbi Adam walked through the city, and saw its streets and markets, and they were crowded with man and beast like sand on the seashore. Rabbi Adam spoke to a man in the marketplace and asked, "Why are so many people all crowded together here?" And the man replied, "Throughout the year the city is quiet and subdued. Only for two weeks of the year does it seethe like a boiling pot, and merchants come here from all corners of the land to sell their wares. These days are the market days, and all the townspeople live for an entire year from the earnings of these two weeks."

Rabbi Adam came to a tavern, and found there many merchants who were eating and drinking, and among them a Jewish merchant from a nearby city. Rabbi Adam sat down beside him and turned to him and said, "Pay heed, for when four hours have passed you will be killed." Now the merchant thought that the old man was mad, so he did not even reply to him. He continued to eat delicacies and drink wine, and then he got up and went over to the men with whom he had traveled to the market, and told them what the old man had said. They laughed and told him not to pay attention to the words of a madman, and not to worry, for what he said was surely nonsense.

An hour later Rabbi Adam returned to the merchant and said, "Know that the hours of life you have left are only three." The merchant laughed at these words, and again told his friends, and they also laughed.

When he left the tavern, the merchant returned to the market and arranged his merchandise, and before long the old man appeared before him again and said, "One hour ago I spoke to you and your mouth was filled with laughter. Now there are only two hours left of your life." And when the merchant heard this, he grew afraid for the first time, and he went to his friends and told them of his fear. They said to him, "Why didn't you stop him before he left you, for perhaps *he* is plotting to kill you." Then the merchant said to them, "When he comes back to me again I will not let him go until he tells me everything, but I am convinced he intends me no harm."

One hour passed, and Rabbi Adam came to the merchant and said, "Know that in one hour you will leave this world." Then the merchant grabbed his arms and shouted, "I will not release you until you tell me who you are, and who it is that is plotting to kill me." The rabbi replied, "You have spoken truly, for there are those who are plotting to kill you. I have discovered this plot, and I have come here to save you from descending into the grave." And this time the merchant recognized that what Rabbi Adam said must be the truth, and he grew afraid for his life. Then he said, "If this is the case, tell me what I should do." And the rabbi said, "Come with me and do everything that I command." The merchant stood there as rigid as a statue, and then he said, "I am ready to follow you."

Rabbi Adam and the merchant walked together until they came to an inn. There Rabbi Adam said to the innkeeper, "How much do you earn a day at the inn?" "Twenty silver shekels a day" was the reply. "If that is so," said Rabbi Adam, "behold I am giving you twenty silver shekels on the condition that you do not allow anyone else to enter your inn for the rest of the day, neither to eat nor to drink. Nor must you allow any wagon drivers to rest in your courtyard."

The innkeeper heeded his words and closed the inn. After this Rabbi Adam turned to the servant of the inn, and requested that a bathtub be brought to the merchant's room, and that it be filled with water. The servant did as Rabbi Adam asked, and then Rabbi Adam commanded the merchant to climb into the tub. The merchant took off his clothes, and climbed in as he was commanded to do. Then Rabbi Adam took out his magic mirror and told the merchant to look within it and to tell him all that he saw. The merchant stretched out his hand and took the mirror and gazed into it, and a great terror descended upon him, and he was silent. Then Rabbi Adam said, "Did I not tell you to reveal to me all that you have seen? Speak!" After this the merchant said, "I see my wife in the company of a man of my town who is known as a sorcerer. They are sitting together, eating and drinking and hugging and kissing, and on the table is a bow and arrow."

Then Rabbi Adam said, "Know that your wife has betrayed you with the evil sorcerer, and even now they are plotting your death. The danger is very great, for the sorcerer has the powers of evil at his command. He is about to shoot an arrow from that bow, and the powers of evil will guide it to you so that it pierces your heart. And after your death the sorcerer and your wife will marry, and will live together without fear of any man. But with the help of God this evil plan will not succeed. Now look again and tell me what you see in the mirror."

The merchant gazed into the mirror again, and said, "Your words are true and correct. Now the sorcerer is making ready to shoot it with his own wicked hands."

Rabbi Adam then said to him, "Do not be afraid or let your heart be faint, for now there is no turning back. Watch carefully what he does, and when you see that he is about to shoot the arrow, then put your head under the water at once. For you must hold your breath and remain submerged until the arrow has passed by you and gone astray. Afterward I will signal for you to lift your head out of the water and sit up." And this is what the merchant did, and a few seconds after he was submerged in the water, a sound was heard in the room like the hissing of an arrow, and when Rabbi Adam signaled him, the merchant lifted his head out of the water. Then Rabbi Adam had him look into the mirror once more, and asked him what he saw, and the merchant replied, "I see my wife and she is in a black mood, and the spirit of the sorcerer is raging within him."

Then Rabbi Adam said, "Good! Now continue to watch closely, and if he sends forth another arrow, do as you did the first time." And when the merchant saw the sorcerer readying the arrow to be shot, he immersed himself fully in the water, and again saved his life.

After this Rabbi Adam said to him, "Look once more into the looking glass, and tell me what you see." And the merchant gazed into the mirror, and saw that his wife was unhappy and that the sorcerer's anger had become like a sea that could not be calmed. He reported this to Rabbi Adam, who said to him, "Look directly at him in the mirror, and if you see that he is going to attempt this evil deed a third time, do as I commanded you at first, but this time while you are submerged extend the little finger of your right hand out of the water."

Once more the merchant looked into the mirror of Rabbi Adam, and once more he saw the sorcerer take up the bow and arrow. Then he immersed himself in the water, but left the tip of his little finger exposed, just as Rabbi Adam had commanded. And as he was holding his breath under water he felt a sharp pain in his finger, and his hand fell back into the water. After this he lifted up his head, and the rabbi gave him the mirror to look into again. Gazing into the mirror, the merchant said, "Now I see that the sorcerer and my wife are rejoicing." And Rabbi Adam said, "That is because they have been deceived into thinking that they have succeeded in killing you, for your little finger stopped the enchanted arrow, and did not permit it to pass through the inn as it did the first two times. Now you can come out of the tub and put on your clothes. So far you have been saved, but danger still hovers over your head. Still, do not be afraid, just do as I tell you to do and your life will be saved." And the merchant left the tub and got dressed, as the rabbi had directed.

The next day the merchant intended to return to his own city, for the market days had ended. But Rabbi Adam said to him, "You may return to your city, but when you get there do not go to your own house. Go instead to that of relatives, and dwell there in secret. After three weeks have passed go forth from that house and go the market. Remain there until the sorcerer sees you. Go up to him and greet him and reply truthfully to any questions that he may ask. Do not hesitate to tell him about me, and if he wants to know where I can be found, tell him that I am willing to stand in his presence to test whose powers are stronger. He will surely not decline this challenge, for he is confident of his powers. Then fix a place and time, and I will meet him there."

The merchant did as Rabbi Adam had commanded. He traveled to his home town, but when he arrived there he dwelt in secret in the house of a relative. When three weeks had passed he left the house and walked to the market in the center of town. Before he had been there very long he saw the sorcerer, who turned pale when he saw him, and approached the merchant and said, "It was said in town that you had gone to the grave." The merchant replied, "I was saved from an early grave." "Who saved you?" asked the sorcerer. "A fellow Jew saved me from the hands of those who sought to slay me." Then the sorcerer said, "Who is this man?" "A holy man, whose name is Rabbi Adam," said the merchant. Then the eyes of the sorcerer grew narrow, and he hissed, "If you do not bring this man before me, you are a dead man." And even though the evil sorcerer had revealed himself, the merchant remained calm and said, "Fix a time and a place, and I will send for him. You can be certain that he will meet you there." So it was that a meeting of the sorcerer and Rabbi Adam was set to take place in the sorcerer's home.

Now the evil sorcerer was so confident that he could defeat Rabbi Adam with his powers that he invited all the nobles of that province to witness the contest. And when the appointed hour had arrived, Rabbi Adam came there accompanied by the merchant, and they found many nobles in the house, who were eating and drinking at the sorcerer's table. One drunken noble said to Rabbi Adam, "Perform wonders for us, show us your powers!" And Rabbi Adam said, "I do not perform wonders, but I put my faith and trust in the Lord, whose powers have never failed me."

The nobles, who were not fond of Jews in the first place, did not like this reply. And they urged the sorcerer to begin the contest at once. The sorcerer complied by bringing out an empty bowl, into which he poured water. Then he passed his staff over it, and the water in the bowl vanished. The nobles gasped when they saw this, and the sorcerer passed the bowl around among them, so that they could confirm it was empty. Then, when they gave it back to him, the sorcerer passed his staff over it in the other direction, and the water reappeared, much to the amazement of the nobles.

Then the sorcerer, looking very smug, asked Rabbi Adam to perform the same feat. "Gladly," said Rabbi Adam. He stepped forward and passed his hand over the bowl of water, and again all the water disappeared. Then he passed the bowl around among the nobles, as the sorcerer had done, and when they saw that it was empty and returned it to him, he passed his hand over it in the other direction and it was filled again. But this time it was filled not with water, but with wine! The nobles were even more amazed at this, and the face of the sorcerer was pale with anger.

Then the sorcerer took down a cage in which he kept a dove. He opened the cage and took out the bird. Then he placed it on the table and passed his staff over it. All at once the dove collapsed, and lay there stiff and dead. Then the sorcerer passed his staff over it in the other direction, and the dove came back to life, flapping its wings. The nobles applauded when they saw this, and all were certain that Rabbi Adam could not duplicate this feat.

Then Rabbi Adam took his place before the dove, and passed his hand over it. Immediately the dove dropped to the table with a thump, its feet in the air. The nobles examined it and all agreed that it was surely dead. Then Rabbi Adam passed his hand over it in the other direction, and the wings of the dove began to flap, and it flew around the room. After this it landed on the table and, to the amazement of all, laid an egg. And only a moment later the egg broke open and a small fledgling inside it stretched its wings. And when the evil sorcerer saw this, a look of terrible hatred crossed his face. Then he said, "I am ready to perform one more wonder, which I am quite certain the Jewish magician cannot duplicate. But I must ask that he leave the room as I perform it, so that he does not overhear the spell that I pronounce."

Rabbi Adam departed from the room, and the sorcerer faced the nobles, his staff in his hand. He held his staff upright on the floor and pronounced a spell over it, and lo, the staff began to blossom and branch, and before long it produced green leaves and apples on the ends of the branches, which quickly grew ripe. The nobles were astonished at this wonder, and they applauded the sorcerer's accomplishment. Then the sorcerer bowed to the nobles and called Rabbi Adam into the room. And when he came in there, the sorcerer said, "Observe this tree and its delightful fruit. Now let us see how great is your power, and if you can cause the tree to wither, and become a staff once more." Then Rabbi Adam turned to the nobles and said, "Since the master of the house commanded me to leave the room when he performed this wonder, I request that he also depart the room at this time." The nobles agreed that this was only proper, and they asked the sorcerer to leave the room until they called on him to return.

After the sorcerer left, Rabbi Adam walked around and around the tree, all the time remarking, "How good are these apples and how pleasant this tree!" As he was circling the tree, seven times in all, his eyes were fixed on an apple at the top of the tree which was exceptionally red, a delight to the eyes. He turned to the chief noble among them and said, "Honored sir, would you be so kind as to cut off this very red apple at the top of the tree?" The nobleman agreed to do this, took a knife, and cut off the desired apple and gave it to Rabbi Adam. And no sooner did he do this than the apples left on the tree began to wither, the leaves fell off, the branches withdrew, and the trunk withered until it was the staff that the sorcerer had begun with. All that remained was the apple in Rabbi Adam's hand, which had remained as ripe as ever.

After this Rabbi Adam commanded that the sorcerer be brought back into the room. One of the nobles went out to get him, and behold, he found the body of the sorcerer in one corner of the room, and his head in another. The nobles were greatly shocked at this turn of events, and they asked Rabbi Adam to explain. He said, "Whoever undertakes to perform magic puts his life at risk, for every wonder created contains one weakness, which can be the undoing of the person who has cast the spell. And in this case it was the apple at the top of the tree that was the one weakness."

Then the nobles sat in judgment over Rabbi Adam, to decide if he had sinned in bringing about the death of the sorcerer. They considered this matter for some time, and concluded that Rabbi Adam had only performed his part of the wonder, by returning the flourishing tree to a staff, and that it was the evil sorcerer's fault for putting himself at risk. The Rabbi left the nobles with great honor, and they sent him home in peace.

And the merchant, who had witnessed all that had taken place, rejoiced greatly over the miracle, and thanked Rabbi Adam for saving him from the hands of the powerful sorcerer. But Rabbi Adam told him to give thanks to God, for all great miracles come from Him. After that the merchant went with his wife to a rabbinical court and divorced her. The wife left her husband's house, but in her heart were thoughts of repentance. She began to fast and pray, and eventually she returned to God with her whole heart. And the Lord, who does not desire the death of the wicked but only that they return to the ways of the righteous, accepted her repentance. But the evil sorcerer who sinned and led her to sin was lost and cut off from the earth for all time.

THE OLD WOMAN WHO LIVED IN
A VINEGAR BOTTLE
England

Once upon a time there was a woman who lived in a vinegar bottle. One day a fairy was passing that way, and she heard the old woman talking to herself.

"It is a shame, it is a shame, it is a shame," said the old woman. "I didn't ought to live in a vinegar bottle. I ought to live in a nice little cottage with a thatched roof, and roses growing all up the wall, that I ought."

So the fairy said, "Very well, when you go to bed tonight you turn round three times, and shut your eyes, and in the morning you'll see what you will see."

So the old woman went to bed, and turned round three times and shut her eyes, and in the morning there she was, in a pretty little cottage with a thatched roof, and roses growing up the walls. And she was very surprised, and very pleased, but she quite forgot to thank the fairy.

And the fairy went north, and she went south, and she went east, and she went west, all about the business she had to do. And presently she thought, "I'll go and see how that old woman is getting on. She must be very happy in her little cottage."

And as she got up to the front door, she heard the old woman talking to herself.

"It is a shame, it is a shame, it is a shame," said the old woman. "I didn't ought to live in a little cottage like this, all by myself. I ought to live in a nice little house in a row of houses, with lace curtains at the windows, and a brass knocker on the door, and people calling mussels and cockles outside, all merry and cheerful."

The fairy was rather surprised; but she said, "Very well. You go to bed tonight, and turn round three times, and shut your eyes, and in the morning you shall see what you shall see."

So the old woman went to bed, and turned round three times and shut her eyes, and in the morning there she was in a nice little house, in a row of little houses, with lace curtains at the windows, and a brass knocker on the door, and people calling mussels and cockles outside, all merry and cheerful. And she was very much surprised, and very much pleased. But she quite forgot to thank the fairy.

And the fairy went north, and she went south, and she went east, and she went west, all about the business she had to do; and after a time she thought to herself, "I'll go and see how that old woman is getting on. Surely she must be happy now."

And when she got to the little row of houses, she heard the old woman talking to herself. "It is a shame, it is a shame," said the old woman. "I didn't ought to live in a row of houses like this, with common people on each side of me. I ought to live in a great mansion in the country, with a big garden all round it, and servants to answer the bell."

And the fairy was very surprised, and rather annoyed, but she said, "Very well, go to bed and turn round three times, and shut your eyes, and in the morning you will see what you will see."

And the old woman went to bed and turned round three times, and shut her eyes, and in the morning there she was, in a great mansion in the country, surrounded by a fine garden, and servants to answer the bell. And she was very pleased and very surprised, and she learned how to speak genteelly, but she quite forgot to thank the fairy.

And the fairy went north, and she went south, and she went east, and she went west, all about the business she had to do; and after a time she thought to herself, "I'll go and see how that old woman is getting on. Surely she must be happy now."

But no sooner had she got near the old woman's drawing-room window than she heard the old woman talking to herself in a genteel voice.

"It certainly is a very great shame," said the old woman, "that I should be living alone here, where there is no society. I ought to be a duchess, driving in my own coach to wait on the queen, with footmen running beside me."

The fairy was very much surprised, and very much disappointed, but she said, "Very well. Go to bed tonight, and turn round three times and shut your eyes, and in the morning you shall see what you shall see."

So the old woman went to bed, and turned round three times, and shut her eyes, and in the morning, there she was, a duchess with a coach of her own, to wait on the queen, and footmen running beside her. And she was very much surprised, and very much pleased. BUT she quite forgot to thank the fairy.

And the fairy went north, and she went south, and she went east, and she went west, all about the business she had to do; and after a while she thought to herself, "I'd better go and see how that old woman is getting on. Surely she is happy, now she's a duchess."

But no sooner had she come to the window of the old woman's great town mansion, than she heard her saying in a more genteel tone than ever, "It is indeed a very great shame that I should be a mere duchess, and have to curtsey to the queen. Why can't I be a queen myself, and sit on a golden throne, with a golden crown on my head, and courtiers all around me?"

The fairy was very much disappointed and very angry; but she said, "Very well. Go to bed and turn round three times, and shut your eyes, and in the morning you shall see what you shall see."

So the old woman went to bed, and turned round three times, and shut her eyes, and in the morning there she was in a royal palace, a queen in her own right, sitting on a golden throne, with a golden crown on her head, and her courtiers all around her. And she was highly delighted, and ordered them right and left. BUT she quite forgot to thank the fairy.

And the fairy went north, and she went south, and she went east, and she went west, all about the business she had to do; and after a while she thought to herself, "I'll go and see how that old woman is getting on. Surely she must be satisfied now!"

But as soon as she got near the throne room, she heard the old woman talking.

"It is a great shame, a very great shame," she said, "that I should be queen of a paltry little country like this instead of ruling the whole round world. What I am really fitted for is to be *Pope*, to govern the minds of everyone on earth."

"Very well," said the fairy. "Go to bed. Turn round three times, and shut your eyes, and in the morning you shall see what you shall see."

So the old woman went to bed, full of proud thoughts. She turned round three times and shut her eyes. And in the morning she was back in her vinegar bottle.

THE MAGIC PEAR TREE
China

A farmer came from the country to sell his pears in the market. They were juicy and fragrant, and his sales were booming, when a Taoist priest wearing tattered scarves and coarse cotton clothes appeared at the wagon and begged for some fruit. The farmer shooed him away, but he refused to leave. The farmer's voice rose until he was screaming and cursing.

"Your wagon holds hundreds of pears," said the priest, "and I ask for only one. That's no great loss, sir. Why get so angry?"

The crowd tried to persuade the farmer to part with a bruised pear and be rid of the man, but the farmer indignantly refused. At last a market guard saw that the uproar was getting out of hand and put up a few coins for a piece of fruit to throw to the priest.

Hands clasped above his head, the priest thanked the guard. Then he turned to the crowd and said, "We who have left the world find man's greed hard to understand. Let me offer some choice pears to all you good customers."

"Now that you have your pear," someone said, "why don't you eat it yourself?"

"All I needed was a seed for planting," replied the priest. And holding the fruit in both hands, he gobbled it up. Then he took the little shovel that he carried on his back and dug several inches into the ground. He placed the seed in the hole and covered it with earth.

The priest called for hot water, and a bystander with a taste for mischief fetched some from a nearby shop. The priest poured the water over the seed he had planted. Every eye was now on him.

Behold! a tiny shoot appeared. Steadily it increased in size until it became a full-grown tree, with twigs and leaves in unruly profusion. In a flash it burst into bloom and then into fruit. Masses of large, luscious pears filled its branches.

The priest turned to the tree, plucked the pears, and began presenting them to the onlookers. In a short while the fruit was gone. Then with his shovel the priest started to chop the tree. *Teng! Teng!*

the blows rang out in the air until finally the tree fell. Taking the upper part of the tree onto his shoulders, the priest departed with a relaxed gait and untroubled air.

During all this the farmer had been part of the crowd, gaping with outstretched neck and forgetting his business. But when the priest departed the farmer noticed that his wagon was empty. And then the suspicion came to him that it was his own pears which had been presented to the crowd. Looking more carefully, he saw that a handle had been chopped off the wagon. In vexation he searched until he found it lying discarded at the foot of a wall. And now he realized that the pear tree he had seen cut down was the handle of his wagon.

Of the priest there was no sign at all, but the marketplace was in an uproar of laughter.

FAITHFUL JOHN
Germany

There was once upon a time an old king who was ill, and thought to himself, "I am lying on what must be my deathbed." Then said he, "Tell Faithful John to come to me." Faithful John was his favorite servant, and was so called, because he had for his whole life long been so true to him. When therefore he came beside the bed, the king said to him, "Most faithful John, I feel my end approaching, and have no anxiety except about my son. He is still of tender age, and cannot always know how to guide himself. If you do not promise me to teach him everything that he ought to know, and to be his foster-father, I cannot close my eyes in peace."

Then answered Faithful John, "I will not forsake him, and will serve him with fidelity, even if it should cost me my life."

At this, the old king said, "Now I die in comfort and peace." Then he added, "After my death, you shall show him the whole castle: all the chambers, halls, and vaults, and all the treasures which lie therein, but the last chamber in the long gallery, in which is the picture of the princess of the Golden Dwelling, shall you not show.

If he sees that picture, he will fall violently in love with her, and will drop down in a swoon, and go through great danger for her sake. Therefore you must protect him from that." And when Faithful John had once more given his promise to the old king about this, the king said no more, but laid his head on his pillow and died.

When the old king had been carried to his grave, Faithful John told the younger king all that he had promised his father on his deathbed, and said, "This will I assuredly keep, and will be faithful to you as I have been faithful to him, even if it should cost me my life."

When the mourning was over, Faithful John said to him, "It is now time that you should see your inheritance. I will show you your father's palace." Then he took him about everywhere, up and down, and let him see all the riches, and the magnificent apartments, only there was one room which he did not open, that in which hung the dangerous picture. The picture, however, was so placed that when the door was opened you looked straight on it, and it was so admirably painted that it seemed to breathe and live, and there was nothing more charming or more beautiful in the whole world.

The young king noticed, however, that Faithful John always walked past this one door, and said, "Why do you never open this one for me?"

"There is something within it," he replied, "which would terrify you."

But the king answered, "I have seen all the palace, and I want to know what is in this room also," and he went and tried to break open the door by force.

Then Faithful John held him back and said, "I promised your father before his death that you should not see that which is in this chamber, it might bring the greatest misfortune on you and on me."

"Ah, no," replied the young king, "if I do not go in, it will be my certain destruction. I should have no rest day or night until I had seen it with my own eyes. I shall not leave the place now until you have unlocked the door."

Then Faithful John saw that there was no help for it now, and with a heavy heart and many sighs, sought out the key from the great bunch. When he had opened the door, he went in first, and thought by standing before him he could hide the portrait so that the king should not see it in front of him. But what good was this? The king stood on tiptoe and saw it over his shoulder. And when he saw the portrait of the maiden, which was so magnificent and shone with gold and precious stones, he fell fainting to the ground. Faithful John took him up, carried him to his bed, and sorrowfully thought, "The misfortune has befallen us. Lord God, what will be the end of it?" Then he strengthened him with wine, until he came to himself again.

The first words the king said were, "Ah, the beautiful portrait! whose is it?"

"That is the princess of the Golden Dwelling," answered Faithful John.

Then the king continued, "My love for her is so great, that if all the leaves on all the trees were tongues, they could not declare it. I will give my life to win her. You are my most faithful John, you must help me."

The faithful servant considered within himself for a long time how to set about the matter, for it was difficult even to obtain a sight of the king's daughter. At length he thought of a way, and said to the king, "Everything which she has about her is of gold—tables, chairs, dishes, glasses, bowls, and household furniture. Among your treasures are five tons of gold; let one of the goldsmiths of the kingdom fashion these into all manner of vessels and utensils, into all kinds of birds, wild beasts, and strange animals, such as may please her, and we will go there with them and try our luck."

The king ordered all the goldsmiths to be brought to him, and they had to work night and day until at last the most splendid things were prepared. When everything was stowed on board a ship, Faithful John put on the dress of a merchant, and the king was forced to do the same in order to make himself quite unrecognizable. Then they sailed across the sea, and sailed on until they came to the town wherein dwelt the princess of the Golden Dwelling.

Faithful John bade the king stay behind on the ship, and wait for him. "Perhaps I shall bring the princess with me," said he, "therefore see that everything is in order; have the golden vessels set out and the whole ship decorated." Then he gathered together in his apron all kinds of golden things, went on shore and walked straight to the royal palace. When he entered the courtyard of the palace, a beautiful girl was standing there by the well with two golden buckets in her hand, drawing water with them. And when she was just turning round to carry away the sparkling water she saw the stranger, and asked who he was. So he answered, "I am a merchant," and opened his apron, and let her look in.

Then she cried, "Oh, what beautiful golden things!" and put her pails down and looked at the golden wares one after the other. Then said the girl, "The princess must see these. She has such great pleasure in golden things that she will buy all you have." She took him by the hand and led him upstairs, for she was the waiting maid.

When the king's daughter saw the wares, she was quite delighted and said, "They are so beautifully worked that I will buy them all from you."

But Faithful John said, "I am only the servant of a rich merchant. The things I have here are not to be compared with those my master has in his ship. They are the most beautiful and valuable things that have ever been made in gold." When she wanted to have everything brought up to her, he said, "There are so many of them that it would take a great many days to do that, and so many rooms would be required to exhibit them, that your house is not big enough."

Then her curiosity and longing were still more excited, until at last she said, "Conduct me to the ship, I will go there myself, and behold the treasures of your master."

At this Faithful John was quite delighted, and led her to the ship, and when the king saw her, he perceived that her beauty was even greater than the picture had represented it to be, and thought no other than that his heart would burst in twain. Then she boarded the ship, and the king led her within. Faithful John, however, remained with the helmsman, and ordered the ship to be pushed off, saying, "Set all sail, till it fly like a bird in the air."

Within, the king showed her the golden vessels, every one of them, also the wild beasts and strange animals. Many hours went by whilst she was seeing everything, and in her delight she did not observe that the ship was sailing away. After she had looked at the last, she thanked the merchant and wanted to go home, but when she came to the side of the ship, she saw that it was on the high seas far from land, and hurrying onwards with all sail set. "Ah," cried she in her alarm, "I am betrayed! I am carried away and have fallen into the power of a merchant—I would rather die!"

The king, however, seized her hand, and said, "I am not a merchant. I am a king, and of no meaner origin than you are, and if I have carried you away with subtlety, that has come to pass because of my exceeding great love for you. The first time that I looked on your portrait, I fell fainting to the ground." When the princess of the Golden Dwelling heard this, she was comforted, and her heart was drawn to him, so that she willingly consented to be his wife.

It so happened, while they were sailing onwards over the deep sea, that Faithful John, who was sitting on the fore part of the vessel, making music, saw three ravens in the air, which came flying towards them. At this he stopped playing and listened to what they were saying to each other, for that he well understood. One cried, "Oh, there he is carrying home the princess of the Golden Dwelling."

"Yes," replied the second, "but he has not got her yet."

Said the third, "But he has got her. She is sitting beside him in the ship."

Then the first began again, and cried, "What good will that do him? When they reach land a chestnut horse will leap forward to meet him, and the prince will want to mount it, but if he does that, it will run away with him, and rise up into the air, and he will never see his maiden more."

Spoke the second, "But is there no escape?"

"Oh, yes, if someone else mounts it swiftly, and takes out the pistol which he will find in its holster and shoots the horse dead, the young king is saved. But who knows that? And whosoever does know it, and tells it to him, will be turned to stone from the toe to the knee."

Then said the second, "I know more than that: even if the horse be killed, the young king will still not keep his bride. When they go into the castle together, a wrought bridal garment will be lying there in the dish, and looking as if it were woven of gold and silver. It is, however, nothing but sulphur and pitch, and if he put it on, it will burn him to the very bone and marrow."

Said the third, "Is there no escape at all?"

"Oh, yes, replied the second, "if anyone with gloves on seizes the garment and throws it into the fire and burns it, the young king will be saved. But what good will that do? Whosoever knows it and tells it to him, half his body will become stone from the knee to the heart."

Then said the third, "I know still more: even if the bridal garment be burned, the young king will still not have his bride. After the wedding, when the dancing begins and the young queen is dancing, she will suddenly turn pale and fall down as if dead, and if someone does not lift her up and draw three drops of blood from her right breast and spit them out again, she will die. But if anyone who knows that were to declare it, he would become stone from the crown of his head to the sole of his foot."

When the ravens had spoken of this together, they flew onwards, and Faithful John had well understood everything, but from that time forth he became quiet and sad, for if he concealed what he had heard from his master, the latter would be unfortunate, and if he disclosed it to him, he himself must sacrifice his life. At length, however, he said to himself, "I will save my master, even if it bring destruction on myself."

When therefore they came to shore, all happened as had been foretold by the ravens, and a magnificent chestnut horse sprang forward. "Good," said the king, "he shall carry me to my palace," and was about to mount it when Faithful John got before him, jumped quickly on it, drew the pistol out of the holster, and shot the horse. Then the other attendants of the king, who were not very fond of Faithful John, cried, "How shameful to kill the beautiful animal, that was to have carried the king to the palace!"

But the king said, "Hold your peace and leave him alone, he is my most faithful John. Who knows what good may come of this!"

They went into the palace, and in the hall there stood a dish, and therein lay the bridal garment looking no otherwise than as if it were made of gold and silver. The young king went towards it and was about to take hold of it, but Faithful John pushed him away, seized it with gloves on, carried it quickly to the fire, and burned it. The other attendants again began to murmur, and said, "Behold, now he is even burning the king's bridal garment!"

But the young king said, "Who knows what good he may have done, leave him alone, he is my most faithful John."

And now the wedding was solemnized: the dance began, and the bride also took part in it. Faithful John was watchful and looked into her face, and suddenly she turned pale and fell to the ground as if she were dead. On this he ran hastily to her, lifted her up, and bore her into a chamber—then he laid her down, and knelt and sucked the three drops of blood from her right breast, and spat them out. Immediately she breathed again and recovered herself, but the young king had seen this, and being ignorant why Faithful John had done it, was angry and cried, "Throw him into a dungeon."

Next morning Faithful John was condemned, and led to the gallows, and when he stood on high, and was about to be executed, he said, "Everyone who has to die is permitted before his end to make one last speech; may I too claim the right?"

"Yes," answered the king, "it shall be granted unto you."

Then said Faithful John, "I am unjustly condemned, and have always been true to you," and he related how he had hearkened to the conversation of the ravens when on the sea, and how he had been obliged to do all these things in order to save his master. Then cried the king, "Oh, my most faithful John. Pardon, pardon—bring him down," But as Faithful John spoke the last word he had fallen down lifeless and become a stone.

Thereupon the king and the queen suffered great anguish, and the king said, "Ah, how ill I have requited great fidelity!" and ordered the stone figure to be taken up and placed in his bedroom beside his bed. And as often as he looked on it he wept and said, "Ah, if I could bring you to life again, my most faithful John."

Some time passed and the queen bore twins, two sons who grew fast and were her delight. Once when the queen was at church and the father was sitting with his two children playing beside him, he looked at the stone figure again, sighed, and full of grief he said, "Ah, if I could but bring you to life again, my most faithful John."

Then the stone began to speak and said, "You can bring me to life again if you will use for that purpose what is dearest to you."

Then cried the king, "I will give everything I have in the world for you."

The stone continued, "If you will cut off the heads of your two children with your own hand, and sprinkle me with their blood, I shall be restored to life."

The king was terrified when he heard that he himself must kill his dearest children, but he thought of Faithful John's great fidelity, and how he had died for him, drew his sword, and with his own hand cut off the children's heads. And when he had smeared the stone with their blood, life returned to it, and Faithful John stood once more safe and healthy before him. He said to the king, "Your truth shall not go unrewarded," and took the heads of the children, put them on again, and rubbed the wounds with their blood, at which they became whole again immediately, and jumped about, and went on playing as if nothing had happened.

Then the king was full of joy, and when he saw the queen coming he hid Faithful John and the two children in a great cupboard. When she entered, he said to her, "Have you been praying in the church?"

"Yes," answered she, "but I have constantly been thinking of Faithful John and what misfortune has befallen him through us."

Then said he, "Dear wife, we can give him his life again, but it will cost us our two little sons, whom we must sacrifice."

The queen turned pale, and her heart was full of terror, but she said, "We owe it to him, for his great fidelity."

Then the king was rejoiced that she thought as he had thought, and went and opened the cupboard, and brought forth Faithful John and the children, and said, "God be praised, he is delivered, and we have our little sons again also," and told her how everything had occurred. Then they dwelt together in much happiness until their death.

Four Hound-Dog Stories
Ireland and United States

THE BEST COON-AND-POSSUM DOG

Old Bob had a hound that he called the best coon-and-possum dog in Mississippi. All he had to do was to show the dog a board, and the dog would go off and find a possum or coon whose hide would fit the board. This saved Bob the trouble of hunting up a board to fit a hide, and he never had to worry about the quality of the possum or coon skin.

One day, though, the dog disappeared and when he had been missing for three days, Bob took to the woods himself to see if he could find any trace of the faithful animal. After hours of searching, he found the dog, so worn out and exhausted that Bob had to carry him home in his arms.

The incident puzzled Bob for a while, but he finally figured it out. His wife had left the ironing board out leaning against the back porch, and the dog saw it and went out in the woods and wore himself out trying to find a possum or coon with a hide big enough to fit the ironing board.—UNITED STATES

HARE AND HOUND

John McLoughlin that lived out the Point road had this hound. There never was the beating of her. She pupped in a teapot.

One time she was carrying the pups, and a hare riz and she made after it and ripped the belly out of herself on this ditch, on wire or something; and the pups, the greyhound pups, spilled out of her. And one of them up like hell, and after the hare and stuck till her till he caught and killed her.

And when the greyhound died, John McLoughlin had her skinned and he put a back in a waistcoat with her skin. And one day he was out over the water hunting and this hare started up; and begod, he said, the back of the waistcoat on him barked!—IRELAND

There was this fella down here one time and he had a wonderful rabbit dog. Well, this dog died and he decided that he had to do something to remember him by so he had him skinned and made himself a pair of gloves out of that dog's hide. One time he was out in the forest working, and he pulled his gloves off and laid them on this stump and set down to eat his lunch. All of a sudden this rabbit run out of the underbrush and those two gloves jumped off of that stump and grabbed that rabbit and choked him to death.

—UNITED STATES

THE SPLIT DOG

Had me a little dog once was the best rabbit dog you ever saw. Well, he was runnin' a rabbit one day, and some fool had left a scythe lyin' in the grass with the blade straight up. That poor little dog ran smack into it and it split him open from the tip of his nose right straight on down his tail.

Well I saw him fall apart and I ran and slapped him back together. I had jerked off my shirt, so I wrapped him up in that right quick and ran to the house. Set him in a box and poured turpentine all over the shirt. I kept him near the stove. Set him out in the sun part of the time. Oh, I could see him still breathin' a little, and I hoped I wouldn't lose him. And after about three weeks I could see him tryin' to wiggle now and then. Let him stay bandaged another three weeks— and then one morning I heard him bark. So I started unwrappin' him and in a few minutes out he jumped, spry as ever.

But—don't you know!—in my excitement, blame if I hadn't put him together wrong-way-to. He had two legs up and two legs down.

Anyhow, it turned out he was twice as good a rabbit dog after that. He'd run on two legs till he got tired, and then flip over and just keep right on.

Ah Lord! That little dog could run goin' and comin', and bark at both ends.—UNITED STATES

SHAPE
SHIFTERS

There are really three ways to be a shape shifter—one who metamorphoses into another creature. First, you can be a sorcerer or witch and learn the ability to change at will. Second, you can be enchanted by a magic maker, perhaps by eating or touching something that causes you to change. And third, you can be a born shape shifter and be transformed, sometimes unwittingly, by natural forces: the pull of the moon, the turn of the tide, or the sloughing off of the skin.

The most feared shape shifter in the world was the werewolf, and there are many who still believe in the dreaded *loup-garou*. However, as so many of the tales about lycanthropes are bloody, psychological horror stories, none are included here. But were-creatures, man-animal transformations, told of around the globe concerned more than wolves. In Japan and Korea, tales were told about were-foxes. In China, there were stories about were-bullfrogs; in Russia, were-snakes; in India, were-leopards and were-tigers. Anthropologists point to such tales as remnants of primitive totemism or as a storytelling response to a belief in reincarnation.

The stories in this section are sometimes love stories, such as "The Swan-Maiden," and sometimes about the getting of wisdom—if somewhat late—as in "The Wounded Seal." The animals in the stories range from a lovely swan to a fearsome serpent; seals, horses, snakes, and deer abound.

If after you read these stories you still desire werewolves, there is a charm from Russia that might help. Stand in a circle drawn on the ground and recite the following words. You may feel the change, the crack of bone and stretch of sinew, come upon you. The entire charm may be found in Montague Summers's *The Werewolf.*

In the ocean sea, on the island Buyán, in the open plain, shines the moon upon an aspen stump, into the green wood, into the spreading vale. Around the stump goes a shaggy wolf; under his teeth are all the horned cattle; but into the wood the wolf goes not; into the vale the wolf does not roam. Moon! moon! golden horns! Melt the bullet, blunt the knife, rot the cudgel, strike fear into man, beast, and reptile, so that they may not seize the grey wolf, nor tear from him his warm hide. My word is firm, firmer than sleep or the strength of heroes.

THE DOCTOR AND HIS PUPIL
France

There was once a poor man who had a twelve-year-old son. He sent him to find work.

The boy departed wearing a jacket that was red in front and white behind. He passed in front of a castle; it was the residence of a doctor, who happened to be standing at the window. As he needed a servant, the master of the castle called the boy.

"What are you looking for in these parts?"

"Since I'd like to make a living, I'm looking for work."

"Do you know how to read?"

"Yes, for I've been to school for six months."

"Then you won't do."

The boy went away; but in a few days he came back with his jacket on backwards and passed once more in front of the castle. Again the master was at his window.

"What are you looking for in these parts?"

"I'd like to make a living; I'm looking for work."

"Do you know how to read?"

"No, for I've never been to school."

"Well, then, come in; I'll hire you. I'll give you one hundred francs a year and board."

The boy entered and his master gave him something to eat. Then he showed him his book of secrets and gave him a duster.

"You will dust my book carefully every day, and that's all you'll have to do."

Then the doctor left on a trip and was gone a whole year. The boy took advantage of this absence to read his master's book and get acquainted with the doctor's skills.

The physician returned. He was very happy with his servant and departed for another year. During this second absence, the boy learned half of the book by heart.

The doctor returned and was so happy with his servant that he doubled his wages and departed for another year. During this third absence the young man learned the remainder of the book by heart. When his master returned he left the doctor's employ to return to his parents, who were as poor as ever.

On the eve of the village fair the young man said to his father, "Tomorrow go into the stable; you will find a beautiful horse that you must take to the fair. Sell him, but above all be sure to keep the halter."

The next day the father entered the stable and found a magnificent horse. He took it to the fair and buyers hastened around to admire the handsome animal. The father sold it for a good price, but he kept the halter and put it in his pocket. Then he set out on the road to his village and shortly he heard footsteps behind him: it was his son, who, having transformed himself into a horse and then retransformed himself into his natural shape while the buyer of the horse was celebrating in the tavern, was hastening to catch up with his father. And both were delighted with the fine deal they had made.

After a time there was no money left in the house.

"Don't worry about it," said the boy to his father. "I'll see that you get more. Go in the stable tomorrow; you will find a steer that you can take to the fair. But when you sell it be sure to keep the rope that you are leading it with."

All took place at the fair as before, and the boy caught up with his father, whose appetite had been whetted by this money which was so easily earned, and who now proposed to take his son again to the next fair in the form of a horse.

But the doctor, by consulting his book, had become aware of what his former servant was doing. He went to the fair, recognized the horse, and bought it. He took the father to the inn to conclude the bargain and made him drink a great deal so that he forgot to keep the halter.

The doctor took the horse quickly away to a blacksmith. "Give him a good shoeing," he advised.

The horse was tied to the door. The children came out of school and a group of them came to hang around the blacksmith shop. The horse extended its muzzle toward a child and whispered to him:

"Untie me!"

The child was afraid and withdrew a bit, but the horse repeated, "Child, untie me!"

The schoolboy approached and untied him. Immediately the horse transformed itself into a hare and ran away. The doctor saw it and turned six boys into hunting dogs. The hare came to the edge of a reservoir, jumped in, and turned into a carp. The doctor arrived, bought all the fish in the reservoir, and had it fished clean. He recognized the carp and was about to grab it when it turned into a lark. He turned into an eagle and pursued the lark, which flew over a castle and fell down the chimney, where it turned into a grain of wheat, which rolled under the table in the bedroom of the girl of the castle.

The day passed. In the evening when the girl had gone to bed, the young man said:

"Mademoiselle, if you wish—"

The girl, hearing his voice, cried out to her parents, who came at once.

"What's the matter?"

"There's someone talking in here!"

But the young man turned back into a grain of wheat and rolled under the table. The parents turned on the lights, looked everywhere, and, finding nothing, departed.

The young man took his own shape and made more advances. The girl cried and her parents returned.

"There's been more talking in the room."

"Have you gone mad?" said the father.

"Well! Go to bed here if you want to hear it."

The father stayed a moment, then went away. The young man reappeared and the girl ended by acceding to him.

"Nights I shall sleep with you and days you may wear me as an engagement ring on your finger."

But the doctor found out all that was going on by consulting his books. He caused the father to become ill and came as a doctor to cure him.

"Heal me and I will pay you well," said the father.

"All I want is the ring on your daughter's finger."

The father promised. But the young man was aware of what was going on.

"The doctor is going to ask you for your ring," he said to the girl. "Don't give it to him; let it fall on the floor."

When the father was cured he called his daughter and told her to give the ring to the doctor. She took it off and let it fall; the ring turned into grains of wheat, which scattered out on the floor. The doctor turned into a rooster to pick them up. The young man turned into a fox and ate the rooster.

THE SWAN-MAIDEN
Sweden

A young peasant, in the parish of Mellby, who often amused himself with hunting, saw one day three swans flying toward him, which settled down upon the strand of a sound nearby. Approaching the place, he was astonished at seeing the three swans divest themselves of their feathery attire, which they threw into the grass, and three maidens of dazzling beauty step forth and spring into the water.

After sporting in the waves awhile they returned to the land, where they resumed their former garb and shape and flew away in the same direction from which they came.

One of them, the youngest and fairest, had, in the meantime, so smitten the young hunter that neither night nor day could he tear his thoughts from the bright image.

His mother, noticing that something was wrong with her son, and that the chase, which had formerly been his favorite pleasure, had lost its attractions, asked him finally the cause of his melancholy, whereupon he related to her what he had seen, and declared that there was no longer any happiness in this life for him if he would not possess the fair swan-maiden.

"Nothing is easier," said the mother. "Go at sunset next Thursday evening to the place where you last saw her. When the three swans come give attention to where your chosen one lays her feathery garb, take it, and hasten away."

The young man listened to his mother's instructions, and, betaking himself, the following Thursday evening, to a convenient hiding place near the sound, he waited, with impatience, the coming of the swans. The sun was just sinking behind the trees when the young man's ears were greeted by a whizzing in the air, and the three swans settled down upon the beach, as on their former visit. As soon as they had laid off their swan attire they were again transformed into the most beautiful maidens, and, springing out upon the white sand, they were soon enjoying themselves in the water.

From his hiding place the young hunter had taken careful note of where his enchantress had laid her swan feathers. Stealing softly forth, he took them and returned to his place of concealment in the surrounding foliage.

Soon thereafter two of the swans were heard to fly away, but the third, in search of her clothes, discovered the young man, before whom, believing him responsible for their disappearance, she fell upon her knees and prayed that her swan attire might be returned to her. The hunter was, however, unwilling to yield the beautiful prize, and, casting a cloak around her shoulders, carried her home.

Preparations were soon made for a magnificent wedding, which took place in due form, and the young couple dwelt lovingly and contentedly together.

One Thursday evening, seven years later, the hunter related to her how he had sought and won his wife. He brought forth and showed her, also, the white swan feathers of her former days. No sooner were they placed in her hands than she was transformed once more into a swan, and instantly took flight through the open window. In breathless astonishment, the man stared wildly after his rapidly vanishing wife, and before a year and a day had passed, he was laid, with his longings and sorrows, in his allotted place in the village churchyard.

SISTER ALIONUSHKA,
BROTHER IVANUSHKA
Russia

Once there lived a king and a queen; they had a son and a daughter, called Ivanushka and Alionushka. When their parents died the children remained alone and went wandering in the wide world. They walked and walked and walked till they saw a pond, and near the pond a herd of cows was grazing.

"I am thirsty," said Ivanushka. "I want to drink."

"Do not drink, little brother, or you will become a calf," said Alionushka. The brother heeded her and they went on farther; they walked and walked and saw a river, and near it a drove of horses.

"Ah, little sister," Ivanushka said, "if you only knew how thirsty I am!"

"Do not drink, little brother, or you will become a colt." Ivanushka heeded her, and they went on farther; they walked and walked and saw a lake, and near it a flock of sheep.

"Ah, little sister, I am terribly thirsty," Ivanushka said.

"Do not drink, little brother, or you will become a sheep." Ivanuska heeded her and they went on farther; they walked and walked and saw a stream, and near it pigs were feeding.

"Ah, little sister, I must drink," Ivanuska said. "I am terribly thirsty."

"Do not drink, little brother, or you will become a piglet." Ivanuska heeded her again and they went on farther; they walked and walked and saw a flock of goats grazing near a well.

"Ah, little sister, now I must drink," Ivanuska said.

"Do not drink, little brother, or you will become a kid." But he could not restrain himself and did not heed his sister; he drank from the well, and became a kid. He leaped before Alionushka and cried, "*Maa-ka-ka! maa-ka-ka!*"

Alionushka tied him with a silken belt and led him on, shedding tears, bitter tears. The kid ran and ran till he ran into the garden of a certain king. The servants saw him and at once reported to the king. "Your Majesty," they said, "in our garden there is a kid; a maiden is leading him on a belt, and she is a great beauty."

The king ordered them to find out who she was. The servants asked her whence she came and of what parentage she was.

"There were a king and a queen and they died," said Alionushka. "We children remained—I, the princess, and my little brother, the prince. He could not restrain himself, drank water from a well, and became a kid."

The servants reported all this to the king. He called Alionushka before him and questioned her about everything. She pleased him and he wanted to marry her. Soon they celebrated their wedding and began to live together, and the kid lived with them. He walked in the garden and ate and drank with the king and queen.

One day the king went hunting. While he was away a sorceress came and cast a spell on the queen. Alionushka fell ill and became thin and pale. Everything became gloomy at the king's palace; the flowers in the garden began to fade, the trees to dry, and the grass to wither. The king returned and asked the queen, "Are you sick?"

"Yes, I am sick," answered the queen.

Next day the king again went hunting. Alionushka lay ill; the sorceress came to her and said, "Do you want me to heal you? Go to such and such a sea at twilight and drink water there."

The queen heeded her and at twilight went to that sea. The sorceress was waiting for her, seized her, tied a stone around her neck, and cast her into the sea. Alionushka sank to the bottom; the kid ran to the shore and wept bitterly. But the sorceress turned herself into the likeness of the queen and went back to the palace.

The king came home and was overjoyed to find that the queen was well again. They set the table and began to dine. "But where is the kid?" asked the king.

"We don't want him with us," said the sorceress. "I gave orders that he be shut out; he has a goatlike smell." Next day, as soon as the king went hunting, the sorceress beat and beat the kid and threatened, "When the king returns I will ask him to slaughter you."

The king returned and the sorceress begged him over and over again to have the kid slaughtered. "I am annoyed with him, I am tired of him," she said.

The king pitied the kid, but there was nothing to be done; the queen insisted and urged him so much that in the end he consented and gave leave to have the kid slaughtered. The kid saw that steel knives were being sharpened for him, and he wept. He ran to the king and implored him, "King, give me leave to go to the sea, to drink water, to rinse my insides."

The king let him go. The kid ran to the sea, stood on the shore, and cried plaintively:

> *Alionushka, my little sister,*
> *Come up, come up to the shore.*
> *Hot fires are burning*
> *Big kettles are boiling,*
> *Steel knives are being sharpened—*
> *They want to slaughter me!*

She answered him:

> *Ivanushka, my little brother,*
> *The heavy stone is pulling me down,*
> *The cruel serpent has sucked out my heart.*

The kid wept and returned home. In the middle of the day he again asked the king, "King, give me leave to go to the sea, to drink water and rinse my insides." The king allowed him to go. The kid ran to the sea and cried plaintively:

> *Alionushka, my little sister,*
> *Come up, come up to the shore.*
> *Hot fires are burning,*
> *Big kettles are boiling,*
> *Steel knives are being sharpened—*
> *They want to slaughter me!*

She answered him:

> *Ivanushka, my little brother,*
> *The heavy stone is pulling me down,*
> *The cruel serpent has sucked out my heart.*

The kid wept and returned home. The king wondered why the kid kept running to the sea. Now the kid asked him for the third time, "King, give me leave to go to the sea, to drink water and rinse my insides." The king let him go and followed him. When he came to the sea he heard the kid calling to his sister:

Alionushka, my little sister,
Come up, come up to the shore.
Hot fires are burning,
Big kettles are boiling,
Steel knives are being sharpened—
They want to slaughter me!

She answered him:

Ivanushka, my little brother,
The heavy stone is pulling me down,
The cruel serpent has sucked out my heart.

The kid again called to his sister. Alionushka swam up and came to the surface. The king snatched her, tore the stone from her neck, pulled her ashore, and asked her how all this had happened. She told him everything.

The king was overjoyed and so also was the kid; he capered, and everything in the garden grew green and blossomed again. The king ordered the sorceress to be put to death; a stake of wood was set up in the courtyard and she was burned. After that the king, the queen, and the kid began to live happily and to prosper and to eat and drink together as before.

THE BLACKSMITH'S WIFE OF YARROWFOOT
Scotland

Some years back, the blacksmith of Yarrowfoot had for apprentices two brothers, both steady lads, and, when bound to him, fine healthy fellows. After a few months, however, the younger of the two began to grow pale and lean, lose his appetite, and show other marks of declining health. His brother, much concerned, often questioned him as to what ailed him, but to no purpose. At last, however, the poor lad burst into an agony of tears, and confessed that he was quite worn out, and should soon be brought to the grave through the usage of his mistress, who was in truth a witch, though none suspected it. "Every night," he sobbed out, "she comes to my bedside, puts a magic bridle on me, and changes me into a horse. Then, seated on my back, she urges me on for many a mile to the wild moors, where she and I know not what other vile creatures hold their hideous feasts. There she keeps me all night, and at early morning I carry her home. She takes off my bridle, and there I am, but so weary I can ill stand. And thus I pass my nights while you are soundly sleeping."

The elder brother at once declared he would take his chance of a night among the witches, so he put the younger one in his own place next to the wall, and lay awake himself till the usual time of the witch-woman's arrival. She came, bridle in hand, and flinging it over the elder brother's head, up sprang a fine hunting horse. The lady leaped on his back, and started for the trysting place, which on this occasion, as it chances, was the cellar of a neighboring laird.

While she and the rest of the vile crew were regaling themselves with claret and sack, the hunter, who was left in a spare stall of the stable, rubbed and rubbed his head against the wall till he loosened the bridle, and finally got it off, on which he recovered his human form. Holding the bridle firmly in his hand, he concealed himself at the back of the stall till his mistress came within reach, when in an instant he flung the magic bridle over her head, and behold, a fine grey mare! He mounted her and dashed off, riding through hedge and ditch, till, looking down, he perceived she had lost a shoe from one of her forefeet. He took her to the first smithy that was open, had the shoe replaced, and a new one put on the other forefoot, and then rode her up and down a plowed field till he was nearly worn out. At last he took her home, and pulled the bridle off just in time for her to creep into bed before her husband awoke and got up for his day's work.

The honest blacksmith arose, little thinking what had been going on all night; but his wife complained of being very ill, almost dying, and begged him to send for a doctor. He accordingly aroused his apprentices; the elder one went out, and soon returned with one whom he had chanced to meet already abroad. The doctor wished to feel his patient's pulse, but she resolutely hid her hands, and refused to show them. The village Esculapius was perplexed; but the husband, impatient at her obstinacy, pulled off the bedclothes, and found, to his horror, that horseshoes were tightly nailed to both her hands! On further examination, her sides appeared galled with kicks, the same that the apprentice had given her during his ride up and down the plowed field.

The brothers now came forward, and related all that had passed. On the following day the witch was tried by the magistrates of Selkirk, and condemned to be burned to death on a stone at the Bullsheugh, a sentence which was promptly carried into effect. It is added that the younger apprentice was at last restored to health by eating butter made from the milk of cows fed in kirkyards, a sovereign remedy for consumption brought on through being witch-ridden.

THE SEAL'S SKIN
Iceland

There was once some man from Myrdal in eastern Iceland who went walking among the rocks by the sea one morning before anyone else was up. He came to the mouth of a cave, and inside the cave he could hear merriment and dancing, but outside it he saw a great many sealskins. He took one skin away with him, carried it home, and locked it away in a chest. Later in the day he went back to the mouth of the cave; there was a young and lovely woman sitting there, and she was stark naked, and weeping bitterly. This was the seal whose skin it was that the man had taken. He gave the girl some clothes, comforted her, and took her home with him. She grew very fond of him, but did not get on so well with other people. Often she would sit alone and stare out to sea.

After some while the man married her, and they got on well together, and had several children. As for the skin, the man always kept it locked up in the chest, and kept the key on him wherever he went. But after many years, he went fishing one day and forgot it under his pillow at home. Other people say that he went to church one Christmas with the rest of his household, but that his wife was ill and stayed at home; he had forgotten to take the key out of the pocket of his everyday clothes when he changed. Be that as it may, when he came home again the chest was open, and both wife and skin were gone. She had taken the key and examined the chest, and there she had found the skin; she had been been unable to resist the temptation, but had said farewell to her children, put the skin on, and flung herself into the sea.

Before the woman flung herself into the sea, it is said that she spoke these words:

> *Woe is me! Ah, woe is me!*
> *I have seven bairns on land,*
> *And seven in the sea.*

It is said that the man was broken-hearted about this. Whenever he rowed out fishing afterwards, a seal would often swim round and round his boat, and it looked as if tears were running from its eyes. From that time on, he had excellent luck in his fishing, and various valuable things were washed ashore on his beach. People often noticed, too, that when the children he had had by this woman went walking along the seashore, a seal would show itself near the edge of the water and keep level with them as they walked along the shore, and would toss them jellyfish and pretty shells. But never did their mother come back to land again.

THE WOUNDED SEAL
Scotland

There once dwelt on the northern coast, not far from John o' Groat's House, a man who gained his living by fishing. He was particularly devoted to the killing of the seals, in which he had great success.

One evening just as he had returned home from his usual occupation, he was called upon by a man on horseback who was an utter stranger to him, but who said that he was to come on the part of a person who wished to make a large purchase of sealskins from him, and wanted to see him for that purpose that very evening. He therefore desired him to get up behind him and come away without any delay.

Urged by the hope of profit he consented, and away they went with such speed that the wind which was in their backs seemed to be in their faces. At length they reached the verge of a stupendous precipice overhanging the sea, where his guide bade him alight, as they were now at the end of their journey,

"But where," says he, "is the person you spoke of?"

"You'll see him presently," said the guide, and, catching hold of him, he plunged with him into the sea.

They went down and down, till at last they came to a door which led into a range of apartments inhabited by seals, and the man to his amazement now saw that he himself was become one of these animals. They seemed all in low spirits, but they spoke kindly to him, and assured him of his safety. His guide now produced a huge *gully* or *joctaleg*, at sight of which, thinking his life was to be taken away, he began to cry for mercy.

"Did you ever see this knife before?" said the guide. He looked at it and saw it was his own, which he had that very day stuck into a seal who had made his escape with it sticking in him. He did not, therefore, attempt to deny that it had been his property.

"Well," said the guide, "that seal was my father. He now lies dangerously ill, and as it is only you that can cure him, I have brought you hither." He then led him into an inner room, where the old seal lay suffering grievously from a cut in his hind quarters. The man was then desired to lay his hand on the wound, at which it instantly healed, and the patient arose hale and sound.

All now was joy and festivity in the abode of the seals, and the guide, turning to the seal hunter, said, "I will now take you back to your family, but you must first take a solemn oath never again to kill a seal as long as you live."

Hard as the condition was, he cheerfully accepted it. His guide then laid hold on him, and they rose up, up, till they reached the surface of the sea, and landed at the cliff. The guide breathed on him and they resumed the human form. They then mounted the horse and sped away like lightning till they reached the fisherman's house. At parting his companion left with him such a present as made him think light of giving over his seal hunting.

The Cat-Woman
France

One winter eve some villagers of Des Haies had gathered to tell and listen to stories about sorcerers, ghosts and *loups-garous*. When it came to Père Pichard's turn to spin a yarn, he knocked out his pipe against the knucklebone of his thumb and asked, "Which story do you want?"

"The tale of the cat-woman," came from all sides.

"Very well," he said. "But it isn't a tale but a true story, and I shall tell it to you just as it happened, without keeping back or changing anything." And this is what he told:

When I was courting my wife I went to and fro on the Croix-des-Haies road, which got its name from the calvary standing at the crossroads midway between her house and mine. One night I stayed at my sweetheart's house later than usual. In those days there was a great happiness in my heart, and I sang as I walked toward home. When I came to the crossroads, I was surprised to see a great white cat at the foot of the calvary. The beast walked right up to me, rubbed her back against my legs, and meowed tenderly. Then she accompanied me as far as the edge of the village, where she jumped into a ditch and disappeared.

From that night on the cat met me at the crossroads and followed me home. I became so used to her that I paid her very little attention. And I forgot all about the animal after I married and had no further occasion for walking at night on the Croix-des-Haies road.

After five or six months of marriage I awoke one night towards midnight and found that my wife was not beside me. I was greatly astonished and called out, "Nanon! Nanon!" There was no response. I lit the candle and searched through the house. Nanon was not there. I found this very strange. Finally I returned to my bed and went back to sleep. When I awoke in the morning, Nanon was there in bed beside me.

"Where did you go last night?" I asked.

"Me?" said she, and her face turned red. But she would say no more.

I did not press her further then. That night, however, I was on the alert, and when she got out of bed about midnight I was aware of it. I glanced toward the door, and although the room was dark I was able to make out something that looked like a hugh white cat, and it went out the door. At dawn Nanon returned to bed.

One morning as she was doing her housework, a spider fell down her neck. She ran to a closet to take off her clothing. I was curious, put my eye to the keyhole, and saw a very odd thing. On her neck just above her left shoulder there was a red mark shaped like a cat's paw. I had heard it said that people who run as *garous* have a mark somewhere upon their bodies. Now that mark and Nanon's leaving the house at night convinced me that she was a cat-woman.

The realization that this was a fact had a terrible effect upon me. For many days I could hardly eat a thing, and for a long time I wandered about the fields like a man who had lost his mind. One day, I remember, I mustered up enough courage to ask her what that mark on her neck was. She refused to answer me, and as she walked away I saw that there was fury in her great glittering green eyes.

Now the cathole in the door was not large enough to admit a cat-woman of her size. As I always took care to bolt the door before going to bed, I wondered how she got back into the house after her nocturnal prowlings. Late one night when Nanon was away, I lit the candle and awaited her return. An hour or two after midnight I heard scratching at the door. Then I observed a paw come in the hole, reach up, and pull back the bolt, and the door opened. I snuffed out the candle immediately, crept into bed, and feigned sleep.

The next day I put a sharp edge on my short-handled axe. An hour before dawn I heard scratching at the door. In an instant I was there with my axe in my hand. When the paw appeared, I struck with all my might. I heard a piercing scream, a scream that still makes me shudder every time I think of it, although all this happened forty years ago. Nanon did not come near the house for three days. On the fourth day she came home. One of her hands was missing. After this she never went out at night. The cat-woman of Croix-des-Haies never prowled again.

THE SERPENT-WOMAN
Spain

There lived in the twelfth century a certain Don Juan de Amarillo, who dwelt not far from Cordova. Although not very young himself, he had a handsome young wife, whom he adored. He introduced her to all his friends; but though she made great sensation by her beauty wherever she appeared, yet, in some way or other, she contrived to make enemies and no friends among either sex.

No one knew where she came from, nor what her name was before she was married. All that was certain was that Don Juan had been absent from home for many years, that he had never been heard of by either friend or foe in all that time, and that he had returned as suddenly as he had departed, but bringing with him a wife.

There were many stories afloat of her origin and character. Some said that she was a strolling player, whom Don Juan had rescued from ill-treatment and persuaded to marry him for his name and position. Others said that she was a witch, and had bewitched the old Don Juan by means of love-philters and noxious herbs.

These stories were none of them true. But people repeated them to each other, and were quite satisfied to believe them. Meanwhile, Doña Pepa want about and enjoyed herself, unconscious of the tales that were told of her, but not unconscious of the terror she inspired. She was quite aware that prople shunned her, and avoided her whenever they could. She was a wonderfully handsome woman, with regular features, dark eyes, and a head like that of a beautiful statue. Her figure was singularly flexible and lithe. But in spite of her beauty, people looked askance at her and felt, without being able to say why, that there was something wrong about her. She had some curious tricks of manner which were startling. When she was pleased, she would raise her head so that it seemed really to lengthen two or three inches, and she would sway her body to and fro with delight. Whereas, if anything displeased her, or she disliked anyone, her head seemed to flatten out, and the touch of her hand was like a bite. She delighted in hearing and repeating all the ill-natured stories that she could about her neighbors, and, in short, seemed as spiteful as a woman could possibly be.

To all outward appearances, she and Don Juan got on excellently well together. But the servants of the household told a different tale. They said that at home they wrangled from morning till night, and that sometimes Don Juan was positively afraid of his wife, especially when her head flattened, for then she looked, and really was, dangerous. People said that they also had seen a look of alarm creep over the old man's face, even in company, when she showed any signs of anger.

Things went on like this for many years, but still Don Juan and his wife seemed to live in peace and harmony. To be sure, the servants, who had been in the family for years, left one after another, and when questioned as to their leaving, answered that the señora was a witch and that the angel Gabriel himself could not live with her. How their master managed, they could not imagine, unless she had bewitched him.

Then it was rumored about that a favorite nephew of Don Juan was coming from Aragon to pay him a visit and to be formally acknowledged as his heir. As he and his wife had no children, he wished to leave his wealth to this nephew, the son of an only sister who was dead; and in course of time the friends and neighbors of Don Juan were invited to meet the stranger.

He was a frank, open-faced, and open-hearted young man, about twenty-seven years old, who at once won the hearts of all who saw him. He was not at all jubilant or overweening at the honors thrust upon him as his uncle's heir, but spoke quite ingenuously of his former poverty and the disadvantages as well as the pleasures of his boyhood, to his aunt's intense disgust.

Doña Pepa could not bear to hear of poor relations, much less to let the world know that Don Juan de Amarillo had any such belongings. And she gave young Don Luis such a look of mingled scorn, hatred, and disgust as made him shudder and kept his tongue quiet for the rest of the evening. The guests tried in vain to draw him into conversation; he had received such a rebuff in Doña Pepa's glance that he became utterly silenced and wondered what sort of woman she could be. He had seen what the guests had not observed (for nobody else had at that moment noticed her), that her head had flattened and that her eyes had grown long and narrow, that she had moistened her lips (which were white with rage) with a hissing sound, and that *her tongue was forked*. He had heard queer stories about his aunt, but had hitherto never paid much attention to them. Now everything he had ever heard in his life came back to his memory, and it was with the utmost effort that he forced himself to sit through the evening, and tried to appear interested in all that went on.

The more Don Luis was known, the more popular he became. Everyone liked him. His uncle worshipped him and could hardly bear him out of his sight, for he reminded him of his dearly loved lost sister and of his own past youth, before he became entangled in the world's wickedness and folly.

Even Doña Pepa could not withstand the freshness and charm of her innocent young nephew, and although she was continually angry with him for his careful avoidance of her, she could not retaliate upon him as she had often retaliated on others—for as time went on she had learned to love him.

He lived in constant fear of her, and tried to keep out of her way by every courteous means in his power. But she would not let him escape from her. She dogged his footsteps everywhere. If he went out for a walk, she was sure to come and meet him, and he felt certain that he was watched—not for his good, but with a jealous eye.

One evening he went to see a friend who was having a sort of reception, and stayed out rather later than usual. When he got to his uncle's house he lit his little taper and proceeded to his room. As he did so, he stumbled over what he supposed to be a coil of rope. To his horror the rope unwound itself, and proved to be a large black snake, whick glided upstairs before him and disappeared under his uncle's door. The thought instantly flashed across his mind that his uncle was in danger of his life, and without hesitation he pounded and knocked and shouted at the door for at least five minutes. They seemed to him five hours. But his uncle was old and sleepy, and it took him some time to wake up. However, at last he came to the door and demanded crossly what his nephew meant by disturbing his rest at that time of night.

"I saw a large black snake creep under this door, my dear uncle, and I was afraid that you might suffer from it before I could help you," replied his nephew.

"Nonsense!" said Don Juan, turning pale, "there is no serpent here," and he tried to shut the door again. But Don Luis was determined to search the room. Doña Pepa was apparently asleep.

The room was carefully searched, but nothing could be found. His uncle was very angry; but as Don Luis was leaving the room, crestfallen at his failure and wondering whether he was losing his mind, Doña Pepa opened her eyes and gave him one of her evil glances; her head flattened, and her eyes grew long and narrow. He left the room with an undefined sensation of terror. He could not sleep, and when he dozed for a few minutes, his dreams were of snakes and of loathsome reptiles.

The next morning he found only his aunt when he went down. His uncle had gone out, Doña Pepa said. Don Luis had taken such an aversion to her that he could hardly bring himself to speak to her, and she took intense delight in plying him with questions, which he felt himself obliged to answer as became a Spanish gentleman.

But at last he could bear it no longer. Doña Pepa was giving very evident signs of rage, and he was hastily beating a retreat, when she strode across the room, seized him by the arm, and said, "You shall not treat me with such disdain. You shall learn to fear me if you cannot learn to love me."

At the same moment that her hand touched his wrist, he felt a sharp sensation as if something had stung him. He threw her hand off and hurried out, thinking for the time no more about his pain. But in the course of the day his arm began to swell rapidly and to throb painfully, until at last the hand and fingers were swollen to such a degree that he could neither close them nor hold anything with them. He then became rather alarmed, and decided to go to a hermit who lived not far off, and who was renowned for his skill in the treatment of poisons as well as for his piety.

After examining the arm the old man said, "It is a serpent bite."

"No, it is not," interrupted Don Luis. "My aunt grasped my arm, in a frenzy of rage, and this is the result."

"Worse still," answered the hermit. "A serpent-woman's bite is sometimes deadly."

"Can you do nothing for me?" cried Don Luis, in despair. "I hate her, and I have been persecuted by her for weeks."

"Yes, and you will be persecuted by her still more. She will take refuge in your room instead of on the landing. Put these leaves upon your arm, and keep wetting them when they become dry, and your arm will probably get better. As to conquering her, that will be a more difficult matter. If you can keep awake you will get the better of her. But if you sleep one minute, you will be at her mercy."

"What shall I do to her? I would do anything short of murdering her," said Don Luis excitedly.

"Take your sword, when you find her a little way from the door, and hack off a piece of the snake, and see the effect. Then come to me again."

With this advice Don Luis was obliged to be content. His arm was so much soothed by the hermit's treatment that he determined to try the rest of his advice.

That night, when he went to his room, he undressed and was just getting into bed when he espied the snake coiled in a high mass at the foot of it. Without a sound he drew his sword, gave a stroke at the snake, and cut off a piece of the tail. The snake reared its head and showed its fangs, preparing apparently for a spring, but Don Luis gave another blow, and another piece of the tail came off. With a hiss the snake uncoiled, dragged itself to the door, disappeared down the stairs, and crept under Don Juan's door.

The next morning Doña Pepa did not appear. His uncle said that she had a habit of sleepwalking, and had run something sharp into her foot.

"I can guess what ails her," thought Don Luis to himself, as he condoled with his uncle, who seemed really troubled.

Don Luis had carefully preserved in a drawer the pieces of the tail which he had cut off, and on looking at them the next morning had found that they were the toes and instep of a human foot.

For some days he neither saw nor heard anything more of his aunt in any shape. But at last she appeared and greeted him most cordially. He noticed, however, that she halted decidedly in her gait, and reported everything to the hermit.

"Have no pity for her, my son," replied the hermit, "for she intends your destruction. If you have any mercy upon her, she will have none for you. The next time strike about a foot from the head, where she cannot hide her disfigurement."

A few evenings after this conversation with the hermit, he found the snake awaiting him in the courtyard, and as usual it went upstairs before him, and coiled itself on a chest in the farthest corner of the room. All the doors in the house seemed to be constructed for harboring and helping snakes, for they were scooped away underneath for two inches.

Don Luis drew his sword and struck as nearly a foot from the head as he could. The snake made a bound to the door and disappeared, the head first and the body following and joining it outside, and it then disappeared under his uncle's door.

The next day Doña Pepa disappeared from human ken for a month, "She had a dreadful abscess on her finger," his uncle said, "which had kept her awake for many nights, and she must lie by for a time and have it lanced."

"I can guess what ails her," thought Don Luis, and went to his friend the hermit to report matters.

On the way he met an old servant who had been in his grand-father's family, and had lived with Don Juan after his marriage, but had been amongst the first to leave. The old servant stopped him and said:

"I have been anxious for a long time about my master and you. Is he well? and what is going on there? I did not like to call at the house, as I left of my own accord. But I had to leave, for I could not bear to live with that horrid snake in the house, Doña Pepa."

"What do you mean by 'snake in the house,' Jorge?" asked Don Luis. "Did you ever *see* a snake in that house?"

"Indeed I have," replied the old servant indignantly. "She followed me all over the house, until I nearly lost my wits. If I went into the kitchen, it was there; in my room, it was there; and at last I went away because when I spoke to my master about it, he grew angry that I saw he thought I was lying. Have you never seen the snake yourself, señor? for everyone else who lived there has."

"Yes, I have seen the same thing myself, if you press me so hard," answered Don Luis; "but what can I do more than I have? In snake form, I have cut off one foot and one hand. What can I do more short of murder?"

"One thing more," said old Jorge earnestly, "one thing more, and that is to watch until she is out. Go to the chest in the master's room, under the left-hand window, and open it. You will find a queer skin, striped like a serpent's, folded up in the right-hand corner. Burn that, and you will find that the snake will not torment you any more."

"Are you sure?" inquired Don Luis, earnestly.

"Quite sure," answered Jorge, as earnestly.

Then they parted.

But the more Don Luis thought over the advice of the old servant, the less inclined he felt to act upon it. It seemed a treacherous thing to do, to go into his uncle's room, steal a serpent's skin out of his chest, and burn it without knowing what might be the consequences of such a deed. So he resolved to go to his friend the hermit, and ask him what he thought. When he had told his story, the old man sat a long while musing and silent. At last he said, "I can quite understand your scruples, and sympathize with you in your feeling for your uncle. But I am afraid that there is no other way of destroying an influence so pernicious as that of Doña Pepa; for you are not the only one whom she has either utterly depraved or injured in some way. And such people are better out of the world than in it, as the mischief they do is incomparably greater than the pleasure they give by their beauty. However, for a month at least, she cannot do you much harm. She is too much injured to show herself until she can hide her misfortune. But if she begins her torments again, I should be inclined to tell the whole case to your uncle, and then say to him what you intend to do."

Upon this advice Don Luis acted. For a month Doña Pepa kept her room, and he saw no more of the snake. After that time, however, she reappeared, and he watched to see how she concealed her wounded hand. It was all covered with a silk handkerchief, and he asked after it with apparent zeal. Doña Pepa colored deeply, but answered with much dignity; she looked thin and pale, and her face was worn with pain. Don Luis's kind heart ached when he saw how he had hurt her. His uncle took great pains to tell every one that poor Doña Pepa had had to have her hand amputated for a wound which had mortified and which had threatened her life. Very few people believed the story, for somehow or other Don Luis's adventures with the serpent had got wind and everyone suspected that Doña Pepa's sufferings were the first punishment for her many deeds of sorcery.

But after a short interval the same troubles began again. Don Luis found the serpent rolled up anywhere and everywhere: in the courtyard, on the stairs, in his room, in every nook and corner, in his boots, under his rug, over his clothes, until he began to think that he was going mad and saw snakes *everywhere*. One morning, however, he awoke and found the snake on his bed, winding itself around his body. He gave it several hard blows, and wounded it in various places, till it glided quietly out of the room. He then at last decided that the time had come to tell his uncle the whole story. When he saw him in the dining hall, he asked him how Doña Pepa was.

The old man looked very much disturbed, and said hesitatingly:

"I have not seen her this morning. But I suppose she is well."

"Have not seen her this morning!" repeated Don Luis, feigning surprise. "Is she not at home?"

"Well, yes, she is at home," replied his uncle, more embarrassed than ever. "But sometimes she is not well enough to see me."

"Oh," said Don Luis significantly; and the matter dropped for the time.

Later in the day, however, Don Luis contrived to find his uncle alone, and then he told him all that he had heard. At first Don Juan was very angry, but as his nephew proceeded and he heard the long list of annoyances and torments to which he had been subjected under his roof, he became very pale and silent.

There was a long pause after Don Luis had finished, and then his uncle said:

"Well, I can say nothing—nor can I help you in any way. This much I *can* tell you, that I sympathize most deeply with you—for—for that snake has been the bane of my life."

"Then," said Don Luis earnestly, "you will not blame me if I punish the snake the next time as it deserves."

"No, I should not blame you, if you can do it," sighed old Don Juan, little dreaming that his nephew already possessed the secret of killing her.

And the conversation ended.

For his uncle's sake Don Luis bore with patience the annoying attentions of the snake as long as he could; but after a month more of torment he watched his opportunity when Don Juan and Doña Pepa were out, and went into his uncle's room. There he found the chest under the left window, just as old Jorge had said. On one side was a queer striped skin, which he immediately recognized as the snake's. He was preparing to light a fire and burn it, when he heard his uncle and Doña Pepa returning. He had only time to close the chest, slip away to his room, and hide the skin, before they entered their room.

As soon as he heard them descend into the hall, he prepared and lit a fire, and took out the skin, rolling it in his hands to make it smaller, when he heard fearful shrieks below. He rushed out to learn the cause, and was told by one of the servants that Doña Pepa had had fearful cramps, as though her body had been folded up. Then Don Luis knew that what he had heard was true; and, without giving himself time to think, he threw the skin upon the fire. In a moment it was in a blaze, and crisped and curled into nothing.

Having watched it burn to the end, he went down to his uncle. Don Juan was walking up and down the room, wringing his hands. Doña Pepa was stretched out upon a couch, looking very white and ill. The family physician was sitting beside her, holding her hand and feeling her pulse.

"What has happened?" asked Don Luis. "Is Doña Pepa ill?"

"She is dead," replied the physician solemnly, "and I cannot discover what was the matter nor what can have killed her. She was in excellent health, as far as I could make out, an hour ago, when I was called in to see her for convulsions; and now, with no bad symptoms at all, she has suddenly died. I cannot understand the cause at all."

Don Luis thought to himself that he perhaps could throw a good deal of light upon the subject. But he held his tongue.

When Doña Pepa was laid out for burial, the old nun who had

prepared her for her last resting place confessed that she had seen the figure of a large snake distinctly traced upon the entire length of her body.

Don Luis and Don Juan lived very happily together for years after the death of Doña Pepa. His uncle seemed like a boy again, so light-hearted and gay was he. When his friends came to see him, he would say, "I have not been so happy for many a long year."

And Don Juan's friends thought it strange, but Don Luis did not. The hermit and one or two others only knew the secret of the serpent-woman.

♦   ♦   ♦   ♦   ♦

THE SNAKE'S LOVER
Peru

There was once a young girl who was the only daughter of a married couple. Because her mother and father had no other children, they would send her up the mountain every day to take the cattle to pasture. The girl was now old enough to be married, well developed and very beautiful.

One day, at the top of a hill, a very refined and very thin young man approached her. "Be my lover," he said. And he kept on talking to her of love.

Seeing that he was tall and strong, the girl consented. From then on they met on the mountain, and there they made love.

"I wish that you would bring me freshly toasted flour to eat," said the young man to the girl. She did what her lover asked her and brought him freshly cooked flour every day. They ate together and served each other. They lived like this for a long time.

The young man walked and ran with his nose to the ground; he crept along, because he had many tiny little feet. This was because he was not a man—he was a snake. But in the girl's eyes he seemed always to be a tall and thin young man.

After some time had gone by, the young girl told her lover, "I am pregnant. When my parents find out, they will scold me and ask me who is the father of my child. We must decide whether we will go to your house or mine."

The young man answered, "We'll have to go to your house. But I can't enter it openly—that's not possible. Tell me, is there a hole in the wall by the mortar where you grind the flour in your house? Isn't there always a hole next to the mortar to hold the rag for cleaning the stone?"

"Yes, there's a hole next to the mortar," she answered.

"Then you must take me there," said the young man.

"But what will you do in that hole?"

"I will live there, day and night."

"You won't fit," she said. "It's a very little hole."

"It will do—it will serve me for a house. Now I want to know where you sleep, in the kitchen or in the storeroom?"

"I sleep in the kitchen," she said. "I sleep with my parents."

"And where is the mortar?"

"It's in the storeroom."

"When I come, you must sleep on the ground next to the mortar."

"And how am I to get away from my parents?" she asked. "They won't want me to sleep alone."

"You must pretend to be afraid that thieves will come and steal from the storeroom. Tell them, 'I'll sleep there to keep watch.' And you must be the only one to use the mortar—don't let your parents use it. Every time you grind the flour, you must throw a little into the hole where I'll be living—I won't eat anything else. And you must take care to cover the hole with the cleaning rag so nobody will see me."

Then the young girl asked, "Can't you present yourself openly to my parents?"

"No, I can't," he answered. "Little by little, I will appear to them."

"And how are you going to live in that hole? It's so small that only a tuft of wool would fit."

"You'll have to make it bigger from the inside."

"All right," she said. "You know what's best for you."

"But you'll have to take me there," the young fellow said, "and leave me behind the house. Then at night you can take me to the storehouse."

"Good," his lover answered.

That night the young girl went home alone. She sneaked into

the storehouse and made the hole by the mortar bigger. The next day she went to the mountain with the cattle and met her lover in the usual place. "I've made the rag-hole bigger," she said. At nightfall they went to her house. She left the young man behind the house by the corral. In the night she came for him and took him to the hole by the mortar. As the young fellow went into the hole, the girl said to herself, "Impossible! He'll never make it." But the young man slid in smoothly.

That very night the girl said to her parents, "Father, Mother, it's quite possible that thieves may come to steal everything we own. From now on I'm going to stay in the room where we keep our food."

The parents nodded. "Go, daughter," they said.

The girl took her bed into the storeroom and spread it out on the ground next to the mortar. The serpent slipped into the bed, and the lovers slept together. And they were together every night from then on.

When there was flour to be ground on the mortar, the girl wouldn't allow anyone else to do it. She would throw handfuls of flour into the rag-hole, and before going out, she would cover the hole with the cleaning rag, so neither her parents nor anyone else could see what was in there.

The parents suspected nothing; they didn't think to uncover the hole and look inside. Only when they realized their daughter was with child did they begin to worry and decide to speak of it. "It looks like our daughter is pregnant," they said. "We'll have to ask her who the father is."

They called her to them and said, "You're pregnant. Who is the father?" But she would not answer. Then the father and the mother each asked her separately, one by one, but still she kept silent.

Soon she began to feel birth pains, night after night. Her parents took care of her. And those nights the snake wasn't able to slide into the young girl's bed.

The serpent no longer lived in the hole in the wall—he had grown so enormous that he couldn't get into it. Sucking the young girl's blood had made him red and swollen. He scratched out a cave in the base of the mortar and moved in there. In this new home of his the serpent grew so fat that he spread out sideways; he was all bloated. But still in his lover's eyes he was no snake—he was a young man. A young man who kept getting fatter and fatter.

The lovers were no longer able to cover their cave under the mortar, so the girl folded her blankets every morning and piled them around the stone base. In this way they were able to hide the serpent's nest from the mother and father.

Because their daughter remained so stubbornly silent, the parents decided to question the people of the *ayllu*.

"Our daughter has gotten pregnant, out of nowhere," they said. "Have you ever seen her talking to anyone, anywhere, maybe in the fields where she tended the cattle?"

But the people all answered, "No, we've seen nothing."

"Where do you let her sleep?" one of them asked.

"She used to sleep in the same room with us, but now she insists on sleeping in the storeroom. She makes her bed on the ground next to the mortar. And she doesn't want anyone else to grind the flour— she won't let us come near the mortar."

"And why won't she let you come near it?" the people asked. "What does she say about this?"

"She says, 'Father, Mother, don't go near the mortar, you'll get my bed dirty. I will do all the grinding myself,' " the father answered.

"She has already begun to suffer birth pains," the mother said.

Then the people told them, "You'll have to go to the Guesser and ask him to look into this. We common folks can't tell what is going on."

So the father and mother went to see the Guesser. They gave him a little package of coca leaves, and begged him to find out about their daughter. "She is not feeling well," they said, "and we don't know what the trouble is."

"What is going on with your daughter?" the Guesser asked. "What ails her?"

"She has become pregnant, we don't know by whom. She keeps on suffering birth pains night after night, but she cannot give birth. And she won't say who the father is," answered the mother.

The Guesser consulted the coca leaves. After a while he said:

"I can see something! Something under the mortar in your house! And that thing is the father! You see, the father is not like us, he's not a man."

"Then what is he?" cried the old folks, very much frightened. "Keep on guessing—find out more, we beg you!"

So the Guesser went on:

"What's in there is a snake, not a man!"

"But what shall we do?" the parents asked.

The Guesser pondered a few minutes, and spoke again, to the father:

"Your daughter won't want you to kill the serpent. She will say, 'Kill me before you kill my lover!' So you must send her away someplace, a day's journey away. And even that she will refuse, so you must tell her like this, using the name of some town: 'They say that in this town there is a remedy that will help you give birth. Go and buy it and bring it back to me. And if you don't obey me, I will hit you, I will beat you to death'—tell her that, it's the only way you will make her go. Next, you must hire some men armed with sticks, with machetes and big clubs. Make your daughter carry out your orders, and when she is far away, you and the men go into the storehouse and push over the mortar. Underneath it you will find the snake. You must beat it to death. Take care it doesn't jump on you, for if it does, it will kill you. Chop off its head and then dig a grave and bury it."

"Very good, sir," said the father. "We'll do just as you tell us."

The father went at once to look for strong men who would help him kill the serpent. He hired ten men armed with clubs and sharp machetes.

"Tomorrow, when my daughter is gone, you must come to my house," he told them. "But don't let anybody see you."

The next morning the parents made the girl get up early and fix herself a lunch basket. To make it look good, they gave her money and said, "Here is the money to buy the remedy we told you about. You will find it in Sumakk Marka, that town on the other side of the river."

But the girl didn't want to obey them. "I can't go," she insisted. "I don't want to." So the parents threatened her: "If you don't go, if you don't fetch the remedy, we we'll kill you with our sticks. We will beat you until we destroy what you carry in your belly."

That frightened the girl, and she took off. They watched her until she was out of sight. When she had vanished on the horizon, the hired men came to the father's house and gathered in the yard. They shared their coca and chewed it awhile. Afterwards they went into the storehouse and carried everything out into the yard. Last of all, they took out the girl's bed.

Then, with their clubs on their shoulders and gripping their machetes, they entered the storeroom, they surrounded the mortar, and they waited. Then they pushed it over.

A fat snake was stretched out there, with a big head like a man's. When it saw it was discovered—*wat'aakk!* went its heavy body as it reared itself up. The men beat it with their clubs and slashed it with their machetes. They chopped it into pieces and threw the head out into the garden plot, and there it writhed, it jumped, it bubbled around on the ground. The men ran after it and pounded it with their clubs, they tried to flatten it. Blood ran out all over the ground, it gushed and spouted from the mutilated body. But still the serpent would not die.

At that very moment the young wife, the snake's lover, returned. When she saw all the people gathered in the yard, she ran at once to the storeroom. The mortar was bathed in blood, and the serpent's nest was empty. She turned her face toward the yard, and there she saw them hitting her lover's head with their clubs. She screamed as if she were dying:

"Why, why do you destroy my lover's head? Why do you kill him? This was my husband! This was the father of my child!"

When she saw she blood she screamed again; her voice filled the house. She screamed and screamed till at last the effort caused her to abort. A swarm of little snakes came wriggling out onto the ground and spread all over the yard, jumping and crawling.

Finally, the men killed the big snake. Then they went after all the little snakes and squashed them too. Some of the men dug a hole in the ground and the others swept in the blood. They swept out all the blood from the house and into the hole and buried all the serpents and the bloody mud. They brought the young girl to her parents' room so they could care for her. Then they cleaned and straightened up the house, and fixed the storeroom the way it had been. They lugged the mortar down to the river and put the stone under a waterfall and left it there. And when everything was in order, the girl's father gave each man fair payment for his work. The men took their pay and left.

After a time, the parents asked their daughter, "In what way could you live with a serpent? He was no man, that husband of yours—he was a demon."

Only then did the young girl tell her story; she told them about her first meeting with the snake. Everything came to be known and was cleared up. The parents cared for their daughter and healed her, her body and her soul. Then, much later, the girl married a good man, and her life was happy.

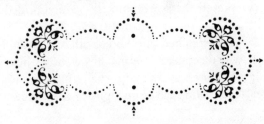

NOT QUITE HUMAN

Every culture has its own resident fairies or trolls or boogers. These are the Others, the Good Folk, the Elfin, the Fey, who have gifts that humans envy. Sometimes it is simply gold, as in "Bridget and the Lurikeen"; sometimes it is second sight, as in "Then the Merman Laughed." The Other Folk have their own morality; they think nothing of tricking humans, eating them, or using them in other, more subtle ways.

It is this question of morality rather than the differences in stature (some of the fairy folk are thought to be tiny, and some, like giants, incredibly tall), length of life, or magical abilities that marks those who are not quite human. As Katharine Briggs points out in *The Vanishing People*: "The kindness of the fairies was often capricious and . . . little mercy mingled with their justice. We are dealing with a pendulous people, trembling on the verge of annihilation, whose mirth is often hollow and whose beauty is precarious and glamorous. From such no great compassion can be expected."

THE WELL-BAKED MAN
American Indian (Pima)

The Magician had made the world but felt that something was missing. "What could it be?" he thought. "What could be missing?" Then it came to him that what he wanted on this earth was some beings like himself, not just animals. "How will I make them?" he thought. First he built himself a *horno*, an oven. Then he took some clay and formed it into a shape like himself.

Now, Coyote was hanging around the way he usually does, and when Magician, who was Man Maker, was off gathering firewood, Coyote quickly changed the shape of that clay image. Man Maker built a fire inside the *horno*, then put the image in without looking at it closely.

After a while the Magician said, "He must be ready now." He took the image and breathed on it, whereupon it came to life. "Why don't you stand up?" said Man Maker. "What's wrong with you?" The creature barked and wagged its tail. "Ah, oh my, Coyote has tricked me," he said. "Coyote changed my being into an animal like himself."

Coyote said, "Well, what's wrong with it? Why can't I have a pretty creature that pleases me?"

"Oh my, well, all right, but don't interfere again." That's why we have the dog; it was Coyote's doing.

So Man Maker tried again. "They should be companions to each other." he thought. "I shouldn't make just one." He shaped some humans who were rather like himself and identical with each other in every part.

"What's wrong here?" Man Maker was thinking. Then he saw. "Oh my, that won't do. How can they increase?" So he pulled a little between the legs of one image, saying, "Ah, that's much better." With his fingernail he made a crack in the other image. He put some pleasant feeling in them somewhere. "Ah, now it's good. Now they'll be able to do all the necessary things." He put them in the *horno* to bake.

"They're done now," Coyote told him. So Man Maker took them out and made them come to life.

"Oh my, what's wrong?" he said. "They're underdone; they're not brown enough. They don't belong here—they belong across the water someplace." He scowled at Coyote. "Why did you tell me they were done? I can't use them here."

So the Magician tried again, making a pair like the last one and placing them in the oven. After a while he said, "I think they're ready now."

"No, they aren't done yet," said Coyote. "You don't want them to come out too light again; leave then in a little longer."

"Well, all right," replied Man Maker. They waited, and then he took them out. "Oh my. What's wrong? These are overdone. They're burned too dark." He put them aside. "Maybe I can use them some other place across the water. They don't belong here."

For the fourth time Man Maker placed his images inside the oven. "Now, don't interfere," he said to Coyote, "you give me bad advice. Leave me alone."

This time the Magician did not listen to Coyote but took them out when he himself thought they were done. He made them come to life, and the two beings walked around, talked, laughed, and behaved in a seemly fashion. They were neither underdone nor overdone.

"These are exactly right," said Man Maker. "These really belong here; these I will use. They are beautiful." So that's why we have the Pueblo Indians.

THE FINN MESSENGER
Norway

Neri Olavsson lived at Sönstveit for a while. His wife ran the farm while he was at sea. A strange thing happened to him one Christmas Eve, while he was off the China coast, and, according to Anne Godlid, it was this.

It had been necessary for him to leave his wife while she was with child, and he was quite worried about her and very homesick.

"If only there was some way of finding out how things are at home!" he said to one of his shipmates, a sailor who happened to be a Finn and was said to know more than the others, "I had to leave my wife when she was with child," he said, "and heaven knows how it's turned out!"

"What'll you give me if I bring word from home for you to-night?" said the other.

"You certainly couldn't do that!" said Neri.

"If you'll give me a pot of spirits, it's in order!" said the sailor.

"I'd gladly give you five, if anything like that is humanly possible," said Neri.

"Well, if you have something at home you'd recognize again, I'll fetch it," said the sailor.

Why yes, they had a queer silver spoon that had come from the *huldre*-folk and which they never used. It stood in a crack in the wall over the window. "Fetch that!" said Neri.

The sailor said they had to stay as quiet as mice as long as it lasted, and this they promised to do. Then he chalked a circle on the deck and lay down inside it just as if he were dead. They all saw how he became paler and paler and lay there without moving a limb until the onlookers were downright terrified. He lay this way for some time, but suddenly he gave a start, got to his feet, and he was holding the spoon in his hands.

"Here's your silver spoon again," he said to Neri. "Now I've been to Sönstveit."

"So I see," said Neri; he recognized the spoon. "How was everything there?"

"Oh, just fine," said the sailor. "Your wife's had a lovely big boy. Your mother was sitting inside a black house, spinning on a distaff. She was a little poorly, she said. But your father was down on his knees, out by the chopping block, cutting wood."

Neri wrote down the date and the hour right away.

When he came home, he found out that everything was just as the sailor had said.

"But the old silver spoon has disappeared!" they said. "One day there was a rumbling so the whole house shook. We never were able to figure out what it was, but since then we haven't seen anything of the spoon!"

"Well, here it is," said Neri. "It's been all the way to China!" And then he told then how it had happened.

VASILISA THE BEAUTIFUL
Russia

In a certain kingdom there lived a merchant. Although he had been married for twelve years, he had only one daughter, called Vasilisa the Beautiful. When the girl was eight years old, her mother died. On her deathbed the merchant's wife called her daughter, took a doll from under her coverlet, gave it to the girl, and said, "Listen, Vasilisushka. Remember and heed my last words. I am dying, and together with my maternal blessing I leave you this doll. Always keep it with you and do not show it to anyone. If you get into trouble, give the doll food, and ask its advice. When it has eaten, it will tell you what to do in your trouble." Then the mother kissed her child and died.

After his wife's death the merchant mourned as is proper, and then began to think of marrying again. He was a handsome man and had no difficulty in finding a bride, but he liked best a certain widow. Because she was elderly and had two daughters on her own, of almost the age as Vasilisa, he thought that she was an experienced housewife and mother. So he married her, but was deceived, for she did not turn out to be a good mother for his Vasilisa.

Vasilisa was the most beautiful girl in the village. Her stepmother and stepsisters were jealous of her beauty and tormented her by giving her all kinds of work to do, hoping that she would grow thin from toil and tanned from the exposure to the wind and sun; in truth, she had a most miserable life. But Vasilisa bore all this without complaint and became lovelier and more buxom every day, while the stepmother and her daughters grew thin and ugly from spite, although they always sat with folded hands like ladies.

How did all this come about? Vasilisa was helped by her doll. Without its aid the girl could never have managed all that work. In return, Vasilisa sometimes did not eat, but kept the choicest morsels for her doll. And at night, when everyone was asleep, she would lock herself in the little room in which she lived, and would give the doll a treat, saying, "Now, little doll, eat, and listen to my troubles. I live in my father's house but am deprived of all joy; a wicked step-mother is driving me from the white world. Tell me how I should live and what I should do." The doll would eat, then would give her advice and comfort her in her trouble, and in the morning she would perform all the chores for Vasilisa, who rested in the shade and picked flowers while the flower beds were weeded, the cabbage sprayed, the water brought in, and the stove fired. The doll even showed Vasilisa an herb that would protect her from sunburn. She led an easy lfe, thanks to her doll.

Several years went by. Vasilisa grew up and reached the marriage age. She was wooed by all the young men in the village, but no one would even look at the stepmother's daughters. The stepmother was more spiteful than ever, and her answer to all the suitors was, "I will not give the youngest in marriage before the elder ones." And each time she sent a suitor away, she vented her anger on Vasilisa in cruel blows.

One day the merchant had to leave home for a long time in order to trade in distant lands. The stepmother moved to another house. Near that house was a thick forest, and in a glade of that forest there stood a hut, and in the hut lived Baba Yaga. She never allowed anyone to come near her and ate human beings as if they were chickens. Having moved into the new house, the merchant's wife, hating Vas-ilisa, repeatedly sent the girl to the woods for one thing or another; but each time Vasilisa returned home safe and sound: her doll had showed her the way and kept her far from Baba Yaga's hut.

Autumn came. The stepmother gave evening work to all three maidens: the oldest had to make lace, the second had to knit stockings, and Vasilisa had to spin; and each one had to finish her task. The stepmother put out the lights all over the house, leaving only one candle in the room where the girls worked, and went to bed. The girls worked. The candle began to smoke; one of the stepsisters took up a scissors to trim it, but instead, following her mother's order, she snuffed it out, as though inadvertently.

"What shall we do now?" said the girls. "There is no light in the house and our tasks are not finished. Someone must run to Baba Yaga and get some light."

"The pins on my lace give me light," said the one who was making lace. "I shall not go."

"I shall not go either," said the one who was knitting stockings. "My knitting needles give me light."

"Then you must go," both of them cried to their stepsister. "Go to Baba Yaga!" And they pushed Vasilisa out of the room.

She went into her own little room, put the supper she had prepared before her doll, and said, "Now, dolly, eat, and aid me in my need. They are sending me to Baba Yaga for a light, and she will eat me up."

The doll ate the supper and its eyes gleamed like two candles. "Fear not, Vasilisushka," it said. "Go where you are sent, only keep me with you all the time. With me in your pocket you will suffer no harm from Baba Yaga." Vasilisa made ready, put her doll in her pocket, and, having made the sign of the cross, went into the deep forest.

She walked in fear and trembling. Suddenly a horseman galloped past her: his face was white, he was dressed in white, his horse was white, and his horse's trappings were white—daybreak came to the woods.

She walked on farther, and a second horseman galloped past her: he was all red, he was dressed in red, and his horse was red—the sun began to rise.

Vasilisa walked the whole night and the whole day, and only on the following evening did she come to the glade where Baba Yaga's hut stood. The fence around the hut was made of human bones, and on the spikes were human skulls with staring eyes; the doors had human legs for doorposts, human hands for bolts, and a mouth with sharp teeth in place of a lock. Vasilisa was numb with horror and stood rooted to the spot. Suddenly another horseman rode by. He was all black, he was dressed in black, and his horse was black. He galloped up to Baba Yaga's door and vanished, as though the earth had swallowed him up—night came. But the darkness did not last long. The eyes of all the skulls on the fence began to gleam, and the glade was as bright as day. Vasilisa shuddered with fear, but not knowing where to run, remained on the spot.

Soon a terrible noise resounded through the woods; the trees crackled, the dry leaves rustled; from the woods Baba Yaga drove out in a mortar, prodding it on with a pestle, and sweeping her traces with a broom. She rode up to the gate, stopped, and sniffing the air around her, cried, "Fie, Fie! I smell a Russian smell! Who is here?"

Vasilisa came up to the old witch and, trembling with fear, bowed low to her and said, "It is I, grandmother. My stepsisters sent me to get some light."

"Very well," said Baba Yaga. "I know them, but before I give you the light you must live with me and work for me; if not, I will eat you up." Then she turned to the gate and cried, "Hey, my strong bolts, unlock! Open up, my wide gate!" The gate opened, and Baba

Yaga drove in whistling. Vasilisa followed her, and then everything closed again.

Having entered the room, Baba Yaga stretched herself out in her chair and said to Vasilisa, "Serve me what is in the stove, I am hungry."

Vasilisa lit a torch from the skulls on the fence and began to serve Yaga the food from the stove—and enough food had been prepared for ten people. She brought kvass, mead, beer, and wine from the cellar. The old witch ate and drank everything, leaving for Vasilisa only a little cabbage soup, a crust of bread, and a piece of pork. Then Baba Yaga made ready to go to bed and said, "Tomorrow after I go, see to it that you sweep the yard, clean the hut, cook the dinner, wash the linen, and go to the cornbin and sort out a bushel of wheat. And let everything be done, or I will eat you up!" Having given these orders, Baba Yaga began to snore.

Vasilisa set the remnants of the old witch's supper before her doll, wept bitter tears, and said, "Here, dolly, eat, and aid me in my need! Baba Yaga has given me a hard task to do and threatens to eat me up if I do not do it all. Help me!"

The doll answered, "Fear not, Vasilisa the Beautiful! Eat your supper, say your prayers, and go to sleep; the morning is wiser than the evening."

Very early next morning Vasilisa awoke, after Baba Yaga had arisen, and looked out of the window. The eyes of the skulls were going out; then the white horseman flashed by, and it was daybreak. Baba Yaga went out into the yard, whistled, and the mortar, pestle, and broom appeared before her. The red horseman flashed by, and the sun rose. Baba Yaga sat in the mortar, prodded it on with the pestle, and swept her traces with the broom.

Vasilisa remained alone, looked about Baba Yaga's hut, was amazed at the abundance of everything, and stopped wondering which work she should do first. For lo and behold, all the work was done; the doll was picking the last shreds of chaff from the wheat. "Ah, my savior," said Vasilisa to her doll, "you have delivered me from death."

"All you have to do," answered the doll, creeping into Vasilisa's pocket, "is to cook the dinner. Cook it with the help of God and then rest, for your health's sake.

When evening came Vasilisa set the table and waited for Baba Yaga. Dusk began to fall, the black horseman flashed by the gate, and night came; only the skull's eyes were shining. The trees crackled, the leaves rustled; Baba Yaga was coming.

Vasilisa met her. "Is everything done?" asked Yaga.

"Please see for yourself, grandmother," said Vasilisa. Baba Yaga looked at everything, was annoyed that there was nothing she could complain about, and said, "Very well, then." Then she cried, "My faithful servants, my dear friends, grind my wheat!" Three pairs of hands appeared, took the wheat, and carried it out of sight. Baba Yaga ate her fill, made ready to go to sleep, and again gave her orders to Vasilisa. "Tomorrow," she commanded, "do the same work you have done today, and in addition take the poppy seed from the bin and get rid of the dust, grain by grain. Someone threw dust into the bins out of spite."

Having said this, the old witch turned to the wall and began to snore, and Vasilisa set about feeding her doll. The doll ate, and spoke as she had spoken the day before: "Pray to God and go to sleep; the morning is wiser than the evening. Everything will be done, Vasilisushka."

Next morning Baba Yaga again left the yard in her mortar, and Vasilisa and the doll soon had all the work done. The old witch came back, looked at everything, and cried, "My faithful servants, my dear friends, press the oil out of the poppy seed!" Three pairs of hands appeared, took the poppy seed, and carried it out of sight. Baba Yaga sat down to dine; she ate, and Vasilisa stood silent. "Why do you not speak to me?" said Baba Yaga. "You stand there as though you were dumb."

"I did not dare to speak," said Vasilisa, "but if you'll give me leave, I'd like to ask you something."

"Go ahead. But not every question has a good answer. If you know too much, you will soon grow old."

"I want to ask you, grandmother, only about what I have seen. As I was on my way to you, a horseman on a white horse, all white himself and dressed in white, overtook me. Who is he?"

"He is my bright day," said Baba Yaga.

"Then another horseman overtook me; he had a red horse, was red himself, and was dressed in red. Who is he?"

"He is my red sun."

"And who is the black horseman whom I met at your very gate, grandmother?"

"He is my dark night—and all of them are my faithful servants."

Vasilisa remembered the three pairs of hands, but kept silent. "Why don't you ask me more?" said Baba Yaga.

"That will be enough," Vasilisa replied. "You said yourself, grandmother, that one who knows too much will grow old soon."

"It is well," said Baba Yaga, "that you ask only about what you have seen outside my house, not inside my house. I do not like to have my dirty linen washed in public, and I eat the overcurious. Now I shall ask you something. How do you manage to do the work I set for you?"

"I am helped by the blessing of my mother." said Vasilisa.

"So that is what it is," shrieked Baba Yaga. "Get you gone, blessed daughter! I want no blessed ones in my house!" She dragged Vasilisa out of the room and pushed her outside the gate, took a skull with burning eyes from the fence, stuck it on a stick, and gave it to the girl, saying, "Here is your light for your stepsisters. Take it; that is what they sent you for."

Vasilisa ran homeward by the light of the skull, which went out only at daybreak, and by nightfall of the following day she reached the house. As she approached the gate, she was about to throw the skull away, thinking that surely they no longer needed a light in the house. But suddenly a dull voice came from the skull, saying, "Do not throw me away, take me to your stepmother." She looked at the stepmother's house and, seeing that there was no light in the windows, decided to enter with her skull. For the first time she was received kindly. Her stepmother and stepsisters told her that since she had left they had had no fire in the house; they were unable to strike a flame themselves, and whatever light was brought by the neighbors went out the moment it was brought into the house. "Perhaps your fire will last," said the stepmother.

The skull was brought into the room, and its eyes kept staring at the stepmother and her daughters, and burned them. They tried to hide, but wherever they went the eyes followed them. By morning they were all burned to ashes; only Vasilisa remained untouched by the fire.

In the morning Vasilisa buried the skull in the ground, locked up the house, and went to the town. A certain childless old woman gave her shelter, and there she lived, waiting for her father's return. One day she said to the woman, "I am weary of sitting without work, grandmother. Buy me some flax, the best you can get; at least I shall be spinning."

The old woman bought good flax and Vasilisa set to work. She spun as fast as lightning, and her threads were even and thin as a hair. She spun a great deal of yarn; it was time to start weaving it, but no comb fine enough for Vasilisa's yarn could be found, and no one would undertake to make one. Vasilisa asked her doll for aid.

The doll said, "Bring me an old comb, and old shuttle, and a horse's mane; I will make a loom for you." Vasilisa got everything that was required and went to sleep, and during the night the doll made a wonderful loom for her.

By the end of the winter the linen was woven, and it was so fine that it could be passed through a needle like a thread. In the spring the linen was bleached, and Vasilisa said to the old woman, "Grandmother, sell this linen and keep the money for yourself."

The old woman looked at the linen and gasped: "No, my child! No one can wear such linen except the tsar. I shall take it to the palace."

The old woman went to the tsar's palace and walked back and forth beneath the windows. The tsar saw her and asked, "What do you want, old woman?"

"Your Majesty," she answered, "I have brought rare merchandise. I do not want to show it to anyone but you."

The tsar ordered her to be brought before him, and when he saw the linen he was amazed. "What do you want for it?" asked he.

"It has no price, little father tsar! I have brought it as a gift to you." The tsar thanked her and rewarded her with gifts.

The tsar ordered shirts to be made of the linen. It was cut, but nowhere could they find a seamstress who was willing to sew them. For a long time they tried to find one, but in the end the tsar summoned the old woman and said, "You have known how to spin and weave such linen, you must know how to sew shirts of it."

"It was not I that spun and wove this linen, Your Majesty," said the woman. "This is the work of a maiden to whom I give shelter."

"Then let her sew the shirts," ordered the tsar.

The old woman returned home and told everything to Vasilisa. "I knew all the time," said Vasilisa to her, "that I would have to do this work." She locked herself in her room and set to work; she sewed without rest and soon a dozen shirts were ready. The old woman took them to the tsar, and Vasilisa washed herself, combed her hair, dressed in her finest clothes, and sat at the window. She sat there waiting to see what would happen.

She saw a servant of the tsar entering the courtyard. The messenger came into the room and said, "The tsar wishes to see the needlewoman who made his shirts, and wishes to reward her with his own hands."

Vasilisa appeared before the tsar. When the tsar saw Vasilisa the Beautiful he fell madly in love with her. "No, my beauty," he said, "I will not separate from you. You shall be my wife." He took Vasilisa by her white hands, seated her by his side, and the wedding was celebrated at once. Soon Vasilisa's father returned, was overjoyed at her good fortune, and came to live in his daughter's house. Vasilisa took the old woman into her home too, and carried her doll in her pocket till the end of her life.

◆　　　　◆　　　　◆　　　　◆　　　　◆

Bridget and the Lurikeen
Ireland

A young girl that lived in sight of Castle Carberry, near Edenderry, was going for a pitcher of water to the neighboring well one summer morning, when who should she see sitting in a sheltery nook under an old thorn, but the Lurikeen, working like vengeance at a little old brogue only fit for the foot of a fairy like himself.

There he was, boring his holes, and jerking his waxed ends, with his little three-cornered hat with gold lace, his knee breeches, his jug of beer by his side, and his pipe in his mouth. He was so busy at his work, and so taken up with an old ballad he was singing in Irish, that he did not mind Breedheen till she had him by the scruff of the neck, as if he was in a vise.

"Ah, what are you doing?" says he, turning his head round as well as he could. "Dear, dear! to think of such a pretty colleen catching a body, as if he was after robbing a hen roost. What did I do to be treated in such a undecent manner? The very vulgarest young ruffin in the townland could do no worse. Come, come, Miss Bridget, take your hands off, sit down, and let us have a chat, like two respectable people."

"Ah, Mr. Lurikeen, I don't care a wisp of borrach for your politeness. It's your money I want, and I won't take hand or eye from you till you put me in possession of a fine lob of it."

"Money, indeed! Ah! where would a poor cobbler like me get it? Anyhow there's no money hereabouts, and if you'll only let go my arms, I'll turn my pockets inside out, and open the drawer of my seat, and give you leave to keep every halfpenny you'll find."

"That won't do. My eyes'll keep going through you like darning needles till I have the gold. Begonies if you don't make haste, I'll carry you, head and pluck, into the village, and there you'll have thirty pair of eyes on you instead of one."

"Well, well, was ever a poor cobbler so circumvented. And if it was an ignorant, ugly bosthoon that done it, I would not wonder. But a decent, comely girl, that can read her 'Poor Man's Manual' at the chapel, and—"

"You may throw your compliments on the stream there. They won't do for me, I tell you. The gold, the gold, the gold! Don't take up my time with your blarney."

"Well, if there's any to be got, it's under the old castle it is. We must have a walk for it. Just put me down, and we'll get on."

"Put you down indeed! I know a trick worth two of that. I'll carry you."

"Well, how suspicious we are! Do you see the castle from this?" Bridget was about turning eyes from the little man to where she knew the castle stood, but she bethought herself in time.

They went up a little hillside, and the Lurikeen was quite reconciled, and laughed and joked. But just as they got to the brow, he looked up over the ditch, gave a great screech, and shouted just as if a bugle horn was blew at her ears: "Oh, murder! Castle Carberry is afire." Poor Biddy gave a great start, and looked up towards the castle. The same moment she missed the weight of the Lurikeen, and when her eyes fell where he was a moment before, there was no more sign of him than if everything that passed was a dream.

THE TWO HUNCHBACKS
Italy

There were two hunchbacks who were brothers. The younger hunchback said, "I'm going out and make a fortune." He set out on foot. After walking for miles and miles he lost his way in the woods.

"What will I do now? What if assassins appeared . . . I'd better climb this tree." Once he was up the tree he heard a noise. "There they are! Help!"

Instead of assassins, out of a hole in the ground climbed a little old woman, then another and another, followed by a whole line of little old women, one right behind the other, who all danced around the tree singing:

> *Saturday and Sunday!*
> *Saturday and Sunday!*

Round and round they went, singing over and over:

> *Saturday and Sunday!*

From his perch in the treetop, the hunchback sang:

> *And Monday!*

The little women became dead silent, looked up, and one of them said, "Oh, the good soul that has given us the lovely line! We never would have thought of it by ourselves!"

Overjoyed, they resumed their dance around the tree, singing all the while:

> *Saturday, Sunday,*
> *And Monday!*
> *Saturday, Sunday,*
> *And Monday!*

After a few rounds they spied the hunchback up in the tree. He trembled for his life. "For goodness' sakes, little old souls, don't kill me. That line just slipped out. I meant no harm, I swear."

"Well, come down and let us reward you. Ask any favor at all, and we will grant it."

The hunchback came down the tree.

"Go on, ask!"

"I'm a poor man. What do you expect me to ask? What I'd really like would be for this hump to come off my back, since the boys all tease me about it."

"All right, the hump will be removed."

The old women took a butter saw, sawed off the hump, and rubbed his back with salve, so that it was now sound and scarless. The hump they hung on the tree.

The hunchback who was no longer a hunchback went home,

and nobody recognized him. "It can't be you!" said his brother.

"It most certainly is me. See how handsome I've become?"

"How did you do it?"

"Just listen." He told him about the tree, the little old women, and their song.

"I'm going to them, too," announced the brother.

So he set out, entered the same woods, and climbed the same tree. At the same time as last, here came the little old women out of their hole singing:

> *Saturday, Sunday,*
> *And Monday!*
> *Saturday, Sunday,*
> *And Monday!*

From the tree the hunchback sang:

> *And Tuesday!*

The old women began singing:

> *Saturday, Sunday,*
> *And Monday!*
> *And Tuesday!*

But the song no longer suited them, its rhythm had been marred.

They looked up, furious. "Who is this criminal, this assassin? We were singing so well and he had to come along and ruin everything! Now we've lost our song!" They finally saw him up in the tree. "Come down, come down!"

"I will not!" said the hunchback, scared to death. "You will kill me!"

"No, we won't. Come on down!"

The hunchback came down, and the little old women grabbed his brother's hump hanging on a tree limb and stuck it on his chest. "That's the punishment you deserve!"

So the poor hunchback went home with two humps instead of one.

THEN THE MERMAN LAUGHED
Iceland

A merman is a dwarf that lives in the sea. There is an old saying in Iceland which many people use as a proverb: "Then the merman laughed." As for how it arose, it is said that a certain farmer drew up in his fishing net a sea-dwarf who called himself a merman, with a big head and broad hands, but shaped like a seal below the navel. He would not teach any of his magic lore to the farmer, so the latter took him ashore, much against his will.

The farmer's wife, a young and lusty woman, came down to the shore and greeted her husband, kissing and fondling him. The farmer was pleased and praised her, but drove his dog away with a blow when it came up with the wife to greet him. Then, when he saw that, the merman laughed. The farmer asks why he laughed, and the merman says, "At stupidity."

As the farmer was making his way home from the sea, he stumbled and tripped over a tussock. He cursed the tussock heartily, asking why it had ever been sent by fate to stand on his land. Then the merman laughed (for he was being carried along, against his will), and said, "This farmer has no sense."

The farmer kept the merman in his house for three days. Some traveling merchants came there, with wares to sell. Now the farmer had never been able to get boots with soles as thick and strong as he wanted, but these merchants thought they had boots of the best quality. The farmer could take his pick among a hundred pairs, and still he said they were all too thin and would be in holes in no time. Then the merman laughed and said, "It's clever men that make the biggest fools."

The farmer could not get any further words of wisdom out of the merman by fair means or foul, except on condition that he took him out to sea again, right back to the very fishing bank where he had been caught, and then he would squat on the blade of the farmer's oar and answer all his questions, but not otherwise. So, after three days, the farmer did this. And when the dwarf was on the oar-blade, the farmer asked what gear fisherman ought to use if they wanted good catches.

The merman answered, "Chewed and trodden iron must be used for the hoods, and the forging must be done where one can hear both river and wave, and the hooks must be tempered in the foam and sweat of tired horses. Use a fishing line made from a grey bull's sinews, and cord from raw horsehide. For bait, use birds' gizzards and flounders, but human flesh on the middle bight, and then if you get no catch you're surely fey. The barb of a fishhook must point outwards."

Then the farmer asked him what was the stupidity he had laughed at when he praised his wife and struck his dog.

The merman answered, "Your own stupidity, farmer. Your dog loves you as dearly as his own life, but your wife wishes you were dead, and she is a whore. The tussock you cursed covers a treasure destined for you, and there's money in plenty under it; that was why you had no sense, farmer, and why I laughed. And the black boots will last you all your life, for you haven't many days to live—three days, they'll last you three days!"

And with this he plunged off the oar-blade, and so they parted. But everything the merman said proved to be true.

PERGRIN AND THE MERMAID
Wales

One fine afternoon in September, in the beginning of the last century, a fisherman, whose name was Pergrin, went to a recess in the rock near Pen Cemmes, where he found a sea maiden doing her hair, and he took the water lady prisoner to his boat.

We know not what language is used by sea maidens, but this one, this time at any rate, talked, it is said, very good Welsh; for when she was in despair in Pergrin's custody, weeping copiously, and with her tresses all disheveled, she called out, "Pergrin, if thou wilt let me go, I will give thee three shouts in the time of thy greatest need."

So, in wonder and fear, he let her go to walk the streets of the deep, and visit her sweethearts there.

Days and weeks passed without Pergrin seeing her after this; but one hot afternoon, when the sea was pretty calm, and the fishermen had no thought of danger, behold his old acquaintance showing her head and locks, and shouting out in a loud voice, "Pergrin! Pergrin! Pergrin! take up thy nets, take up thy nets, take up thy nets!"

Pergrin and his companion instantly obeyed the message and drew their nets in with great haste. In they went, past the bar, and by the time they had reached the Pwll Cam the most terrible storm had overspread the sea, while he and his companion were safe on land. Twice nine others had gone out with them, but they were all drowned without having the chance of obeying the warning of the water lady.

The Ash Lad Who Had an Eating Match with the Troll
Norway

There was once a farmer who had three sons. He was badly off, and old and feeble, and his sons wouldn't turn their hands to a thing. To the farm belonged a large, good forest, and there the father wanted the boys to chop wood and see about paying off some of the debt.

At last he got them around to his way of thinking, and the eldest was to go out chopping first. When he had made his way into the forest, and had started chopping a shaggy fir tree, a big, burly troll came up to him.

"If you're chopping in my forest, I'm going to kill you!" said the troll.

When the boy heard that, he flung aside the axe and headed for home again as best he could. He got home clean out of breath, and told them what had happened to him. But his father said he was chicken-hearted. The trolls had never scared *him* from chopping wood when he was young, he said.

On the next day the second son was to set out, and he fared just like the first. When he had struck the fir tree a few blows with his axe, the troll came up to him, too, and said, "If you're chopping in my forest, I'm going to kill you!"

The boy hardly dared look at him. He flung aside the axe and took to his heels just like his brother, and just as fast. When he came home again, his father became angry and said that the trolls had never scared *him* when he was young.

On the third day the Ash Lad wanted to set out.

"*You?*" said the two eldest. "You'll certainly manage it—you who've never been beyond the front door!"

He didn't say much to *that*, the Ash Lad didn't, but just asked for as big a lunch as possible to take with him. His mother had no curds, so she hung the cauldron over the fire to curdle a little cheese for him. This he put in his knapsack, and set out on his way.

When he had been chopping for a little while, the troll came to him and said, "If you're chopping in my forest, I'm going to kill you!"

But the boy wasn't slow. He ran over to the knapsack to get the cheese, and squeezed it till the whey spurted. "If you don't hold your tongue," he shrieked to the troll, "I'll squeeze you the way I'm squeezing the water out of this white stone!"

"Nay, dear fellow! Spare me!" said the troll. "I'll help you to chop!"

Well, on that condition the boy would spare him, and the troll was clever at chopping, so they managed to fell and cut up many cords of wood during the day.

As evening was drawing nigh, the troll said, "Now you can come home with me. My house is closer than yours."

Well, the boy went along, and when they came to the troll's home, *he* was to make up the fire in the hearth, while the boy was to fetch water for the porridge pot. But the two iron buckets were so big and heavy that he couldn't so much as budge them.

So the boy said, "It's not worth taking along these thimbles. I'm going after the whole well, I am!"

"Nay, my dear fellow," said the troll, "I can't lose my well. *You* make the fire and I'll go after the water."

When he came back with the water, they cooked up a huge pot of porridge.

"If it's all the same to you," said the boy, "let's have an eating match!"

"Oh yes!" replied the troll, for at *that* he felt he could always hold his own.

Well, they sat down at the table, but the boy stole over and took the knapsack and tied it in front of him, and he scooped more into the knapsack than he ate himself. When the knapsack was full, he took up his knife and ripped a gash in it. The troll looked at him, but didn't say anything.

When they had eaten a good while longer, the troll put down his spoon. "Nay! Now I can't manage any more!" he said.

"You *must* eat!" said the boy. "I'm barely half full yet. Do as I did and cut a hole in your stomach, then you can eat as much as you wish!"

"But doesn't that hurt dreadfully?" asked the troll.

"Oh, nothing to speak of," replied the boy.

So the troll did as the boy said, and then, you might know, that was the end of him.

But the boy took all the silver and gold to be found in the mountain, and went home with it. With that he could at least pay some of the debt.

How Mosquitoes Came to Be
American Indian (Tlingit)

Long ago there was a giant who loved to kill humans, eat their flesh, and drink their blood. He was especially fond of human hearts. "Unless we can get rid of this giant," people said, "none of us will be left," and they called a council to discuss ways and means.

One man said, "I think I know how to kill the monster," and he went to the place where the giant had last been seen. There he lay down and pretended to be dead.

Soon the giant came along. Seeing the man lying there, he said, "These humans are making it easy for me. Now I don't even have to catch and kill them; they might die right on my trail, probably from fear of me!"

The giant touched the body. "Ah, good," he said, "this one is still warm and fresh. What a tasty meal he'll make; I can't wait to roast his heart."

The giant flung the man over his shoulder, and the man let his head hang down as if he were dead. Carrying the man home, the giant dropped him in the middle of the floor right near the fireplace. Then he saw that there was no firewood and went to get some.

As soon as the monster had left, the man got up and grabbed the giant's huge skinning knife. Just then the giant's son came in, bending low to enter. He was still small as giants go, and the man held the big knife to his throat. "Quick, tell me, where's your father's heart? Tell me or I'll slit your throat!"

The giant's son was scared. He said, "My father's heart is in his left heel."

Just then the giant's left foot appeared in the entrance, and the man swiftly plunged the knife into the heel. The monster screamed and fell down dead.

Yet the giant still spoke: "Though I'm dead, though you killed me, I'm going to keep on eating you and all the other humans in the world forever!"

"That's what you think!" said the man. "I'm about to make sure that you never eat anyone again." He cut the giant's body into pieces and burned each one in the fire. Then he took the ashes and threw them into the air for the winds to scatter.

Instantly each of the particles turned into a mosquito. The cloud of ashes became a cloud of mosquitoes, and from the midst the man heard the giant's voice laughing, saying, "Yes, I'll eat you people until the end of time."

And as the monster spoke, the man felt a sting, and a mosquito started sucking his blood, and then many mosquitoes stung him, and he began to scratch himself.

THE DEPARTURE OF THE GIANTS
Africa (Mensa et al.)

Before the first Mensa, Habab, Beni-Amer, and Cunama people arrived, a tribe of giants was living in the land. It is said by some that God created the giants first, and that later he made people in the size they are today. The giants were truly giants. They used water skins made of whole elephant hides. Their spears were as tall as euphorbia trees, and the stones they threw from their slings were not pebbles but large boulders. They roasted whole cows over their fires for a single meal, and drank milk from great wooden tubs. When other tribes came into the country looking for water for their cattle and goats, the giants killed them or drove them away. Many courageous Mensa, Beni-Amer, and Habab warriors died trying to hold watering places against the giants.

Today the giants are gone, but you may still see the great stones they used for foundations of their houses, and here or there people find the remains of the enormous tombs in which the giants were buried. This story is about how the giants finally disappeared. It is told by the old people of the tribes.

God concluded that things were not peaceful because of the giants. The world was out of balance. So he sent for the chief of the giants and said to him, "It is time for your tribe to leave the world."

The chief of the giants said, "Master, how have we offended you that we should have to leave?"

God replied, "Your tribe has been too hard with the small people. You have forgotten that water holes were given to all the tribes for their cattle. You drive the people away, though they have done you no harm."

The chief of the giants said, "Master, all tribes guard their wells. All tribes fight to protect their land. What have we done that is different?"

God said, "Because you are so large and the others so small, everything is out of balance. Your tribe consumes everything. While you eat a whole cow for your dinner, the other tribes stand on a hilltop watching you swallow down enough to keep them alive for a month."

The giant chief said, "Master, it was you who created us as we are. Is the fault ours?"

God said, "No, the fault is not yours, yet I have to send your tribe out of this world. Therefore I will be as kind as I can. I will give you a choice. I will let you choose how to depart. You may disappear with my curse or my blessings."

The chief of the giants said, "Who would want to receive God's curse? If we must go, send us on our way with your blessings."

God answered, "Good. Let it be that way. I will lay blessings on you. Because sons are a blessing to all families, henceforth all your children to come will be sons. Because cows are a blessing on account of the calves they bear and the milk they give, henceforth all calves that are born will be females."

The chief of the giants returned to his tribe. He told the people of the blessings God had given them, and they were happy. Things came to pass as God had promised. Women gave birth only to sons, and cows gave birth only to female calves. The sons grew up. It was time for them to marry, but there were no young women to be their wives. The female calves matured, but there were no bulls for them to mate with. So in time no more children were born to the giants, and no more calves were born to the cattle. People grew old and died. Cattle grew old and died. The tribe of giants withered.

At last the chief called a council of the old people who were still alive. He said to them, "As all men can see, we are dying out from our blessings. Let us not linger here any more, waiting for the end. Let every person build a tomb for himself and cover it with a roof of stones. Let each one enter his tomb and close up the entrance. In this way we will finally depart from the world."

So every person built himself a tomb and covered it with a roof of stones, after which he entered, closed up the opening, and remained there until he died. Thus the giants perished and disappeared from the face of the land.

The roofs of the tombs fell long ago, and all that remain are piles of stones. Because they remember what happened to the giants, people of the tribes sometimes say when life seems too generous to them:

"Take care, let us not die from blessings like the giants did."

FOOLING
the
DEVIL

Fooling the Devil or Satan or Old Nick or the Hairy Man is an old game in folklore. Since, for the most part, these stories came through the peasant class, mouth to ear over and over again, they took on a kind of master-slave tone as well. The Devil was, after all, the ultimate master to be bamboozled or tricked.

In some stories the Devil is similar to the ogre in the stupid-ogre cycle, infinitely gullible, and motifs have traveled from the ogre to the Devil and back again. The Finnish tale "The Devil's Hide" and the Cuban "How El Bizarrón Fooled the Devil" show prime examples of this kind of befuddled demon. In other stories the Devil is simply taken in by a sharper. The Irish, especially, love this kind of tale, as seen in "The Lawyer and the Devil." And occasionally the demon is completely browbeaten by a woman, as in "The Bad Wife" and "Katcha and the Devil." There is a strong ballad tradition that concerns the scolding wife who beats the Devil up. Child ballad number 278, "The Farmer's Curst Wife," is very popular in the countrysides of both Britain and America. One version, found in Vermont, ends with the tag: "Now you can see that the women are worse than the men;/They can go to hell and back again!"

THE PEASANT AND THE DEVIL
Germany

There was once upon a time a far-sighted, crafty peasant whose tricks were much talked about. The best story, however, is how he once got hold of the Devil, and made a fool of him.

The peasant had one day been working in his field, and as twilight had set in, was making ready for the journey home, when he saw a heap of burning coals in the middle of his field, and when, full of astonishment, he went up to it, a little black Devil was sitting on the live coals.

"Are you sitting upon a treasure?" said the peasant.

"Yes, in truth," replied the Devil, "on a treasure which contains more gold and silver than you have ever seen in your life!"

"The treasure lies in my field and belongs to me," said the peasant.

"It is yours," answered the Devil, "if you will for two years give me one half of everything your field produces. Money I have enough, but I have a desire for the fruits of the earth."

The peasant agreed to the bargain. "In order, however, that no dispute may arise about the division," said he, "everything that is above ground shall belong to you, and what is under the earth to me."

The Devil was quite satisfied with that, but the cunning peasant had sown turnips.

Now when the time for harvest came, the Devil appeared and wanted to take away his crop; but he found nothing but the yellow withered leaves, while the peasant, full of delight, was digging up his turnips.

"You have had the best of it for once," said the Devil, "but the next time that won't do. What grows above ground shall be yours, and what is under it, mine."

"I am willing," replied the peasant; but when the time came to sow, he did not again sow turnips, but wheat. The grain became ripe, and the peasant went into the field and cut the full stalks down to the ground.

When the Devil came, he found nothing but the stubble, and went away in a fury down into a cleft in the rocks.

"That is the way to cheat the Devil," said the peasant, and went and fetched away the treasure.

WICKED JOHN AND THE DEVIL
United States

One time there was an old blacksmith named John. He was so mean they called him Wicked John. Mean? Aa-aa Lord! He didn't wait till Saturday night for *his* dram. He'd just as soon start in drinkin' of a Sunday . . . Monday . . . Tuesday. It didn't differ. He stayed lit-up all week anyhow. Talked mean. Acted mean. Independent minded. He wasn't afraid of nothin' nor nobody.

One thing about him though: he always did treat a stranger right. And one mornin' Wicked John was workin' there in his shop when an old beggar came to the door: crippled-up with rheumatism, all bent over and walkin' on two sticks. Looked right tired and hungry-like. Stood there till fin'lly Old John hollered at him, says "Well come in! Confound! Come on in and sit down! Rest yourself."

The old beggar he heaved over the sill, stumbled to where there was a nail-keg turned up, sat down. John kept right on workin', talkin' big; but seemed like the old man was so give-out he couldn't talk much. So directly old John threw his hammer down and headed for the house. "You wait now. Just sit right there."

Came back with a plate full of vittles: boiled sweet tater, big chunk of ham-meat, beans, greens, slice of cake—and he'd even gone to the springhouse and fetched a pitcher of sweet milk. "Here, old man! Try these rations. I hope you can find something here you can eat."

"Thank ye. Thank ye."

"Oh hit ain't much. If I can eat it three times a day every day, you can stomach it once I reckon."

Wicked John he went on back to work a-hammerin' and a-poundin'. Watched the old beggar out the corner of his eye: saw him lay the plate and glass to one side directly and start to get up. He let his two walkin' sticks fall to the ground. Commenced straightenin' up, straightenin' up, all the kinks comin' out of him. There was a flash of light all at once. And the next thing old John knew—there, r'ared up in the door, was a fine stout-like old man: had a white beard and white hair, long white robe right down to his feet, and a big gold key swingin' in his hand.

Old John stood there with his jaw hangin', and his eyes popped open.

"Well John, I don't reckon you know me, do ye?"

"Why—now, what happened to that old beggar? And where-in-the-nation did you come from—where folks dress like that?"

"I don't see you've got any way of knowin' me, John, since you never have been inside a church-house your whole life. I'm Saint Peter."

"Aw-w-w, now! You expect me to believe that?"

"It don't differ whether you believe it or not. I'll just tell you how-come I'm down here. Once a year I walk the earth to see can I find any decent folks left on it. And the first man I run across that treats me right I always give him three wishes. So you go ahead, John. Wish for anything you've a mind to, and hit'll be that-a-way. Take your three wishes, and be careful now."

Well, Old John he was grinnin' at Saint Peter like he didn't believe none of it. He was already pretty high that mornin', so he looked around: started wishin' on the first thing would pop into his head.

"Three wishes, huh? Well now—see that old high-back rockin' chair yonder? I keep it there so I can sit and rest everwhen I get done with ar' job-of-work. But—don't you know!—these dad-blame loafers that hang around in here of an evenin'! Nearly every time I go to sit down, there sits one of them lazy no-'count fellers a-wearin' out the seat of his britches in *my* rocker. Hit makes me mad! And I just wish that anybody sits there will stick to the chair-bottom and that old rocker rock 'em till they holler! Hold 'em stuck fast—till I let 'em go."

Saint Peter was writin' it down with a gold pencil in a little gold notebook. "That's one, John."

"Aa-aa Lord! Lemme see now. Well, take my big sledge hammer there. Every day after school these blame school kids come by here and get to messin' with my tools: slip that sledge out and take it across the road. Play pitch-hammer, or see how big a rock they can bust. And—confound!—every time I need it I have to go and hunt the dad-blame thing where them feisty boys have dropped it in the grass. Blame take it! I wish: that *anybody* teches that hammer will stick to the handle and hit pound right on—shake 'em! Shake the daylights out of 'em, till I let 'em go."

Saint Peter was scowlin' and shakin' his head like he thought old John was wastin' his wishes pretty bad.

But John was mean, like I said. *He* didn't care! Looked at Saint Peter mischievous-like, grinned sort of devilish, says, "One more wish, huh, Peter? All right. Now: There's that big firebush just outside the door. Gets full of all them red blooms real early in the spring-of-the-year. I like my old thornbush but hit's been mommicked up right bad here lately: folks backin' their wagons over it, horses tromplin' it—and these here highfalutin' folks comin' over the mountain a-fox-huntin'. Humph! Go gallopin' all around these pasture-fields fox-huntin' on horseback—their little red coats flappin' out behind. Looks like they got to stop and break ridin' switches off that bush every time they pass here. I wish that *anybody* teches that firebush, it will grab 'em and pull 'em headforemost right down in the middle where them stickers are the thickest—hold 'em there till *I* let 'em out."

Saint Peter quit writin', shut his little book, put hit and the gold pencil back inside his white robe, says, "Mighty sorry wishes, John. Looks like you might have made one wish for the good of your soul. You've sure wasted your chance. But that's what you've wished for and hit'll be that-a-way just like I said. Well, I got to go now."

"Oh, just stay the night, Peter."

"Can't stay."

And Saint Peter stepped over the doorsill and he was gone from there, and Wicked John couldn't tell which-a-way he went nor nothin'.

Well you'd a-thought old John might have done a little better one way or another after havin' a saint right there in his shop, but it didn't have no effect on *him*. Aa-aa Lord! He got meaner than ever. Somebody 'uld come and John would tell 'em, "Sit down." He'd trick a man into helpin' him hammer somethin' with that big sledge—and let it shake 'em a while 'fore he'd make it turn loose. And if anybody happened to brush against that firebush hit would grab 'em and they'd get scratched up right pityful, but old John he 'uld just laugh and let 'em stay stuck till he got ready to let 'em go.

So, one way or another, Wicked John turned so cussed he got to be the meanest man in the world. And the Devil—he keeps pretty good track of what's goin' on up here, you know—he got worried. Decided that wouldn't do: havin' anybody out-do him in meanness. So he sent for Old John. Wouldn't wait for him to die. Sent one of the little devils to fetch him right now.

Old John looked up one mornin' and there, standin' in the door, was a little horn-ed devil—about a fifth-grade-size devil—little horns just startin' to bump up on his forehead.

"Come on, old man. Daddy sent me to get ye. Said for me to bring ye right on back."

Old John had his hammer raised up, starin at that little devil— started in hammerin' again. Says, "All right, son. I'll be ready to go with ye in just a few more licks. Got to finish this one horseshoe. Come on in. Hit won't take me but a minute."

"No. Daddy said not to wait."

"All right! All right! Come on in. I'll be as quick as I can."

The little devil he came on inside, frettin'. Watched old John pound a few licks. Looked around the shop—and made for that old rockin' chair. Eased down in it, r'ared back and started rockin'. Says, "You hurry up now. Daddy'll sure get mad if we take too long."

John finished that shoe, soused it in the coolin' tub, throwed it on the ground. The little devil started to get up. Heaved a time or two. And directly poor little devil's head was goin' *whammity-bang!* against the chairback.

"Oh, mister, I'm stuck!"

"Now! Hain't that too bad!"

"Ow! Please mister! Let me up!"

"I'll let you go if you get out of here and not bother me no more."

"Yes, sir! I'll leave right now! And I'll not *never* come back."

"All right. Away with ye!"

And the rockin' chair throwed him out on the ground and— *rippity-tuck!*—out the door, and down the road!

John went on with his work, and in a few minutes there was another'n—a little devil about high-school-size, little horns spike-in' up. Stood there in the door actin' biggity. Says, "You come on here, old man."

"Why hello, son. Come on in." John kept right on workin'.

"You stop that poundin' and come on with me. Ye hear?"

"Why I can't stop now. This thing's red-hot and I'm bound to finish it 'fore we leave."

"No now! You quit right where you're at. Daddy said if I didn't fetch you back in five minutes he'd roast me good."

John kept right on—*bam! bam! bam!*

"Huh? Can't hear ye. I can't talk till I get done with this wagon tire."

Well, that little devil saw old John was havin' it kind of awkward the way he had to hold up that big iron wagon tire and beat it one-handed. So he lumbered right on inside the shop.

"Stand back then, old man. You hold that thing and let me pound it. We got to hurry."

Leaned over and picked up the big sledge hammer, started swingin' it. Wicked John, he held the tire up and turned it this-a-way and that-a-way. Pulled it out from under the hammer directly, cooled it in the big tub, and leaned it against the wall.

"Much obliged. Hit's finished. What ye poundin' so hard for?" And old John went to laughin'.

Well, the way that hammer was swingin' that little devil around, jerkin' him up and down with his legs a-flyin' ever' which-a-way—hit was a sight-in-this-world!

"Ow! My hands is stuck! O please mister! Make this thing turn me loose!"

"You promise to leave here?"

"Shore I promise!"

"And not come back?"

"Yes, sir! No, sir! You won't never catch *me* here again!"

"Then away with ye!"

When the hammer let go, it slung that little devil up in the rafters. He hit the ground, and when he got his legs untangled he streaked out the door and went dustin' down the road.

Then it wasn't hardly no time at all till Wicked John looked up and there standin' in the door—with his old goat horns roached back over his head, and his forked tail a-swishin', and that big cow's foot of his'n propped up on the sill—was the Old Boy. His eyes were just a-blazin'. Old John kept right on with his work. "Howdy do! Come on in."

"YOU COME ON HERE, OLD MAN! AND I AIN'T GOIN' TO TAKE NO FOOLISHNESS OFF YE NEITHER!"

"All right sir. Just as soon as I get done. Promised a man I'd sharpen this mattick head 'fore twelve. Hit won't take but a few more licks. Come on in, confound it, and sit down!"

"NO! I'LL NOT SIT IN NO CHAIR OF YOUR'N!"

"Suit yourself. But we'll be ready to go quicker'n you can waste time argu-in', if *you'll* hit this mattick a lick or two while I hold it with the tongs here. Just grab the big sledge leanin' there on the door jam and . . ."

"NO, I AIN'T GOIN' TO TECH NO SLEDGE HAMMER NEITHER! YOU DONE MADE ME MAD ENOUGH ALREADY, OLD MAN, THE WAY YOU DONE MY BOYS. AND I'M TAKIN' YOU OFF FROM HERE RIGHT NOW!"

Old John r'ared up, says, "You and who else? Jest tech me! I dare ye!"

The Devil made for him and old John let him have it. And such a punchin', knockin', beatin', you never did see! Poundin', scratchin', kickin', buttin', like two horses fightin'. Wicked John was mean, like I said. He wasn't goin' to take nothin' off nobody, not even the Devil himself. They had a round or two there by the door and fin'lly the Devil grabbed old John by the seat of his britches and heaved him outside. John twisted around some way or other and got hold of the Devil's tail—kinked it up, you know, like tryin' to make an unruly cow go in the barn—yanked right hard. Well that really made the Devil mad.

"BLAST YE, OLD MAN! I'M GOIN' TO LICK THE HIDE OFF YOU RIGHT NOW. JUST SEE IF I DON'T. WHERE'LL I GET ME A SWITCH?"

And the Devil reached to break him a switch off that firebush. Time he touched it, hit wropped all around him and jerked him headforemost right down in the middle of all them long stickers. The old Devil he tried to get loose but the more he thrashed around in there the more he got scratched, till fin'lly he had to give up: his legs hangin' limp out the top of the bush and his head 'way down in there.

"Mister?"

Old John was laughin' so hard he had to lean against the shop. "What ye want now?"

"Please sir. Let me out."

"Who was that you was goin' to whip? Huh?"

"Nobody. Now will you let me out of here?"

"I'll let you out of there on one condition: you, nor none of your boys, don't ye never—none of ye—ever come back up here botherin' me no more. You promise me that and I might let ye go."

"Hell yes, I promise—now please will you make this bush turn loose of me?"

The bush let go, and when the old Devil crawled out he had leaves and trash caught on his horns, and his old long black coat torn to rags. He turned around and when he got his legs to workin', such a kickin' up dust you never did see! They tell me that when The Old Boy left there he wasn't moseyin'.

So Wicked John he never was bothered by any more devils after that. Just kept on blacksmithin' there in his shop. Lived on till he was an old old man. Stayed mean, too—just as mean as ever right to the day he died. And when fin'lly he *did* die, he didn't do a thing but go right straight to the Pearly Gates. *Bam! Bam! Bam!*

Saint Peter cracked the door, and when he saw who it was, he backed off a little, says, "*Uh*—oh!" Looked out. "Er—hello, John. Just what did you want?"

"Well Peter—seein' as you knowed me, I thought that maybe . . ."

"Why John, you can't come in here."

"Oh I know I can't *stay*, Peter. But I'd sort of like to take me one look around: see them golden streets, hear me a little harp music, and then I'll go."

"Can't do it, John. Can't do it. You wait a minute. I'm just goin' to show you your accounts here on the record. Hand out the book, one of ye."

Saint Peter reached and took the big book, licked his thumb and turned the pages.

"Here you are—now here's your two pages in the ledger, John. Look there on the good-deed side. All the ninety-two years you've lived, three entries, 'way up at the top of the page. But over here on the *other* side—why!—hit's black, clean to the bottom line. And all the meanness you've done the past twelve years, you can see for yourself, it had to be writ in sideways."

Saint Peter shut the book and took off his spectacles, says, "I'm sorry, John, but you can't put one foot inside here. So if you'll excuse me now—" And Saint Peter backed through the gates and reached and shut 'em to.

Well old John he just shuffled around and headed back down the stairsteps.

That day several devils was there in front of the gate to Hell, playin' catch with a ball of fire. And one of 'em happened to be that first 'un was sent to fetch Wicked John. He chanced to look off down the road directly. His eyes popped open and he missed his catch. Turned and ran through the gates just a-squallin', "Daddy! O Daddy! Run here quick!"

The old Devil came and looked out. And there, headed right that way, with his hands in his pockets, a-whistlin', and just a-weavin' down the road—was Wicked John. The Devil turned around, says, "Bar the door, boys! Bar the door."

So when old John got there, there was the gates to Hell shut and padlocked: the little devils peepin' out from behind the mine-props and coal piles scared to death, and the old Devil standin' 'way back, says, "Un-*unh!* You ain't comin' in *here* now. Don't ye come no closeter. You just turn around right where you're at and put off! I done had enough of you. Now git!"

Old John stood there scratchin' his head, says, "Confound!" Turned to the Devil, says, "Look-a-here. I went up yonder and Saint Peter told me I couldn't get in up *there*, and here *you've* gone and locked me out. Why! I don't know where to go to, now."

The Devil studied a minute, grabbed up some tongs, reached in one of his furnaces and got hold of a hot coal. Edged over 'side the gate and handed the tong-handles out the bars, says, "Here, old man. You just take this chunk of fire and go on off somewhere else—and start you a hell of your own."

Old John took it and put off.

And right to this day, they say that in the Great Dismal Swamps—somewhere over yonder between Virginia and Carolina—you can look out of a night and see a little bob of light movin' around out there.

One old-time name for it is the Will-o'-the-wisp, and some old folks call it the Jacky-my-lantern. Now some people that don't know any better—these schoolteachers and college professors—they'll try to tell you it's nothin' but some kind of marsh gas a-lightin' up out in the swamps.

But you'uns know better now, don't ye?

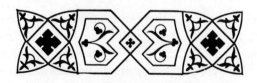

THE BAD WIFE
Russia

There was once a bad wife who made life impossible for her husband and disobeyed him in everything. If he told her to rise early, she slept for three days; if he told her to sleep, she did not sleep at all. If her husband asked her to make pancakes, she said, "You don't deserve pancakes, you scoundrel!" If her husband said, "Don't make pancakes, wife, since I don't deserve them," she made an enormous panful, two whole gallons of pancakes, and said, "Now eat, scoundrel, and be sure that all of them are eaten!" If he said, "Wife, do not wash the clothes nor go out to cut hay—it is too much for you," she answered, "No, you scoundrel, I will go and you shall come with me."

One day, after a quarrel with her, he went in distress to the woods to pick berries, found a currant bush, and saw a bottomless pit in the middle of it. As he looked at it, he thought to himself, "Why do I go on living with a bad wife and struggling with her? Could I not put her in that pit and teach her a lesson?" He went back home and said, "Wife, do not go to the woods for berries." "I shall go, you fool!" "I found a currant bush, don't pick it!" "I shall go and pick it clean—and what is more, I won't give you any currants!"

The husband went out and his wife followed him. He came to the currant bush and his wife jumped toward it and yelled, "Don't go into that bush, you scoundrel, or I'll kill you!" She herself went into the middle of it, and fell plop!—into the bottomless pit.

The husband went home happily and lived there in peace for three days. On the fourth day, he went to see how his wife was getting along. He took a long towrope, let it down into the pit, and dragged out a little imp. He was frightened and was about to drop him back into the pit, when the imp began to shriek and then said imploringly, "Peasant, do not put me back, let me out into the world. A bad wife has come into our pit—she torments, bites, and pinches all of us, we are sick to death of her. If you let me out, I will do you a good turn!" So the peasant let him go free in holy Russia. The imp said, "Well, peasant, let us go to the town of Vologda. I will make people sick and you shall cure them."

Now the imp set to work on merchants' wives and daughters; he would enter into them and they would go mad and fall ill. Our peasant would go to the house of the sick woman; the imp would leave, a blessing would come on the house; everyone thought that the peasant was a doctor, gave him money, and fed him pies. The peasant thus amassed an uncountable sum of money. Then the imp said to him, "You now have plenty, peasant. Are you satisfied? Next I shall enter a boyar's daughter, and mind you do not come to cure her, else I shall eat you."

The boyar sent for the peasant, the famous "doctor." He came to the boyar's beautiful house and told him to have all the townspeople and all the carriages and coachmen gather in the street in front of the house; he gave orders that all the coachmen should crack their whips and cry aloud, "The bad wife has come, the bad wife has come!" Then he went into the sick maiden's room. When he came in, the imp was enraged at him and said, "Why have you come here, Russian man? Now I will eat you!"

He said, "What do you mean? I have not come to drive you out, but to warn you that the bad wife is here!"

The imp jumped on the windowsill, stared fixedly, and listened intently. He heard all the crowd in the street cry in one voice, "The bad wife has come!"

"Peasant," said the imp, "where shall I hide?"

"Return to the pit. She won't go there again!"

The imp went there and joined the bad wife. The boyar rewarded the peasant by giving him half his possessions and his daughter in marriage; but the bad wife to this day sits in the pit in nether darkness.

KATCHA AND THE DEVIL
Czechoslovakia

❧

There was once a woman named Katcha who lived in a village where she owned her own cottage and garden. She had money besides, but little good it did her, because she was such an ill-tempered vixen that nobody, not even the poorest laborer, would marry her. Nobody would even work for her, no matter what she paid, for she couldn't open her mouth without scolding, and whenever she scolded she raised her shrill voice until you could hear it a mile away. The older she grew the worse she became, until by the time she was forty she was as sour as vinegar.

Now as it always happens in a village, every Sunday afternoon there was a dance either at the burgomaster's or at the tavern. As soon as the bagpipes sounded, the boys all crowded into the room and the girls gathered outside and looked in the windows. Katcha was always the first at the window. The music would strike up and the boys would beckon the girls to come in and dance, but no one ever beckoned Katcha. Even when she paid the piper no one ever asked her to dance. Yet she came Sunday after Sunday just the same.

One Sunday afternoon as she was hurrying to the tavern she thought to herself, "Here I am getting old and yet I've never once danced with a boy! Plague take it, today I'd dance with the Devil if he asked me!"

She was in a fine rage by the time she reached the tavern, where she sat down near the stove and looked around to see what girls the boys had invited to dance.

Suddenly a stranger in hunter's green came in. He sat down at a table near Katcha and ordered drink. When the servingmaid brought the beer, he reached over to Katcha and asked her to drink with him. At first she was much taken aback at this attention, then she pursed her lips coyly and pretended to refuse, but finally she accepted.

When they had finished drinking, he pulled a ducat from his pocket, tossed it to the piper, and called out:

"Clear the floor, boys! This is for Katcha and me alone!"

The boys snickered and the girls giggled, hiding behind each other and stuffing their aprons into their mouths so that Katcha wouldn't hear them laughing. But Katcha wasn't noticing them at all. Katcha was dancing with a fine young man! If the whole world had been laughing at her, Katcha wouldn't have cared.

The stranger danced with Katcha all afternoon and all evening. Not once did he dance with anyone else. He brought her marzipan and sweet drinks and, when the hour came to go home, he escorted her through the village.

"Ah," sighed Katcha when they reached her cottage and it was time to part, "I wish I could dance with you forever!"

"Very well," said the stranger. "Come with me."

"Where do you live?"

"Put your arm around my neck and I'll tell you."

Katcha put both arms about his neck, and instantly the man changed into a devil and flew straight down to Hell.

At the gates of Hell he stopped and knocked.

His comrades came and opened the gates and when they saw that he was exhausted, they tried to take Katcha off his neck. But Katcha held on tight and nothing they could do or say would make her budge.

The devil finally had to appear before the Prince of Darkness himself with Katcha still glued to his neck.

"What's that thing you've got around your neck?" the Prince asked.

So the devil told how as he was walking about on earth he had heard Katcha say she would dance with the Devil himself if he asked her. "So I asked her to dance with me," the devil said. "Afterwards just to frighten her a little I brought her down to Hell. And now she won't let go of me!"

"Serve you right, you dunce!" the Prince said. "How often have I told you to use common sense when you go wandering around earth! You might have known Katcha would never let go of a man once she had him!"

"I beg Your Majesty to make her let go!" the poor devil implored.

"I will not!" said the Prince. "You'll have to carry her back to earth yourself and get rid of her as best you can. Perhaps this will be a lesson to you."

So the devil, very tired and very cross, shambled back to earth with Katcha still clinging to his neck. He tried every way to get her off. He promised her wooded hills and rich meadows if she but let him go. He cajoled her, he cursed her, but all to no avail: Katcha still held on.

Breathless and discouraged, he came at last to a meadow where a shepherd, wrapped in a great shaggy sheepskin coat, was tending his flocks. The devil transformed himself into an ordinary-looking man so that the shepherd didn't recognize him.

"Hi, there," the shepherd said, "what's that you're carrying?"

"Don't ask me," the devil said with a sigh. "I'm so worn out I'm nearly dead. I was walking yonder not thinking of anything at all when along comes a woman and jumps on my back and won't let go. I'm trying to carry her to the nearest village to get rid of her there, but I don't believe I'm able. My legs are giving out."

The shepherd, who was a good-natured chap, said, "I tell you what: I'll help you. I can't leave my sheep long, but I'll carry her halfway."

"Oh," said the devil, "I'd be very grateful if you did!"

So the shepherd yelled at Katcha, "Hi, there, you! Catch hold of me!"

When Katcha saw that the shepherd was a handsome youth, she let go of the devil and leaped upon the shepherd's back, catching hold of the collar of his sheepskin coat.

Now the young shepherd soon found that the long shaggy coat and Katcha made a pretty heavy load for walking. In a few moments he was sick of his bargain and began casting about for some way of getting rid of Katcha.

Presently he came to a pond and he thought to himself that he'd like to throw her in. He wondered how he could do it. Perhaps he could manage it by throwing in his greatcoat with her. The coat was so loose that he thought he could slip out of it without Katcha's discovering what he was doing. Very cautiously he slipped out one arm. Katcha didn't move. He slipped out the other arm. Still Katcha didn't move. He unlooped the first button. Katcha noticed nothing. He unlooped the second button. Still Katcha noticed nothing. He unlooped the third button and *kerplunk!* he had pitched coat and Katcha and all into the middle of the pond!

When he got back to his sheep, the devil looked at him in amazement.

"Where's Katcha?" he gasped.

"Oh," the shepherd said, pointing over his shoulder with his thumb, "I decided to leave her up yonder in a pond."

"My dear friend," the devil cried, "I thank you! You have done me a great favor. If it hadn't been for you I might be carrying Katcha till doomsday. I'll never forget you and sometime I'll reward you. As you don't know who it is you've helped, I must tell you I'm a devil."

With these words the devil vanished.

For a moment the shepherd was dazed. Then he laughed and said to himself, "Well, if they're all as stupid as he is, we ought to be able for them!"

The country where the shepherd lived was ruled over by a dissolute young duke who passed his days in riotous living and his nights in carousing. He gave over the affairs of state to two governors who were as bad as he. With extortionate taxes and unjust fines they robbed the people until the whole land was crying out against them.

Now one day for amusement the duke summoned an astrologer to court and ordered him to read in the planets the fate of himself and his two governors. When the astrologer had cast a horoscope for each of the three reprobates, he was greatly disturbed and tried to dissuade the duke from questioning him further.

"Such danger," he said, "threatens your life and the lives of your two governors that I fear to speak."

"Whatever it is," said the duke, "speak. But I warn you to speak the truth, for if what you say does not come to pass you will forfeit your life."

The astrologer bowed and said: "Hear then, oh Duke, what the planets foretell: Before the second quarter of the moon, on such and such a day, at such and such an hour, a devil will come and carry off the two governors. At the full of the moon on such and such a day, at such and such an hour, the same devil will come for Your Highness and carry you off to Hell."

The duke pretended to be unconcerned, but in his heart he was deeply shaken. The voice of the astrologer sounded to him like the voice of judgment, and for the first time conscience began to trouble him.

As for the governors, they couldn't eat a bite of food and were carried from the palace half dead with fright. They piled their ill-gotten wealth into wagons and rode away to their castles, where they barred all the doors and windows in order to keep the devil out.

The duke reformed. He gave up his evil ways and corrected the abuses of state in the hope of averting if possible his cruel fate.

The poor shepherd had no inkling of any of these things. He tended his flocks from day to day and never bothered his head about the happenings in the great world.

Suddenly one day the devil appeared before him and said, "I

have come, my friend, to repay you for your kindness. When the moon is in its first quarter, I was to carry off the former governors of this land because they robbed the poor and gave the duke evil counsel. However, they're behaving themselves now, so they're to be given another chance. But they don't know this. Now on such and such a day do you go to the first castle where a crowd of people will be assembled. When a cry goes up and the gates open and I come dragging out the governor, do you step up to me and say, 'What do you mean by this? Get out of here or there'll be trouble!' I'll pretend to be greatly frightened and make off. Then ask the governor to pay you two bags of gold, and if he haggles just threaten to call me back. After that, go on to the castle of the second governor and do the same thing and demand the same pay. I warn you, though, be prudent with the money and use it only for good. When the moon is full, I'm to carry off the duke himself, for he was so wicked that he's to have no second chance. So don't try to save him, for if you do you'll pay for it with your own skin. Don't forget!"

The shepherd remembered carefully everything the devil told him. When the moon was in its first quarter he went to the first castle. A great crowd of people was gathered outside waiting to see the devil carry away the governor.

Suddenly there was a loud cry of despair, the gates of the castle opened, and there was the devil, as black as night, dragging out the governor. He, poor man, was half dead with fright.

The shepherd elbowed his way through the crowd, took the governor by the hand, and pushed the devil roughly aside.

"What do you mean by this?" he shouted. "Get out of here or there'll be trouble!"

Instantly the devil fled, and the governor fell on his knees before the shepherd and kissed his hands and begged him to state what he wanted in reward. When the shepherd asked for two bags of gold, the governor ordered that they be given him without delay.

Then the shepherd went to the castle of the second governor and went through exactly the same performance.

It goes without saying that the duke soon heard of the shepherd, for he had been anxiously awaiting the fate of the two governors. At once he sent a wagon with four horses to fetch the shepherd to the palace, and when the shepherd arrived he begged him piteously to rescue him likewise from the devil's clutches.

"Master, "The shepherd answered, "I cannot promise you anything. I have to consider my own safety. You have been a great sinner, but if you really want to reform, if you really want to rule your people justly and kindly and wisely as becomes a true ruler, then indeed I will help you even if I have to suffer hellfire in your place."

The duke declared that with God's help he would mend his ways, and the shepherd promised to come back on the fatal day.

With grief and dread the whole country awaited the coming of the full moon. In the first place the people had greeted the astrologer's prophecy with joy, but since the duke had reformed, their feelings for him had changed.

Time sped fast as time does whether joy be coming or sorrow, and all too soon the fatal day arrived.

Dressed in black and pale with fright, the duke sat expecting the arrival of the devil.

Suddenly the door flew open and the devil, black as night, stood before him. He paused a moment and then he said, politely:

"Your time has come, Lord Duke, and I am here to get you!"

Without a word the duke arose and followed the devil to the courtyard, which was filled with a great multitude of people.

At that moment the shepherd, all out of breath, came pushing his way through the crowd, and ran straight at the devil, shouting out:

"What do you mean by this? Get out of here or there'll be trouble!"

"What do *you* mean?" whispered the devil. "Don't you remember what I told you?"

"Hush!" the shepherd whispered back. "I don't care anything about the duke. This is to warn you! You know Katcha? She's alive and she's looking for you!"

The instant the devil heard the name of Katcha he turned and fled.

All the people cheered the shepherd, while the shepherd himself laughed in his sleeve to think that he had taken in the devil so easily.

As for the duke, he was so grateful to the shepherd that he made him his chief counselor and loved him as a brother. And well he might, for the shepherd was a sensible man and always gave him sound advice.

THE LAWYER AND THE DEVIL
Ireland

There was this man in it one time and he had three sons and he wanted to make something of them but hadn't the money. So he sells himself to the Divil to raise money to school the three boys, and he did. He made one a priest, the other a doctor, and the third one was a lawyer. The Divil give him the money to pay for their education.

But anyway, at the end of seven years the Divil showed up to claim the old man and his soul and take him and it down to Hell. He had his three sons there, or one at a time in with him. So when the Divil come the priest began to pray and beg and appeal for sparings for his father, and in the heel of the hunt he got a few years more off the Divil for his father.

When that was up and the Divil come again the doctor was there and he appealed for sparings for his father and got them. And when the Divil come a third time to claim the old fellow the lawyer was there. The lawyer says to the Divil:

"You've given sparings to my father twice already and I know you can't be expected to do it again. But," says he, "as a last request, will you give him sparings while that butt of a candle is there?"

The candle was burning on the table.

The divil said he would; it was only a butt of a candle and wouldn't be long in it.

At that the lawyer picks up the butt of a candle and blows it out and puts it in his pocket. And that was that! The Divil had to keep to his bargain and go without the old man, for the lawyer held on to the butt of a candle. Trust the lawyer to beat the Divil.

Coals on the Devil's Hearth
Ireland

This man, he was very poor, and he was getting it very tight to live, with a wife and family.

And he sold himself to the Devil.

But the bargain was, that he'd have to go with him at the end of a number of years.

But anyway, he got very rich.

And he got his family reared.

And the way it was: when him and the Devil made the bargain, the Devil gave him a *drum*, and a pair of drumsticks.

And he told him that every time that he'd want money, for to go out and give a roll on the drum, when he wanted anything done, and he'd do it for him.

So anyway, he went be the orders of the Devil. But in the long run, he joined to get very nervous and got afraid of the journey that he had to *go*.

So he joined to fret terribly.

And the wife remarked him terribly failed, and in bad form.

He never let on to her how they came to have the *money* or anything like *that*. And she knew nothing about this bargain that he had made off the Devil.

So anyway, he wouldn't tell her what the cause of it was. But she *still* was at him for to tell her what was troubling him.

So in the long run he told her.

So, she says. "There's a plan to get rid of him."

"Well, *what is it?*" says the man. *And he got terrible excited.*

"Well," she says, "you told me there that you had a drum, that you notified him when you wanted anything."

"Aye, I have it," he says.

"Well," says she, "take out the drum now, and give a roll on it, and when he comes, tell him that you want churches and chapels built. *At once!*"

So he went out and gave a roll on the drum and the Devil came along.

Your man says to him, "Well," he says, "I want you to do a thing, but whether you'll do it or not, I don't know. Would you put up churches and chapels here and there through the country?"

"Ah, I will, of course," says the Devil.

So anyway there was churches and chapels erected be night that the people couldn't understand atall.

So, when him and the Devil was parting, the Devil says to him, "Let that be the last thing now that ever you'll ask me *to do.*"

So he was in as bad fettle as ever when he came back to the wife.

But the buildings went *up.*

So, aw, he was getting that she didn't know what was going to happen.

Says she, "There's one plan yet, that ye'll get shut of him forever."

She says, "Get out the drum, and give a *roll* on it, a good *loud* one. When he comes, tell him that you want him to do the last thing that ever you'll ask him to do.

"And when he asks you what it is, tell him that you want him to make all lawyers honest men."

He out with the drum.

And he gave a rattle.

No time till the boyo appeared.

"*Well,*" he says, "*what do you want me to do the day?* You told me the last time that we were talking that you'd never ask me to do more for you."

"Well," he says, "this is going to be the last."

"Well, what is it?" says the Devil.

"I want you," he says, "for to make all lawyers honest men."

"*Ah,*" says the Devil.

"Give me that drum," he says.

"There's women at the back of this. If I done what you want, there's times that I wouldn't have a coal on me hearth."

THE DEVIL'S HIDE
Finland

There was once a Finnish boy who got the best of the Devil. His name was Erkki. Erkki had two brothers who were, of course, older than he. They both tried their luck with the Devil and got the worst of it. Then Erkki tried his luck. They were sure Erkki, too, would be worsted, but he wasn't. Here is the whole story:

One day the oldest brother said, "It's time for me to go out into the world and earn my living. Do you two younger ones wait here at home until you hear how I get on."

The younger boys agreed to this and the oldest brother started out. He was unable to get employment until by chance he met the Devil. The Devil at once offered him a place but on very strange terms.

"Come work for me," the Devil said, "and I promise that you'll be comfortably housed and well fed. We'll make this bargain: the first of us who loses his temper will forfeit to the other enough of his own hide to sole a pair of boots. If I lose my temper first, you may exact from me a big patch of my hide. If you lose your temper first, I'll exact the same from you."

The oldest brother agreed to this and the Devil at once took him home and set him to work. "Take this axe," he said, "and go out behind the house and chop me some firewood."

The oldest brother took the axe and went out to the wood-pile.

"Chopping wood is easy enough," he thought to himself. But at the first blow he found that the axe had no edge. Try as he would he couldn't cut a single log.

"I'd be a fool to stay here and waste my time with such an axe!" he cried.

So he threw down the axe and ran away thinking to escape the Devil and get work somewhere else. But the Devil had no intention of letting him escape. He ran after him, overtook him, and asked him what he meant leaving thus without notice.

"I don't want to work for you!" the oldest brother cried petulantly.

"Very well," the Devil said, "but don't lose your temper about it."

"I will lose my temper!" the oldest brother declared. "The idea—expecting me to cut wood with such an axe!"

"Well," the Devil remarked, "since you insist on losing your temper, you'll have to forfeit me enough of your hide to sole a pair of boots! That was our bargain."

The oldest brother howled and protested, but to no purpose. The Devil was firm. He took out a long knife and slit enough of the oldest brother's hide to sole a pair of big boots.

"Now then, my boy," he said, "now you may go."

The oldest brother went limping home, complaining bitterly at the hard fate that had befallen him. "I'm tired and sick," he told his brothers, "and I'm going to stay home and rest. One of you will have to go out and get work."

The second brother at once said that he'd be delighted to try his luck in the world. So he started out and he had exactly the same experience. At first he could get no work, then he met the Devil and the Devil made exactly the same bargain with him that he had made with the oldest brother. He took the second brother home with him, gave him the same dull axe, and sent him out to the woodpile. After the first stroke the second brother threw down the axe in disgust and tried to run off, and the Devil, of course, wouldn't let him go until he, too, had submitted to the loss of a great patch of hide. So it was no time at all before the second brother came limping home complaining bitterly at fate.

"What ails you two?" Erkki said.

"You go out into the cruel world and hunt work," they told him, "and you'll find out soon enough what ails us! And when you do find out you needn't come limping home expecting sympathy from us, for you won't get it!"

So the very next day Erkki started out, leaving his brothers at home nursing their sore backs and their injured feelings.

Well, Erkki had exactly the same experience. At first he could get work nowhere, then later he met the Devil and went into his employ on exactly the same terms as his brothers.

The Devil handed him the same dull axe and sent him out to the woodpile. At the first blow Erkki knew that the axe had lost its edge and would never cut a single log. But instead of being discouraged and losing his temper, he only laughed.

"I suppose the Devil thinks I'll lose my hide over a trifle like this!" he said. "Well, I just won't!"

He dropped the axe and, going over to the woodpile, began pulling it down. Under all the logs he found the Devil's cat. It was an evil-looking creature with a grey head.

"Ha!" thought Erkki. "I bet anything you've got something to do with this!"

He raised the dull axe and with one blow cut off the evil creature's head. Sure enough the axe instantly recovered its edge, and after that Erkki had no trouble at all in chopping as much firewood as the Devil wanted.

That night at supper the Devil said, "Well, Erkki, did you finish the work I gave you?"

"Yes, master, I've chopped all that wood."

The Devil was surprised. "Really?"

"Yes, Master. You can go out and see for yourself."

"Then you found something in the woodpile, didn't you?"

"Nothing but an awful-looking old cat."

The Devil started. "Did you do anything to that cat?"

"I only chopped its head off and threw it away."

"What!" the Devil cried angrily. "Didn't you know that was my cat!"

"There now, master," Erkki said soothingly, "you're not going to lose your temper over a little thing like a dead cat, are you? Don't forget our bargain!"

The Devil swallowed his anger and murmured, "No, I'm not going to lose my temper, but I must say that was no way to treat my cat."

The next day the Devil ordered Erkki to go out to the forest and bring home some logs on the ox sledge.

"My black dog will go with you," he said, "and as you come home you're to take exactly the same course as the dog takes."

Well, Erkki went out to the forest and loaded the ox sledge with logs and then drove the oxen home following the Devil's black dog. As they reached the Devil's house the black dog jumped through a hole in the gate.

"I must follow master's orders," Erkki said to himself.

So he cut up the oxen into small pieces and put them through the same hole in the gate; he chopped up the logs and pitched them through the hole; and he broke up the sledge into pieces small enough to follow the oxen and the logs. Then he crept through the hole himself.

That night at supper the Devil said, "Well, Erkki, did you come home the way I told you?"

"Yes master, I followed the black dog."

"What!" the Devil cried. "Do you mean to say you brought the oxen and the sledge and the logs through the hole in the gate?"

"Yes, master, that's what I did."

"But you couldn't!" the Devil declared.

"Well, master," Erkki said, "just go out and see."

The Devil went outside and when he saw the method by which Erkki had carried out his orders he was furious. But Erkki quieted him by saying, "There now, master, you're not going to lose your temper over a trifling matter like this, are you? Remember our bargain!"

"N-n-no," the Devil said, again swallowing his anger, "I'm not going to lose my temper, but I want you to understand, Erkki, that I think you've acted very badly in this!"

All that evening the Devil fumed and fussed about Erkki.

"We've got to get rid of the boy! That's all there is about it!" he said to his wife.

Of course, whenever Erkki was in sight the Devil tried to smile and look pleasant, but as soon as Erkki was gone he went back at once to his grievance. He declared emphatically, "There's no living in peace and comfort with such a boy around!"

"Well," his wife said, "if you feel that way about it, why don't you kill him tonight when he's asleep? We could throw his body into the lake and no one be the wiser."

"That's a fine idea!" the Devil said. "Wake me up sometime after midnight and I'll do it!"

Now Erkki overheard this little plan, so that night he kept awake. When he knew from their snoring that the Devil and his wife were sound asleep, he slipped over to their bed, quietly lifted the Devil's wife in his arms, and without awakening her placed her gently in his own bed. Then he put on some of her clothes and laid himself down beside the Devil in the wife's place.

Presently he nudged the Devil awake.

"What do you want?" the Devil mumbled.

"Sst!" Erkki whispered. "Isn't it time we got up and killed Erkki?"

"Yes," the Devil answered, "it is. Come along."

They got up quietly, and the Devil reached down a great sword from the wall. Then they crept over to Erkki's bed, and the Devil with one blow cut off the head of the person who was lying there asleep.

"Now" he said, "we'll just carry out the bed and all and dump it in the lake."

So Erkki took one end of the bed and the Devil the other and, stumbling and slipping in the darkness, they carried it down to the lake and pitched it in.

"That's a good job done!" the Devil said with a laugh.

Then they went back to bed together, and the Devil fell instantly asleep.

The next morning when he got up for breakfast, there was Erkki stirring the porridge.

"How—did you get here?" the Devil asked. "I mean—I mean where is my wife?"

"Your wife? Don't you remember," Erkki said, "you cut off her head last night and then we threw her into the lake, bed and all! But no one will be the wiser!"

"W-wh-what!" the Devil cried, and he was about to fly into an awful rage when Erkki restrained him by saying, "There now, master, you're not going to lose your temper over a little thing like a wife, are you? Remember our bargain!"

So the Devil was forced again to swallow his anger.

"No, I'm not going to lose my temper," he said, "but I tell you frankly, Erkki, I don't think that was a nice trick for you to play on me!"

Well, the Devil felt lonely not having a wife about the house, so in a few days he decided to go off wooing for a new one.

"And, Erkki," he said. "I expect you to keep busy while I'm gone. Here's a keg of red paint. Now get to work and have the house all blazing red by the time I get back."

"All blazing red," Erkki repeated. "Very well, master, trust me to have it all blazing red by the time you get back!"

As soon as the Devil was gone, Erkki set the house afire and in a short time the whole sky was lighted up with the red glow of the flames. In great fright the Devil hurried back and got there in time to see the house one mass of fire.

"You see, master," Erkki said, "I've done as you told me. It looks very pretty, doesn't it? All blazing red!"

The Devil almost choked with rage.

"You—you—" he began, but Erkki restrained him by saying, "There now, master, you're not going to lose your temper over a little thing like a house afire, are you? Remember our bargain!"

The Devil swallowed hard and said, "N-no, I'm not going to

lose my temper, but I must say, Erkki, that I'm very much annoyed with you!"

The next day the Devil wanted to go a-wooing again and before he started he said to Erkki, "Now, no nonsense this time! While I'm gone you're to build three bridges over the lake, but they're not to be built of wood or stone or iron or earth. Do you understand?"

Erkki pretended to be frightened. "That's a pretty hard task you've given me, master!"

"Hard or easy, see that you get it done!" the Devil said.

Erkki waited until the Devil was gone, then he went out to the field and slaughtered all the Devil's cattle. From the bones of the cattle he laid three bridges across the lake, using the skulls for one bridge, the ribs for another, and the legs and the hoofs for the third. Then when the Devil got back, Erkki met him and, pointing to the bridge, said, "See, master, there they are, three bridges put together without stick, stone, iron, or bit of earth!"

When the Devil found out that all his cattle had been slaughtered to give bones for the bridges, he was ready to kill Erkki, but Erkki quieted him by saying, "There now, master, you're not going to lose your temper over a little thing like the slaughter of a few cattle, are you? Remember our bargain!"

So again the Devil had to swallow his anger. "No," he said, "I'm not going to lose my temper exactly, but I tell you, Erkki, that I don't think you're behaving well!"

The Devil's wooing was successful and pretty soon he bought home a new wife. The new wife didn't like having Erkki about, so the Devil promised he'd kill the boy. I'll do it tonight," he said, "when he's asleep."

Erkki overheard this, and that night he put the churn in his bed under the covers, and where his head ordinarily would be, he put a big round stone. Then he himself curled up on the stove and went comfortably to sleep.

During the night the Devil took his great sword from the wall and went over to Erkki's bed. His first blow hit the round stone and nicked the sword. His second blow struck sparks.

"Mercy me!" the Devil thought, "He's got a mighty hard head! I better strike lower!"

With the third stroke he hit the churn a mighty blow. The hoops flew apart and the churn collapsed.

The Devil went chuckling back to bed. "Ha!" he said boastfully to his wife, "I got him that time!"

But the next morning when he woke up he didn't feel like laughing, for there was Erkki as lively as ever and pretending that nothing had happened.

"What!" cried the Devil in amazement, "didn't you feel anything strike you last night while you were asleep?"

"Oh, I did feel a few mosquitoes brushing my cheek," Erkki said. "Nothing else."

"Steel doesn't touch him!" the Devil said to his wife. "I think I'll try fire on him."

So that night the Devil told Erkki to sleep in the threshing barn. Errki carried his cot down to the threshing floor, and then when it was dark he shifted it into the hay barn, where he slept comfortably all night.

During the night the Devil set fire to the threshing barn. In the early dawn Erkki carried his cot back to the place of the threshing barn, and in the morning when the Devil came out the first thing he was was Erkki unharmed and peacefully sleeping among the smoking ruins.

"Mercy me, Erkki!" he shouted, shaking him awake. "Have you been asleep all night?"

Erkki sat up and yawned. "Yes, I've had a fine night's sleep. But I did feel a little chilly."

"Chilly!" the Devil gasped.

After that the Devil's one thought was to get rid of Erkki.

"That boy's getting on my nerves!" he told his wife. "I just can't stand him much longer! What are we going to do about him?"

They discussed one plan after another, and at last decided that the only way they'd ever get rid of him would be to move away and leave him behind.

"I'll send him out to the forest to chop wood all day," the Devil said, "and while he's gone we'll row ourselves and all our belongings out to an island and when he comes back he won't know where we've gone."

Erkki overheard this plan and the next day when they were sure he was safely at work in the forest he slipped back and hid himself in the bedclothes.

Well, when they got to the island and began unpacking their things there was Erkki in the bedclothes!

The Devil's new wife complained bitterly. "If you really loved me," she said, "you'd cut off that boy's head!"

"But I've tried to cut it off!" the Devil declared, "and I never can do it! Plague take such a boy! I've always known the Finns were an obstinate lot but I must say I've never met one as bad as Erkki! He's too much for me!"

But the Devil's wife kept on complaining until at last the Devil promised that he would try once again to cut off Erkki's head.

"Very well," his wife said, "tonight when he's asleep I'll wake you."

Well, what with the moving and everything the wife herself was tired and as soon as she went to bed she fell asleep. That gave Erkki just the very chance he needed to try on the new wife the trick he had played on the old one. Without waking her he carried her to his bed and then laid himself down in her place beside the Devil. Then he waked up the Devil and reminded him that he had promised to cut off Erkki's head.

The poor old Devil got up and went over to Erkki's bed and of course cut off the head of his new wife.

The next morning when he found out what he had done, he was perfectly furious.

"You get right out of here, Erkki!" he roared. "I never want to see you again!"

"There now, master," Erkki said, "you're not going to lose your temper over a little thing like a dead wife, are you?"

"I am so going to lose my temper!" the Devil shouted. "And what's more, it isn't a little thing! I liked this wife, I did, and I don't know where I'll get another one I like as well! So you just clear out of here and be quick about it, too!"

"Very well, master," Erkki said, I'll go, but not until you pay me what you owe me."

"What I owe you!" bellowed the Devil. "What about all you owe me for my house and my cattle and my wife and my dear new wife and everything!"

"You've lost your temper," Erkki said, "and now you've got to pay me a patch of your hide big enough to sole a pair of boots. That was our bargain!"

The Devil roared and blustered but Erkki was firm. He wouldn't budge a step until the Devil had allowed him to slit a great patch of hide off his back.

That piece of the Devil's hide made the finest soles that a pair of boots ever had. It wore for years and years and years. In fact, Erkki is still tramping around on those same soles. The fame of them has spread over all the land and it has got so that now people stop Erkki on the highway to look at his wonderful boots soled with the Devil's hide. Travelers from foreign countries are deeply interested when they hear about the boots and when they meet Erkki they question him closely.

"Tell us," they beg him, "how did you get the Devil's hide in the first place?"

Erkki always laughs and makes the same answer:

"I got it by not losing my temper!"

As for the Devil, he's never again made a bargain like that with a Finn!

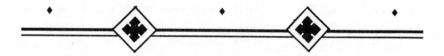

How El Bizarrón Fooled the Devil
Cuba

There was once a man called El Bizarrón who wandered about looking for work. A restless fellow. He wandered here. He wandered there. But more often there than here.

One day he was told that in the house of the Devil there was need for a servant. *"Pues, ten cuidado!"* they warned. (A forceful way of saying, "Watch out!") Two servants the Devil had already slain. He was a mean one. All who worked for him ended up dead. Much sooner than later, too. Clearly a recommendation to avoid *that* house.

But El Bizarrón retorted, "I'm on my way. The Devil won't frighten *me*."

So, to the Devil's front door he went. And knocked.

Who should open the door but the Devil himself.

"Have you work for a strong man?"

"Work enough for six strong men. You are sure there are not five more of you? Ah, well. *Pase adentro.*"

In walked El Bizarrón. The Devil led him to the room where he was to sleep. "Rest," he said. "Tomorrow you will begin your chores."

El Bizarrón stretched himself on the bed. Before long, healthy snores were livening up that corner of the house.

The next day the Devil sent him to fetch water.

But El Bizarrón demanded, "Give me a pick and shovel."

The Devil without any fuss gave them.

El Bizarrón went down to the river. He began digging a ditch from the stream to the Devil's house. Like six men he toiled. Well . . . like three anyway.

At eleven o'clock came the Devil to check up on El Bizarrón. "Water I wish. Not a ditch. Explain yourself," he commanded.

"I am digging a canal to your house. Then there will be no need to go for water. Water will flow to you."

The Devil reflected. This man can dig. The trench is already the depth of a pitchfork. (The Devil knew his pitchforks.) Moreover, this man can *think*. He didn't like that at all. It was such a distasteful thought that he went off home.

A few days later the Devil ordered El Bizarrón to fetch a load of wood. El Bizarrón demanded, "Give me a length of rope. A long length."

Without much ado the Devil gave it.

El Bizarrón took the rope on his shoulder and went off to the mountain. There he set himself to wind the rope around the trees— around the whole forest. The rope was a lengthy length all right. With all his tramping, the heels of El Bizarrón's shoes were worn to a fraction of a millimeter; not enough sole remained to measure a fraction of anything. At eleven o'clock when the Devil came to see what El Bizarrón was up to, he found him with the rope looped around the mountain as a collar wreathes a neck.

Of course he wanted to know, "What are you doing?"

El Bizarrón answered, "Securing this mountain of woods so I can carry it back in one trip."

What a barbarian, thought the Devil. And he directed El Bizarrón to return to the house. Without the mountain. No room for *that* in the backyard.

Soon after, there was a throwing contest on the beach, with metal bars. The Devil thought, ah, I shall send this strong fellow as a competitor. With his muscles he must surely win me a prize. And he led El Bizarrón to the shore, El Bizarrón with a bar balanced on his shoulder.

At the beach everyone was practicing and preparing himself for the match. Except El Bizarrón. That one curled himself on the sunny sand and took a snooze.

The day peeled off its hours. The contest began. Came the turn of El Bizarrón.

Loudly he cried out, "Order those faraway boats to sail away. Otherwise I will sink them with my shot!"

As this was impossible they would not permit him to throw. It was a disappointment to all. In particular to the Devil, who felt more and more uneasy about El Bizarrón's strength. *And* his acuteness. Too dangerous is this ox with his fox's brain, he decided. I must rid myself of him.

The two made their way back to the Devil's house. In a buttery manner the Devil suggested that since he desired to spend that night stretched out on the iron grill of the barbecue, El Bizarrón might wish to sleep beneath.

"Why not?" asked El Bizarrón in an offhand way.

So it was arranged. The Devil then hid two heavy, heavy rocks that he planned to drop on El Bizarrón during the night.

Evening fell, and both lay down in their places: the Devil on the high grill and El Bizarrón underneath. But El Bizarrón noticed that the Devil appeared much bulkier than usual. A suspicious sign. Hmmmmmmm. Unknown to the Devil, El Bizarrón changed his bed to a corner, a far corner. And waited.

At midnight he heard the clangor of falling rocks. At once he shouted, "Ay, what a mosquito has bitten me!"

Naturally the Devil thought, two boulders have dropped on him and to this fellow they are no more than an insect bite. He was impressed. Disturbed. Shaken to his red marrow.

He climbed down to note exactly El Bizarrón's condition. This one was now sitting under the barbecue, unbruised, unscratched, unmarked. And there lay the smashed rocks.

"Ah," said El Bizarrón in a voice of wonder, "I believed it was a mosquito and instead it was these stones. How came they here?"

Now the Devil's teeth clacked with fright. Speaking between clacks he declared, "Fellow, I shall give you a burro loaded with silver if you will leave here—if you leave for a destination far, far away. Preferably the moon. Or farther."

El Bizarrón accepted the offer. Why not? He brought up the burro. The Devil filled the saddlebags with money, till they bulged like sacks of potatoes.

"There you have it. Now go."

El Bizarrón went. After he had been gone a while, the Devil's wife said to him, "That ninny deceived you. He is not so strong as all that." She flung sneers against the Devil as if she were hurling stones at a stray dog.

Her scorn convinced her husband. So, saddling a horse, he set out to find El Bizarrón and take from him the donkey and the riches.

Looking back, El Bizarrón glimpsed the Devil approaching at a distance. Quickly he hid the donkey in a field of sugarcane. Then he lay on his back in the middle of the road with his legs in the air.

The Devil came up. In astonishment he asked, "And what ails *you?*"

"Ah, nothing. That stubbornness of a donkey refused to walk. So I gave him a kick that sent him above the clouds . . . "

The Devil, his teeth clattering again, wanted to know, "But why are you lying here kicking at the wind?"

"I don't want the donkey killed when he drops back to earth. This way I'll ease his fall with my feet."

At that the palsy of the Devil's teeth affected the rest of him. He might have been a flag lashed by a gale. Swiftly he spurred his horse and galloped home.

His wife asked, "Did you catch him?"

"Catch him! Should I want to? There he was. No sign of the burro—he had kicked it to Heaven. And if I had waited to recover the money he might have booted *me* to Heaven. And what place is that for the Devil? Glad am I to be free of him."

BEARSKIN
Germany

There was once a young fellow who enlisted as a soldier, conducted himself bravely, and was always the foremost when it rained bullets. So long as the war lasted all went well, but when peace was made he received his dismissal, and the captain said he might go where he liked. His parents were dead and he had no longer a home, so he went to his brothers and begged them to take him in and keep him until war broke out again.

The brothers, however, were hard-hearted and said, "What can we do with you? You are of no use to us. Go and make a living for yourself."

The soldier had nothing left but his gun, so he took that on his shoulder and went forth into the world. He came to a wide heath, on which nothing was to be seen but a circle of trees; under these he sat sorrowfully down, and began to think over his fate.

"I have no money," thought he, "I have learned no trade but that of fighting, and now that they have made peace they don't want me any longer. So I see beforehand that I shall have to starve."

All at once he heard a rustling, and when he looked round, a strange man stood before him, who wore a green coat and looked right stately, but had a hideous cloven foot. "I know already what you are in need of," said the man. "Gold and possessions shall you have, as much as you can make away with, do what you will, but first I must know if you are fearless, that I may not bestow my money in vain."

"A soldier and fear—how can those two things go together?" he answered. "You can put me to the proof."

"Very well, then," answered the man, "look behind you."

The soldier turned round, and saw a large bear, which came growling towards him. "Oho!" cried the soldier, "I will tickle your nose for you, so that you shall soon lose your fancy for growling." and he aimed at the bear and shot it through the muzzle; it fell down and never stirred again.

"I see quite well," said the stranger, "that you are not wanting in courage, but there is still another condition which you will have to fulfill."

"If it does not endanger my salvation," replied the soldier, who knew very well who was standing by him. "If it does, I'll have nothing to do with it."

"You will look to that for yourself," answered Greencoat. "You shall for the next seven years neither wash yourself, nor comb your beard nor your hair, nor cut your nails, nor once say the Lord's Prayer. I will give you a coat and a cloak, which during this time you must wear. If you die during these seven years, you are mine; if you remain alive, you are free, and rich to boot, for all the rest of your life."

The soldier thought of the great extremity in which he now found himself, and as often had gone to meet death, he resolved to risk it now also, and agreed to the terms. The Devil took off his green coat and gave it to the soldier, and said, "If you have this coat on your back and put your hand into the pocket, you will always find it full of money." Then he pulled the skin off the bear and said; "This shall be your cloak, and your bed also, for thereon shall you sleep, and in no other bed shall you lie, and because of this apparel shall you be called Bearskin." Whereupon the Devil vanished.

The soldier put the coat on, felt at once in the pocket, and found that the thing was really true. Then he put on the bearskin and went forth into the world, and enjoyed himself, refraining from nothing that did him good and his money harm. During the first year his appearance was passable, but during the second he began to look like a monster. His hair covered nearly the whole of his face, his beard was like a piece of coarse felt, his fingers had claws, and his face was so covered with dirt that if cress had been sown on it, it would have come up. Whosoever saw him ran away, but as he everywhere gave the poor money to pray that he might not die during the seven years, and as he paid well for everything, he still always found shelter. In the fourth year, he entered an inn where the landlord would not receive him, and would not even let him have a place in the stable, because he was afraid the horses would be scared. But as Bearskin thrust his hand into his pocket and pulled out a handful of ducats, the host let himself be persuaded and gave him a room in an outhouse. Bearskin, however, was obliged to promise not to let himself be seen, lest the inn should get a bad name.

As Bearskin was sitting alone in the evening, and wishing from the bottom of his heart that the seven years were over, he heard a loud lamenting in a neighboring room. He had a compassionate heart, so he opened the door, and saw an old man weeping bitterly and wringing his hands. Bearskin went nearer, but the man sprang to his feet and tried to escape from him.

At last, when the man perceived that Bearskin's voice was human, he let himself be prevailed upon, and by kind words Bearskin succeeded so far that the old man revealed the cause of his grief. His property had dwindled away by degrees, he and his daughters would have to starve, and he was so poor that he could not pay the innkeeper and was to be put in prison.

"If that is your only trouble," said Bearskin, "I have plenty of money." He caused the innkeeper to be brought thither, paid him, and even put a purse full of gold into the poor old man's pocket.

When the old man saw himself set free from all his troubles, he did not know how to show his gratitude. "Come with me," said he to Bearskin. "My daughters are all miracles of beauty; choose one of them for yourself as a wife. When she hears what you have done for me, she will not refuse you. You do in truth look a little strange, but she will soon put you to rights again."

This pleased Bearskin well, and he went.

When the eldest saw him she was so terribly alarmed at his face that she screamed and ran away. The second stood still and looked at him from head to foot, but then she said," How can I accept a husband who no longer has a human form? The shaven bear that once was here and passed itself off for a man pleased me far better, for at any rate it wore a hussar's dress and white gloves. If he were only ugly, I might get used to that." The youngest, however said, "Dear Father, that must be a good man to have helped you out of your trouble, so if you have promised him a bride for doing it, your promise must be kept."

It was a pity that Bearskin's face was covered with dirt and with hair, for if not they might have seen how delighted he was when he heard these words. He took a ring from his finger, broke it in two, and gave her half; the other he kept for himself. Then he wrote his name on her half, and hers on his, and begged her to keep her piece carefully. Then he took his leave and said, "I must still wander about for three years, and if I do not return then, you are free, for I shall be dead. But pray to God to preserve my life."

The poor betrothed bride dressed herself entirely in black, and when she thought of her future bridegroom, tears came into her eyes. Nothing but contempt and mockery fell to her lot from her sisters.

"Take care," said the eldest, "if you give him your hand, he will strike his claws into it."

"Beware!" said the second. "Bears like sweet things, and if he takes a fancy to you, he will eat you up."

"You must always do as he likes," began the elder again, "or else he will growl." And the second continued, "But the wedding will be a merry one, for bears dance well."

The bride was silent, and did not let them vex her.

Bearskin, however, traveled about the world from one place to another, did good where he was able, and gave generously to the poor that they might pray for him.

At length, as the last day of the seven years dawned, he went once more out onto the heath and seated himself beneath the circle of trees. It was not long before the wind whistled, and the Devil stood before him and looked angrily at him: then he threw Bearskin his old coat and asked for his own green one back.

"We have not got so far as that yet," answered Bearskin. "You must first make me clean." Whether the Devil liked it or not, he was forced to fetch water and wash Bearskin, comb his hair, and cut his nails. After this, he looked like a brave soldier, and was much handsomer than he had ever been before.

When the Devil had gone away, Bearskin was quite lighthearted. He went into the town, put on a magnificent velvet coat, seated himself in a carriage drawn by four white horses, and drove to his bride's house. No one recognized him. The father took him for a distinguished general, and led him into the room where his daughters were sitting. He was forced to place himself between the two eldest, who helped him to wine, gave him the best pieces of meat, and thought that in all the world they had never seen a handsomer man. The bride, however, sat opposite to him in her black dress, and never raised her eyes nor spoke a word.

When at length he asked the father if he would give him one of his daughters to wife, the two eldest jumped up and ran into their bedrooms to put on splendid dresses, for each of them fancied she was the chosen one.

The stranger, as soon as he was alone with his bride, brought out his half of the ring, and threw it in a glass of wine which he handed across the table to her. She took the wine, but when she had drunk it, and found the half ring lying at the bottom, her heart began to beat. She got the other half, which she wore on a ribbon round her neck, joined them, and saw that the two pieces fitted together exactly.

Then said he, "I am your betrothed bridegroom, whom you saw as Bearskin, but through God's grace I have again received my human form and have once more become clean." He went up to her, embraced her, and gave her a kiss.

In the meantime the two sisters came back in full dress, and when they saw that the handsome man had fallen to the share of the youngest, and heard that he was Bearskin, they ran out full of anger and rage. One of them drowned herself in the well, the other hanged herself on a tree.

In the evening, someone knocked at the door, and when the bridegroom opened it, it was the Devil in his green coat, who said, "You see, I have now got two souls in the place of your one!"

The Lad and the Devil
Norway

Once upon a time there was a lad who went along a road cracking nuts. He happened to find one which was worm-eaten, and shortly afterwards he met the Devil.

"Is it true," said the lad, "what they say, that the Devil can make himself as small as he likes, and go through a pinhole?"

"Yes, of course," answered the Devil.

"Well, let me see you do it. Creep into this nut if you can," said the lad.

And the Devil did it. But he had no sooner got through the wormhole than the lad put a small peg in the hole.

"I have got you safe, now," he said, and put the nut in his pocket. When he had walked some distance he came to a smithy. He went in there and asked the smith if he would crack that nut for him.

"Yes, that's easily done," said the smith, and took the smallest hammer he had, laid the nut on the anvil, and gave it a blow, but it didn't break. So he took a somewhat bigger hammer, but that wasn't heavy enough either; then he took a still bigger one, but no—the nut would not break.

This made the smith angry, and he seized the big sledgehammer. "I shall soon make bits of you," he said, and he gave the nut such a blow that it went into a thousand pieces, and sent half the roof of the smithy flying in the air. Such a crash! just as if the hut were tumbling together.

"I think the Devil was in the nut," said the smith.

"So he was," said the lad.

WILEY AND THE HAIRY MAN
United States

Wiley's pappy was a bad man and no-count. He stole watermelons in the dark of the moon. He was lazy, too, and slept while the weeds grew higher than the cotton. Worse still, he killed martins and never even chunked at a crow.

One day he fell off the ferryboat where the river is quicker than anywhere else and no one ever found him. They looked for him a long way down river and in the still pools between the sandbanks, but they never found him. They heard a big man laughing across the river, and everybody said, "That's the Hairy Man." So they stopped looking.

"Wiley," his mammy told him, "the Hairy Man's got your pappy and he's goin' to get you if you don't look out."

"Yas'm," he said. "I'll look out. I'll take my hound-dogs everywhere I go. The Hairy Man can't stand no hound-dog."

Wiley knew that because his mammy had told him. She knew because she came from the swamps by the Tombisbee River and knew conjure magic.

One day Wiley took his axe and went down in the swamp to cut some poles for a hen-roost and his hounds went with him. But they took out after a shoat and ran it so far off Wiley couldn't even hear them yelp.

"Well," he said, "I hope the Hairy Man ain't nowhere round here now."

He picked up his axe to start cutting poles, but he looked up and there came the Hairy Man through the trees grinning. He was sure ugly and his grin didn't help much. He was hairy all over. His eyes burned like fire and spit drooled all over his big teeth.

"Don't look at me like that," said Wiley, but the Hairy Man kept coming and grinning, so Wiley threw down his axe and climbed up a big bay tree. He saw the Hairy Man didn't have feet like a man but like a cow, and Wiley never had seen a cow up a bay tree.

"What for you done climb up there?" the Hairy Man asked Wiley when he got to the bottom of the tree.

Wiley climbed nearly to the top of the tree and looked down. Then he climbed plumb to the top.

"How come you climbin' trees?" the Hairy Man said.

"My mammy done tole me to stay away from you. What you got in that big croaker-sack?"

"I ain't got nothin' yet."

"Gwan away from here," said Wiley, hoping the tree would grow some more.

"Ha," said the Hairy Man and picked up Wiley's axe. He swung it about and the chips flew. Wiley grabbed the tree close, rubbed his belly on it and hollered, "Fly, chips, fly, back in your same old place."

The chips flew and the Hairy Man cussed and damned. Then he swung the axe and Wiley knew he'd have to holler fast. They went to it tooth and toenail then, Wiley hollering and the Hairy Man chopping. He hollered till he was hoarse and he saw the Hairy Man was gaining on him.

"I'll come down part of the way," he said, "if you'll make this bay tree twice as big around."

"I ain't studyin' you," said the Hairy Man, swinging the axe.

"I bet you can't," said Wiley.

"I ain't going to try," said the Hairy Man.

Then they went to it again, Wiley hollering and the Hairy Man chopping. Wiley had about yelled himself out when he heard his hound-dogs yelping way off.

"Hyeaaah, dog," hollered Wiley, and they both heard the hound-dogs yelping and coming jam-up. The Hairy Man looked worried.

"Come on down," he said, "and I'll teach you conjure."

"I can learn all the conjure I want from my mammy."

The Hairy Man cussed some more, but he threw the axe down and took off throught the swamp.

When Wiley got home he told his mammy that the Hairy Man had most got him but his dogs ran him off.

"Did he have his sack?"

"Yas'm."

"Next time he come after you, don't climb no bay tree."

"I ain't," said Wiley. "They ain't big enough around."

"Don't climb no kind o' tree. Just stay on the ground and say 'Hello, Hairy Man.' You hear me, Wiley?"

"No'm."

"He ain't goin' to hurt you, child. You can put the Hairy Man in the dirt when I tell you how to do him."

"I puts him in the dirt and he puts me in that croaker-sack. I ain't puttin' no Hairy Man in the dirt."

"You just do like I say. You say, 'Hello, Hairy Man.' He says, 'Hello, Wiley,' You say, 'Hello Hairy Man, I done heard you about the best conjure man round here.' 'I reckon I am.' You say, 'I bet you cain't turn yourself into no giraffe.' You keep tellin' him he cain't and he will. Then you say, 'I bet you cain't turn yourself into no possum.' Then he will, and you grab him and throw him in the sack."

"It don't sound just right somehow," said Wiley, "but I will." So he tied up his dogs so they wouldn't scare away the Hairy Man, and went down to the swamp again. He hadn't been there long when he looked up and there came the Hairy Man grinning through the trees, hairy all over and his big teeth showing more than ever. He knew Wiley came off without his hound-dogs. Wiley nearly climbed a tree when he saw the croaker-sack, but he didn't.

"Hello, Hairy Man," he said.

"Hello, Wiley." He took the sack off his shoulder and started opening it up.

"Hairy Man, I done heard you are about the best conjure man round here."

"I reckon I is."

"I bet you cain't turn yourself into no giraffe."

"Shucks, that ain't no trouble," said the Hairy Man.

"I bet you cain't do it."

So the Hairy Man twisted round and turned himself into a giraffe.

"I bet you cain't turn yourself into no alligator," said Wiley.

The giraffe twisted around and turned into an alligator, all the time watching Wiley to see he didn't try to run.

"Anybody can turn theyself into something big as a man," said Wiley, "but I bet you cain't turn yourself into no possum."

The alligator twisted around and turned into a possum, and Wiley grabbed it and threw it in the sack.

Wiley tied the sack up as tight as he could and then he threw it in the river. He started home through the swamp and he looked up and there came the Hairy Man grinning through the trees. Wiley had to scramble up the nearest tree.

The Hairy Man gloated: "I turned myself into the wind and blew out. Wiley, I'm going to set right here till you get hungry and fall out of that bay tree. You want me to learn you some more conjure?"

Wiley studied awhile. He studied about the Hairy Man and he studied about his hound-dogs tied up most a mile away.

"Well," he said, "you done some pretty smart tricks. But I bet you cain't make things disappear and go where nobody knows."

"Huh, that's what I'm good at. Look at that old bird-nest on the limb. Now look. It's done gone."

"How I know it was there in the first place? I bet you cain't make something I know is there disappear."

"Ha ha!" said the Hairy Man. "Look at your shirt."

Wiley looked down and his shirt was gone, but he didn't care, because that was just what he wanted the Hairy Man to do.

"That was just a plain old shirt," he said. "But this rope I got tied round my breeches has been conjured. I bet you cain't make it disappear."

"Huh, I can make all the rope in this county disappear."

"Ha ha ha," said Wiley.

The Hairy Man looked mad and threw his chest way out. He opened his mouth wide and hollered loud.

"From now on all the rope in this county has done disappeared."

Wiley reared back, holding his breeches with one hand and a tree-limb with the other.

"Hyeaaah, dog," he hollered loud enough to be heard more than a mile off.

When Wiley and his dogs got back home his mammy asked him did he put the Hairy Man in the sack.

"Yes'm, but he done turned himself into the wind and blew right through that old croaker-sack."

"That *is* bad," said his mammy. "But you done fool him twice. If you fool him again he'll leave you alone. He'll be mighty hard to fool the third time."

"We got to study up a way to fool him, Mammy."

"I'll study up a way tereckly," she said, and sat down by the fire and held her chin between her hands and studied real hard. But Wiley wasn't studying anything except how to keep the Hairy Man away. He took his hound-dogs out and tied one at the back door and one at the front door. Then he crossed a broom and an axe-handle over the window and built a fire in the fire-place. Feeling a lot safer, he sat down and helped his mammy study. After a little while his mammy said, "Wiley, you go down to the pen and get that little suckin' pig away from that old sow."

Wiley went down and snatched the sucking pig through the rails and left the sow grunting and heaving in the pen. He took the pig back to his mammy and she put it in his bed.

"Now, Wiley," she said, "you go on up to the loft and hide."

So he did. Before long he heard the wind howling and the trees shaking, and then dogs started growling. He looked out through a knothole in the planks and saw the dog at the front door looking down toward the swamps, with his hair standing up and his lips drawn back in a snarl. Then an animal as big as a mule with horns on its head ran out of the swamp past the house. The dog jerked and jumped, but he couldn't get loose. Then an animal bigger than a great big dog with a long nose and big teeth ran out of the swamp and growled at the cabin. This time the dog broke loose and took after the big animal, who ran back down into the swamp. Wiley looked out another chink at the back end of the loft just in time to see his other dog jerk loose and take out after an animal which might have been a possum, but wasn't.

"Law-dee," said Wiley. "The Hairy Man is coming here, sure."

He didn't have long to wait, because soon enough he heard something with feet like a cow scrambling around on the roof. He knew it was the Hairy Man, because he heard him swear when he touched the hot chimney. The Hairy Man jumped off the roof when he found out there was a fire in the fireplace and came up and knocked on the front door as big as you please.

"Mammy," he hollered, "I done come after your baby."

"You ain't going to get him," Mammy hollered back.

"Give him here or I'll set your house on fire with lightning."

"I got plenty of sweet milk to put it out with."

"Give him here or I'll dry up your spring, make your cow go dry, and send a million boll weevils out of the ground to eat up your cotton."

"Hairy Man, you wouldn't do all that. That's mighty mean."

"I'm a mighty mean man. I ain't never seen a man as mean as I am."

"If I give you my baby will you go on way from here and leave everything else alone?"

"I swear that's just what I'll do," said the Hairy Man, so Mammy opened the door and let him in.

"He's over there in that bed," she said.

The Hairy Man came in grinning like he was meaner than he said. He walked over to the bed and snatched the covers back.

"Hey," he hollered. "there ain't nothing in this bed but a old suckin pig."

"I ain't said what kind of baby I was giving you, and that suckin' pig sure belong to me before I gave it to you."

The Hairy Man raged and yelled. He stomped all over the house gnashing his teeth. Then he grabbed up the pig and tore out through the swamp, knocking down trees right and left. The next morning the swamp had a wide path like a cyclone had cut through it, with trees torn loose at the roots and lying on the ground. When the Hairy Man was gone Wiley came down from the loft.

"Is he done gone, Mammy?"

"Yes, child. That old Hairy Man cain't ever hurt you again. We done fool him three times."

The
GETTING
of
WISDOM

Aeschylus tells us that by suffering comes wisdom; the wag, that through wisdom comes suffering; and the Bible, that fear of the Lord is the beginning of wisdom. Every great figure in world literature has taken it upon himself to comment upon wisdom: Shakespeare, Homer, Montaigne, Milton, Wordsworth, Byron, Cervantes, and the rest. But long before the literati were commenting, the world's folk were having their own say about wisdom's many faces in the stories and tales—most often short and pithy—that they passed around.

Whether those stories are allegories such as the Greek "Truth and Falsehood," the legends such as the English story "The Peddler of Swaffham," or full-scale extravaganzas such as the Italian tale "The Happy Man's Shirt," they are entertainments culled from the hearts and minds of the folk and are therefore human wisdom in its most encapsulated form.

TRUTH AND FALSEHOOD
Greece

Once, Truth and Falsehood met at a crossroads, and after they had greeted each other, Falsehood asked Truth how the world went with him. "How goes it with me?" said Truth. "Each year worse than the last." "I can see the plight you are in," said Falsehood, glancing at Truth's ragged clothes, "Why, even your breath stinks." "Not a bite has passed my lips these three days," said Truth. "Wherever I go, I get troubles, not only for myself, but for the few who love me still. It's no way to live, this." "You have only yourself to blame," said Falsehood to him. "Come with me. You'll see better days, dress in fine clothes like mine, and eat plenty, only you must not gainsay anything I say."

Truth consented, just that once, to go and eat with Falsehood because he was so hungry he could hardly keep upright. They set out together and came to a great city, went into the best hotel, which was full of people, and sat and ate of the best. When many hours had gone by, and most of the people had gone, Falsehood rapped with his fist on the table, and the hotelkeeper himself came up to see to their wants, for Falsehood looked like a great nobleman. He asked what they desired.

"How much longer am I to wait for the change from the sovereign I gave the boy who sets the table?" said Falsehood. The host called the boy, who said that he had had no sovereign. Then Falsehood grew angry and began to shout, saying he would never have believed that such a hotel would rob the people who went in there to eat, but he would bear it in mind another time, and he threw a sovereign at the hotelkeeper. "There," he said, "bring me the change."

Fearing that his hotel would get a bad name, the hotelkeeper would not take the sovereign, but gave change from the reputed sovereign of the argument, and boxed the ears of the boy who could not remember taking the coin. The boy began to cry, and protest that he had not had the sovereign, but as no one believed him, he sighed deeply and said, "Alas, where are you, unhappy Truth? Are you no more?"

"No, I'm here," said Truth, through clenched teeth, "but I had not eaten for three days, and now I may not speak. You must find the right of it by yourself, my tongue is tied."

When they got outside, Falsehood burst out laughing and said to Truth, "You see how I contrive things?"

"Better I should die of hunger," said Truth, "than do the things you do." So they parted forever.

GETTING COMMON SENSE
Jamaica

Once upon a time, Anansi thought to himself that if he could collect all the common sense in the world and keep it for himself, then he was bound to get plenty of money and plenty of power, for everybody would have to come to him with their worries, and he would charge them a whole lot when he advised them.

Anansi started to collect up and collect up all the common sense he could find and put it all into one huge calabash. When he searched and searched and couldn't find any more common sense, Anansi decided to hide his calabash on the top of a very tall tree so that nobody else could reach it.

So Anansi tied a rope around the neck of the calabash and tied the two ends of the rope together and hung the rope around his neck so that the calabash was on his belly. He started up the tall tree, but he couldn't climb very well or very fast because the calabash kept getting in his way. He was trying and trying so hard when all of a sudden he heard a voice burst out laughing in back of him. And when he looked he saw a little boy standing on the tree's root: "What a foolish man! If you want to climb the tree frontways, why don't you put the calabash behind you?"

Well, Anansi was so angry to hear that big piece of common sense coming out of the mouth of such a little boy after he had thought he had collected all the common sense in the world that Anansi took off the calabash, broke it into pieces, and the common sense scattered out in the breeze all over the world. Everybody got a little bit of it, but no one got it all. It was Anansi who made it happen that way.

Jack Mandora, me no choose none.

RICH MAN, POOR MAN
Africa (Akamba)

It happened one time, long, long ago, that in one of the villages of the Akamba, there were two men who lived as neighbors. One was rich, and the other was poor, but they were friends. The poor man worked for the rich man, helping him. Now a famine came to the land. And when the suffering became very severe, the rich man forgot the poor man, and the poor man who used to eat at his friend's house now had to beg from him. Finally, the rich man chased him away altogether, because a rich man cannot remain a friend of a poor person for too long, and he felt that even the scraps he now gave his poor neighbor were just too much.

One day, this poor man was scrounging about in the village for something to eat. He was given maize by a man who took pity on him, and he took it home to his wife, and she cooked it. But they had no meat with which to make it into soup; nor did they have salt with which to season it. So the man said, "I will go to see if my rich friend is having a good soup tonight." He went and found that the meal cooking there gave out a nice sweet smell. So he returned back to his house, got the cooked maize, and brought it back to the rich man's house, where he sat against the wall and ate it, breathing in the smell that came from the rich man's meal. When he had eaten, he returned to his own home.

Another day, the poor man saw the rich man and went up to him and said, "I came a few days ago, while you were eating your food, and I sat by the wall, and ate my food together with the delicious smell that came from your food."

The rich man was furious, and he said, "So that's why my food was completely tasteless that day! It was you who ate the good taste from my food, and you must pay me for it! I'm taking you to the judge to file a case against you." And he did that, and the poor man was told to pay one goat to the rich man for eating the sweet smell from his food. But the poor man could not afford even one goat, and he broke down and cried as he went back to his house.

On his way home, he met a wise man and speechmaker, and he told him what had happened. The wise man gave him a goat, and told him to keep that goat until he came back. Now, the judge had appointed a certain day when the poor man was to pay the rich man; and on that day, many people came together to witness the payment. The wise man came also, and when he saw the people talking, he asked. "Why are you making so much fuss here?" The judge said, "This poor man is supposed to pay this rich man a goat, for the smell he breathed from the rich man's food." The wise man asked his first question again, and he was given the same answer. So the wise man said, "Will you let me give another judgment on this case?" The people said, "Yes, if you are a good judge!" So he went on to say, "A man who steals must give back only as much as he has taken, no more, no less."

When the people asked him how he could pay back just the smell of good food, the wise man replied, "I will show you!" Then he turned to the rich man, and said to him, "Rich man, I am going to hit this goat, and when it bleats, I want you to take its bleating sound! You are not to touch this poor man's goat, unless he touched your food." Then he said again to the people, "Listen now, while I pay back the rich man." So he beat the goat, and it bleated, and he said to the rich man, "Take that sound as payment for the smell of your good food!"

THE LOST HORSE
China

A man who lived on the northern frontier of China was skilled in interpreting events. One day for no reason, his horse ran away to the nomads across the border. Everyone tried to console him, but his father said, "What makes you so sure this isn't a blessing?" Some months later his horse returned, bringing a splendid nomad stallion. Everyone congratulated him, but his father said, "What makes you so sure this isn't a disaster?" Their household was richer by a fine horse, which the son loved to ride. One day he fell and broke his hip. Everyone tried to console him, but his father said, "What makes you so sure this isn't a blessing?"

A year later the nomads came in force across the border, and every able-bodied man took his bow and went into battle. The Chinese frontiersmen lost nine of every ten men. Only because the son was lame did father and son survive to take care of each other. Truly, blessing turns to disaster, and disaster to blessing: the changes have no end, nor can the mystery be fathomed.

IT COULD ALWAYS BE WORSE
Jewish

The poor Jew had come to the end of his rope. So he went to his rabbi for advice.

"Holy Rabbi!" he cried. "Things are in a bad way with me, and are getting worse all the time! We are poor, so poor, that my wife, my six children, my in-laws, and I have to live in a one-room hut. We get in each other's way all the time. Our nerves are frayed and, because we have plenty of troubles, we quarrel. Believe me—my home is a hell and I'd sooner die than continue living this way!"

The rabbi pondered the matter gravely. "My son," he said, "promise to do as I tell you and your condition will improve."

"I promise, Rabbi," answered the troubled man. "I'll do anything you say."

"Tell me—what animals do you own?"

"I have a cow, a goat, and some chickens."

"Very well! Go home now and take all these animals into your house to live with you."

The poor man was dumbfounded, but since he had promised the rabbi, he went home and brought all the animals into his house.

The following day the poor man returned to the rabbi and cried, "Rabbi, what a misfortune have you brought upon me! I did as you told me and brought the animals into the house. And now what have I got? Things are worse than ever! My life is a perfect hell—the house is turned into a barn! Save me, Rabbi—help me!"

"My son," replied the rabbi serenely, "go home and take the chickens out of your house. God will help you!"

So the poor man went home and took the chickens out of his house. But it was not long before he again came running to the rabbi.

"Holy Rabbi!" he wailed. "Help me, save me! The goat is smashing everything in the house—she's turning my life into a nightmare."

"Go home," said the rabbi gently, "and take the goat out of the house. God will help you!"

The poor man returned to his house and removed the goat. But it wasn't long before he again came running to the rabbi, lamenting loudly, "What a misfortune you've brought upon my head, Rabbi! The cow has turned my house into a stable! How can you expect a human being to live side by side with an animal?"

"You're right—a hundred times right!" agreed the rabbi. "Go straight home and take the cow out of your house!"

And the poor unfortunate hastened home and took the cow out of his house.

Not a day had passed before he came running again to the rabbi.

"Rabbi!" cried the poor man, his face beaming. "You've made life sweet again for me. With all the animals out, the house is so quiet, so roomy, and so clean! What a pleasure!"

His Just Reward
Sweden

Once there was a man who went out into the forest looking for a runaway horse. At one point he had to climb across a gap in the mountain, where he saw that a large snake had got its tail caught under some large rocks.

The snake said to the man, "If you help free me, I'll see that you get your just reward!"

So the man took his staff and pried the rocks apart so the snake could get out.

"Thanks," said the snake. "Now be so kind as to come over here and take your just reward!"

The man asked what his just reward might be?

"Death," said the snake. "Death is your just reward."

The man said that he'd never heard of that before, and he'd like to ask the first living creature they met if the snake really was right about this.

They walked along until they met a bear. The man asked the bear what one's just reward ought to be, and the bear answered that it was death.

Then the snake said, "You see, death *is* your just reward. Now I'm coming to get you!"

But the man said, "Let's walk a little farther and ask someone else."

After a while they met a wolf. The man asked him what one's just reward ought to be.

The wolf answered, "Death. That's one's just reward."

"Well!" said the snake. "Let's get on with it."

"No," said the man. "I want to hear one more judge in the case, whoever it might be."

A little while later they met a fox, and the man asked him what, in his opinion, was a just reward.

Like the others the fox answered, "Death."

"So now I'm going to eat you up," said the snake.

"No," said the fox when he heard the snake's words. "I don't think we ought to make a final judgment in this case until we have examined it thoroughly. To begin with, what actually happened?"

"Well," said the man, "the snake had got its tail caught in a rock crevice."

Then the fox said, "I think we'd better go back to the spot and take a look."

And so they did. When they arrived the fox asked the man to use his staff to pry the rocks apart again, and he told the snake to place his tail just where it had been when he'd got it caught. When the tail was again in place, the fox told the man to let go of the staff a little bit.

Then he asked the snake, "Was it tighter than this before?"

"Yes," said the snake.

"Then let go a little more," said the fox to the man. "Was it still tighter?"

"Yes," said the snake.

"Then let go altogether," said the fox to the man. "Now," he said to the snake, "were you stuck even more tightly?"

"No! Now I'm stuck even worse than I was before."

And the fox said, "Well then, you might as well just stay here, so that the two of you will be even again."

And so the snake was forced to stay in the crevice while the man walked away, happy not to have received his just reward.

DJUHA'S SLEEVE
Syria

One day Djuha arrived at a banquet in his usual rags, only to be turned away at the door. After changing into his costliest clothes and saddling his mule, he returned to his host's house looking like a man of substance. This time the servant welcomed him respectfully and seated him near the guests of honor. As Djuha reached for a piece of roast meat, his sleeve happened to slip down into the food. "Pull back your sleeve," whispered the man sitting next to him. "No," replied Djuha, "that I shall not do!" Then, addressing his sleeve, he said, "Eat, my sleeve, eat and take your fill! You have more right to this feast than I, since they respect you above me in this house."

King Mátyás and His Scholars
Hungary

Once the king and his scholars were walking past a reedy swamp. A hot day it was.

"A bit of rain would be just in time for these reeds," said the king, though the reeds stood in water.

The scholars caught each other's eye and began to laugh. What need was there of rain when the reeds stood in water?

The king made no reply.

When they got home, he gave orders to serve them the finest dishes generously salted and without any drink to wash the meal down. And at his order big bowls were placed under the table, at the feet of each scholar. The bowls were filled with water, and the scholars had to put their feet into the bowls. When they had finished supping, the scholars desired some drink as the good dishes made them thirsty. They asked the king to let them have some water as they were nearly dying with thirst.

Said the king, "What for? Your feet are in water. You were laughing at me when I said the reeds wanted a good rain. You said, 'Why should they want rain as they stood in water?' Well, why should you want water when your feet are in it? You will get none."

The Missing Axe
China

A man whose axe was missing suspected his neighbor's son. The boy walked like a thief, looked like a thief, and spoke like a thief. But the man found his axe while he was digging in the valley, and the next time he saw his neighbor's son, the boy walked, looked, and spoke like any other child.

◆   ◆   ◆   ◆   ◆

WHAT MELODY IS THE SWEETEST?
Afghanistan

Shah Abbas of Persia was a man of wit who liked to converse in parables. Among his ministers was Merza Zaki, who understood his parables well.

One day the shah was holding court with his ministers, discussing the ways of this world. Thereon he asked his ministers, "What is the sweetest melody?"

One answered, "The melody of the flute."

"No," answered another minister. "The melody of the harp is the most pleasant to the ear."

The third remarked, "Neither one nor the other! The violin has the finest tone."

Thus a bitter dispute arose.

Merza Zaki was silent and did not say anything. Days passed. Then Merza Zaki invited the shah and the rulers of the state to a banquet arranged in their honor. Musicians entertained the honored guests on all kinds of instruments. But how strange, the table bore no refreshments. The guests were without food and drink. You must know that in the East the tables are always laden with delicacies at a banquet, and when the guests have eaten and drunk their fill, there is still more food, and copper vessels of meat and rice are brought to the loaded tables. Now where was the food? It was embarrassing to ask, so the guests just went on sitting till midnight. Then Merza Zaki beckoned to the headwaiter, and he brought a vessel of cooked food into the room and beat the lid of the pot with a big spoon. *Clink! Clink!*

All the guests breathed a sigh of relief. Indeed it was time. Then Shah Abbas said, "The clink of dishes in the ears of a hungry man— this is the sweetest melody."

The Peddler of Swaffham
England

There lived in former times in Swaffham in Norfolk a certain peddler named John Chapman who dreamed that if he went to London Bridge and stood there, he would hear very joyful news. At first he slighted this dream, but afterwards, his dream being doubled and trebled upon him, he resolved to test it. And so he went to London and stood upon the bridge there two or three days, looking about him. But he heard nothing that might yield him any comfort.

At last a shopkeeper who stood close by noted John Chapman's fruitless standing, seeing he neither sold any wares nor asked any alms. The shopkeeper went over to him and most earnestly begged to know he wanted there, or what his business was.

To that the peddler honestly answered that he had dreamed that if he came to London and stood there upon the bridge, he should hear good news.

The shopkeeper laughed heartily at that. "What a fool you are, taking such a long journey on such a silly errand. I'll tell thee, country fellow, last night I dreamed that I was in Swaffham in Norfolk, a place utterly unknown to me. I dreamed that behind the house of a man named Chapman in a certain orchard is a great oak tree. I dreamed that if I dug under that great oak I would find a vast treasure. Now think you that I am such a fool to take a long journey on the instigation of a silly dream?" He laughed again. "No, no, I am the wiser. Therefore, good fellow, learn wit from me and get you home and mind your own business."

John Chapman, observing the shopkeeper's words and what he'd dreamed, and knowing they concentered on him and glad of such joyful news, went speedily home.

There he dug under the great oak and found a prodigious great treasure in the box. The box contained a Latin inscription on the lid, which, of course, John Chapman could not decipher. He craftily put the lid in his window, and very soon two schoolboys turned the Latin sentences into English:

Under me doth lie
Another much richer than I.

So he went to work, digging much deeper than before, and found a much richer treasure than the former.

And Swaffham Church being for the most part fallen down; he set on workmen and re-edified it most sumptuously at his own charge. And to this day John Chapman's statue stands therein in stone, with his pack on his back and his dog at his heels. And his memory is also preserved by the same form or picture in most of the old glass windows, taverns, and alehouses of that town to this day.

THE BEDUIN'S GAZELLE
Saudi Arabia

A Beduin set out one day with his young son to graze his she-camel and look for wild herbs and roots to take back for his wife to cook. When they had loaded the camel and were heading toward home, a herd of magnificent gazelles suddenly appeared across their path. Silently and quickly the father made the camel lower herself onto her knees, and he slid from her back. Warning the boy not to stray until he returned, he hurried after the gazelles. The wild things leaped into the air and streaked off as soon as he stepped toward them, but the Beduin was a keen hunter and loved nothing better than the chase. Eagerly he followed on their trail.

Meanwhile the tender child waited alone. From destiny there is no escape. It was his fate that a She-Ghoul, that monster of the wilderness who loves to feed on human flesh, should spy him as he stood unprotected. With one leap she sprang upon him and greedily devoured him.

The father hunted long and far but could not catch a single deer. At last he resigned himself and returned without the game. Though the camel was kneeling where he had left it, he could not see his son. He looked on every side, but the boy was gone. Then on the ground he found dark drops of blood. "My son! My son is killed! My son is dead!" he shrieked. Yet what could he do but lead his camel home?

On the way he rode past a cave, and there he saw the She-Ghoul dancing, fresh from her feast, her hanging breasts swinging from side to side like the empty sleeves of the women's cloaks when they rock in mourning over the dead. The Beduin took careful aim and shot the She-Ghoul dead. He slashed open her belly, and in it he found his son. He laid the boy upon his cloak, pulled the woolen cloth around him tight, and so carried him home.

When he reached his tent the Beduin called his wife and said, "I have brought you back a gazelle, dear wife, but as God is my witness, it can be cooked only in a cauldron that has never been used for a meal of sorrow."

The woman went from tent to tent for the loan of such a pot. But one neighbor said, "Sister, we used the large cauldron to cook the rice for the people who came to weep with us when my husband died." And another told her, "We last heated our big cooking pot on the day of my son's funeral." She knocked at every door but did not find what she sought. So she returned to her husband empty-handed.

"Haven't you found the right kind of cauldron?" asked the Beduin. "There is no household but has seen misfortune," she answered. "There is no cauldron but has cooked a meal of mourning." Only then did the Beduin fold back his woolen cloak and say to her, "They have all tasted their share of sorrow. Today the turn is ours. This is my gazelle."

> *Of such things and the like is the world made,*
> *But lucky is the soul that God loves and calls to Himself.*

THE HAPPY MAN'S SHIRT
Italy

A king had an only son that he thought the world of. But this prince was always unhappy. He would spend days on end at his window staring into space.

"What on earth do you lack?" asked the king. "What's wrong with you?"

"I don't even know myself, Father."

"Are you in love? If there's a particular girl you fancy, tell me, and I'll arrange for you to marry her, no matter whether she's the daughter of the most powerful king on earth or the poorest peasant girl alive!"

"No, Father, I'm not in love."

The king tried in every way imaginable to cheer him up, but theaters, balls, concerts, and singing were all useless, and day by day the rosy hue drained from the prince's face.

The king issued a decree, and from every corner of the earth came the most learned philosophers, doctors, and professors. The king showed them to the prince and asked for their advice. The wise men withdrew to think, then returned to the king. "Majesty, we have given the matter close thought and we have studied the stars. Here's what you must do. Look for a happy man, a man who's happy through and through, and exchange your son's shirt for his."

That same day the king sent ambassadors to all parts of the world in search of the happy man.

A priest was taken to the king. "Are you happy?" asked the king.

"Yes, indeed, Majesty."

"Fine. How would you like to be my bishop?"

"Oh, Majesty, if only it were so!"

"Away with you! Get out of my sight! I'm seeking a man who's happy just as he is, not one who's trying to better his lot."

Thus the search resumed, and before long the king was told about a neighboring king, who everybody said was a truly happy man. He had a wife as good as she was beautiful and a whole slew of children. He had conquered all his enemies, and his country was at peace. Again hopeful, the king immediately sent ambassadors to him to ask for his shirt.

The neighboring king received the ambassadors and said, "Yes, indeed, I have everything anybody could possibly want. But at the same time I worry because I'll have to die one day and leave it all. I can't sleep at night for worrying about that!" The ambassadors thought it wiser to go home without this man's shirt.

At his wit's end, the king went hunting. He fired at a hare but only wounded it, and the hare scampered away on three legs. The king pursued it, leaving the hunting party far behind him. Out in the open field he heard a man singing a refrain. The king stopped in his tracks. "Whoever sings like that is bound to be happy!" The song led him into a vineyard, where he found a young man singing and pruning the vines.

"Good day, Majesty," said the youth. "So early and already out in the country?"

"Bless you! Would you like me to take you to the capital? You will be my friend."

"Much obliged, Majesty, but I wouldn't even consider it. I wouldn't even change places with the Pope."

"Why not? Such a fine young man like you . . ."

"No, no, I tell you. I'm content with just what I have and want nothing more."

"A happy man at last!" thought the king. "Listen, young man. Do me a favor."

"With all my heart, Majesty, if I can."

"Wait just a minute," said the king, who, unable to contain his joy any longer, ran to get his retinue. "Come with me! My son is saved! My son is saved!" And he took them to the young man. "My dear lad," he began, "I'll give you whatever you want! But give me . . . give me . . ."

"What, Majesty?"

"My son is dying! Only you can save him. Come here!"

The king grabbed him and started unbuttoning the youth's jacket. All of a sudden he stopped, and his arms fell to his sides.

The happy man wore no shirt.

GHOSTS
and
REVENANTS

According to Stith Thompson, "the living tradition and active faith of nearly all countries abound in ghost legends. Not only may thousands of people be found who testify to having seen ghosts, but practices are all but universal which assume for their justification a substratum of such belief."

The varieties and types of ghosts seem to be infinite. Some ghosts are insubstantial mists, some walking bones, and some are as substantial as Tabb's man in white who carries him away in a fierce hold. Some are angry, some are sad, and some are still in love. Some return for vengeance, some for pleasure, and some to earn their way into heaven, like the ghost in the Chinese "Drinking Companions."

Likewise, stories of ghosts and revenants inspire varying reactions in the listener. Some tales cause the hearer to shiver, even blanch. A few, like "One Night in Paradise" or "The Spirit-Wife," make us sigh, or even shed a tear. Some are delicious surprises, like the Irish story "The Dream House." And some, like "The Ostler and the Grave Robbers," make an audience laugh out loud.

There is something about ghost stories that causes the listener to look around warily. And that, so we learned long ago in the ever-young story of Orpheus and Eurydice, may dispel the following spirit—whether we want to or not.

ORPHEUS AND EURYDICE
Greece

Orpheus was the son of Apollo and the Muse Calliope. He was presented by his father with a lyre and taught to play upon it, which he did to such perfection that nothing could withstand the charm of his music. Not only his fellow mortals but wild beasts were softened by his strains, and gathering round him laid by their fierceness, and stood entranced with his lay. Nay, the very trees and rocks were sensible to the charm. The former crowded round him and the latter relaxed somewhat of their hardness, softened by his notes.

Hymen had been called to bless with his presence the nuptials of Orpheus with Eurydice; but though he attended, he brought no happy omens with him. His very torch smoked and brought tears into their eyes.

In coincidence with such prognostics, Eurydice, shortly after her marriage, while wandering with the nymphs, her companions, was seen by the shepherd Aristaeus, who was stuck by her beauty and made advances to her. She fled, and in flying trod upon a snake in the grass, was bitten in the foot, and died.

Orpheus sang his grief to all who breathed the upper air, both gods and men, and finding it all unavailing resolved to seek his wife in the regions of the dead. He descended by a cave situated on the side of the promontory of Taenarus and arrived at the Stygian realm. He passed through crowds of ghosts and presented himself before the throne of Pluto and Proserpine.

Accompanying the words with the lyre, he sung, "O deities of the underworld, to whom all we who live must come, hear my words, for they are true. I come not to spy out the secrets of Tartarus, nor to try my strength against the three-headed dog with snaky hair who guards the entrance. I come to seek my wife, whose opening years the poisonous viper's fang has brought to an untimely end. Love has led me here, Love, a god all powerful with us who dwell on the earth, and, if old traditions say true, not less so here. I implore you by these abodes full of terror, these realms of silence and uncreated things, unite again the thread of Eurydice's life. We all are destined to you, and sooner or later must pass to your domain. She too, when she shall have filled her term of life, will rightly be yours. But till then grant her to me, I beseech you. If you deny me, I cannot return alone; you shall triumph in the death of us both."

As he sang these tender strains, the very ghosts shed tears. Tantalus, in spite of his thirst, stopped for a moment his efforts for water, Ixion's wheel stood still, the vulture ceased to tear the giant's liver, the daughters of Danaus rested from their task of drawing water in a sieve, and Sisyphus sat on his rock to listen. Then for the first time, it is said, the cheeks of the Furies were wet with tears. Proserpine could not resist, and Pluto himself gave way.

Eurydice was called. She came from among the new-arrived ghosts, limping with her wounded foot. Orpheus was permitted to take her away with him on one condition, that he should not turn around to look at her till they should have reached the upper air.

Under this condition they proceeded on their way, he leading, she following, through passages dark and steep, in total silence, till they had nearly reached the outlet into the cheerful upper world, when Orpheus, in a moment of forgetfulness, to assure himself that she was still following him, cast a glance behind him, when she was instantly borne away. Stretching out their arms to embrace each other, they grasped only the air!

Dying now a second time, she yet cannot reproach her husband, for how can she blame his impatience to behold her? "Farewell," she said, "a last farewell"—and was hurried away, so fast that the sound hardly reached his ears.

THE SPIRIT-WIFE
American Indian (Zuni)

A young man was grieving because the beautiful young wife whom he loved was dead. As he sat at the graveside weeping, he decided to follow her to the land of the dead. He made many prayer sticks and sprinkled sacred corn pollen. He took a downy eagle plume and colored it with red earth color. He waited until nightfall, when the spirit of his departed wife came out of the grave and sat beside him. She was not sad, but smiling. The spirit-woman told her husband, "I am just leaving one life for another. Therefore do not weep for me."

"I cannot let you go," said the young man. "I love you so much that I will go with you to the land of the dead."

The spirit-wife tried to dissuade him, but could not overcome his determination. So at last she gave in to his wishes, saying, "If you must follow me, know that I shall be invisible to you as long as the sun shines. You must tie this red eagle plume to my hair. It will be visible in daylight, and if you want to come with me, you must follow the plume."

The young husband tied the red plume to his wife's hair, and at daybreak, as the sun slowly began to light up the world, bathing the mountaintops in a pale pink light, the spirit-wife started to fade from his view. The lighter it became, the more the form of his wife dissolved and grew transparent, until at last it vanished altogether. But the red plume did not disappear. It waved before the young man, a mere arm's length away, and then, as if rising and falling on a dancer's head, began leading the way out of the village, moving through the streets out into the cornfields, moving through a shallow stream, moving into the foothills of the mountains, leading the young husband ever westward toward the land of the evening.

The red plume moved swiftly, evenly, floating without effort over the roughest trails, and soon the young man had trouble following it. He grew tireder and tireder, and finally was totally exhausted as the plume left him farther behind. Then he called out, panting, "Beloved wife, wait for me. I can't run any longer."

The red plume stopped, waiting for him to catch up, and when he did so, hastened on. For many days the young man traveled, following the plume by day, resting during the nights, when his spirit-bride would sometimes appear to him, speaking encouraging words. Most of the time, however, he was merely aware of her presence in some mysterious way. Day by day the trail became rougher and rougher. The days were long, the nights short, and the young man grew wearier and wearier, until at last he had hardly enough strength to set one foot before the other.

One day the trail led to a deep, almost bottomless chasm, and as the husband came to its edge, the red plume began to float away from him into nothingness. He reached out to seize it, but the plume was already beyond his reach, floating straight across the canyon, because spirits can fly through the air.

The young man called across the chasm, "Dear wife of mine, I love you. Wait!"

He tried to descend one side of the canyon, hoping to climb up the opposite side, but the rock walls were sheer, with nothing to hold on to. Soon he found himself on a ledge barely wider than a thumb, from which he could go neither forward nor back. It seemed that he must fall into the abyss and be dashed into pieces. His foot had already begun to slip, when a tiny striped squirrel scooted up the cliff, chattering, "You young fool, do you think you have the wings of a bird or the feet of a spirit? Hold on for just a little while and I'll help you." The little creature reached into its cheek pouch and brought out a little seed, which it moistened with saliva and stuck into a crack in the wall. With its tiny feet the squirrel danced above the crack, singing, "*Tsithl, tsithl, tsithl*, tall stalk, tall stalk, tall stalk, sprout, sprout quickly." Out of the crack sprouted a long, slender stalk, growing quickly in length and breadth, sprouting leaves and tendrils, spanning the chasm so that the young man could cross over without any trouble.

On the other side of the canyon, the young man found the red plume waiting, dancing before him as ever. Again he followed it at a pace so fast that it often seemed that his heart would burst. At last the plume led him to a large, dark, deep lake, and the plume plunged into the water to disappear below the surface. Then the husband knew that the spirit land lay at the bottom of the lake. He was in despair because he could not follow the plume into the deep. In vain did he call for his spirit-wife to come back. The surface of the lake remained undisturbed and unruffled like a sheet of mica. Not even at night did his spirit-wife reappear. The lake, the land of the dead, had swallowed her up. As the sun rose above the mountains, the young man buried his face in his hands and wept.

Then he heard someone gently calling, "Hu-hu-hu," and felt the soft beating of wings on his back and shoulders. He looked up and saw an owl hovering above him. The owl said, "Young man, why are you weeping?"

He pointed to the lake saying, "My beloved wife is down there in the land of the dead, where I cannot follow her."

"I know, poor man," said the owl. "Follow me to my house in the mountains, where I will tell you what to do. If you follow my advice, all will be well and you will be reunited with the one you love."

The owl led the husband to a cave in the mountains and, as they entered, the young man found himself in a large room full of owl-men and owl-women. The owls greeted him warmly, inviting him to sit down and rest, to eat and drink. Gratefully he took his seat.

The old owl who had brought him took his owl clothing off, hanging it on an antler jutting out from the wall, and revealed himself as a manlike spirit. From a bundle in the wall this mysterious being took a small bag, showing it to the young man, telling him, "I will give this to you, but first I must instruct you in what you must do and must not do."

The young man eagerly stretched out his hand to grasp the medicine bag, but the owl drew back. "Foolish fellow, suffering from the impatience of youth! If you cannot curb your eagerness and your youthful desires, then even this medicine will be of no help to you."

"I promise to be patient," said the husband.

"Well then," said the owl-man, "this is sleep medicine. It will make you fall into a deep sleep and transport you to some other place. When you awake, you will walk toward the Morning Star. Following the trail to the middle anthill, you will find your spirit-wife there. As the sun rises, so she will rise and smile at you, rise in the flesh, a spirit no more, and so you will live happily.

"But remember to be patient; remember to curb your eagerness. Let not your desire to touch and embrace her get the better of you, for if you touch her before bringing her safely home to the village of your birth, she will be lost to you forever."

Having finished this speech, the old owl-man blew some of the medicine on the face of the young husband, who instantly fell into a deep sleep. Then all the strange owl-men put on their owl coats and, lifting the sleeper, flew with him to a place at the beginning of the trail to the middle anthill. There thay laid him down underneath some trees.

Then the strange owl-beings flew on to the big lake at the bottom of which the land of the dead was located. The old owl-man's magic sleep medicine, and the feathered prayer sticks which the young man had carved, enabled them to dive down to the bottom of the lake and enter the land of the dead. Once inside, they used the sleep medicine to put to sleep the spirits who are in charge of that strange land beneath the waters. The owl-beings reverently laid their feathered prayer sticks before the altar of that netherworld, took up the beautiful young spirit-wife, and lifted her gently to the surface of the lake. Then, taking her upon their wings, they flew with her to the place where the young husband was sleeping.

When the husband awoke, he saw first the Morning Star, then the middle anthill, and then his wife at his side, still in deep slumber. Then she too awoke and opened her eyes wide, at first not knowing where she was or what had happened to her. When she discovered her lover right by her side, she smiled at him, saying, "Truly, your love for me is strong, stronger than love has been; otherwise we would not be here."

They got up and began to walk toward the pueblo of their birth. The young man did not forget the advice the old owl-man had given him, especially the warning to be patient and shun all desire until they had safely arrived at their home. In that way they traveled for four days, and all was well.

On the fourth day they arrived at Thunder Mountain and came to the river that flows by Salt Town. Then the young wife said, "My husband, I am very tired. The journey has been long and the days hot. Let me rest here awhile, let me sleep awhile, and then, refreshed, we can walk the last short distance home together." And her husband said, "We will do as you say."

The wife lay down and fell asleep. As her lover was watching over her, gazing at her loveliness, desire so strong that he could not resist it overcame him, and he stretched out his hand and touched her.

She awoke instantly with a start, and , looking at him and at his hand upon her body, began to weep, the tears streaming down her face. At last she said, "You loved me, but you did not love me enough; otherwise you would have waited. Now I shall die again." And before his eyes her form faded and became transparent, and at the place where she had rested a few moments before, there was nothing. On a branch of a tree above him the old owl-man hooted mournfully, "Shame, shame, shame." Then the young man sank down in despair, burying his face in his hands, and ever after his mind wandered as his eyes stared vacantly.

If the young lover had controlled his desire, if he had not longed to embrace his beautiful wife, if he had not touched her, if he had practiced patience and self-denial for only a short time, then death would have been overcome. There would be no journeying to the land below the lake, and no mourning for others lost.

But then, if there were no death, men would crowd each other with more people on this earth than the earth can hold. Then there would be hunger and war, with people fighting over a tiny patch of earth, over an ear of corn, over a scrap of meat. So maybe what happened was for the best.

One Night in Paradise
Italy

Once upon a time there were two close friends who, out of affection for each other, made this pledge: the first to get married would call on the other to be his best man, even if he should be at the ends of the earth.

Shortly therafter one of the friends died. The survivor, who was planning to get married, had no idea what he should now do, so he sought the advice of his confessor.

"This is a ticklish situation," said the priest, "but you must keep your promise. Call on him even if he is dead. Go to his grave and say what you're supposed to say. It will then be up to him whether to come to your wedding or not."

The youth went to the grave and said, "Friend, the time has come for you to be my best man!"

The earth yawned, and out jumped the friend. "By all means. I have to keep my word, or else I'd end up in Purgatory for no telling how long."

They went home, and from there to church for the wedding. Then came the wedding banquet, where the dead youth told all kinds of stories, but not a word did he say about what he'd witnessed in the next world. The bridegroom longed to ask him some questions, but he didn't have the nerve. At the end of the banquet the dead man rose and said, "Friend, since I've done you this favor, would you walk me back a part of the way?"

"Why, certainly! But I can't go far, naturally, since this is my wedding night."

"I understand. You can turn back any time you like."

The bridegroom kissed his bride. "I'm going to step outside for a moment, and I'll be right back." He walked out with the dead man. They chatted about the first one thing and then another, and before you knew it, they were at the grave. There they embraced, and the living man thought, If I don't ask him now, I'll never ask him. He therefore took heart and said, "Let me ask you something, since you are dead. What's it like in the hereafter?"

"I really can't say," answered the dead man. "If you want to find out, come along with me to Paradise."

The grave opened, and the living man followed the dead one inside. Thus they found themselves in Paradise. The dead man took his friend to a handsome crystal palace with gold doors, where angels played their harps for blessed souls to dance, with Saint Peter strumming the double bass. The living man gaped at all the splendor, and goodness knows how long he would have remained in the palace if there hadn't been all the rest of Paradise to see. "Come on to another spot now," said the dead man, who led him into a garden whose trees, instead of foliage, displayed songbirds of every color. "Wake up, let's move on!" said the dead man, guiding his visitor onto a lawn where angels danced as joyously and gracefully as lovers. "Next we'll go to see a star!" He could have gazed at the stars forever. Instead of water, their rivers ran with wine, and their land was of cheese.

All of a sudden, he started. "Oh, my goodness, friend, it's later than I thought. I have to get back to my bride, who's surely worried about me."

"Have you had enough of Paradise so soon?"

"Enough? If I had my choice . . ."

"And there's still so much to see.

"I believe you, but I'd better be getting back."

"Very well, suit yourself." The dead man walked him back to the grave and vanished.

The living man stepped from the grave, but no longer recognized the cemetery. It was packed with monuments, statues, and tall trees. He left the cemetery and saw huge buildings in place of the simple stone cottages that used to line the streets. The streets were full of automobiles and streetcars, while airplanes flew through the skies. "Where on earth am I? Did I take the wrong street? And look how these people are dressed!"

He stopped a little old man on the street. "Sir, what is this town?"

"This city, you mean."

"All right, this city. But I don't recognize it, for the life of me. Can you please direct me to the house of the man who got married yesterday?"

"Yesterday? I happen to be the sacristan, and I can assure you no one got married yesterday!"

"What do you mean? I got married myself!" Then he gave an account of accompanying his dead friend to Paradise.

"You're dreaming," said the old man. "That's an old story people tell about the bridegroom who followed his friend into the grave and never came back, while his bride died of sorrow."

"That's not so, I'm the bridegroom myself!"

"Listen, the only thing for you to do is to go and speak with our bishop."

"Bishop? But here in town there's only the parish priest."

"What parish priest? For years and years we've had a bishop." And the sacristan took him to the bishop.

The youth told his story to the bishop, who recalled an event he'd heard about as a boy. He took down the parish books and began flipping back the pages. Thirty years ago, no. Fifty years ago, no. One hundred, no. Two hundred, no. He went on thumbing the pages. Finally on a yellowed, crumbling page he put his finger on those very names. "It was three hundred years ago. The young man disapppeared from the cemetery, and the bride died of a broken heart. Read right here if you don't believe it!"

"But I'm the bridegroom myself!"

"And you went to the next world? Tell me about it!"

But the young man turned deathly pale, sank to the ground, and died before he could tell one single thing he had seen.

A Pretty Girl in the Road
United States

One time there was a fellow a-riding along and it was getting dark and coming on to rain besides. He seen a girl a-standing beside the road, where an old house had burnt down but the chimney was still there. She was a tall slim girl with a poke bonnet on, but he seen her face plain. He stopped and says if you are going somewheres I will give you a ride, because my horse carries double. She says her name is Stapleton, and her folks live down the road a piece. So then she jumped up behind him light as a feather. Pretty soon he spurred the horse a little, so she had to put her arms round his waist.

They rode on about a mile and he found out her first name was Lucy, and she wasn't married neither. He could feel her breath on his neck while they was a-talking, and he liked it fine. He got to thinking this was the kind of a girl he'd like to marry up with, because he liked her better than any girl he ever seen before.

So they rode another mile and it was pretty dark by this time, and they come to a graveyard. And there was a big house with lights in the windows just a little way off. She says that's where my folks live, but I'd better get down here. He figured she was going to take a short cut home, so her paw wouldn't know she had been riding with a stranger. Folks was awful particular about what their daughters done in them days. The girl jumped off and walked over to the gate. He says, "I'll be seein' you pretty soon." but Lucy just waved him goodbye and went into the graveyard.

The fellow waited awhile so she would have time to get home, and then he rode up in front of the big house. Soon as the dogs begun to bark an old man come out, and he says, "My name is Stapleton." He says the fellow is welcome to have supper with them and stay all night, as they have got plenty of room. And then he hollered a boy out of the barn to take care of the traveler's horse.

They had a mighty good supper, but there wasn't nobody at the table only Judge Stapleton and his wife. The fellow kept looking for Lucy to show up any minute, but she never come. So after while he went to bed in the spare room. It was a fine shuck mattress too, but he didn't sleep very good.

Next morning after breakfast they got to talking, and the judge says to him and his wife just moved here a year ago. "We used to live two miles down the road," he says, "but our house was lightnin'-struck and burnt plumb down. There ain't nothing left now but the old chimney." The fellow says yes, he seen that chimney when he rode by there last night. "I don't mind losing the house," says the judge, "only our daughter was sick in bed. We carried her out to the gate, but the shock was too much for her, and she died that same night."

The fellow just set there, and the judge went on a-talkin' about what a fine girl his daughter was, and how him and the old woman was pretty lonesome nowadays. "We buried her in that little grave-yard," says the judge. "You can see her stone from the front gallery. There ain't one day goes by, rain or shine, that my wife don't walk over there an' set by the grave awhile."

Everything was mighty still for a minute, and then the traveler says, "What was your daughter's name?" It sounded kind of funny, the way he said it, but he was obliged to know.

"Her name was Lucy," says the judge.

The Dream House
Ireland

A few years ago there was a lady living in Ireland—a Mrs. Butler—clever, handsome, popular, prosperous, and perfectly happy. One morning she said to her husband, and to anyone who was staying there, "Last night I had the most wonderful night. I seemed to be spending hours in the most delightful place, in the most enchanting house I ever saw—not large, you know, but just the sort of house one might live in oneself, and oh! so perfectly, so deliciously comfortable. Then there was the loveliest conservatory, and the garden was so enchanting! I wonder if anything half so perfect can really exist."

And the next morning she said, "Well, I have been to my house again. I must have been there for hours. I sat in the library; I walked on the terrace; I examined all the bedrooms; and it is simply the most perfect house in the world."

So it grew to be quite a joke in the family. People would ask Mrs. Butler in the beginning if she had been to her house in the night, and often she had, and always with more intense enjoyment. She would say, "I count the hours till bedtime, that I may get back to my house!" Then gradually the current of outside life flowed in, and gave a turn to their thoughts; the house ceased to be talked about.

Two years ago the Butlers grew weary of their life in Ireland. The district was wild and disturbed. The people were insolent and ungrateful. At last they said, "We are well off. We have no children. There's no reason why we should put up with this, and we'll go and live altogether in England."

So they came to London, and sent for all the house agents' lists of places within forty miles of London, and many were the places they went to see. At last they heard of a house in Hampshire. They went to it by rail, and drove from the station. As they came to the lodge, Mrs. Butler said, "Do you know, this is the lodge of my house." They drove down an avenue— "But this *is* my house!" she said.

When the housekeeper came, she said, "You will think it very odd, but do you mind my showing you the house? That passage leads to the library, and through that there is a conservatory, and then through a window you enter the drawing-room," etc., and it was all so. At last, in an upstairs passage, they came upon a baize door. Mrs. Butler, for the first time, looked puzzled. "But that door is not in my house," she said. "I don't understand about your house, ma'am," said the housekeeper, "but that door has only been there six weeks."

Well, the house was for sale, and the price asked was very small, and they decided at once to buy it. But when it was bought and paid for, the price had been so extraordinarily small, that they could not help a misgiving that there must be something wrong with the place. So they went to the agent of the people who had sold it, and said, "Well, now the purchase is made, and the deeds are signed, *will* you mind telling us why the price asked was so small?"

The agent had started violently when they came in, but recovered himself. Then he said to Mrs. Butler, "Yes; it is quite true, the matter is quite settled, so there can be no harm in telling you now. The fact is that the house has had a great reputation for being haunted, but you, madam, need be under no apprehensions, for you are yourself the ghost!"

The Peasant and the Fiend
Estonia

A horse belonging to a peasant who was performing husbandry work for a landowner, fell down. Deprived of his horse's aid, the peasant could do nothing; he was lost! With but a single ruble in his possession, he set out to a horse fair at Kukerversky Inn, which stood twenty miles away; there he hoped to exchange his ruble for a horse. He took with him the end-crust of a loaf, some sprats and a bottle of kvass and, halfway, sat down to eat.

A gentleman who was riding along the road upon a fine horse came up level with the peasant and stopped; then he entered into conversation and, learning the object of the peasant's journey, offered to sell his horse and whip for a ruble, saying, "Never feed this horse, but flog him frequently with the whip; the more you punish him the better will he thrive and the harder will he work." Next the gentleman vanished.

The astonished peasant took the horse and, riding off, from time to time used the whip. The horse worked excellently during some years, and without food.

On the evening of Christmas Day, when the peasant and his family sat at table feasting, the horse thrust his muzzle through the open door into the room. It seemed to the master of the house that there were tears in the horse's intelligent eyes, and, pitying his faithful assistant, he took a piece of bread from the table and gave it to the poor creature.

Suddenly the horse became transformed into a man, and stood before the astounded peasant as his old landlord, who had died several years previously. "Know, March," said he, "that the gentleman who sold you the horse was the Fiend himself; he tortures thus many who on earth have not feared God and have wrought evil. In my lifetime I was not concerned with the salvation of my soul and served Mammon. I did not fear to do injustice, and even rejoiced when I defrauded. I tormented many peasants and in their hearts they desired my death, which came and consigned me to the Fiend's claws. I know that I shall never escape from him. Although I stand before you in the form of your old lord, my Fiend-master will soon arrive and lead me to a place where live many unhappy condemned souls." Having spoken thus, the lord wept bitterly.

Suddenly a noise and cracking sounded in the stable, and the same gentleman presented himself as had sold the horse to the peasant. He said to the latter, "Not having obeyed me and having given the horse food, March, you will now be deprived of his services."

The gentleman seized the whip and struck the landlord several times on the back. The landlord again became a horse, the gentleman jumped on him, flogged him with the whip, and vanished like a whirlwind. Thus the Fiend had forced the unhappy landlord to serve the peasant during three years.

The Tinker and the Ghost
Spain

On the wide plain not far from the city of Toledo there once stood a great grey castle. For many years before this story begins no one had dwelt there, because the castle was haunted. There was no living soul within its walls, and yet on almost every night in the year a thin, sad voice moaned and wept and wailed through the huge, empty rooms. And on All Hallow's Eve a ghostly light appeared in the chimney, a light that flared and died and flared again against the dark sky.

Learned doctors and brave adventurers had tried to exorcise the ghost. And the next morning they had been found in the great hall of the castle, sitting lifeless before the empty fireplace.

Now one day in late October there came to the little village that nestled around the castle walls a brave and jolly tinker whose name was Esteban. And while he sat in the marketplace mending the pots and pans the good wives told him about the haunted castle. It was All Hallows' Eve, they said, and if he would wait until nightfall he could see the strange, ghostly light flare up from the chimney. He might, if he dared go near enough, hear the thin, sad voice echo through the silent rooms.

"If I dare!" Esteban repeated scornfully." You must know, good wives, that I—Esteban—fear nothing, neither ghost nor human. I will gladly sleep in the castle tonight, and keep this dismal spirit company."

The good wives looked at him in amazement. Did Esteban know that if he succeeded in banishing the ghost the owner of the castle would give him a thousand gold *reales*?

Esteban chuckled. If that was how matters stood, he would go to the castle at nightfall and do his best to get rid of the thing that haunted it. But he was a man who liked plenty to eat and drink and a fire to keep him company. They must bring to him a load of faggots, a side of bacon, a flask of wine, a dozen fresh eggs and a frying pan. This the good wives gladly did. And as the dusk fell, Esteban loaded these things on the donkey's back and set out for the castle. And you may be very sure that not one of the village people went very far along the way with him!

It was a dark night with a chill wind blowing and a hint of rain in the air. Esteban unsaddled his donkey and set him to graze on the short grass of the deserted courtyard. Then he carried his food and his faggots into the great hall. It was dark as pitch there. Bats beat their soft wings in his face and the air felt cold and musty. He lost no time in piling some of his faggots in one corner of the huge stone fireplace and in lighting them. As the red and golden flames leaped up the chimney Esteban rubbed his hands. Then he settled himself comfortably on the hearth.

"*That* is the thing to keep off both cold and fear," he said.

Carefully slicing some bacon he laid it in the pan and set it over the flames. How good it smelled! And how cheerful the sound of its crisp sizzling!

He had just lifted his flask to take a deep drink of the good wine when down the chimney there came a voice—a thin, sad voice—and "*Oh me!*" it wailed, "*Oh me! Oh me!*"

Esteban swallowed the wine and set the flask carefully down beside him.

"Not a very cheerful greeting, my friend," he said, as he moved the bacon on the pan so that it should be equally brown in all its parts. "But bearable to a man who is used to the braying of his donkey."

And "*Oh me!*" sobbed the voice, "*Oh me! Oh me!*"

Esteban lifted the bacon carefully from the hot fat and laid it on a bit of brown paper to drain. Then he broke an egg into the frying pan. As he gently shook the pan so that the edges of his egg should be crisp and brown and the yolk soft, the voice came again. Only this time it was shrill and frightened.

"*Look out below,*" it called. "*I'm falling.*"

"All right," answered Esteban, "only don't fall into the frying pan."

With that there was a thump, and there on the hearth lay a man's leg! It was a good leg enough and it was clothed in the half of a pair of brown corduroy trousers.

Esteban ate his egg, a piece of bacon and drank again from the flask of wine. The wind howled around the castle and the rain beat against the windows.

Then, "*Look out below,*" called the voice sharply. "*I'm falling!*"

There was a thump, and on the hearth there lay a second leg, just like the first!

Esteban moved it away from the fire and piled on more faggots. Then he warmed the fat in the frying pan and broke into it a second egg.

And, *"Look out below!"* roared the voice. And now it was no longer thin, but strong and lusty. *"Look out below! I'm falling!"*

"Fall away," Esteban answered cheerfully. "Only don't spill my egg."

There was a thump, heavier than the first two, and on the hearth there lay a trunk. It was clothed in a blue shirt and a brown corduroy coat.

Esteban was eating his third egg and the last of the cooked bacon when the voice called again, and down fell first one arm and then the other.

"Now," thought Esteban, as he put the frying pan on the fire and began to cook more bacon. "Now there is only the head. I confess that I am rather curious to see the head."

And, "LOOK OUT BELOW!" thundered the voice. "I'M FALLING—FALLING!"

And down the chimney there came tumbling a head!

It was a good head enough, with thick black hair, a long black beard and dark eyes that looked a little strained and anxious. Esteban's bacon was only half cooked. Nevertheless, he removed the pan from the fire and laid it on the hearth. And it is a good thing that he did, because before his eyes the parts of the body joined together, and a living man—or his ghost—stood before him! And *that* was a sight that might have startled Esteban into burning his fingers with the bacon fat.

"Good evening," said Esteban. "Will you have an egg and a bit of bacon?"

"No, I want no food," the ghost answered. "But I will tell you this, right here and now. You are the only man, out of all those who have come to the castle, to stay here until I could get my body together again. The others died of sheer fright before I was half finished."

"That is because they did not have sense enough to bring food and fire with them," Esteban replied coolly. And he turned back to his frying pan.

"Wait a minute!" pleaded the ghost. "If you will help me a bit more, you will save my soul and get me into the Kingdom of Heaven. Out in the courtyard, under a cypress tree, there are buried three bags—one of copper coins, one of silver coins, and one of gold coins. I stole then from some thieves and brought them here to the castle to hide. But no sooner did I have them buried than the thieves overtook me, murdered me and cut my body into pieces. But they did not find the coins. Now you come with me and dig them up. Give the copper coins to the Church, the silver coins to the poor, and keep the gold coins for yourself. Then I will have expiated my sins and can go to the Kingdom of Heaven."

This suited Esteban. So he went out into the courtyard with the ghost. And you should have heard how the donkey brayed when he saw them!

When they reached the cypress tree in a corner of the courtyard: "Dig," said the ghost.

"Dig yourself," answered Esteban.

So the ghost dug, and after a time the three bags of money appeared.

"Now will you promise to do just what I asked you to do?" asked the ghost.

"Yes, I promise," Esteban answered.

"Then," said the ghost, "strip my garments from me."

This Esteban did, and instantly the ghost disappeared, leaving his clothes lying there on the short grass of the courtyard. It went straight up to Heaven and knocked on the gate. Saint Peter opened it, and when the spirit explained that he had expiated his sins, gave him a cordial welcome.

Esteban carried the coins into the great hall of the castle, fried and ate another egg and then went peacefully to sleep before the fire.

The next morning when the village people came to carry away Esteban's body, they found him making an omelette out of the last of the fresh eggs.

"Are you alive?" they gasped.

"I am," Esteban answered. "And the food and the faggots lasted through very nicely. Now I will go the owner of the castle and collect my thousand gold *reales*. The ghost has gone for good and all. You will find his clothes lying out in the courtyard."

And before their astonished eyes he loaded the bags of coins on the donkey's back and departed.

First he collected the thousand gold *reales* from the grateful lord of the castle. Then he returned to Toledo, gave the copper coins to the *cura* of his church, and faithfully distributed the silver ones among the poor. And on the thousand *reales* and the golden coins he lived in idleness and great contentment for many years.

Hold Him, Tabb
Afro-American

A number of wagons were traveling together one afternoon in December. It was extremely cold, and about the middle of the afternoon it began to snow. They soon came to an abandoned settlement by the roadside, and decided it would be a good place to camp out of the storm, as there were stalls for their horses and an old dwelling-house in which they themselves could stay.

When they had nearly finished unhooking their horses a man came along and said that he was the owner of the place, and that the men were welcome to stay there as long as they wanted to, but that the house was haunted, and not a single person had stayed in it alive for twenty-five years. On hearing this the men immediately moved their camp to a body of woods about one-half mile further up the road. One of them, whose name was Tabb, and who was braver than the rest, said that he was not afraid of haunts, and that he did not mean to take himself and horses into the woods to perish in the snow, but that he'd stay where he was.

So Tabb stayed in the house. He built a big fire, cooked and ate his supper, and rested well through the night without being disturbed. About daybreak he awoke and said, "What fools those other fellows are to have stayed in the woods when they might have stayed in here, and been as warm as I am!"

Just as he had finished speaking he looked up to the ceiling, and there was a large man dressed in white clothes just stretched out under the ceiling and sticking up to it. Before he could get from under the man, the man fell right down upon him, and then commenced a great tussle between Tabb and the man. They made so much noise that the men in the woods heard it and ran to see what was going on.

When they looked in at the window and saw the struggle, first Tabb was on top and then the other man. One of them cried, "Hold him, Tabb, hold him!"

"You can bet your soul I got him!" said Tabb.

Soon the man got Tabb out of the window.

"Hold him, Tabb, hold him!" one of the men shouted.

"You can bet your life I got him!" came from Tabb.

Soon the man got Tabb upon the roof of the house.

"Hold him, Tabb, hold him!" said one of the men.

"You can bet your boots I got him!" answered Tabb.

Finally the man got Tabb up off the roof into the air.

"Hold him, Tabb, hold him!" shouted one of the men.

"I got him and he got me, too!" said Tabb.

The man, who was a ghost, carried Tabb straight up into the air until they were both out of sight. Nothing was ever seen of him again.

DRINKING COMPANIONS
China

A fisherman named Hsü made his home outside the north gate of Tzu, a township in present-day Shantung. Every night he took along some wine to the riverside to drink while he fished. And each time, he poured a little offering on the ground "so that the spirits of those who have drowned in the river may have some wine too." When other fishermen had caught nothing, Hsü usually went home with a basketful.

One evening as Hsü was tippling by himself, a young man approached him and paced back and forth. Hsü offered him a drink and grandly shared his winejar. It was a disappointing night, however, for he failed to catch a single fish. "Let me go downstream and drive them up for you," said the young man, who rose and departed in a manner that seemed to be airborne. He returned shortly and said, "A number of fish will be arriving." And indeed, Hsü could hear a chorus of splashing as the approaching fish struck at insects. He took up his net and got several, each a foot long.

Delighted, Hsü thanked the young man and started home. Then he turned to offer his benefactor some fish, but the young man declined, saying, "I have often enjoyed your delicious brew. For my trifling assistance it's not worth speaking of reciprocity. In fact, if you wouldn't refuse my company, I'd like to make a custom of it."

"We have spent only an evening together," answered Hsü. "What do you mean by 'often enjoyed?' But it would be a pleasure if you kept visiting me, though I'm afraid I don't have anything to repay your kindness." Then he asked the young man his name.

"I am a Wang," was the reply, "but have no given name. You could call me 'Liu-lang,' or 'Sixth-born,' when we meet." And thus they parted.

Next day Hsü sold his fish and bought more wine. In the evening the young man was already there when Hsü arrived at the riverbank, so they had the pleasure of drinking together again. And again after several rounds the young man suddenly whisked away to drive the fish for Hsü.

Things went on agreeably like this for half a year when out of the blue Liu-lang announced to Hsü, "Ever since I had the honor of your acquaintance, we have been closer than closest kin. But the day of parting has come." His voice was filled with sadness.

Hsü was surprised and asked why. The young man started to speak and then stopped several times until he said at last, "Close as we are, the reason may shock you. But now that we are to part, there's no harm in telling you the plain truth: I'm a ghost, one with a weakness for wine. I died by drowning when I was drunk, and I have been here several years. The reason you always caught more fish than anyone else is that I was secretly driving them toward you in thanks for your libations. But tomorrow my term of karma ends, and a replacement for me will be coming. I'm to be reborn into another life on earth. This evening is all that remains for us to share, and it is hard not to feel sad."

Hsü was frightened at first, but they had been close friends for so long that his fear abated. He sighed deeply over the news, poured a drink, and said, "Liu-lang, drink this up and don't despair. If our ways must part, that's reason enough for regret; but if your karmic lot is fulfilled and your term of suffering relieved, that's cause for congratulation, not sorrow." And together they shared a deep swig of wine. "Who will replace you?" asked Hsü.

"You'll see from the riverbank. At high noon a woman will drown as she crosses the river. That will be the one!" As the roosters in the hamlet called forth the dawn, the two drinkers parted, shedding tears.

The next day Hsü watched expectantly from the edge of the river. A woman came carrying a baby in her arms. As she reached the river, she fell. She tossed the child to shore, then began crying and flailing her hands and feet. She surfaced and sank several times until she pulled herself out, streaming water. Then she rested a little while, took her child in her arms, and left.

When the woman was sinking, Hsü could not bear it and wished he could rush to her rescue. He held back only because he remembered that she was to replace Liu-lang. But when the woman got herself out he began to doubt what Liu-lang had told him.

At dusk Hsü went fishing in the usual spot. Again his friend came and said to him, "Now we are together again and need not speak of parting for the time being." When Hsü asked why, Liu-lang replied, "The woman had already taken my place, but I had pity for the child in her arms. Two should not be lost for one, and so I spared them. When I will be replaced is not known, and so it seems that the brotherhood between us shall continue."

Hsü sighed with deep feeling. "Such a humane heart should be seen by the Highest of Heaven." And so they had the pleasure of each other's company as before.

Several days later, however, Liu-lang came to say goodbye again. Hsü thought he had found another replacement, but Liu-lang said, "No, my compassionate thought for the drowning woman actually reached to Heaven, and I have been rewarded with a position as local deity in Wu township of Chauyüan county. I assume office tomorrow. Please remember our friendship and visit me; don't worry about the length or difficulty of the journey."

"What a comfort to have someone as upright as you for a deity," said Hsü, offering his congratulations. "But no road connects men and gods. Even if the distance did not daunt me, how could I manage to go?"

"Simply go; don't think about it," replied the young man. After repeating the invitation, he left.

Hsü went home to put his things in order and set out at once, though his wife mocked him. "You're going hundreds of miles? Even if this place exists, I don't think you can hold a conversation with a clay idol!" she sneered. Hsü paid no attention. He started off and eventually arrived in Chauyüan county, where he learned that there really was a Wu township. On his way there he stopped at a hostel and asked for directions to the temple. The host said with an air of pleasant surprise, "By any chance is our guest's surname Hsü?"

"Yes, how did you know?"

The host left abruptly without making a reply. Presently a mixed throng approached and circled Hsü like a wall; men carried their babies, women peeped around their doors. The crowd announced to an amazed Hsü, "Several nights ago we had a dream in which our deity said that a friend named Hsü would be coming and that we should help him out with his traveling expenses. We have been respectfully awaiting you." Marveling at this reception, Hsü went to sacrifice at the temple.

"Since we parted," he prayed, "my thoughts have dwelled on you night and day. I have come far to keep our agreement, and I am both favored and deeply moved by the sign you gave the local people. But I am embarrassed to have come without a fitting gift. All I brought was a flask of wine. If it is acceptable, let us drink as we used to on the riverbank." His prayer done, Hsü burned paper money. Shortly he saw a wind arise behind the shrine. The smoke swirled around for a time and then disappeared.

That night Liu-lang, looking altogether different now that he was capped and garbed in finery, entered Hsü's dreams. Expressing his appreciation, Liu-lang said, "For you to come so far to see me moves me to tears, but I am unable to meet you directly because I hold such a trivial position. It saddens me to be so near to the living and yet so far. The people here have some meager presents for you as a token of our past association. Whenever you are to return home, I shall see you off myself.

Hsü remained in Wu township a few more days before preparing to leave. The people of Wu tried to keep him longer, making earnest appeals and inviting him to daylong feasts with different hosts. But Hsü was set on returning home. The people outdid themselves in generosity, and before the morning passed his bags were filled with gifts. The grey-haired and the young gathered to see him out of the village. And a whirlwind followed him some three or four miles farther. Hsü bowed again and again. "Take care of yourself, Liu-lang," he said. "Don't bother coming so far. With your humane and loving heart, you can surely bring good fortune to this township without advice from old friends." The wind swirled around for a time and then was gone. The villagers, exclaiming in wonder at these events, also went to their homes.

When Hsü arrived back in his own village, his family's circumstances had improved so much that he did not return to fishing. Later he saw people from Chauyüan county who told him that the deity was working miracles and had become widely known.

The Recorder of Things Strange says: To attain the heights of ambition without forgetting the friends one made when poor and lowly—that is what made Wang Liu-lang a god! Nowadays, when do the high and noble in their carriages recognize those still wearing a bamboo hat?

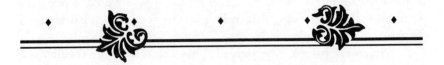

THE OSTLER AND THE GRAVE ROBBERS
Scotland

One dark night, at a wayside inn, a pony and trap drove up, and stopped. There was two men and a woman. The woman was setting between the two men, with a hood on her head, and her face was covered with a veil.

The men jumped out, and left the woman setting. They went into the pub for a drink.

The ostlers was busy in the stable, and one looked out, and when he saw the woman setting by herself, he went up to the trap, and said to the woman, "It's a cauld night the night!" But he got no answer. He spoke again, but still no answer. He had a close look at her, and he saw it was a corpse.

He got up and got hold of her, and carried her into the stable, and took off her disguise, and put it on himself. Then he got into the trap in the woman's place, and was setting bolt upright and just like the woman when the men came out, and jumped in, one at either side. They just thought it was the dead woman.

After traveling some distance along the road, one of the men said to the other, "D'ye ken that body's getting warm?"

The other said, "I was just thinking the same."

Then the ostler spoke up and said, "If ye had been as lang in Hell as me, ye'd be warm too!"

That was enough. The men jumped out and ran for their life. The ostler saw no more of them; he just turned the pony and trap, and took it back to the inn.

It was now his property, as he knew they dare not come back to claim it.

DEATH
and the
WORLD'S
END

According to tradition, the Roman emperors rode in their chariots with a slave behind holding the laurel crown over the royal head and whispering, "Remember, thou art mortal" in the royal ear. Just so, these final stories are the folk way of whispering in our own ears about mortality.

There are many explanations in folklore of how death came into the world in the first place. Often it is by mistake—the woman who "didn't know anything yet, because she had been walking on earth for just a few hours" in the Blackfoot tale "Woman Chooses Death." There are also many reminders of mortality and of why death is necessary: the Italian "Jump into My Sack" and its variant from Turkey, "Youth Without Age and Life Without Death," are prime examples.

Of course, the fact of death doesn't stop people from wanting to cheat death, But no one does forever, as the boy finds out in "Godfather Death" and as the miser finds out in the Russian" Death of a Miser."

And after death, what then? There are so many different heavens—the Isles of the Blessed, Valhalla, Tir-Nan-Og—and varieties of hell that only a sampling can be given here.

But this section ends—and the book ends—with a story about the end of the world and what keeps Armageddon at bay. It is, according to the White River Sioux, the task of an old, old lady, "so old that her face looks like a shriveled-up walnut." And if she reminds us somewhat of the Greek Fates or of Penelope at her loom or the master weaver creating all the patterns of the world, that is how it should be. Stories lean on stories, and what the old woman is weaving, after all, is Story. It is the story of the world. And when that story is finally at an end, so too ends the world.

THE DURATION OF LIFE
Germany

When God created the world and was about to fix the length of each creature's life, the ass came and asked, "Lord, how long shall I live?"

"Thirty years," replied God. "Does that content you?"

"Ah, Lord," answered the ass, "that is a long time. Think of my painful existence! To carry heavy burdens from morning to night, to drag sacks of corn to the mill that others may eat bread, to be cheered and refreshed with nothing but blows and kicks. Relieve me of a portion of this long time." Then God had pity on him and relieved him of eighteen years, and the ass went away comforted.

Then the dog appeared. "How long would you like to live?" said God to him. "Thirty years are too many for the ass, but you will be satisfied with that."

"Lord," answered the dog, "is that Thy will? Consider how I shall have to run, my feet will never hold out so long, and when I have once lost my voice for barking, and my teeth for biting, what will be left for me to do but run from one corner to another and growl?" God saw was that he was right, and released him from twelve years of life.

Then came the monkey. "You will certainly live thirty years willingly?" said the Lord to him. "You have no need to work as the ass and the dog have to, and will always enjoy yourself."

"Ah, Lord," he answered, "it may seem as if that were the case, but it is quite different. When it rains millet porridge I have no spoon. I am always to play merry pranks, and make faces which force people to laugh, and if they give me an apple, and I bite into it, why, it is sour! How often sadness hides itself behind mirth! I shall never be able to hold out for thirty years." God was gracious and took off ten.

At last man appeared, joyous, healthy and vigorous, and begged God to appoint his time for him.

"Thirty years shall you live," said the Lord. "Is that enough for you?"

"What a short time," cried man, "when I have built my house

• 448 •

and my fire burns on my own hearth; when I have planted trees which blossom and bear fruit, and am just intending to enjoy my life, I am to die! O Lord, lengthen my time."

"I will add to it the ass's eighteen years," said God.

"That is not enough," replied the man.

"You shall also have the dog's twelve years."

"Still too little!"

"Well, then," said God, "I will give you the monkey's ten years also, but more you shall not have." The man went away, but was not satisfied.

So man lives seventy years. The first thirty are his human years, which are soon gone; then is he healthy, merry, works with pleasure, and is glad of his life. Then follow the ass's eighteen years, when one burden after another is laid on him: he has to carry the corn which feeds others, and blows and kicks are the reward of his faithful services. Then come the dog's twelve years, when he lies in the corner, and growls and has no longer any teeth to bite with, and when this time is over the monkey's ten years form the end. Then man is weak-headed and foolish, does silly things, and becomes the jest of children.

WOMAN CHOOSES DEATH
American Indian (Blackfoot)

Old Man decided that something was missing in the world he had made. He thought it would be a good thing to create a woman and a child. He didn't quite know how they should look, but he took some clay and mud and for four days tried out different shapes. At first he didn't like the looks of the beings he formed. On the fourth day, however, he shaped a woman in a pleasing form, round and nice, with everything in front and back, above and below, just right.

"This is good," Old Man said, "this the kind of woman I like to have in my world." Then he made a little child resembling the woman. "Well," said Old Man, "this is just what I wanted, but they're not alive yet."

Old Man covered them up for four days. On the first day he looked under the cover and saw a faint trembling. On the second day the figures could raise their heads. On the third day they moved their arms and legs. "Soon they will be ready," said Old Man. And on the fourth day he looked underneath the cover and saw his figures crawling around. "They're ready now to walk upon my world," thought Old Man. He took the cover off and told the woman and the child, "Walk upright like human beings." The woman and the child stood up. They began to walk, and they were perfect.

They followed Old Man down to the river, where he gave them the power of speech. At once the woman asked, "What is that state we are in, walking, moving, breathing, eating?"

"That is life," said Old Man. "Before, you were just lumps of mud. Now, you live."

"When we were lumps of mud, were we alive then?" asked the woman.

"No, said Old Man, "you were not alive."

"What do you call the state we were in then?" asked the woman.

"It is called death," answered Old Man. "When you are not alive, then you are dead."

"Will we be alive always?" asked the woman. "Will we go on living forever, or shall we be dead again at some time?"

Old Man pondered. He said, "I didn't think about that at all. Let's decide it right now. Here's a buffalo chip. If it floats, then people will die and come back to life four days later."

"No," said the woman. "This buffalo chip will dissolve in the water. I'll throw in this stone. If it floats, we'll live forever and there will be no death. If it sinks, then we'll die." The woman didn't know anything yet, because she had been walking on earth for just a few hours. She didn't know about stones and water, so she threw the stone into the river and it sank.

"You made a choice there," said Old Man. "Now nothing can be done about it. Now people will die."

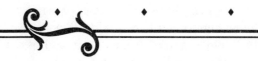

Jump into My Sack
Italy

Many, many years ago, in the barren mountains of Niolo, lived a father with twelve sons. A famine was raging, and the father said, "My sons, I have no more bread to give you. Go out into the world, where you will certainly fare better than here at home."

The eleven older boys were getting ready to leave, when the twelfth and youngest, who was lame, started weeping. "And what will a cripple like me do to earn his bread?"

"My child," said his father, "don't cry. Go with your brothers, and what they earn will be yours as well."

So the twelve promised to stay together always and departed. They walked a whole day, then a second, and the little lame boy fell constantly behind. On the third day, the oldest brother said, "Our little brother Francis, who's always lagging, is nothing but a nuisance! Let's walk off and leave him on the road. That will be best for him too, for some kind-hearted soul will come along and take pity on him."

So they stopped no more to wait for him to catch up, but walked on, asking alms of everyone they met, all the way to Bonifacio.

In Bonifacio they saw a boat moored at the dock. "What if we climbed in and sailed to Sardinia?" said the oldest boy. "Maybe there's less hunger there than in our land."

The brothers got into the boat and set sail. When they were halfway across the straits, a fierce storm arose and the boat was dashed to pieces on the reefs, and all eleven brothers drowned.

Meanwhile the little cripple Francis, exhausted and frantic when he missed his brothers, screamed and cried and then fell asleep by the roadside. The fairy guardian of that particular spot had seen and heard everything from a treetop. As soon as Francis was asleep, she came down the tree, picked certain special herbs, and prepared a plaster, which she smoothed on the lame leg; immediately the leg became sound. Then she disguised herself as a poor little old woman and sat down on a bundle of firewood to wait for Francis to wake up.

Francis awakened, got up, prepared to limp off, and then realized he was no longer lame but could walk like everyone else. He saw the little old woman sitting there, and asked, "Madam, have you by chance seen a doctor around here?"

"A doctor? What do you want with a doctor?"

"I want to thank him. A great doctor must certainly have come by while I was sleeping and cured my lame leg."

"I am the one who cured your lame leg," replied the little old woman, "since I know all about herbs, including the one that heals lame legs."

As pleased as Punch, Francis threw his arms around the little old woman and kissed her on both cheeks. "How can I thank you, ma'am? Here, let me carry your bundle of wood for you."

He bent over to pick up the bundle, but when he stood up, he faced not the old woman, but the most beautiful maiden imaginable, all radiant with diamonds and blond hair down to her waist; she wore a deep blue dress embroidered with gold, and two stars of precious stones sparkled on her ankle-boots. Dumbfounded, Francis fell at the fairy's feet.

"Get up," she said. "I am well aware that you are grateful, and I shall help you. Make two wishes, and I will grant them at once. I am the queen of the fairies of Lake Creno, mind you."

The boy thought a bit, then replied, "I desire a sack that will suck in whatever I name."

"And just such a sack shall you have. Now make one more wish."

"I desire a stick that will do whatever I command."

"And just such a stick shall you have," replied the fairy, and vanished. At Francis's feet lay a sack and a stick.

Overjoyed, the boy decided to try them out. Being hungry, he cried, "A roasted partridge into my sack!" *Zoom!* A partridge fully roasted flew into the sack. "Along with bread!" *Zoom!* A loaf of bread came sailing into the sack. "Also a bottle of wine!" *Zoom!* There was the bottle of wine. Francis ate a first-rate meal.

Then he set out again, limping no longer, and the next day he found himself in Mariana, where the most famous gamblers of Corsica and the Continent were meeting. Francis didn't have a cent to his name, so he ordered, "One hundred thousand crowns into my sack!" and the sack filled with crowns. The news spread like wildfire through Mariana that the fabulously wealthy prince of Santo Francesco had arrived.

At that particular time, mind you, the Devil was especially partial to the city of Mariana. Disguised as a handsome young man, he beat everybody at cards, and when the players ran out of money, he would purchase their souls. Hearing of this rich foreigner who went by the name of prince of Santo Francesco, the Devil in disguise approached him without delay. "Noble prince, pardon my boldness in coming to you, but your fame as a gambler is so great that I couldn't resist calling on you."

"You put me to shame," replied Francis. "To tell the truth, I don't know how to play any game at all, nor have I ever had a deck of cards in my hand. However, I would be happy to play a hand with you, just for the sake of learning the game, and I'm sure that with you as a teacher I'll be an expert in no time."

The Devil was so gratified by the visit that upon taking leave and bowing goodbye, he negligently stretched out a leg and showed his cloven hoof. "Oh, me!" said Francis to himself. "So this is old Satan himself who has honored me with a visit. Very well, he will meet his match." Once more alone, he commanded of the sack a fine dinner.

The next day Francis went to the casino. There was a great turmoil, with all the people crowded around one particular spot. Francis pushed through and saw, on the ground, the body of a young man with a blood-stained chest. "He was a gambler," someone explained, "who lost his entire fortune and thrust a dagger into his heart, not a minute ago."

All the gamblers were sad-faced. But one, noted Francis, stood in their midst laughing up his sleeve; it was the Devil who had paid Francis a visit.

"Quick!" said the Devil, "Let's take this unfortunate man out, and get on with the game!" And they all picked up their cards once more.

Francis, who didn't even know how to hold the cards in his hand, lost everything he had with him that day. By the second day he knew a little bit about the game, but lost still more than the day before. By the third day he was an expert, and lost so much that everyone was sure he was ruined. But the loss did not trouble him in the least, since there was his sack he could command and then find inside all the money he needed.

He lost so much that the Devil thought to himself, He might have been the richest man in existence to start with, but he's surely about to end up now with nothing to his name. "Noble prince," he said, taking him aside, "I can't tell you how sorry I am over the misfortune that has befallen you. But I have good news for you: heed my words and you will recover half of what you lost!"

"How?"

The Devil looked around, then whispered, "Sell me your soul!"

"Ah!" cried Francis. "So that's your advice to me, Satan? Go on, jump into my sack!"

The Devil smirked and aimed to flee, but there was no escape: he flew head-first into the yawning sack, which Francis closed, then addressed the stick, "Now pound him for all you're worth!"

Blows rained fast and furious. Inside, the Devil writhed, cried, cursed. "Let me out! Let me out! Stop, or you'll kill me!"

"Really? You'll give up the ghost? Would that be a loss, do you think?" And the stick went right on beating him.

After three hours of that shower, Francis spoke. "That will do, at least for today."

"What will you take in return for setting me free?" asked the Devil in a weak voice.

"Listen carefully: if you want your freedom back, you must bring back to life at once every one of those poor souls who killed themselves in the casino because of you!"

"It's a bargain!" replied the Devil.

"Come on out, then. But remember, I can catch you again any time I feel like it."

The Devil dared not go back on his word. He disappeared underground and, in almost no time, up came a throng of young men pale of face and with feverish eyes. "My friends," said Francis, "you ruined yourselves gambling, and the only way out was to kill yourselves. I was able to have you brought back this time, but I might not be able to do so another time. Will you promise me to gamble no more?"

"Yes, yes, we promise!"

"Fine! Here are a thousand crowns for each of you. Go in peace, and earn your bread honestly."

Overjoyed, the revived youths departed, some returning to families in mourning, others striking out on their own, their past misdeeds having been the death of their parents.

Francis, too, thought of his old father. He set out for his village but, along the way, met a boy wringing his hands in despair.

"How now, young man? Do you make wry faces for sale?" asked Francis, in high spirits. "How much are they by the dozen?"

"I don't feel like laughing, sir," replied the boy.

"What's the matter?"

"My father's a woodcutter and the sole support of our family. This morning he fell out of a chestnut tree and broke his arm. I ran into town for the doctor but he knows we are poor and refused to come."

"Is that all that's worrying you? Set your mind at rest. I'll take care of things."

"You're a doctor?"

"No, but I'll make that one come. What is his name?"

"Doctor Pancrazio."

"Fine! Doctor Pancrazio, jump into my sack!"

Into the sack, head-first, went a doctor with all his instruments.

"Stick, pound him for all you're worth!" And the stick began its dance. "Help! Mercy!"

"Do you promise to cure the woodcutter free of charge?"

"I promise whatever you ask."

"Get out of the sack, then." And the doctor ran to the woodcutter's bedside.

Francis continued on his way and, in a few days, came to his village, where even greater hunger now raged than before. By constantly repeating, "Into my sack a roasted chicken, a bottle of wine," Francis managed to provision an inn where all could go and eat their fill without paying a penny.

He did this for as long as the famine lasted. But he stopped, once times of plenty returned, so as not to encourage laziness.

Do you think he was happy, though? Of course not! He was sad without any news of his eleven brothers. He had long since forgiven them for running off and leaving him, a helpless cripple. He tried saying, "Brother John, jump into my sack!"

Something stirred inside the sack. Francis opened it and found a heap of bones.

"Brother Paul, jump into my sack!"

Another heap of bones.

"Brother Peter, jump into my sack!" Calling them all, up to the eleventh, he found each time, alas, only a little pile of bones half gnawed in two. There was no doubt about it: his brothers had all died together.

Francis was sad. His father also died, leaving him all alone. Then it was his turn to grow old.

His last remaining desire before dying was to see again the fairy of Lake Creno who had made him so properous. He therefore set out and reached the place where he had first met her. He waited and waited, but the fairy did not come. "Where are you, good queen? Please appear one more time! I can't die until I've seen you again!"

Night had fallen and there was still no sign of the fairy. Instead, here came Death down the road. In one hand she held a black banner and, in the other, her scythe. She approached Francis, saying, "Well, old man, are you not yet weary of life? Haven't you been over enough hills and dales? Isn't it time you did as everyone else and came along with me?"

"O Death," replied Francis. "Bless you! Yes, I have seen enough of the world and everything in it. I have had my fill of everything. But before coming with you, I must first bid someone farewell. Allow me one more day."

"Say your prayers, if you don't want to die like a heathen, and hurry after me."

"Please, wait until the cock crows in the morning."

"No."

"Just one hour more, then?"

"Not even one minute more."

"Since you are so cruel, then, jump into my sack!"

Death shuddered, all her bones rattled, but she had no choice but jump into the sack. In the same instant appeared the queen of the fairies, as radiant and youthful as the first time. "Fairy," said Francis, "I thank you!" Then he addressed Death: "Jump out of the sack and attend to me."

"You have never abused the power I gave you, Francis," said the fairy. "Your sack and your stick have always been put to good use. I shall reward you, if you tell me what you would like."

"I have no more desires."

"Would you like to be a chieftain?"

"No."

"Would you like to be king?"

"I wish nothing more."

"Now that you're an old man, would you like health and youth again?"

"I have seen you, and I'm content to die."

"Farewell, Francis. But first burn the sack and the stick." And the fairy vanished.

The good Francis built a big fire, warmed his frozen limbs briefly, then threw the sack and the stick into the flames, so that no one could put them to evil use.

Death was hiding behind a bush. "Cockadoodledo! Cockadoodledo!" crowed the first cock.

Francis did not hear. Age had made him deaf.

"There's the cock crowing!" announced Death, and struck the old man with her scythe. Then she vanished, bearing his mortal remains.

YOUTH WITHOUT AGE AND
LIFE WITHOUT DEATH
Turkey

Once upon a time there was a great emperor and an empress. Both were young and beautiful, and as they would fain have been blessed with offspring they went to all the wise men and all the wise women and bade them read the stars to see if they would have children or not, but all in vain. At last the emperor heard that in a certain village, hard by, dwelt a wiser old man than all the rest, so he sent and commanded him to appear at court. But the wise old man sent the messengers back with the answer that those who needed him must come to him. So the emperor and the empress set out, with their lords and their ladies, and their servants and their soldiers, and came to the house of the wise old man. And when the old man saw them coming from afar he went out to meet them.

"Welcome," cried he. "But I tell thee, O emperor! that the wish of thy heart will only work thee woe."

"I came not hither to take counsel of thee," replied the emperor, "but to know if thou hast herbs by eating whereof we may get us children."

"Such herbs have I," replied the old man. "But ye will have but one child, and him ye will not be able to keep, though he be never so nice and charming."

So when the emperor and the empress had gotten the wondrous herbs, they returned joyfully back to their palace, and a few days afterward the empress became a mother. At his birth the child screamed so loudly that all the enchantments of the magicians could not make him silent. Then the emperor began to promise him everything in the wide world, but even this would not quiet him.

"Be silent, my heart's darling," he said, "and I will give thee all the kingdoms east of the sun and west of the moon! Be silent, my son, and I will give thee a consort more lovely than the fairy queen herself." Then at last, when he perceived that the child still kept on screaming, he said, "Silence, my son, and I will give thee Youth Without Age, and Life Without Death!"

Then the child ceased to cry and all the courtiers beat the drums and blew the trumpets, and there was great joy in the whole realm for many days.

The older the child grew the more pensive and melancholy he became. He went to school, and to the wise men, and there was no learning and wisdom that he did not make his own, so the the emperor, his father, died and came to life again for sheer joy. And the whole realm was proud that it was going to have so wise and goodly an emperor, and all men looked up to him as to a second Solomon. But one day, when the child had already completed his fifteenth year, and the emperor and all his lords and great men were at table diverting themselves, the fair young prince arose and said, "Father, the time has now come when thou must give me what thou didst promise me at my birth!"

At these words the emperor was sorely troubled. "Nay, but, my son," said he, "how can I give thee a thing which the world has never heard of? If I did promise it to thee, it was but to make thee quiet."

"Then, O my father, if thou canst not give it to me, I must needs go forth into the world, and seek until I find that fair thing for which I was born."

Then the emperor and his nobles all fell down on their knees and besought him not to leave the empire. "For," said the nobles, "thy father is now growing old, and we would place thee on the throne, and give thee to wife the most beautiful empress under the sun." But they were unable to turn him from his purpose, for he was as steadfast as a rock, so at last his father gave him leave to go forth into the wide world to find what he sought.

Then Boy Beautiful went into his father's stables, where were the most beautiful chargers in the whole empire, that he might choose one from among them; but no sooner had he laid his hand on one of them than it fell to the ground trembling, and so it was with all the other stately chargers. At last, just as he was about to leave the stable in despair, he cast his eye over it once more, and there in one corner he beheld a poor knacker, all weak, spavined, and covered with boils and sores. Up to it he went, and laid his hand upon its tail, and then the horse turned its head and said to him, "What are thy commands, my master? God be praised who hath had mercy upon me and sent a warrior to lay his hand over me!"

Then the horse shook itself and became straight in the legs again, and Boy Beautiful asked him what he should do next.

"In order that thou mayest attain thy heart's desire," said the horse, "ask thy father for the sword and lance, the bow, quiver, and armor which he himself wore when he was a youth. But thou must comb and curry me with thine own hand six weeks, and give me barley to eat cooked in milk."

So the emperor called the steward of his household, and ordered him to open all the coffers and wardrobes that his son might choose what he would; and Boy Beautiful, after searching for three days and three nights, found at last, at the bottom of an old armory, the arms and armor which his father had worn as a youth. Very rusty were these ancient weapons, but he set to work with his own hands to polish them up and rub off the rust, and at the end of six weeks they shone like mirrors. He also cherished the steed as he had been told. Grievous was the labor, but it came to an end at last.

When the good steed heard that Boy Beautiful had cleansed and polished his armor, he shook himself once more, and all his boils and sores fell off from him. There he now stood a stout horse and strong, and with four large wings growing out of his body. Then said Boy Beautiful, "We go hence in three days!"—"Long life to thee, my master!" replied the steed. "I will go wherever thou dost command."

When the third day came the emperor and all his court were full of grief. Boy Beautiful, attired as became a hero, with his sword in his hand, bounded onto his horse, took leave of the emperor and the empress, of all the great nobles and all the little nobles, of all the warriors and all the courtiers. With tears in their eyes, they besought him not to depart on this quest; but he, giving spurs to his horse, departed like a whirlwind, and after him went sumpter horses with money and provisions, and some hundreds of chosen warriors whom the emperor had ordered to accompany him on his journey.

But when he had reached a wilderness on the confines of his father's realm, Boy Beautiful took leave of the warriors, and sent them back to his father, taking of the provisions only so much as his good steed could carry. Then he pursued his way toward sunrise, and went on and on for three days and three nights till he came to an immense plain covered with the bones of many dead men. Here they stopped to rest, and the horse said to him, "Know, my master, that we are now in the domains of the witch Gheonoea, who is so evil a being that none can set a foot on her domains and live. Once she was a woman like other women, but the curse of her parents, whom she would never obey, fell like a withering blast upon her, and she became what she now is. At this moment she is with her children in the forest, but she will come speedily to seek and destroy thee. Great and terrible is she, yet fear not, but make ready thy bows and arrows, thy sword and lance, that thou mayst make use of them when the time comes."

Then they rested, and while one slept the other watched.

When the day dawned they prepared to traverse the forest. Boy Beautiful bridled and saddled his horse, drew the reins tighter than at other times, and set out. At that moment they heard a terrible racket.

Then the horse said, "Beware, my master, Gheonoea is approaching." The trees of the forest fell to this side and to that as the witch drew nigh like the tempest, but Boy Beautiful struck off one of her feet with an arrow from his bow, and he was about to shoot a second time when she cried, "Stay thy hand, Boy Beautiful, for I'll do thee no harm!" And seeing he did not believe her, she gave him a promise written in her blood.

"Look well to thy horse, Boy Beautiful," said she, "for he is a greater magician than I. But for him I should have roasted thee, but now thou must dine at my table. Know too that no mortal hath yet succeeded in reaching this spot, though some have got as far as the plain where thou didst see all the bones."

Then Gheonoea hospitably entertained Boy Beautiful as men entertain travelers. Now and then, as they conversed together, Gheonoea groaned with pain, but as soon as Boy Beautiful threw her her foot which he had shot off, she put it in its place and immediately it grew fast on to her leg again. Then, in her joy, Gheonoea feasted him for three days and begged him to take for his consort one of her three daughters, who were divinely beautiful, but he would not. Then he asked her concerning his quest. "With such valor and such a good steed as thine," she answered, "thou must needs succeed."

So after the three days were over they went on their way again. Boy Beautiful went on and on, and the way was very long, but when they had passed the boundaries of Gheonoea they came to a beauteous meadowland, but on one side the grass was fresh and bright and full of flowers, and on the other side it was burnt to cinders. Then Boy Beautiful asked the horse the meaning of the singed grass, and this is what the horse replied: "We are now in the territory of Scorpia, the sister of Gheonoea. Yet so evil-minded are these two sisters that they cannot live together in one place. The curse of their parents has blasted them, and they have become witches as thou dost see. Their hatred of each other is great, and each of them is ever striving to wrest a bit of land from the dominions of the other. And when Scorpia is angry she vomits forth fire and flame, and so when she comes to her sister's boundaries the grass of the border withers up before her. She is even more dreadful than her sister, and has, besides, three heads. But be of good cheer, my master, and tomorrow morning be ready to meet her."

At dawn next day, they were preparing to depart when they heard a roaring and a crashing noise, the like of which man has never heard since the world began.

"Be ready, my master, for now Scorpia is approaching," cried the faithful steed.

And indeed, Scorpia it was. With jaws reaching from earth to heaven, and spitting forth fire as she approached, Scorpia drew near, and the noise of her coming was like the roar of a whirlwind. But the good steed rose into the air like a dart, and Boy Beautiful shot an arrow which struck off one of the witch's three heads. He was about to lay another arrow on his bow, when Scorpia begged him to forgive her and she would do him no harm, and by way of assurance she gave him a promise written in her blood.

Then she feasted him as her sister had done before, and he gave her back her severed head, which she stuck in its place again. Then, after three days, Boy Beautiful and his faithful steed took to the road again.

When they had crossed Scorpia's borders, they went on and on without stopping till they came to a vast meadow covered with nothing but flowers, where Spring reigned eternally. Every flower was wondrously beautiful and full of a fragrance that comforted the soul, and a light zephyr ran continually over the flowery billows. Here then they sat them down to rest, and the good steed said:

"Hitherto, oh my master! we have prospered, but now a great danger awaits us, which if by the help of the Lord God we overcome, then shall we be heroes indeed. Not far from here stands the palace of Youth Without Age, and Life Without Death, but it is surrounded by a high and deep forest, and in this forest are all the savage monsters of the wide world.

"Day and night they guard it, and if a man can count the grains of sand on the seashore, then also can he count the number of these monsters. We cannot fight them; they would tear us to pieces before we were halfway through the forest. So we must try if we can to leap clean over it without touching it."

So they rested them two days to gather strength, and then the steed drew a long breath and said to Boy Beautiful, "Draw my saddle girths as tightly as thou art able, and when thou hast mounted me, hold on fast with all thy might to my mane, and press thy feet on my neck instead of on my flanks, that thou mayest not hinder me."

Boy Beautiful arose and did as his steed told him, and the next moment they were close up to the forest.

"Now is the time, my master," cried the good steed. "This wild monsters are now being fed, and are gathered together in one place. Now let us spring over!"

"I am with thee, and the Lord have mercy upon us both," replied Boy Beautiful.

Then up in the air they flew, and before them lay the palace, and so gloriously bright was it that a man could sooner look into the face of the midday sun than upon the glory of the palace of Youth Without Age, and Life Without Death. Right over the forest they flew, and just as they were about to descend at the foot of the palace staircase, the steed with the tip of his hind leg touched lightly, oh, ever so lightly! a twig on the topmost summit of the tallest tree of the forest. Instantly the whole forest was alive and alert, and the monsters began to howl so awfully that, brave as he was, the hair of Boy Beautiful stood up on his head. Hastily they descended, but had not the mistress of the palace been outside there in order to feed her kittens (for so she called the monsters), Boy Beautiful and his faithful steed would have been torn to pieces. But the mistress of the monsters, for pure joy at the sight of a human being, held the monsters back, and sent them back to their places. Fair, tall, and of goodly stature was the Fairy of the Palace, and Boy Beautiful felt his heart die away within him as he beheld her. But she was full of compassion at the sight of him, and said, "Welcome, Boy Beautiful! What dost thou seek?"

"We seek Youth Without Age, and Life Without Death," he replied.

Then he dismounted from his steed and entered the palace, and there he met two other fair dames of equal beauty: these were the elder sisters of the Fairy of the Palace. They regaled Boy Beautiful with a banquet served on gold plate, and the good steed had leave to graze where he would, and the Fairy made him known to all her monsters, that so he might wander through the woods in peace. Then the fair dames begged Boy Beautiful to abide with them always, and Boy Beautiful did not want to be asked twice, for to stay with the Fairy of the Palace was his darling desire.

Then he told them his story, and of all the dangers he had passed

through to get there, and so the Fairy of the Palace became his bride, and she gave him leave to roam at will throughout her domains. "Nevertheless," said she, "there is one valley thou must enter or it will work thee woe, and the name of that valley is the Vale of Complaint."

There then Boy Beautiful abode, and he took no count of time, for though many days passed away, he was yet as young and strong as when he first came there. He went through leagues of forest without once feeling weary. He rejoiced in the golden palace, and lived in peace and tranquillity with his bride and her sisters. Oftentimes too he went a-hunting.

One day he was pursuing a hare, and shot an arrow after it, and then another, but neither of them hit the hare. Never before had Boy Beautiful missed his prey, and his heart was vexed within him. He pursued the hare still more hotly, and sent another arrow after her. This time he did bring her down, but in his haste the unhappy man had not perceived that in following the hare he had passed through the Vale of Complaint! He took up the hare and returned homeward, but while he was still on the way a strange yearning after his father and his mother came over him. He durst not tell his bride of it, but she and her sisters immediately guessed the cause of his heaviness.

"Wretched man!" they cried. "Thou hast passed through the Vale of Complaint!"

"I have done so, darling, without meaning it," he replied. "But now I am perishing with longing for my father and mother. Yet need I desert thee for that? I have now been many days with thee, and am as hale and well as ever. Suffer me then to go and see my parents but once, and then I will return to thee to part no more."

"Forsake us not, O beloved!" cried his bride and her sisters. "Hundreds of years have passed away since thy parents were alive; and thou also, if thou dost leave us, wilt never return more. Abide with us, or, an evil omen tells us, thou wilt perish!"

But the supplications of the three ladies and his faithful steed likewise could not prevail against the gnawing longing to see his parents which consumed him.

At last the horse said to him, "If thou wilt not listen to me, my master, then 'tis thine own fault alone if evil befall thee. Yet I will promise to bring thee back on one condition."

"I consent, whatever it may be," said Boy Beautiful. "Speak, and I will listen gratefully."

"I will bring thee back to thy father's palace, but if thou dismount but for a moment, I shall return without thee."

"Be it so," replied Boy Beautiful.

So they made them ready for their journey, and Boy Beautiful embraced his bride and departed, but the ladies stood there looking after him, and their eyes were filled with tears.

And now Boy Beautiful and his faithful steed came to the place where the domains of Scorpia had been, but the forests had become fields of corn, and cities stood thickly on what had once been desolate places. Boy Beautiful asked all whom he met concerning Scorpia and her habitations, but they only answered that these were but idle fables which their grandfathers had heard from their great-grandfathers.

"But how is that possible?" replied Boy Beautiful. " 'Twas but the other day that I passed by—" and he told them all he knew. Then they laughed at him as at one who raves or talks in his sleep; but he rode away wrathfully without noticing that his beard and the hair of his head had grown white.

When he came to the domain of Gheonoea, he put the same questions and received the same answers. He could not understand how the whole region could have utterly changed in a few days, and again he rode away, full of anger, with a white beard that now reached down to his girdle and with legs that began to tremble beneath him.

At length he came to the empire of his father. Here there were new men and new buildings, and the old ones had so altered that he scarce knew them.

So he came to the palace where he had first seen the light of day. As he dismounted the horse kissed his hand and said, "Fare thee well, my master! I return from whence I came. But if thou also wouldst return, mount again and we'll be off instantly."

"Nay," he replied, "fare thee well. I also will return soon."

Then the horse flew away like a dart.

But when Boy Beautiful beheld the palace all in ruins and over-grown with evil weeds, he sighed deeply, and with tears in his eyes he sought to recall the glories of that fallen palace. Round about the place he went, not once nor twice: he searched in every room, in every corner for some vestige of the past; he searched the stable in which he had found his steed; and then he went down into the cellar, the entrance to which was choked up by fallen rubbish.

Here and there and everywhere he searched about, and now his long white beard reached below his knee, and his eyelids were so heavy that he had to raise them on high with his hands, and he found he could scarce totter along. All he found there was a huge old coffer, which he opened, but inside it there was nothing. Yet he lifted up

the cover, and then a voice spoke to him out of the depths of the coffer and said:

"Welcome, for hadst thou kept me waiting much longer, I also would have perished."

Then his Death, who was already shriveled up like a withered leaf at the bottom of the coffer, rose up and laid his hand upon him, and Boy Beautiful instantly fell dead to the ground and crumbled into dust. But had he remained away but a little time longer, his Death would have died, and he himself would have been living now. And so I mount my nag and utter an "Our Father" ere I go.

GOHA ON THE DEATHBED
Egypt

Once Goha got very ill and was about to die. He called his wife and said to her, "Beloved wife, put on your best clothes and perfume, and comb your hair—in short, do all you can to look as beautiful as you can be!"

She answered sobbing, "Don't say things like that! How can I do all these things with you dying! I will never think of these things again after you have passed away!"

Goha said; "Do it for me, and come and sit at the head of my bed."

The woman did all she could to fix her looks and sat down next to him. She asked him, "Did you want to look at my beauty before you die?"

Goha answered, "No. They say 'Death chooses the best,' and I thought Azrael might see you and decide to take you instead of me."

DEATH OF A MISER
Russia

There was once an old miser who had two sons and a great deal of money. When he heard Death coming, he locked himself up in his room, sat on his oaken chest, swallowed his gold coins, chewed up his bills, and thus ended his life. His sons came, laid out the dead body under the holy icons, and invited the sexton to chant the psalms. At midnight a devil in human form suddenly appeared, took the old man on his shoulders, and said, "Hold up the flap of your coat, sexton!" And he shook the dead man, saying, "The money is yours, but the bag is mine." And he vanished, taking the body with him.

GODFATHER DEATH
Germany

A poor man had twelve children and was forced to work night and day to give them even bread. When therefore the thirteenth came into the world, he knew not what to do in his trouble, but ran out into the great highway, and resolved to ask the first person whom he met to be godfather.

The first to met him was the good God, who already knew what filled his heart, and said to him, "Poor man, I pity you. I will hold your child at its christening, and will take charge of it and make it happy on earth."

The man said, "Who are you?"

"I am God."

"Then I do not desire to have you for a godfather," said the man. "You give to the rich, and leave the poor to hunger." Thus spoke the man, for he did not know how wisely God apportions riches and poverty. He turned therefore away from the Lord, and went farther.

Then the Devil came to him and said, "What do you seek? If you will take me as a godfather for your child, I will give him gold in plenty and all the joys of the world as well."

The man asked, "Who are you?"

"I am the Devil."

"Then I do not desire to have you for godfather," said the man. "You deceive men and lead them astray."

He went onwards, and then came Death striding up to him with withered legs, and said, "Take me as godfather."

The man asked, "Who are you?"

"I am Death, and I make all equal."

Then said the man, "You are the right one, you take the rich as well as the poor, without distinction. You shall be godfather."

Death answered, "I will make your child rich and famous, for he who has me for a friend can lack nothing."

The man said, "Next Sunday is the christening; be there at the right time."

Death appeared as he had promised, and stood godfather quite in the usual way.

When the boy had grown up, his godfather one day appeared and bade him go with him. He led him forth into a forest, and showed him a herb which grew there, and said, "Now you shall receive your godfather's present. I make you a celebrated physician. When you are called to a patient, I will always appear to you. If I stand by the head of the sick man, you may say with confidence that you will make him well again, and if you give him of this herb he will recover; but if I stand by the patient's feet, he is mine, and you must say that all remedies are in vain, and that no physician in the world could save him. But beware of using the herb against my will, or it might fare ill with you."

It was not long before the youth was the most famous physician in the whole world. "He had only to look at the patient and he knew his condition at once, whether he would recover, or must needs die." So they said of him, and from far and wide people came to him, sent for him when they had anyone ill, and gave him so much money that he soon became a rich man.

Now it so befell that the king became ill, and the physician was summoned, and was to say if recovery were possible. But when he came to the bed, Death was standing by the feet of the sick man, and the herb did not grow which could save him. "If I could but cheat Death for once," thought the physician, "he is sure to take it ill if I do but, as I am his godson, he will shut one eye. I will risk it." He therefore took up the sick man, and laid him the other way, so that now Death was standing by his head. Then he gave the king some of the herb, and he recovered and grew healthy again.

But Death came to the physician, looking very black and angry, threatened him with his finger, and said, "You have betrayed me. This time I will pardon it, as you are my godson; but if you venture it again, it will cost you your neck, for I will take you yourself away with me."

Soon afterwards the king's daughter fell into a severe illness. She was his only child, and he wept day and night, so that he began to lose the sight of his eyes, and he caused it to be made known that whosoever rescued her from death should be her husband and inherit the crown.

When the physician came to the sick girl's bed, he saw Death by her feet. He ought to have remembered the warning given by his godfather, but he was so infatuated by the great beauty of the king's daughter, and the happiness of becoming her husband, that he flung all thought to the winds. He did not see that Death was casting angry glances on him, that he was raising his hand in the air, and threatening him with his withered fist. He raised up the sick girl, and placed her head where her feet had lain. Then he gave her some of the herb, and instantly her cheeks flushed red, and life stirred afresh in her.

When Death saw that for a seconed time his own property had been misused, he walked up to the physician with long strides, and said, "All is over with you, and now the lot falls on you," and seized him so firmly with his ice-cold hand that he could not resist, and led him into a cave below the earth. There he saw how thousands and thousands of candles were burning in countless rows, some large, some medium-sized, others small. Every instant some were extinguished, and others again burnt up, so that the flames seemed to leap hither and thither in perpetual change.

"See," said Death, "these are the lights of men's lives. The large ones belong to children, the medium-sized ones to married people in their prime, the little ones belong to old people; but children and young folks likewise have often only a tiny candle."

"Show me the light of my life," said the physician, and he thought that it would be still very tall. Death pointed to a little end which was just threatening to go out, and said, "Behold, it is there."

"Ah, dear godfather," said the horrified physician, "light a new one for me, do it for love of me, that I may enjoy my life, be king, and the husband of the king's beautiful daughter."

"I cannot," answered Death, "one must go out before a new one is lighted."

"Then place the old one on a new one, that will go on burning at once when the old one has come to an end," pleaded the physician.

Death behaved as if he were going to fulfill his wish, and took hold of a tall new candle; but as he desired to revenge himself, he purposely made a mistake in fixing it, and the little piece fell down and was extinguished. Immediately the physician fell on the ground, and now he himself was in the hands of Death.

THE HUNGRY PEASANT, GOD, AND DEATH
Mexico

Not far from the city of Zacatecas there lived a poor peasant, whose harvest was never sufficient to keep hunger away from himself, his wife and children. Every year his harvests grew worse, his family more numerous. Thus as time passed, the man had less and less to eat for himself, since he sacrificed a part of his own rations on behalf of his wife and children.

One day, tired of so much privation, the peasant stole a chicken with the determination to go far away, very far, to eat it, where no one could see him and expect him to share it. He took a pot and climbed up the most broken side of a nearby mountain. Upon finding a suitable spot, he made a fire, cleaned his chicken, and put it to cook with herbs.

When it was ready, he took the pot off the fire and waited impatiently for it to cool off. As he was about to eat it, he saw a man coming along one of the paths in his direction. The peasant hurriedly hid the pot in the bushes and said to himself, "Curse the luck! Not even here in the mountains is one permitted to eat in peace."

At this moment the stranger approached and greeted, "Good morning, friend!"

"May God grant you a good morning," he answered.

"What are you doing here, friend?"

"Well, nothing, señor, just resting. And, Your Grace, where are you going?"

"Oh, I was just passing by and stopped to see if you could give me something to eat."

"No, señor, I haven't anything."

"How's that, when you have a fire burning?"

"Oh, this little fire; that's just for warming myself."

"Don't tell me that. Haven't you a pot hidden in the bushes? Even from here I can smell the cooked hen."

"Well yes, señor, I have some chicken but I shall not give you any; I would not even give any to my own children. I came way up here because for once in my life I wanted to eat my fill. I shall certainly not share my food with you."

"Come friend, don't be unkind. Give me just a little of it!"

"No, señor, I shall not give you any. In my whole life I have not been able to satisfy my hunger, not even for one day."

"Yes, you will give me some. You refuse because you don't know who I am.

"I shall not give you anything, no matter who you are, I shall not give you anything!"

"Yes, you will as soon as I tell you who I am."

"Well then, who are you?"

"I am God, your Lord."

"Uh, hm, now less than ever shall I share my food with you. You are very bad to the poor. You only give to those whom you like. To some you give haciendas, palaces, trains, carriages, horses; to others, like me, nothing. You have never even given me enough to eat. So I shall not give you any chicken."

God continued arguing with him, but the man would not even give Him a mouthful of broth, so He went His way.

When the peasant was about to eat his chicken, another stranger came along; this one was very thin and pale.

"Good morning, friend!" he said. "Haven't you anything there you can give me to eat?"

"No, señor, nothing."

"Come, don't be a bad fellow! Give me a little piece of that chicken you're hiding."

"No, señor, I shall not give you any."

"Oh yes, you will. You refuse me now because you don't know who I am."

"Who can you be? God, Our Lord Himself, just left and not even to Him would I give anything, less to you."

"But you will, when you know who I am."

"All right; tell me then who you are."

"I am Death!"

"You were right. To you I shall give some chicken, because you are just. You, yes, you take away the fat and thin ones, old and young, poor and rich. You make no distinctions nor show any favoritism. To you, yes, I shall give some of my chicken!"

THE WORD THE DEVIL MADE UP
Afro-American (Florida)

The old Devil looked around Hell one day and saw that his place was short of help, so he thought he'd run up to Heaven and kidnap some angels to keep things running till he got reinforcements from Miami.

Well, he slipped up behind a great crowd of angels on the outskirts of Heaven and stuffed a couple of thousand in his mouth, a few hundred under each arm, and wrapped his tail around another thousand. And he darted off toward Hell.

When he was flying low over the earth looking for a place to land, a man looked up and saw the Devil and asked him, "Old Devil, I see you have a load of angels. Are you going back for more!"

Devil opened his mouth and told him, "Yeah," and all the little angels flew out of his mouth and went on back to Heaven. While he was trying to catch them, he lost all the others. So he had to go back after another load.

He was flying low again and the same man saw him and said, "Old Devil, I see you got another load of angels."

Devil nodded his head and mumbled, "Unh hunh," and that's why we say it that way today.

A Paddock in Heaven
England

There was a man who had just died, and arrived in Heaven, and Saint
Peter was showing him around. Presently they came to a high wall.
"Hush," said Saint Peter. He fetched a ladder very quietly, and climbed
up, beckoning the newcomer to follow him. They went stealthily up
and peered over the wall. It was one of the Heavenly Meadows, and
there were a lot of rather ordinary-looking people walking about in
twos and threes.

"Who are they?" said the newcomer.

"Sh! said Saint Peter. "Don't let them hear you. They're the
Primitive Methodists, and if they knew anyone else was in the place,
they'd leave Heaven at once."

How a Man Found His Wife
in the Land of the Dead
Papua

When our dead leave us none knoweth whither they go, nor by much
searching hath any man found the way to Ioloa, the Land of the Dead,
save one, and of him will I tell thee.

This man lived in the hills where ariseth the Uruam, the river
which flows into the sea between Wamira and Divari. It came to pass
that the man's wife died, and he mourned for her many days. But
when it was time for the death feast to be made for her, he went
forth with his dog to hunt for a cuscus that it might be eaten at the
feast. (This tale doth my father tell, and I who have heard it tell it
now to thee.)

Now a cuscus sleeps all day, but in the softness of the evening it comes forth to seek its food. Therefore, it was at this time that the man set out to hunt. In a little he had found one, which he killed, and having no one with him who might carry it, he hung it upon a tree and went on. Once more he found one, which also he killed and hung on a tree. Then he saw a third, and the dog ran after it to catch it. But the cuscus ran also, and went down a hole in the earth. Now it went to its home in Ioloa, for it belonged to the Dead.

When the man reached the hole, he found that his dog had also gone down, and he feared lest it might lose its way and come not back to him. Therefore he rolled away the great stone which lay over the hole and looked down. There far below he saw coconuts growing, so he said within himself, "This is a village."

Then he too went down the hole far into the earth. His dog was before him, and he caught him in his arms. Now so it is in Ioloa that all the day the bones of the Dead lie on the ground, but at evening each takes his own bones, and lives thus till the dawn. And as the man drew near, it was the time that the bones should live. It so befell that his wife was already walking, and was coming toward him. When she saw him, she said in her heart, "My husband hath died on the earth, and hath come to me." Then she went to him, and with her fingers pinched his arm until the blood showed on his skin. Then said she, "Thou are not dead. Wherefore hast thou come hither?" And when he had told her how it had befallen him to find the hole in the earth, and that he had followed his dog, she said, "Hold thy dog closely lest he go after the bones of men, which lie upon the ground, and come thou with me while I hide thee, for it may be that the Dead will slay thee if they find thee here."

Then she took him to her house and bade him lie still nor let the voice of the dog be heard, for it was now time for the Dead to arise. The man did as she bade him, and he watched as the Dead laid hold of each his own bones. "This is my thigh," and "Here is my arm," he heard them say. Now it was night, and the Dead began to dance, while some of them beat also upon drums. And the man was much afraid as he watched from the house. But his wife remained with him, and he cared not for fear nor any other thing while he had her with him once more. "Ah, my wife," he cried, "how hot was my heart with grief till I found thee!"

But his wife feared for him that the Dead would find him in their land and would work him some evil; therefore she said, "Thou must not tarry here, for the Dead if they find thee will certainly fall upon thee."

Then said the man, "How can I leave thee when I have but now found thee?"

"Ah, my lord," answered the wife, "of a truth thou must not linger here. Yet if thou wouldst see me once more go now, and after three nights are past come again to me, and I will be here."

Then the man, after she had thus spoken, rose up to go. But on the way he stayed to pick coconuts, and scented herbs, and wild limes, that he might show them to the people of Uruam. And as he thus did, the Dead saw him and made haste after him in great numbers, and seized from his hands the coconuts, the scented herbs, and the wild limes, and he being beset by them could but escape with his life. And when he had come up to the face of the earth, the Dead closed the hole with a great stone that no man might lift.

Therefore when the man returned after the three nights were past, he found no place where he might enter, and he saw his wife no more. Nor since that day have any found the way to Ioloa. But if the stone had not been placed over the hole we might even now have seen and talked with our dead after they had left us for their own land.

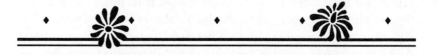

THE END OF THE WORLD
American Indian (White River Sioux)

Somewhere at a place where the prairie and the Maka Sicha, the Badlands, meet, there is a hidden cave. Not for a long, long time has anyone been able to find it. Even now, with so many highways, cars, and tourists, no one has discovered this cave.

In it lives a woman so old that her face looks a shriveled-up walnut. She is dressed in rawhide, the way people used to be before the white man came. She has been sitting there for a thousand years or more, working on a blanket strip for her buffalo robe. She is making the strip out of dyed porcupine quills, the way our ancestors did before white traders brought glass beads to this turtle continent. Resting beside her, licking his paws, watching her all the time is

Shunka Sapa, a huge black dog. His eyes never wander from the old woman, whose teeth are worn flat, worn down to little stumps, she has used them to flatten so many porcupine quills.

A few steps from where the old woman sits working on her blanket strip, a huge fire is kept going. She lit this fire a thousand or more years ago and has kept it alive ever since. Over the fire hangs a big earthen pot, the kind some Indian peoples used to make before the white man came with his kettles of iron. Inside the big pot, *wojapi* is boiling and bubbling. *Wojapi* is berry soup, good and sweet and red. That soup has been boiling in the pot for a long time, ever since the fire was lit.

Every now and then the old woman gets up to stir the *wojapi* in the huge earthen pot. She is so old and feeble that it takes her a while to get up and hobble over to the fire. The moment her back is turned, the huge black dog starts pulling the porcupine quills out of her blanket strip. This way she never makes any progress, and her quill-work remains forever unfinished. The Sioux people used to say that if the old woman ever finishes her blanket strip, then at the very moment that she threads the last porcupine quill to complete the design, the world will come to an end.

NOTES

INTRODUCTION

"Tell all the Truth . . .": Emily Dickinson, poem no. 1129, *The Complete Poems of Emily Dickinson*, ed. Thomas H. Johnson (Boston: Little, Brown, 1960), p. 506. The poem ends, "The Truth must dazzle gradually/Or every man be blind—"

"Whining like forest dogs . . .": Vachel Lindsay, "Eden in Winter," *Collected Poems*, rev. ed. (New York: Macmillan, 1925).

"He woke up frightened . . .": Katharine Briggs, *British Folktales* (New York: Pantheon Books, 1977), p. 170.

"Tales are, in the ears . . .": Roger D. Abrahams, *African Folktales* (New York: Pantheon Books, 1983), p. 2.

The Old Lady in the Cave: My own reconstruction of a story told me—punchline only—by storyteller Carol Birch, who does not know where it comes from. All attempts to trace it have failed so far.

"There is a kind of death . . .": Ruth Sawyer, *The Way of the Storyteller* (New York: Penguin Books, 1977), p. 59.

"Tends to absorb something . . .": Italo Calvino, *Italian Folktales* (1980; New York: Pantheon Books, 1981), p. xxi.

"Man has to resort . . .": Graham Greene, as quoted in Reidar Christiansen, *Folktales of Norway* (Chicago: University of Chicago Press, 1964), p. xxi.

The Talking Skull: Leo Frobenius and Douglas C. Fox, *African Genesis* (Berkeley, Calif.: Turtle Island Foundation, 1983), p. 236.

For more about this particular story, see either Abrahams, *African Folktales*, Introduction, pp. 1–27, or William Bascom, "The Talking Skull Refuses to Talk," *Researches in African Literatures* 8 (1977): 226–91.

"Compassion and humanness . . .": Kornei Chukovsky, *From Two to Five*, trans. and ed. Miriam Morton (Berkeley: University of California Press, 1963), p. 138.

"Bright is the ring of words . . .": Robert Louis Stevenson, *Poems of Robert Louis Stevenson*, selected by Helen Plotz (New York: Thomas Y. Crowell, 1973), p. 57.

"The fairy tale takes these existential anxieties . . .": Bruno Bettelheim, *The Uses of Enchantment* (New York: Alfred A. Knopf, 1976), p. 10.

"The breath of life . . .": quoted by Laura Simms to the author.

"Whenever misfortune threatened the Jews . . .": a Hasidic tale that has been retold many ways, this version by John Shea, "Theology and Autobiography: Relating Theology to Lived Experience," *Commonweal*, June 16, 1978, pp. 358–62.

"There is a romantic idea . . .": Joseph Campbell, "Exploring Myth with Joseph Campbell," *The Inward Light* (Proceedings of the Friends General Conference on Religion and Psychology) 39, nos. 8–9 (Winter 1976–77): 50.

"The younger generations . . .": Don Futterman, "Allah Yassadi: Among the

Moroccan Storytellers of Yeroham," in *The Calendar of Storytelling Arts*, produced by the New England Storytelling Center, Lesley College Graduate School, Cambridge, Mass., 1985.

"Sociology, Anthropology . . .": Briggs, *British Folktales*, p. 2.

"The ancient beldame . . .": my own retelling of a popular literary anecdote about the philosopher William James.

"It was a dark and stormy night . . .": Katharine Briggs and Ruth L. Tongue, *Folktales of England* (Chicago: University of Chicago Press, 1965), p. 149.

This story—tale type 2320, "Rounds," motif Z17—is very popular; over 100 versions have been collected for Lithuania alone. Edward Bulwer-Lytton began one of his novels "It was a dark and stormy night"; and Charles Schultz, the creator of *Peanuts*, has had his writing dog, Snoopy, use the same classic opener.

Why We Tell Stories: Lisel Mueller, *The Need to Hold Still* (Baton Rouge: Louisiana State University Press, 1981), pp. 62–63.

TELLING TALES

The Man Who Had No Story: Séamas Ó Catháin, *The Bedside Book of Irish Folklore* (Cork: Mercier Press, 1980), pp. 81–86.

Collected in 1965 in Donegal, this is tale type 2412B in Sean O'Sullivan and Reidar Th. Christiansen, *The Types of the Irish Folktale*, Folklore Fellows' Communications no. 188 (Helsinki: Suomalainen Tiedeakatemia, 1967).

How Spider Obtained the Sky God's Stories: R. S. Rattray, *Akan-Ashanti Folk Tales* (Oxford: Oxford University Press, 1930).

Kwaku Anansi the spider is the incomparable African trickster who stars in hundreds of stories. Roger Abrahams talks about "the vitality and the protean abilities" of such characters. A children's picture book of this tale, *A Story, a Story*, illustrated by Gail Haley, won the Caldecott Medal in 1971.

Helping to Lie: Kurt Ranke, *Folktales of Germany* (Chicago: University of Chicago Press, 1966), p. 193.

This little German tale is only one version of a widespread story of lying, the oldest of which is by the Persian poet Firdausi (A.D. 935–1020). It entered the European tradition in the twelfth century in the *Exempla* of the Bishop of Akkon.

The Ash Lad Who Made the Princess Say "You're a Liar!" Peter Christen Asbjørnsen and Jørgen Moe, *Norwegian Folk Tales* (1960; New York: Pantheon Books, 1982), pp. 17–18.

This is tale type 852. Versions of this popular story are scattered throughout Europe as well as Indonesia, Virginia, and Missouri , and a single version has been collected in Africa.

The Parson and the Sexton: Asbjørnsen and Moe, *Norwegian Folk Tales*, pp. 15–16.

This is the Norwegian version of an extremely popular story, "The Emperor and the Abbot" (tale type 922). In the English tradition it is a folk ballad, "King John and the Bishop." While the emperor or king always propounds three riddles, some eighteen different riddles have been used. Walter Anderson, in his classic study of the tale, suggests that it originated in some Jewish community in the Near East, possibly Egypt, about the seventh century, The earliest literary versions date back to the ninth century.

The Tall Tales: I. K. Junne, *Floating Clouds, Floating Dreams: Favorite Asian Folktales* (Garden City, N.Y.: Doubleday, 1974), pp. 3–5.

This Burmese version of the trickster tricked is related to tale type 1920, "Contests in lying," where cleverness and absurd logic win the day.

Catherine, Sly Country Lass: Italo Calvino, *Italian Folktales* (1980; New York: Pantheon Books, 1981), pp. 261–66.

This extraordinarily popular tale (type 875), is known in the Grimm collection as "The Peasant's Wise Daughter," in Czechoslovakia as "Clever Manka," and in hundreds of other tellings. It can be traced back to India, though its finest development has been in Europe. This is the Italian version. The set of tasks in which Catherine must appear "neither naked nor clothed" was also imposed upon the daughter of Brunhild and Sigurd in the great German cycle, as well as in the Icelandic *Saga of Ragnar Lodbrok* and in the Welsh hero cycle *The Mabinogion*, in the account of the death of Llew Llaw Gyffes.

The Wise Little Girl: Aleksandr Afanas'ev, *Russian Fairy Tales* (New York: Pantheon Books, 1945, 1973), pp. 252–55.

A Russian tale with many of the same motifs as "Catherine, Sly Country Lass": the three questions by the king, the task-countertask. The line about a cart giving birth to a foal is found in stories around the world.

Clever Answers: Afanas'ev, *Russian Fairy Tales*, pp. 578–79.

In this Russian variant of tale type 922B, the king and the soldier are in collusion and there is a further riddle to be solved: that of the plucked geese. In the Yiddish version, the "plucked pigeon" is the king's vizier.

A Dispute in Sign Language: Dov Noy, *Folktales of Israel* (Chicago: University of Chicago Press, 1963), pp. 95–97.

This ebullient Israeli story is a favorite among modern tellers because of the ease with which gesture can be incorporated in the telling. Tale type 924A, "Discussion between priest and Jew carried on by symbols," it was first written down in the thirteenth century in the *Gloss of Accursius*. Versions have been found in England ("The Professor of Signs"), in the Turkish tales of Nasr-ed-Din Hodja, and even set down in literary form by Rabelais.

Leopard, Goat, and Yam: Roger D. Abrahams, *African Folktales* (New York: Pantheon Books, 1983), p. 110.

This is an African version of the famous classical logic puzzle with the answer built in.

An Endless Story: Keigo Seki, *Folktales of Japan*, trans. Robert J. Adams (Chicago: University of Chicago Press, 1963).

This version of the endless tale, type 2300, has a distinctly Oriental flavor.

THE VERY YOUNG AND THE VERY OLD

Glooscap and the Baby: Richard Erdoes and Alfonso Ortiz, *American Indian Myths and Legends* (New York: Pantheon Books, 1984), pp. 25–26.

The Algonquian tribes told many stories about Glooscap, or First Man, who was a combination of trickster and god.

The Brewery of Eggshells: William Butler Yeats, *Irish Fairy and Folk Tales* (New York: Modern Library, 1925, 1950), pp. 51–54.

This method of detecting a changeling is widespread in European folk stories. Versions have been found in Germany (where the changeling is made to laugh), in Denmark (where it remarks on pudding that is made with pig's hide and hair), and Brittany. Stories about changelings fall under motif F321.1.

Father of Eighteen Elves: Jacqueline Simpson, *Icelandic Folktales and Legends* (Berkeley: University of California Press, 1972), pp. 28–30.

This Icelandic variation of "The Brewery of Eggshells" has the porridge stirrer in common with some Norwegian versions. The elf-woman's complaint that the human mother is not treating her charge as well as the fairies are caring for the human child can also be found in Danish variants of this tale. In one Danish story, the changeling says, "I am so old that I have been suckled by eighteen mothers."

The Fly: Mai Vo-Dinh, *The Toad Is the Emperor's Uncle: Animal Folktales from Viet-Nam* (Garden City, N.Y.: Doubleday, 1970).

Stories about wise children abound in folklore. In this Vietnamese tale, the child outwits the usurious landlord in a very sophisticated manner.

The Two Pickpockets: Katharine Briggs, *British Folktales* (New York: Pantheon Books, 1977), p. 64.

This jocular tale from England is still current. There are similar stories in India and Hawaii.

The Seventh Father of the House: Peter Christen Asbjørnsen and Jørgen Moe, *Norwegian Folk Tales* (1960; New York: Pantheon Books, 1982), pp. 13–14.

Unlike most cumulative tales, this repetitious Norwegian story has an incantatory power that doesn't change the essential narrative flow.

The King's Favorite: Moss Roberts, *Chinese Fairy Tales and Fantasies* (New York: Pantheon Books, 1979), p. 151.

Wagging My Tail in the Mud: Roberts, *Chinese Fairy Tales and Fantasies*, p. 126. The great Taoist philosopher Chuang Tzu published this Chinese gem.

When One Man Has Two Wives: Inea Bushnaq, *Arab Folktales* (New York: Pantheon Books, 1986), p. 352.

This jest story from Syria has found its way into American and English music-hall comedy routines.

The Old Man and His Grandson: Jakob and Wilhelm Grimm, *The Complete Grimm's Fairy Tales* (New York: Pantheon Books, 1944, 1972), pp. 363–64.

Variants of this tale (type 980A) have been found in countries as far apart as Brazil, Japan, and Greece.

Half a Blanket: Michael J. Murphy, *Now You're Talking . . . Folk Tales from the North of Ireland* (Belfast: Blackstaff Press, 1975), p. 42.

This Irish version of "The Old Man and His Grandson" is only one of the many variants. The Korean story, "The Aged Father," has the old man taken to a mountaintop and put over the side in a basket. The child advises his father to save the basket so that he, in his turn, may put his own father in it.

TRUE LOVES AND FALSE

How Men and Women Got Together: Richard Erdoes and Alfonso Ortiz, *American Indian Myths and Legends* (New York: Pantheon Books, 1984), pp. 41–45.

The Bloods and the Piegans, two of the allied Algonquian tribes that made up the Blackfoot people of Montana Territory, tell this story. It is similar to a rather more graphically sexual tale, "Bringing Men and Women Together," from the Afro-American tradition in Surinam.

The Little Old Woman with Five Cows: C. Fillingham Coxwell, *Siberian and Other Folk-Tales* (London: C. W. Daniel, 1925), pp. 262–69.

This Siberian tale comes from the Yakut people of the middle Lena Basin, whose language is closely related to Turkish. The story has many common motifs: the miraculous birth, the maid of "indescribable beauty," the wedding taboos, the false bride, the talking animal helper, and the happy ending.

The Prayer That Was Answered: Frederick and Audrey Hyde-Chambers, *Tibetan Folktales* (Boulder, Colo.: Shambhala Publications, 1981), pp. 152–55.

This Tibetan tale of the "false bridegroom" (motif K1915) has a particular ironic twist, a variant of motif K1600, "The deceiver falls into own trap."

The Merchant's Daughter and the Slanderer: Aleksandr Afanas'ev, *Russian Fairy Tales* (New York: Pantheon Books, 1945, 1973), pp. 415–18.

This Russian tale combines three major motifs: the king falling in love with a picture (see "Faithful John"), the deceptive wager (which Shakespeare uses in *Cymbeline*), and the ending in which the young woman accuses the liar with his own words. It is a much-traveled tale, having found its way even into a Tiwa American Indian story, "The Faithful Wife and the Woman Warrior."

What Happened to Hadji: Allan Ramsay and Francis McCullagh, *Tales from Turkey* (London: Simpkin, Marshall, Hamilton, Kent, 1914).

This tale from Turkey incorporates type 924, "Discussion between priest and Jew carried on by symbols" (see "A Dispute in Sign Language" in the "Telling Tales" section) into a story of a faithful wife. The stupid Hadji is a popular Turkish character.

Mr. Fox: Katharine Briggs, *British Folktales* (New York: Pantheon Books, 1977), pp. 87–89.

This Bluebeard variant is connected to the cellar-of-blood and robber-bridegroom tales (type 956). The Grimm version is "Fitcher's Bird." The American Appalachian "Old Foster" is so similar to "Mr. Fox" as to be the same story with only regional accents making the difference. The "Be bold" formula can also be found in Spenser's

Faerie Queene, book 3, canto 2, stanza 54. In her book of essays *Daguerreotypes*, Isak Dinesen recalls a similar story and incantation she heard as a child in Denmark.

The Waiting Maid's Parrot: Moss Roberts, *Chinese Fairy Tales and Fantasies* (New York: Pantheon Books, 1979), pp. 9–14.

From China, this story incorporates romantic elements which Oriental societies usually discouraged. Arranged marriages were the norm, but this story uses a magical animal helper (the reincarnation of the waiting maid's sister) to aid the two lovers.

The White Cat: Kate Douglas Wiggin and Nora Archibald Smith, *The Fairy Ring* (Garden City, N.Y.: Doubleday, 1967), pp. 312–25.

This is the classic French tale of an animal bride (type 402), made popular in 1710 through a retelling by Mme. D' Aulnoy. The same story is found throughout Europe in over 300 versions, as well as in Armenia and North Africa. Different animals appear as the bride: in Finland, a mouse; in Czechoslovakia, a frog. The gifts differ, too: sometimes a ring, a kerchief, a loaf of bread, a bouquet, the finest dog or horse is demanded by the father. The status of the hero and his family also differs from story to story: sometimes he is royal, ofttimes a farmer (Czech) or a laborer (Finnish).

Sedna: Ronald Melzack, *The Day Tuk Became a Hunter* (New York: Dodd, Mead, 1967).

This demon-lover story told by the Eskimo people is one of their most popular and widespread tales. Sedna is the goddess of the sea, though she is also called by other names. Nuliajuk, a similar goddess of the sea and sea animals, loses her fingers when she tries to leap onto a raft with other boys and girls.

Urashima the Fisherman: Royall Tyler, *Japanese Tales* (New York: Pantheon Books, 1987).

This fragment taken from the *Tango Fudoki* is one of the best-known and most widespread of Japanese folktales. It dates from as early as the eighth century A.D. In the variant published by Edmund Dulac in the *Allies Fairy Book* in 1916, Urashima crumbles into dust at the end of the story. The supernatural lapse of time is a familiar motif (see "One Night in Paradise" in the "Ghosts and Revenants" section).

The Spirit of the Van: Thomas Keightley, *The Fairy Mythology* (1892; London: Wildwood House, 1981), pp. 409–11.

A Welsh story that has made its way as a legend attaching itself to a particular place, this tale nevertheless is a familiar one. The warning against striking the fairy lover three times ("That's once . . .") is a usual taboo. As Katharine Briggs says in *The Vanishing People* (New York: Pantheon Books, 1978): "In the Fairy Wife tales and legends the fairy is wooed and consents to the marriage with a stipulation, which is generally not arbitrary, but arises out of the conditions of her being. This is almost always contravened and the wife departs" (p. 148). This particular story was written down in the late nineteenth century.

The Toad-Bridegroom: Zong In-Sob, *Folk Tales from Korea* (London: Routledge & Kegan Paul, 1952), pp. 175–78.

This is a variant of the frog-prince tale (type 440), that classic Grimm favorite, collected throughout Europe, America, Scandinavia, and the Russias back to the thirteenth century; it is also related to "Beauty and the Beast." The provocative core of all the variants is that the loathsome-looking hero must be loved for himself alone. Note that in this version it is the toad's rank rather than his extreme ugliness that causes him to be refused at first.

Taken: Robin Flower, *The Western Island: Or, The Great Blasket* (New York: Oxford University Press, 1945), pp. 135–37.

This Irish tale is a very Christian version of the "captive in Faery" stories. Katharine Briggs wrote that "too hasty a re-marriage is often the cause of failure to rescue a captive in Fairyland," but here it is the hard judgment of the priest that dooms the taken woman. The clash between Christendom and Faery is given full treatment in Maureen Duffy's *The Erotic World of Faery* (New York: Avon Books, 1980).

The Girl at the Shieling: Jacqueline Simpson, *Icelandic Folktales and Legends* (Berkeley: University of California Press, 1972), pp. 35–40.

The love between a girl, especially a girl on a lonely mountain pasturage, and an elf or fairy man is common in Scandinavian lore. This lovely, tragic Icelandic tale is motif ML6005, "The interrupted fairy wedding."

Deer Hunter and White Corn Maiden: Erdoes and Ortiz, *American Indian Myths and Legends,* pp. 173–75.

From the Tewa tribe of the Pueblos, this story of an all-consuming love that ignores tribal traditions and taboos even after death is similar to another Tewa tale, "The Husband's Promise."

TRICKSTERS, ROGUES, AND CHEATS

"The advocate of uncertainty . . .": Alan Garner, *The Guizer* (New York: Greenwillow Books, 1976), Introduction, p. 1.

Tyll Ulenspiegel's Merry Prank: M. A. Jagendorf, *Tyll Ulenspiegel's Merry Pranks* (New York: Vanguard Press, 1938).

The German trickster supreme (also spelled Till Eulenspiegel) is a historical personage who lived in the fourteenth century and is said to have died in 1350 at Mölln, Schlweswig-Holstein, where his grave has been a popular tourist site since the sixteenth century. By the fifteenth century, legends, jokes, and anecdotes were attributed to him; in fact, a collection of these were printed in one or more Low German books about that time.

The Hodja and the Cauldron: Allan Ramsay and Francis McCullagh, *Tales from Turkey* (London: Simpkin, Marshall, Hamilton, Kent, 1914).

The Hodja, or Nasr-ed-Din Hodja, is a popular figure in Turkish tales, as well as in the folklore of other Near and Middle Eastern countries. There is no agreement as to whether the Hodja actually lived, though there is a government-sanctioned tombstone at Akeshehir, dated 1284. Like many national tricksters, the Hodja figures in a cycle of tales, most of them familiar stories found in other countries. This one has a Jewish parallel tale in which the rabbi trades spoons and says, "If a spoon can bear little spoons and if a goblet can bear little goblets, why should it surprise you that a watch can die?" An Indian variant puts it this way: "In a country where a large balance of iron was eaten by mice, a hawk might easily carry off an elephant." In Syria the same cycle of stories clusters around the trickster Djuha; the story "Djuha Borrows a Pot" is a popular one.

Being Greedy Chokes Anansi: Roger D. Abrahams, *Afro-American Folktales* (New York: Pantheon Books, 1985), p. 122.

The stories about Kwaku Anansi the spider began in West Africa and made their way across the ocean to America on the slave ships. Anansi is the classic trickster, both having godlike qualities and occasionally playing the fool. This tale is motif C496, "Tabu using certain words."

Quevedo and the King: Américo Paredes, *Folktales of Mexico* (Chicago: University of Chicago Press, 1970), p. 34.

Don Francisco de Quevedo y Villegas, a Spanish poet and satirist, lived in the late sixteenth century and the early seventeenth (1580–1645). He became a legendary character, and trickster stories clustered around his name in both the folklore and the literature of the time (the borrowing in both from the trickster cycles of other countries was enormous). The principal motifs in this short tale from Mexico are H1050, "Paradoxical tasks"; J1485, "Mistaken identity: I did not know it was you"; and J1160, "Clever pleadings."

Why the Hare Runs Away: Roger D. Abrahams, *African Folktales* (New York: Pantheon Books, 1983), pp. 74–75.

This Ewe tale from Africa is a bareboned version of the famous tarbaby story (tale type 175) that first appeared in the Indian *Jataka* tales and then spread worldwide as an oral story. Here, birdlime instead of tar is used. Tarbabies come in all shapes, sizes, and materials: pitch, wax, gum, and clay are some of the things out of which the figure is made.

Coyote Fights a Lump of Pitch: Richard Erdoes and Alfonso Ortiz, *American Indian Myths and Legends* (New York: Pantheon Books, 1984), pp. 359–61.

This White Mountain Apache variant of the tarbaby story (type 175) stars the American Indian trickster Coyote. The tarbaby is linked to the original *Jataka* tale "The Demon with the Matted Hair," in which the Buddha himself fights the demon and sticks to the figure in five places—hands, feet, and head.

Crack and Crook: Italo Calvino, *Italian Folktales* (1980; New York: Pantheon Books, 1981), pp. 50–52.

This Italian version of tale type 1525, "The master thief," has retained only the final episode, the bedsheet. The red mark on the door is reminiscent of the trick played by the great dog in Hans Christian Andersen's story "The Tinderbox."

The Master Thief: Jakob and Wilhelm Grimm, *The Complete Grimm's Fairy Tales* (New York: Pantheon Books, 1944, 1972), pp. 773–80.

This story is tale type 1525, and there are versions of it throughout the world. The American is "Jack and the Rich Old Man"; the Irish, "Jack, the Cunning Thief"; the Mexican, "Ite'que"; and the French, "The Skillful Thief." Herodotus told a similar story about King Rhampsinitus in 450 B.C. In most of the variants the horse and the bedsheet are consistent, though in the Mexican it is a poncho rather than a sheet that must be taken.

Peik: Claire Booss, *Scandinavian Folk and Fairy Tales* (New York: Avenel Books/ Crown Publishers, 1984), pp. 44–49.

Known elsewhere in Europe as "The Clever Boy" (tale type 1542), this is the Norwegian version. Motif K341.8.1, "Trickster pretends to ride home for tools to perform tricks," can also be found in parallel stories of the American Indians, most notably the Kiowa "Coyote Tricks the White Man," and "Coyote and Wasichu" from the Brule Sioux. The life-restoring-object trick is a familiar motif. There are examples of it in the American Ozarks ("The Magic Horn"), in the West Highlands of Scotland, in the Afro-American tradition, and in several American Indian tales, as well as in India.

The Monkey and the Crocodile: Ellen C. Babbitt, *Jataka Tales: Animal Stories* (Englewood Cliffs, N.J.: Prentice-Hall, 1912, 1940).

From the Indian *Jataka* tales, this story of clever deception is popular throughout the world. It is quite old and has been found as "The Fox and the Foolish Fishes" in the seventh- or eighth-century Jewish *Alphabet of Ben Sera*. In Japan the story is known as "The Jelly Fish and the Monkey" and is a pourquoi tale about why the jellyfish is pulp.

The Race Between Toad and Donkey: Abrahams, *Afro-American Folktales*, pp. 194–96.

This is the Jamaican version of motif K11.1, tale type 1074, a story popular in East Asia, in Africa, among the American Indians, and in the Portuguese tradition of Brazil. According to Stith Thompson, it is a story that can star either animals or men.

The King's Son Goes Bear Hunting: C. Fillingham Coxwell, *Siberian and Other Folk-Tales* (London: C. W. Daniel, 1925), pp. 655–56.

This Finnish tale is type 154, "Bear food," without the second and third episodes in which the man's dogs chase the fox into the hole and the fox then holds a conversation with the parts of his body. This first section may be found in the *Roman de Renart*, indicating that it was in common European usage from the tenth or eleventh century.

John Brodison and the Policeman: Henry Glassie, *Irish Folktales* (New York: Pantheon Books, 1985), pp. 103–4.

This Irish short tale is possibly related to tale type 1529, "The peasant betrays the Jew through the substitution of a horse," according to Henry Glassie, though that is stretching things a bit.

The Rabbi and the Inquisitor: Nathan Ausubel, *A Treasury of Jewish Folklore* (New York: Crown Publishers, 1948), p. 36.

Escape by deception is a common folkloric theme, though this Jewish tale is different from most.

The Ugly Son: Royall Tyler, *Japanese Tales* (New York: Pantheon Books, 1987).

This Japanese story of a deceptive marriage is unique.

Dividing the Goose: Aleksandr Afanas'ev, *Russian Fairy Tales* (New York: Pantheon Books, 1945, 1973), pp. 579–80.

Part of the body of stories called "deceptive bargains," this tale from Russia has made its way west. In America the clever peasant's place is taken by an Irish tramp in a joke story called "Dividing the Chicken."

The Men Who Wouldn't Stay Dead: Milton Rugoff, *A Harvest of World Folk Tales* (New York: Viking Press, 1949), pp. 331–33.

This famous French story (motif K2321, tale type 1536A) began as a literary jest story of a decidedly gruesome nature, and has made its way out of the medieval *fabliaux* and into the oral tradition.

The Story of Campriano: Calvino, *Italian Folktales*, pp. 298–301.

A more elegant and artistic Italian version of the bloody Indian story "The Greatest Cheat of Seven," it still has its dash of gore at the finale. It is also a variant of tale type 753, "Christ and the smith," a saint's legend told throughout Europe.

THE FOOL: NUMBSKULLS AND NOODLEHEADS

"The comic counterpart of solemnity . . .": Richard Erdoes and Alfonso Ortiz, *American Indian Myths and Legends* (New York: Pantheon Books, 1984), p. 279.

"The element I think marks us most . . .": Alan Garner, *The Guizer* (New York: Greenwillow Books, 1976), Introduction, p. 1.

The Three Sillies: Katharine Briggs, *British Folktales* (New York: Pantheon Books, 1977), pp. 61–63.

This English noodle story is the classic silly tale, known throughout the world. In the Grimm collection it is "Clever Elsie," and it is that version which gives it its tale type, 1450. Thompson says that it is probably Oriental and literary in origin, but it is now widespread in the oral tradition. The Indian version, "The Silly Weaver Girl," is quite short, and her audience merely laughs at her instead of joining in her foolishness. Some variants, such as "What Shall Baby's Name Be?" conclude without the search for the other sillies. In the Siberian tale "The Fools," it is the girl's hiccoughs and the need to keep them from her suitors that start off the silliness. In the search many different kinds of fools are discovered. Besides the cow, trousers, and moon incidents in the English tale, there are such incidents as a tall man trying to get into a small house (Greece), watering oxen with a spoon (Italy), leading a camel from the field (Siberia), and even the scatological Greek incident of someone showing his backside to an old woman who promises to recognize him again by his lovely face. "It seems *everybody* is dumber than my wife," concludes the husband in the Italian "Cicco Petrillo," "so I'd better go back home."

Nasr-ed-Din Hodja in the Pulpit: Allan Ramsay and Francis McCullagh, *Tales from Turkey* (London: Simpkin, Marshall, Hamilton, Kent, 1914).

From Turkey, the Hodja is both gull and rogue. The Turkish government has put its imprimatur on the historical Hodja, claiming officially that he was born in the village of Hortu and died in 1284. There are Afro-American as well as Italian versions of this story. It is tale type 1826, "The parson has no need to preach."

Lazy Jack: James Orchard Halliwell, *Popular Rhymes and Nursery Tales of England* (London: John Russell Smith, 1849), pp. 37–39.

This classic English numbskull tale is about a boy so literal-minded that he does exactly what he has been told whether or not it fits the situation. Tale type 1696, this story seems to have its origins in Chinese Buddhistic sources. It can be traced up through Renaissance jestbooks. A highly popular tale, it has been collected all over Europe in some 200 versions as well as throughout Asia, Africa, and America in both the white and the Native American cultures.

Chelm Justice: Nathan Ausubel, *A Treasury of Jewish Folklore* (New York: Crown Publishers, 1948), p. 337.

The Jewish inhabitants of Chelm, like the English Gothamites, are considered collectively stupid and have a cycle of stories attributed to them.

Those Stubborn Souls, the Biellese: Italo Calvino, *Italian Folktales* (1980; New York: Pantheon Books, 1981), p. 60.

The Biellese are not only considered stupid, like their counterparts in Chelm, but stubborn as well. In Trieste it is not the Biellese but the Friulians who star in this Italian tale.

The Drovers Who Lost Their Feet: Américo Paredes, *Folktales of Mexico* (Chicago: University of Chicago Press, 1970), p. 151.

This is the Mexican version of a famous noodle tale, type 1288, which is popular in Europe, India, and America.

The Old Man and Woman Who Switched Jobs: Lone Thygesen-Blecher and George Blecher, *Swedish Folktales* (New York: Pantheon Books, forthcoming).

Commonly known as "The Husband Who Would Mind the House," this Swedish tale is type 1408 and is found in the ballad tradition as "The Cow on the Roof." In Scandinavia almost 200 variants have been collected. The story has had a renaissance in American feminist circles.

The Two Old Women's Bet: Richard Chase, *Grandfather Tales* (Boston: Houghton Mifflin, 1948), pp. 156–60.

"The merry wives' wager," type 1406, is here given an Appalachian setting. There are parallel stories from Turkey and Israel and all the way to the Scandinavian countries. Included in this story is tale type 1313, "The man who thought himself dead." The incident about the naked man who believes himself clothed in the finest cloth served, in its Scandinavian versions, as a pattern for Hans Christian Andersen's "The Emperor's New Clothes."

A Stroke of Luck: Linda Degh, *Folktales of Hungary* (Chicago: University of Chicago Press, 1965), pp. 147–49.

This variant is from Hungary, but this tale, type 1381, has been found all over Europe and North Africa. It was extremely popular in medieval literature, finding its way into both jest books and *fabliaux.*

The Sausage: Claire Booss, *Scandinavian Folk and Fairy Tales* (New York: Avenel Books/Crown Publishers, 1984), pp. 179–81.

This story (motif J2071, "Foolish wishes") comes from Sweden, but the story itself is much older than this version, having originally to do with the wanderings of the saints over the earth. The brothers Grimm printed it as "The Poor Man and the Rich Man," with different incidents but the same basic motif.

Nail Soup: Booss, *Scandinavian Folk and Fairy Tales,* pp. 181–86.

A variant of tale type 1548, "The soup-stone," this Swedish story is also known as "The Old Woman and the Tramp." It is popular worldwide. Other soup starters have included stones (France) and an axe (Russia).

Old Dry Frye: Chase, *Grandfather Tales,* pp. 100–105.

This American Southern mountain thigh-slapper is a variant of the basic tale type 1537, "The corpse killed five times." It is well known through the medieval *fabliau* tradition and has been collected in Europe, Asia, and Africa as well as in America in both the white and the Native American cycles. There is even a Siberian version, "The Unlucky Corpse."

Bye-bye: Diane Wolkenstein, *The Magic Orange Tree and Other Haitian Folktales* (New York: Alfred A. Knopf, 1978), pp. 190–91.

This Haitian story is closely related to the Oriental tale type 225, "The crane teaches the fox to fly."

The Barn Is Burning: Roger D. Abrahams, *Afro-American Folktales* (New York: Pantheon Books, 1985), pp. 293–95.

An Afro-American version of the popular English story "Master of All Masters," greatly elaborated and used in the master-slave tradition of the American South. Versions of this tale (type 1562A) have been collected all over Europe and the Americas. In Mexico, the trickster Pedro de Urdemalas is credited with fooling the mistress of the house.

HEROES: LIKELY AND UNLIKELY

The Birth of Finn MacCumhail: Jeremiah Curtin, *Myths and Folk-Lore of Ireland* (Boston: Little, Brown, 1906), pp. 204–20.

One of the great Irish folk heroes, Finn is born in a typical mythic-hero way: fulfilling a prophecy. The slaughter of all the male children born on a certain day comes from long Oriental tradition (see Herod's edict about the sons of the Israelites at the time of Jesus' birth; likewise the pharaoh's edict at the time of Moses). Other common motifs include the blinding of the one-eyed giant (tale type 1137, as in the Greek Polyphemus story), escaping in ram disguise (same story, motif K603), and the talking ring (similar to a Florentine story). In any Irish story, Finn can always be recognized: he is the one chewing on his thumb to get knowledge, a trait so outstanding as to have its own motif (D1811.1).

Li Chi Slays the Serpent: Moss Roberts, *Chinese Fairy Tales and Fantasies* (New York: Pantheon Books, 1979), pp. 129–31.

There are many stories of brave women in folklore, though the late-nineteenth-century collectors who anthologized world folklore for children (especially Andrew Lang) tended to leave women warriors out. The idea of offering a young woman (or maiden or virgin) to a dragon as a sacrifice is an old one, but in China dragons were beneficent fertility gods, which is why the "dragon" in this tale is a "serpent." Nevertheless, the story is well within the dragon-slayer tradition (tale type 300).

The Devil with the Three Golden Hairs: Jakob and Wilhelm Grimm, *The Complete Grimm's Fairy Tales* (New York: Pantheon Books, 1944, 1972), pp. 151–58.

This story is tale type 461 crossed with type 930, "The rich man and his son-in-law." As an independent tale it has been found all over Europe; more than 300 variants have been collected. In the combined version, the story has gotten as far as China, Africa, the Thompson River Indians in British Columbia, and the Portuguese in Massachusetts. It is one of the most studied tale types in the world.

The Longwitton Dragon: Katharine Briggs, *British Folktales* (New York: Pantheon Books, 1977), pp. 147–49.

From the North Country of England comes this strange dragon-slayer story (tale type 300). The idea of a dragon drawing its strength from the water is similar to the Greek traditional belief that dryads drew their strength from their trees. This dragon, though, may have come originally from the Orient, as it is there that dragons are associated with the element of water.

The Orphan Boy and the Elk Dog: Richard Erdoes and Alfonso Ortiz, *American Indian Myths and Legends* (New York: Pantheon Books, 1984), pp. 53–60.

This story is about the introduction of horses (called Elk Dogs) to the Blackfoot tribe.

Molly Whuppie: Joseph Jacobs, *English Fairy Tales* (London: David Nutt, 1898), pp. 130–35.

From England comes this tale of a hardy heroine. The giant's variation from the traditional "Fee-fi-fo-fum" is slight. The trick of the substituted necklaces (caps in some variants) is motif K1611. Clarkson and Cross make much of the line "bridge of one hair," likening it to the Norse Bifrost, the bridge giants could not cross, and linking it to the Scottish belief that witches could ride over a single-hair bridge (see Atelia Clarkson and Gilbert B. Cross, *World Folktales: A Scribner Resource Collection* [New York: Scribner's, 1984]).

The Beginning of the Narran Lake: Henrietta Drake-Brockman, *Australian Legendary Tales* (Sydney: Angus & Robertson, 1953), pp. 12–14.

This is an Aboriginal pourquoi tale starring a brave if formidable husband, "who having wooed his wives with a *nulla-nulla* kept them obedient by fear of the same weapon." The wives are swallowed by Kurrias (crocodiles). Only in a wonder tale could the digestive process be so avoided (see "Red Riding Hood" et al.).

The Flying Head: Erdoes and Ortiz, *American Indian Myths and Legends*, pp. 227–28.

This Iroquois tale stars a young mother who, in the traditional manner of the unlikely hero, says, "Someone must make a stand against this monster. It might as well be me." Her method of dispatching him is reminiscent of the European story, type 1131, in which hot porridge burns the giant's throat.

The Story of the Youth Who Went Forth to Learn What Fear Was: The Complete Grimm's Fairy Tales, pp. 29–39.

This is the classic German tale, type 326. Note similarities to "The Man Who Had No Story," in the "Telling Tales" section.

WONDER TALES, TALL TALES, AND BRAG

"Having heard, for the first time . . .": Rudolf Erich Raspe, *The Adventures of Baron Munchausen* (London: Shenval Press, 1948), p. 3.

Talk: Harold Courlander and George Herzog, *The Cow-Tail Switch and Other West African Stories* (New York: Henry Holt, 1947), pp. 25–29.

This African tale of the Ashanti people is a cumulative story that gets its power from the repetitious pattern and the joking last line. Motif B210.2, "Talking animal or object refuses to talk on demand" (like "The Talking Skull" in the Introduction to this book), is the progenitor of the tale. There are parallel stories in England and America, and of course throughout Africa.

The King of Ireland's Son: Brendan Behan, *Brendan Behan's Ireland: An Irish Sketchbook* (New York: Bernard Geis Associates, Random House, 1962), pp. 136–41.

The opening sentence of this Irish wonder tale is a mini–tall tale in itself. It is related to tale type 550, "The bird, the horse and the princess." The hiding game may be found in many tales of type 329, "Hiding from the Devil."

The Goose Girl: Jakob and Wilhelm Grimm, *The Complete Grimm's Fairy Tales* (New York: Pantheon Books, 1944, 1972), pp. 404–11.

This Cinderella cousin is from Germany, tale type 533, with 14 European variants from France to Russia and a single instance in Africa. In America there is a Zuni Indian version in which the girl herds turkeys.

The Princess on the Glass Hill: Joanna Cole, *Best-Loved Folktales of the World* (Garden City, N.Y.: Doubleday, 1982), pp. 345–52.

A popular Norwegian tale, this is type 530. It falls into two sections: the acquisition of the magic horse, and the ride up the mountain. The first part is related to tale type 300, "The dragon slayer," found throughout the world. A similar Egyptian story has a prince who reaches the princess's chamber "seventy ells above the ground."

The Promises of the Three Sisters: Hasan M. El-Shamy, *Folktales of Egypt* (Chicago: University of Chicago Press, 1980), pp. 63–72.

Hasan El-Shamy says in his notes that this is an extremely popular story, normally told by women. There are 14 variants in Egypt as well as North Africa and the Berber communities, and it is found as far west as Ireland. It is tale type 707, "The three golden sons," and has a literary history and, in Stith Thompson's words, "one of the eight or ten best known plots in the world."

The Magic Mirror of Rabbi Adam: Howard Schwartz, *Elijah's Violin and Other Jewish Fairy Tales* (New York: Harper & Row, 1983), pp. 187–95.

This story is from a sixteenth-century Jewish source in Eastern Europe. Sorcerors' duels are motif D1719.1, "Contest in magic."

The Old Woman Who Lived in a Vinegar Bottle: Katharine Briggs, *British Folktales* (New York: Pantheon Books, 1977), pp. 40–42.

This English version of the Grimm "The Fisher and His Wife," tale type 555, leaves out both the fisherman and the magic fish, but the moral of the story is certainly the same. It is a widely distributed tale in both Eastern and Western Europe and in such widely scattered areas as Puerto Rico and parts of Asia.

The Magic Pear Tree: Moss Roberts, *Chinese Fairy Tales and Fantasies* (New York; Pantheon Books, 1979), pp. 51–52.

The Taoist priest in this Chinese story is from the White Lotus Society tradition.

Faithful John: The Complete Grimm's Fairy Tales, pp. 43–51.

Tale type 516, "The faithful servant," is a Grimm story which includes a number of traveling motifs such as the language of animals and the resuscitation by blood (motif E113), to name just two. Its distribution ranges from Portugal to India. The

Indian variants have been around for some two thousand years: the eleventh-century *Ocean Streams of Story* included a fully developed version. The turning-to-stone and disenchantment-by-blood themes can also be found in a literary story, the thirteenth-century romance *Amis and Amiloun*.

Four Hound-Dog Stories: "The Best Coon-and-Possum Dog," B. A. Botkin, *A Treasury of Mississippi River Folklore* (New York: American Legacy Press/Crown Publishers, 1955); "Hare and Hound," Michael J. Murphy, "The Folk Stories of Dan Rooney of Lurgancanty," *Ulster Folklife* 11 (1965): 80–86; "The Maryland Dog," George G. Carey, *Maryland Folklore and Folklife* (Cambridge, Md.: Tidewater Publishers, 1970), p. 44; "The Split Dog," Richard Chase, *American Folk Tales and Songs* (1956; New York: Dover Publications, 1971), pp. 97–98.

These four short tall tales come from Ireland and America. Variations occur all over the American South. Literary versions have been printed in hunting magazines, folklore volumes, and regional newspaper columns. Motif X1215.11, "Lie: The split dog," is an example of how popular these hound-dog stories can be. Sometimes they are even attributed to historical personages: "Davy Crockett and Old Bounce" is a Kentucky version of the split dog.

SHAPE SHIFTERS

"In the ocean sea . . .": Montague Summers, *The Werewolf* (New York: University Books/Crown Publishers, 1966), quoted from Nancy Garden, *Werewolves* (Philadelphia: J. B. Lippincott, 1973), pp. 37–38.

The Doctor and His Pupil: Paul Delarue, *The Borzoi Book of French Folk Tales* (New York: Alfred A. Knopf, 1956).

From France, this is tale type 325, "The magician and his pupil," a story that is well known in India (where it probably originated) and Europe. Its literary history in Europe begins with Straparola in the sixteenth century. The story can also be found in the Near East, parts of America, Siberia, the Philippines, and North Africa. The battle of the sorcerers is older than the tale, dating back at least to the Early Middle Kingdom of Egypt, 1200 B.C.

The Swan-Maiden: Claire Booss, *Scandinavian Folk and Fairy Tales* (New York: Avenel Books/Crown Publishers, 1984), pp. 248–50.

Stories of swan-maidens are found throughout Europe; this one comes from Sweden. As usual in this type of story, the swan-maiden is seen first in a group of her peers. In E.S. Hartland's *The Science of Fairy Tales* (1891), an entire chapter is dedicated to swan-maiden stories.

Sister Alionushka, Brother Ivanushka: Aleksandr Afanas'ev, *Russian Fairy Tales* (New York: Pantheon Books, 1945, 1973), pp. 406–10.

This is the Russian version of the Grimm's "Little Brother, Little Sister," type 450. A puzzling story since the kid is never disenchanted, it seems to be missing the ending to bring it to a completely satisfying conclusion. A literary version appeared in Basile's *Pentamarone* in the seventeenth century, and the tale is popular in Germany, the Balkans, Russia, Italy, and the Near East.

The Blacksmith's Wife of Yarrowfoot: Katharine Briggs, *British Folktales* (New York: Pantheon Books, 1977), pp. 277–79.

This Scottish tale has versions throughout the British Isles, in the Southern United States, and even in Scandinavia. Motif G241.2.1, "Witch transforms man to horse and rides him," and motif G243, "Witch's Sabbath," are included in this tale.

The Seal's Skin: Jacqueline Simpson, *Icelandic Folktales and Legends* (Berkeley: University of California Press, 1972), pp. 100–102.

This is the Icelandic version of the classic selchie (selkie, selky, or silky) story. Selchies were thought to be men on the land and seals in the sea, as the folk ballad "The Great Silkie of Sule Skerry" has it. Stories about them are common along the coasts of the northern seas—in Iceland, the Scandinavian countries, and Scotland. Like the swan-maiden stories, the selchie tales concern transformation by skin, type 400. The earliest known selchie story from Iceland is from a manuscript by Jon Gudmundsson the Learned, 1641.

The Wounded Seal: Thomas Keightley, *The Fairy Mythology* (1892; London: Wildwood House, 1981), pp. 394–95.

This selchie story from Scotland deals with "sympathetic magic," the like-calls-to-like idea. The seal-folk, also known by the Celts as the roane, were thought by some to be the original fairies. The Shetlanders call them sea trows.

The Cat-Woman: James R. Foster, *Lovers, Mates, and Strange Bedfellows: Old World Folktales* (New York: Harper & Brothers, 1960), pp. 146–48.

This French story is a werewolf variant. Widely known, it ends with motif D702.1.1, "Cat's paw cut off, woman's hand missing."

The Serpent-Woman: F. H. Lee, *Folk Tales of All Nations* (New York: Coward McCann, 1930), pp. 895–902.

This Spanish version of the loathly-wife tale is the distaff side of the marriage-to-a-monster story. The burning of the snake's skin (motif D721.3, "Disenchantment by destroying skin") is a death sentence, unlike the same action in the swan-maiden tales. In Spain there used to be a superstition that an evil woman becomes a snake every night for a certain number of years and has the power to inflict painful and often fatal bites.

The Snake's Lover: David Guss, *Legends of the South American Indians* (New York: Pantheon Books, forthcoming). This Peruvian story is similar to "The Serpent-Woman" in that the shape shifter is an evil snake. However, though snake wife/husband stories can be found from Scandinavia to India (tale types 433A and B), this story seems more appropriately in the tradition of the loathly-bridegroom motif (D733).

NOT QUITE HUMAN

"The kindness of the fairies . . .": Katharine Briggs, *The Vanishing People* (New York: Pantheon Books, 1978), p. 161.

The Well-Baked Man: Richard Erdoes and Alfonso Ortiz, *American Indian Myths and Legends* (New York: Pantheon Books, 1984), pp. 46–47.

This Pima story is one of the pointed jocular tales that are popular among various American Indian tribes. It is also well established on the summer-camp circuit.

The Finn Messenger: Reidar Christiansen, *Folktales of Norway* (Chicago: University of Chicago Press, 1964), pp. 40–41.

In Norway, where this story comes from, the Finns (Laplanders) were thought to be great shape changers and masters of magic. Astral messengers are common occult characters. This story includes motif E721.2, "Body in trance while soul is absent." This particular tale has been collected in some 15 variants in Norway, as well as in Sweden, Lapland, and Denmark.

Vasilisa the Beautiful: Aleksandr Afanas'ev, *Russian Fairy Tales* (New York: Pantheon Books, 1945, 1973), pp. 439–47.

A Russian Cinderella variant, this story includes the famous Russian witch Baba Yaga, whose hut moved about the forest on chicken's legs. Baba Yaga's mode of transportation is unique in folklore annals: flying in a mortar steered by a pestle.

Bridget and the Lurikeen: Henry Glassie, *Irish Folktales* (New York: Pantheon Books, 1985), pp. 164–65.

The lurikeen in this Irish tale is the same as the leprachaun, the fairy cobbler with a secret stash of gold. He is also called a lubarkin, logheryman (Ulster), cluricaun (Cork), luricaun (Kerry), lurigadaun (Tipperary), lubberkin (England), or *lojemand* (Norse, meaning Loki Playman).

The Two Hunchbacks: Italo Calvino, *Italian Folktales* (1980; New York: Pantheon Books, 1981), pp. 332–34.

This is the Italian version of a popular story, type 503, that has been found in Ireland, Japan, France, Spain, Brittany, England, and Germany. There is also a folk ballad in the Irish tradition called "Monday, Tuesday," which tells only the first part of the tale, omitting the second hunchback altogether.

Then the Merman Laughed: Jacqueline Simpson, *Icelandic Folktales and Legends* (Berkeley: University of California Press, 1972), pp. 92–93.

The motif of the three laughs (N456, "Enigmatic smile/laugh reveals a secret knowledge") is popular in Scandinavia and the British Isles. This variant is from Iceland, where tales of merfolk are common. In Ireland, 78 versions of the story have been collected. It is also in the Arthurian tradition, having been included in a story about Merlin in Geoffrey of Monmouth's *Vita Merlini*. In Babylon the motif can be found in a fifth-century tale, "King Solomon and Asmodeus."

Pergrin and the Mermaid: John Rhys, *Celtic Folklore: Welsh and Manx* (1901; London: Wildwood House, 1980), pp. 163–64.

This Welsh tale demonstrates the kind of morality or tit-for-tat that the merfolk offer fishermen. It is a popular story that has attached itself to particular spots and become legend. Other localities in Wales have claimed the same tale.

The Ash Lad Who Had an Eating Match with the Troll: Peter Christen Asbjørnsen and Jorgen Møe, *Norwegian Folk Tales* (1960; New York: Pantheon Books, 1982), pp. 81–82.

This is the classic Norwegian tale, type 1060, in which the stupid ogre is outwitted by squeezing a substituted stone (see also "The old man and the wood sprite," type 1640, and the eating contest itself, type 1088). The stories can all be found in Northern Europe and in the tales of North American Indians as well.

How Mosquitoes Came to Be: Erdoes and Ortiz, *American Indian Myths and Legends*, pp. 192–93.

This charming pourquoi tale is from the Tlinglit Indians. This particular version was retold by Erdoes and Ortiz from English-language sources.

The Departure of the Giants: Harold Courlander, *The Crest and the Hide and Other African Stories* (New York: Coward McCann & Geoghegan, 1982), pp. 97–99.

This African tale from the Mesa, Habab, Beni-Amar, and Cunama people is a legend that grew up to account for large stone cairns in the area. The blessing that is really a curse is a typical jest of a trickster god.

FOOLING THE DEVIL

The Peasant and the Devil: Jakob and Wilhelm Grimm, *The Complete Grimm's Fairy Tales* (New York: Pantheon Books, 1944, 1972), pp. 767–68.

This is the classic Grimm tale, types 1030 and 9B, known as "Crop division." In this version a peasant and the Devil bargain over the crops, but the actors in the drama vary around the world. In Egypt, a wolf and a mouse quarrel. In the Afro-American tradition, it is a rabbit and a bear; in Norway, a bear and a fox; in China, a landlord and a peasant. The crops vary too: in this Grimm story, they are turnips and grain, but potatoes, wheat, corn, taro, and even popcorn have appeared in variants.

Wicked John and the Devil: Richard Chase, *American Folk Tales and Songs* (1956; New York: Dover Publications, 1971), pp. 22–30.

This European import to America can be found throughout the South; variants can be found in Germany, France, Estonia, Ireland, Finland, Denmark, Norway, Palestine, Lapland, and the Russias. It is tale type 330, "The smith and the Devil" and "The smith and death." The motif "Devil sticking to a tree or stool or chair" can be traced as far back as ancient Greek and Hebrew sources.

The Bad Wife: Aleksandr Afanas'ev, *Russian Fairy Tales* (New York: Pantheon Books, 1945, 1973), pp. 56–57.

This Russian tale and the story that follows, "Katcha and the Devil," fall into the "curst wife" tradition. There is a lively ballad tradition as well on the same subject. Child Ballad 278, "The Farmer's Curst Wife," has wide distribution in America and England.

Katcha and the Devil: Parker Fillmore, *Czechoslovak Fairy Tales* (New York: Harcourt, Brace & Howe, 1919, pp. 101–12.

This is an elaborate Czechoslovakian version of the Russian "Bad Wife," both of which fall into the "curst wife" tradition. The threat in this story, "You know Katcha? She's alive and looking for you!" finds its answer in the Vermont ballad "The Farmer's Curst Wife":

> Oh, one little devil peeks over the wall,
> Saying, "Take her back—she'll kill us all!"

The Lawyer and the Devil: Michael J. Murphy, *Now You're Talking . . . Folk Tales from the North of Ireland* (Belfast: Blackstaff Press, 1975), pp. 116–17.

This little Irish jocular tale is type 1187. Found in Greek myth and across Europe, it has attained its greatest popularity in Ireland.

Coals on the Devil's Hearth: Henry Glassie, *Irish Folktales* (New York: Pantheon Books, 1985), pp. 117–18.

Related to tale type 1187 (see "The Lawyer and the Devil"), this Irish story ends up with a bit of wisdom about the cleverness of women.

The Devil's Hide: F. H. Lee, *Folk Tales of All Nations* (New York: Coward McCann, 1932), pp. 416–23.

This Finnish story is part of the "stupid ogre" cycle, with the Devil taking the ogre's place. It is also an "impossible tasks" tale. Such stories, widely scattered throughout Europe, are especially popular in Scandinavia.

How El Bizarrón Fooled the Devil: Dorothy Sharp Carter, *Greedy Mariani and Other Folktales of the Antilles* (New York: Atheneum Publishers, 1974), pp. 24–29.

This is a Cuban variant of a popular South American story that is related to "The Devil's Hide" and is a version of tale type 1640, "The brave tailor."

Bearskin: The Complete Grimm's Fairy Tales, pp. 467–72.

This strange German fairy tale combines a more classic magic tale with a "fool-the-Devil" story. The ending, with its ironic twist, "You see, I have now got two souls in the place of your one!" shows a different morality than the usual Devil tale.

The Lad and the Devil: Claire Booss, *Scandinavian Folk and Fairy Tales* (New York: Avenel Books/Crown Publishers, 1984), pp. 12–13.

This short Norwegian story makes use of the same kind of trick as Puss-in-Boots played on the ogre.

Wiley and the Hairy Man: Virginia Haviland, *North American Legends* (New York: William Collins Publishers, 1979), pp. 126–33.

This tale from the American South is a Devil story: the Hairy Man "didn't have feet like a man but like a cow"—the cloven hoofs give him away. Employing the same trick as that in "The Lad and the Devil," this is a much more elaborated story.

THE GETTING OF WISDOM

Truth and Falsehood: Georgios A. Megas, *Folktales of Greece* (Chicago: University of Chicago Press, 1970), pp. 133–34.

A variation of tale type 613, "The two travelers," in which the nature of truth and falsehood is disputed, this Greek story was found in Argos in the Peloponnesus. Versions of this tale can be found throughout the Middle East as well.

Getting Common Sense: Roger D. Abrahams, *Afro-American Folktales* (New York: Pantheon Books, 1985), p. 52.

This is the Jamaican version of an Anansi story that is widely distributed in the West Indies and the Guianas.

Rich Man, Poor Man: Roger D. Abrahams, *African Folktales* (New York: Pantheon Books, 1983), pp. 145–47.

This African story is one variant of a popular wisdom tale that has been found as far away as Burma and Israel and throughout Europe. Rabelais published a version called "The Theft of a Smell." In each version payment is in a slightly different currency: in Burma, for example, the greedy stallkeeper gets paid with the shadow of a coin. There is an interesting Egyptian version in which a whore complains that a man has dreamed of sleeping with her and so owes her money.

The Lost Horse: Moss Roberts, *Chinese Fairy Tales and Fantasies* (New York: Pantheon Books, 1979), p. 82.

This blessing/curse story from China has a number of close relatives throughout the Middle East.

It Could Always Be Worse: Nathan Ausubel, *A Treasury of Jewish Folklore* (New York: Crown Publishers, 1948), pp. 69–70.

This popular Jewish story has made its way into the American nursery by means of a number of popular picture books such as *Too Much Noise*, by Ann McGovern.

His Just Reward: Lone Thygesen-Blecher and George Blecher, *Swedish Folktales* (New York: Pantheon Books, forthcoming).

This is the Swedish variant of a very popular tale, type 155, "The ungrateful serpent returned to captivity." Its roots are literary, but the story has been found worldwide, from India to China, throughout Africa, in Egypt, and in Mexico. Usually the animal is a serpent or snake, but occasionally it is a crocodile, tiger, or wolf.

Djuha's Sleeve: Inea Bushnaq, *Arab Folktales* (New York: Pantheon Books, 1986), p. 253.

The Syrian fool Djuha, who traveled to Italy, where he became "Giufa," is as often wise as foolish. The Sicilian version, "Eat Your Fill, My Fine Clothes," is almost word for word the same. In Nubia the fool is Djawha; in Mala, Djahan; and in Turkey, Hodja.

King Mátyás and His Scholars: Linda Degh, *Folktales of Hungary* (Chicago: University of Chicago Press, 1965), p. 172.

King Mátyás stars in a number of Hungarian stories, This particular exempla has been recorded in six variants, the first published in 1890.

The Missing Axe: Roberts, *Chinese Fairy Tales and Fantasies*, p. 58.

The Chinese specialize in short, pithy, anecdotal teaching stories. This one is from Lieh Tzu.

What Melody Is the Sweetest? Dov Noy, *Folktales of Israel* (Chicago: University of Chicago Press, 1963), p. 172.

This tale was told by an Afghanistani living in Israel, and its roots are quite old. Variants are found all over the Middle East. For example, in Morocco the answer to the question "What is the sweetest?" Is "Nothing is sweeter than a bed full of playing sons and daughters." The question in this variant, "What melody . . .?" is motif H635, "Riddle: What is the sweetest sound?" and the riddle itself is sometimes part of "The clever peasant girl" (tale type 875; see "Catherine, Sly Country Lass" and "The Wise Little Girl" in the "Telling Tales" section) as well as of "The Emperor and the Abbot" (type 922). But the core story here is quite different from any of those.

The Peddler of Swaffham: Adapted by Jane Yolen from Katharine Briggs, *British Folktales* (New York: Pantheon Books, 1977), pp. 244–45.

This legend from Norfolk, England, about the efficacy of dreams concerns a peddler named John Chapman—"chapman" being the old word for a peddler. In the fifteenth-century *Black Book* (still in the Swaffham Church library) is a list of the benefactors of the church, and it records that Chapman paid for the new north aisle as well as contributing to the spire fund in 1462.

The Beduin's Gazelle: Bushnaq, *Arab Folktales*, pp. 55–56.

This story is from Saudi Arabia and is related at the core to the story that follows, "The Happy Man's Shirt," which has its origins in Greece.

The Happy Man's Shirt: Italo Calvino, *Italian Folktales* (1980; New York: Pantheon Books, 1981), pp. 117–19.

This is the Italian version of tale type 844, "The luck-bringing shirt," which Hans Christian Andersen gave its finest literary form in "The Shoes of Happiness" (Lykkens Galosher). The ultimate source, though, is a legend about Alexander the Great in the *Pseudo-Callisthenes*. From the Greek, the story made its way into medieval Latin and spread throughout the Orient and Europe.

GHOSTS AND REVENANTS

Orpheus and Eurydice: Bulfinch's Mythology (New York: Doubleday, 1968), pp. 192–94.

The classic Greek myth of the husband who seeks his dead wife in the bowels of the earth (motif F81.1) was popular throughout the Middle Ages in ballads and literary romances.

The Spirit-Wife: Richard Erdoes and Alfonso Ortiz, *American Indian Myths and Legends* (New York: Pantheon Books, 1984), pp. 447–51.

This Zuni tale is but one of the many American Indian Orpheus stories. There are forty versions, and according to Stith Thompson, in only three of them does the wife successfully return. There is a study by A. H. Gayton, "The Orpheus Myth in North America," in the *Journal of American Folklore* 48 (1935).

One Night in Paradise: Italo Calvino, *Italian Folktales* (1980; New York: Pantheon Books, 1981), pp. 119–21.

This Italian story is a ghostly version of the supernatural-passage-of-time-in-fairyland motif, itself tale type 470, "Friends in life and death." E. S. Hartland, in *The Science of Fairy Tales*, has two chapters on this subject. Katharine Briggs, in *The Vanishing People*, devotes one chapter to it. There is a medieval Christian legend of a monk who listens to a heavenly bird singing, and when he stops listening, three hundred years have passed. Such stories are common throughout Europe, America (see the literary tale "Rip Van Winkle," by Washington Irving), the Middle East, and the Orient (see "Urashima the Fisherman" in the "True Loves and False" section). The story has been in the European literary tradition since the thirteenth century.

A Pretty Girl in the Road: Vance Randolph, *The Devil's Pretty Daughter and Other Ozark Tales* (New York: Columbia University Press, 1955), pp. 80–81.

America has fostered many similar ghost stories, legends attached to particular localities. Known in general as "The Vanishing Hitch-hiker," this is probably the most popular ghost story still in circulation today.

The Dream House: Katharine Briggs, *British Folktales* (New York: Pantheon Books, 1977), pp. 265–66.

This one of the many Irish ghost stories is unusual in that the dreamer who is the ghost is very much alive.

The Peasant and the Fiend: C. Fillingham Coxwell, *Siberian and Other Folk-Tales* (London: C. W. Daniel, 1925), pp. 664–65.

This Estonian transformation story is a variant of tale type 761, "The cruel rich man as the Devil's horse," which is popular in Finland as well.

The Tinker and the Ghost: Ralph Steele Boggs and Mary Gould Davis, *Three Golden Oranges and Other Spanish Folk Tales* (London: Longmans, Green, 1936), pp. 99–108.

This Spanish story incorporates some of the action in "The Story of the Youth Who Went Forth to Learn What Fear Was" (see the "Heroes" section), tale type 326, with motif E351, "Dead returns to pay money debt."

Hold Him, Tabb: Langston Hughes and Arna Bontemps, *The Book of Negro Folklore* (New York: Dodd, Mead, 1958), pp. 167–68.

This jocular ghost story, funny despite its tragic ending, is from the Afro-American tradition.

Drinking Companions: Moss Roberts, *Chinese Fairy Tales and Fantasies* (New York: Pantheon Books, 1979), pp. 178–82.

This charming ghost story is from China.

The Ostler and the Grave Robbers: Briggs, *British Folktales*, pp. 208–9.

This jocular anecdote comes from the Burke and Hare period of British history, when grave robbers (or "resurrection men") were digging up newly buried corpses and selling them to medical schools.

DEATH AND THE WORLD'S END

The Duration of Life: Jakob and Wilhelm Grimm, *The Complete Grimm's Fairy Tales* (New York: Pantheon Books, 1944, 1972), pp. 716–17.

This etiological story is about the length of life—surely the proper way to begin a section on death!

Woman Chooses Death: Richard Erdoes and Alfonso Ortiz, *American Indian Myths and Legends* (New York: Pantheon Books, 1984), pp. 469–70.

This story about the creation of death (motif A1335, "Origin of Death") is from the Blackfoot tribe of American Indians. In a number of primitive stories about death's beginning, it is woman who unwittingly brings death into the world, like Eve in the Garden of Eden.

Jump into My Sack: Italo Calvino, *Italian Folktales* (1980; New York: Pantheon Books, 1981), pp. 708–13.

This Italian version of "The table, the ass, and the stick" (tale type 563), crossed with "The magic providing purse" (type 564), is here provided with another idea—that of holding off death for a certain amount of time.

Youth Without Age and Life Without Death: F. H. Lee, *Folk Tales of All Nations* (New York: Coward McCann, 1930), pp. 935–42.

This Turkish wonder tale is reminiscent of the end of the Irish tale of the hero-singer Oisin, who was half mortal. He had outlived everyone he had known on earth during the years he spent in the fairy world, Tir-Nan-Og, and when he came out again and set his foot on the ground, he turned to dust.

Goha on the Deathbed: Hasan M. El-Shamy, *Folktakes of Egypt* (Chicago: University of Chicago Press, 1980), pp. 224–25.

This jocular tale from Egypt is part of the Goha cycle of trickster stories. According to Hasan El-Shamy, Goha is the most popular of the tricksters in the Arabic world, a variant of the Turkish Nasr-ed-Din Hodja. Stories about Goha were known before the eleventh century. This tale is a variation of motif T211.1, "Wife dies so that husband's death may be postponed."

Death of a Miser: Aleksandr Afanas'ev, *Russian Fairy Tales* (New York: Pantheon Books, 1945, 1973), p. 268.

This Russian story is one of the many miser tales told worldwide.

Godfather Death: The Complete Grimm's Fairy Tales, pp. 209–12.

This is the German version of a story (tale type 332) that has been around at least since 1300. It has both a literary and an oral tradition throughout Europe and as far away as Iceland and Palestine.

The Hungry Peasant, God, and Death: Frances Toor, *A Treasury of Mexican Folkways* (New York: Crown Publishers, 1947), pp. 492–95.

This ironic little story is from Mexico, but it has its origins in Europe.

The Word the Devil Made Up: Roger D. Abrahams, *Afro-American Folktales* (New York: Pantheon Books, 1985), p. 48.

This jocular Afro-American story, with its irresistible line about the Devil getting reinforcements from Miami, is from Florida.

A Paddock in Heaven: Katharine Briggs and Ruth L. Tongue, *Folktales of England* (Chicago: University of Chicago Press, 1965), p. 113.

According to Katharine Briggs, this English jest is part of "a large modern cycle of stories about St. Peter and exclusive sects and individuals in Heaven." At Indiana University there is a collection of 31 comic stories on the same theme.

How a Man Found His Wife in the Land of the Dead: F. H. Lee, *Folk Tales of All Nations* (New York: Coward McCann, 1930), pp. 798–99.

In this Papuan Orpheus tale, the man is given no chance at all to save his wife.

The End of the World: Erdoes and Ortiz, *American Indian Myths and Legends,* pp. 485–86.

The White River Sioux tell this story, which has echoes of the Greek tale of Penelope who wove during the day and ripped out her weaving at night to keep her unwanted suitors at bay, as well as a suggestion of the Greek stories of the Fates. There is a children's book based on this legend, *Annie and the Old One,* by Miska Miles, in which the Navajo grandmother tells her grandchild she will die when her weaving is finished. To keep her beloved grandmother alive, the child picks out each night what has been woven during the day.

PERMISSIONS ACKNOWLEDGMENTS

Grateful acknowledgment is made to the following for permission to reprint and adapt from previously published material. In the case of adaptation, the author may have retitled the tale.

"Coyote Fights a Lump of Pitch" from *Memoirs of the American Folklore Society*, vol. 33, 1939. Reprinted by permission of the American Folklore Society.

"A Pretty Girl in the Road" from *The Devil's Pretty Daughter and Other Ozark Tales* by Vance Randolph, 1955. Reprinted by permission of Columbia University Press.

Excerpt ("Whenever misfortune threatened . . .") from John Shea, "Theology and Autobiography: Relating Theology to Lived Experience," *Commonweal*, June 16, 1978. Reprinted by permission of *Commonweal*.

"Talk" from *The Cow-Tail Switch and Other West African Stories* by Harold Courlander and George Herzog. Copyright 1947 by Henry Holt & Co., © 1981 by Harold Courlander and George Herzog. Reprinted by permission of Harold Courlander.

"The Departure of the Giants" from *The Crest and the Hide and Other African Stories* by Harold Courlander. Copyright © 1982 by Harold Courlander. Reprinted by permission of Coward, McCann & Geoghegan.

"The Lad and the Devil," "Peik," "The Sausage," "The Old Woman and the Tramp," and "The Swan-Maiden" from *Scandinavian Folk and Fairy Tales*, edited by Claire Booss. Copyright © 1984 by Crown Publishers, Inc. Used by permission of Avenel Books, distributed by Crown Publishers, Inc.

"How El Bizarrón Fooled the Devil" from *Greedy Mariani and Other Folktales of the Antilles* by Dorothy Sharp Carter. Copyright © 1974 by Dorothy Sharp Carter. Reprinted by permission of Curtis Brown, Ltd.

"The Sedna Legend" from *The Day Tuk Became a Hunter* by Ronald Melzack. Copyright © 1967 by Ronald Melzack. Reprinted by permission of Dodd, Mead & Company, Inc.

"The Tall Tales" from *Floating Clouds, Floating Dreams* by I. K. Junne. Copyright © 1974 by I. K. Junne. "The White Cat" from *The Fairy Ring* by Kate Douglas Wiggin and Nora Archibald Smith. Copyright 1906 by McClure & Phillips. Reprinted by permission of Doubleday & Company, Inc.